Erotic Subjects

Erotic Subjects

The Sexuality of Politics in Early Modern English Literature

Melissa E. Sanchez

OXFORD
UNIVERSITY PRESS

OXFORD
UNIVERSITY PRESS

Oxford University Press is a department of the University of Oxford.
It furthers the University's objective of excellence in research, scholarship,
and education by publishing worldwide.

Oxford   New York

Auckland   Cape Town   Dar es Salaam   Hong Kong   Karachi
Kuala Lumpur   Madrid   Melbourne   Mexico City   Nairobi
New Delhi   Shanghai   Taipei   Toronto

With offices in

Argentina   Austria   Brazil   Chile   Czech Republic   France   Greece
Guatemala   Hungary   Italy   Japan   Poland   Portugal   Singapore
South Korea   Switzerland   Thailand   Turkey   Ukraine   Vietnam

Oxford is a registered trade mark of Oxford University Press
in the UK and certain other countries.

Published in the United States of America by
Oxford University Press
198 Madison Avenue, New York, NY 10016

© Oxford University Press 2011

First issued as an Oxford University Press paperback, 2013.

Library of Congress Cataloging-in-Publication Data
Sanchez, Melissa E.
Erotic subjects : the sexuality of politics in early modern English literature / Melissa E. Sanchez.
p. cm.
Includes bibliographical references and index.
ISBN 978-0-19-975475-5 (cloth : acid-free paper); 978-0-19-935436-8 (paperback)
1. English literature—Early modern, 1500–1700—History and criticism.
2. Politics and literature.
3. Sexuality—Psychology.
4. Literature and society—England—History—16th century.
5. Literature and society—England—History—17th century. I. Title.
PR428.P6S36   2011
820.9'3581—dc22   2010029641

For Chris
¿Quién más?

CONTENTS

ACKNOWLEDGMENTS

I have incurred many debts in the process of writing this book, and it is a pleasure to acknowledge them here. Without generous institutional support, I never could have begun, much less completed, this project. This book saw its start with an Andrew C. Mellon summer fellowship at the Huntington Library; years later, support from the USC-Huntington Early Modern Studies Institute allowed me to return to the Huntington to pursue research that proved critical to the book's completion. San Francisco State University and the University of Pennsylvania facilitated my writing with course relief, sabbatical leave, and research and travel grants. In particular, support from Penn's Alice Paul Center for Research on Women Gender, and Sexuality made it possible for me to conduct essential research at the Bodleian, Folger, and British Libraries.

I thank *The Sidney Journal*, *English Literary Renaissance*, and *ELH* for permission to reproduce versions of arguments that first appeared in their pages. An early version of chapter 2 appeared as "'The True Vowed Sacrifice of Unfeigned Love': Eros and Authority in *The Countess of Pembroke's Arcadia*" in *The Sidney Journal* 22 (2004): 90–105; portions of chapter 3 appeared as "Fantasies of Friendship in *The Faerie Queene*, Book IV" in *English Literary Renaissance* 37 (2007): 250–273; and chapter 5 appeared in an early form as "The Politics of Masochism in Mary Wroth's *Urania*" in *ELH* 74 (2007): 449–478.

I am especially happy to acknowledge my personal and intellectual debts, and I regret that space does not allow me to describe these in the detail they deserve. I wrote several early chapters of this book at San Francisco State, where Paul Sherwin, Julie Paulson, and Sara Hackenberg were insightful readers. At the University of Pennsylvania, I have benefited from the brilliance and friendship of my colleagues. Toni Bowers, Margreta de Grazia, Suvir Kaul, Zack Lesser, Ania Loomba, Phyllis Rackin, and Peter Stallybrass read substantial portions of this book, and their rigorous comments helped me to see what it was really about. Rita Barnard, Rita Copeland, David Eng, Jim English, David Kazanjian, Yolanda Padilla, Josephine Park, Emily Steiner, David Wallace, and Chi-ming Yang gave me advice and encouragement when I needed it most. Nancy Bentley, Rebecca Bushnell, Tim Corrigan, Stuart Curran, Peter de Cherney, Jed Esty, Michael Gamer, Amy Kaplan, Demie Kurz, Heather Love, Cary Mazer, Ann Matter, Paul Saint-Amour, Wendy

Steiner, and Salamishah Tillet have gone out of their way to offer support and share expertise.

Many of the ideas here saw their genesis in a dissertation at the University of California, Irvine. And although only one of that dissertation's chapters ultimately made it into this book, my mentors at Irvine taught me standards of scholarly creativity and integrity that I have tried to live up to in all of my work. I owe particular thanks to Victoria Silver, Jane Newman, Julia Lupton, Bob Folkenflik, Linda Georgianna, Ann Van Sant, and Andrzej Warminski. I never would have gone to graduate school in the first place if it had not been for Richard Kroll, and this book bears his influence in countless ways. I wish that he were here to read it.

Over the course of writing this book, I have had many occasions to marvel at the wisdom and generosity of my fellow early modernists. I am particularly beholden to Joe Loewenstein, Peter Mancall, and Anne Lake Prescott for their thoughtful criticism and unfailing encouragement. I have learned a lot (much more than many of them probably know) from exchanges with Michael Brennan, Jean Brink, Kim Coles, Julie Crawford, Jeff Dolven, Andrew Escobedo, Kirby Farrell, Carla Freccero, Barbara Fuchs, Paul Hammer, Graham Hammill, Margaret Hannay, Paul Hecht, Derek Hirst, Jean Howard, Heather James, Victoria Kahn, Carol Kaske, Arthur Kinney, Clare Kinney, Mary Ellen Lamb, Jeff Masten, Bill Oram, Jonathan Post, Roy Ritchie, Jen Rust, Lauren Silberman, Nigel Smith, Malcolm Smuts, Thomas Roche, Chris Warley, Bart Van Es, Steve Zwicker, and, especially, Valerie Traub. I have also benefited from the opportunity to present portions of this book at the Columbia University Early Modern Studies Seminar, the Huntington Library Early Modern Studies Institute, the Princeton University Early Modern Studies Seminar, the Temple University PreModern Studies Colloquium, and Washington University in St. Louis. Thanks to those audiences for their feedback and to Molly Murray and Alan Stewart; Heather James and Peter Mancall; Nigel Smith; Nichole Miller and Shannon Miller; and Joe Lowenstein and Vincent Sherry for those invitations.

My two anonymous readers at Oxford University Press offered wonderfully astute suggestions for revision. I have been grateful to my editor, Brendan O'Neill, for the care with which he has shepherded this book through every stage of the publication process, and to Oxford's production editor, Marc Schneider, for his unfailing efficiency. I also want to thank Erika Wetter at Routledge for encouraging this project, along with my two anonymous Routledge readers for their helpful and enthusiastic comments on the manuscript.

In addition to these professional debts, I owe thanks to the many people whose love and friendship have sustained me over the years. My father, Ruben Sanchez, has never wavered in his support and confidence. I am also grateful to my sister, Tiffany Sanchez, and my friends Jason Denman, Jeannine DiLorenzo, Lisa Keffer, Richard and Sharon Madden, Ann Mikkelsen, Helen and Richard Oesterheld, Samantha Robson, Gerald Turpin, and Samantha Wexler-Morin. They have been important parts of my life both before and during the writing of this book, as were my grandmother Clara Rosenbrock and my friend Rachel Meyer, both of whom I miss very much.

My gratitude to Newman, Algernon, and Chris is constant and incalculable. Since long before this project began, Newman and Algernon have been my most dependable sources of delight and distraction. Last and most loving thanks go to my husband, Chris Diffee, to whom I dedicate this book. He has read every word on every page, talked exhaustively over every idea, and had faith in this project when I did not. This book, like my life, is unimaginable without him.

Erotic Subjects

⚬⚬

Introduction

Erotic Subjects examines the intricate relationship between sexuality, politics, and literature in early modern England. A good deal of important recent scholarship has studied the politics of sexuality; this book studies the sexual dimension of politics. Throughout the following pages, I examine some surprising implications of the commonplace early modern equation of political and erotic unions—the claim that sovereign and subject, like husband and wife, are bound as much by reciprocal love as by law or necessity. Numerous scholars have observed that this translation of hierarchy into a romance between ruler and ruled shaped political discourse from the reign of Elizabeth I through that of Charles II. This work has taught us, as Arthur F. Marotti memorably insists, that "love is not love" in early modern literature. Rather, it is a discourse about power and influence, ambition and anxiety.[1]

This book argues that love is not "love" in another sense, one that has received little critical attention but that is equally important for understanding sixteenth- and seventeenth-century political thought. What we typically think of as "love"—a beautiful and benevolent attachment to an other—rarely appears in early modern erotic literature. Instead, love tends to show up as what Lauren Berlant has called a "queer feeling."[2] Narratives of masochism, erotic violence, and cross-gendered

1. Marotti, "Elizabethan Sonnet Sequences and the Social Order." Other insightful accounts of the ideological force of early modern erotic discourses include Montrose, "Figurations of Gender and Power"; Goldberg, *James I and the Politics of Literature*; Norbrook, *Poetry and Politics*; Sharpe, *Criticism*; Victoria Kahn, *Wayward Contracts*; Purkiss, *Literature, Gender, and Politics*; and Bowers, *British Seduction Stories*.

2. As Berlant insists, love shares the complexities of sexuality. Despite the "absorption of the fantasy of love by normativity," love remains charged with ambivalent, aggressive, masochistic, and narcissistic impulses that disrupt the ideals it is invoked to serve ("Love, A Queer Feeling," 443–444).

identification repeatedly supplant those of courtship and marriage in the work of politically active writers from Sidney to Milton. For these authors, love almost invariably inspires desires and fantasies that resist normalizing, rational structures. As we shall see, since love was thought to inspire political consent and service, attention to the "queer"—peculiar and eccentric—nature of eros also accentuates the queer side of politics.[3] Allegiance and agency appear far less conscious and deliberate than rationalist accounts of politics would have it when Philip Sidney depicts abjection as a source of both moral authority and sexual arousal; when Spenser and Shakespeare make it hard to tell the difference between rape and seduction; when Mary Wroth and Margaret Cavendish depict women who adore treacherous or abusive lovers; when court masques by Ben Jonson, Aurelian Townshend, Thomas Carew, and William Davenant stress the pleasures of enslavement; or when Milton represents Adam's admiration for Eve as equally composed of contempt and self-loathing. Because these and other early modern authors understand political subjection in sexual terms, their analyses of desire are also analyses of how power works. This literature thus constitutes an alternate tradition of political theory that stresses a perverse component of sovereignty, one that disrupts more conventional accounts of politics as driven by rational choice, false consciousness, or brute force.[4]

In the late sixteenth century, the insight that political behavior is often shaped by baffling, even self-destructive, desires inspires a strain of political writing concerned with the psychological roots of tyranny. The association of eros and politics appears throughout early modern political tracts, as well as early modern literature,

---

3. *Oxford English Dictionary*, 2d ed., s.v. "queer." Throughout *Erotic Subjects*, I bring together the early modern meaning of "queer" with Michael Warner's definition of the term as signifying not only desires that reject heteronormativity but modes of being that challenge the "regimes of the normal" more largely ("Introduction" to *Fear of a Queer Planet*, xxvii). I also draw on Dollimore's definition of the "perverse dynamic" as that which "denotes certain instabilities and contradictions within dominant structures which exist by virtue of exactly what those structures simultaneously contain and exclude" (*Sexual Dissidence*, 33) and Freccero's argument that queer theory works to critique identitarian constructs by examining how not only gay and lesbian identities but also "certain forms of heterosexual, transsexual, and transgender identities and bisexuality" destabilize ideas of normativity (*Queer/Early/Modern*, 13-30; 14). I do, however, take caution from work that has detailed some of the pitfalls of using the word "queer" to describe any and all sexualities that do not conform to married, procreative ideals (see Schlichter, "Queer at Last?"; and Sharon Marcus, "Review Essay"). I consequently limit my use of the term to describe representations of literary and political affects that prominently run counter to ideals of rational and "normal" desire and practice, regardless of the gender of the persons involved. For further discussion, see chapter 1, below.

4. Foucault's critical insight that power sustains itself not by prohibiting desire but by producing it has long offered an important challenge to views of the libido as a free, natural force that is distinct from the legal and political systems that would manage it. For Foucault, such systems themselves generate an unruly range of attachments and perversions; see *History of Sexuality*.

and the discourse of love was a central part of what Quentin Skinner has called the "normative vocabulary" of sixteenth- and seventeenth-century thinkers.[5] Consequently, the period's depictions of love can help us understand how people explained and experienced subjection in an era of personal monarchy. As a long tradition of classical and medieval literature attests, love is experienced as both the most private and voluntary and the most alien and invasive of emotions. Actions can be externally compelled, but desires cannot—yet when one does fall in love, it rarely feels like an entirely conscious or voluntary decision. Elizabethan writers retain those classical descriptions of desire as both choice and compulsion, but the period also sees significant shifts in the definition of pleasure. For it is at this time that we have the emergence in England of two discourses that explore the sadomasochistic potential of unlimited devotion: Protestant hagiography and Petrarchan courtship.[6] Although they differ radically in their structures, the hagiographic and Petrarchan traditions both see suffering, not joy, as evidence of true love: if we love someone even though it hurts us, our affections must be both selfless and sincere. As early modern erotic literature recognizes, this association of pain with love may lead both political and erotic subjects to accept, or even enjoy, their own abuse. Love still offers considerable comforts and pleasures, but narratives of redemption and fulfillment do not tell the full story of its effects.

I begin with a discussion of the historical and theoretical frameworks of this book. I then turn to an analysis of two of the most influential and extensive sixteenth-century studies of the relation between love, pain, and power: Sidney's *Arcadia* and Spenser's *Faerie Queene*. These Elizabethan romances adopt many of the generic and formal conventions that Barbara Fuchs has called the "strategies" of romance—love, nostalgia, chivalry, magic, questing, interlaced plots, and deferred closure, among others—to examine the problem of political obedience in Elizabethan England.[7] For my analytic purposes, the most important of these strategies is romance's depiction of undying love as both a sign of virtue and a potentially destructive force. The *Arcadia* and *The Faerie Queene* challenge Elizabethan idealizations of love and loyalty by showing that loving someone no matter what may not be such a good thing after all. For Sidney and Spenser not only recognize that

---

5. For Skinner, a "normative vocabulary" is the set of terms available for discussion of a given problem or issue (*Foundations*, 1:x–xv).

6. For an analysis of the role that these traditions played in Elizabethan propaganda, see Yates, *Astraea*, 29–120. Petrarchan poetry, of course, had been long been available in England, but it is in the Elizabethan period that it achieves the height of its popularity. I discuss the relation between Foxe's *Acts and Monuments* and English Petrarchan poetry in more detail in chapter 1.

7. Fuchs, *Romance*, 2. Important general studies of the ideological work of romance include Northrop Frye, *Anatomy of Criticism*, 186–205, and *Secular Scripture*; Jameson, *Political Unconscious*, 103–150; Patterson, *Censorship and Interpretation*; McKeon, *Origins of the English Novel*; and Victoria Kahn, *Wayward Contracts*. For the history of the English romance tradition, see Cooper, *English Romance in Time*.

absolute commitment to another may look more like masochism or obsession than like what we think of as love. They also stress the political implications of such steadfast passion. If submission and even suffering are desirable in themselves, then it becomes hard to determine when injustice calls for resistance. This irrational, addictive aspect of human desire is a problem that politically engaged writers continued to explore by drawing on Sidneian and Spenserian romance throughout the late sixteenth and seventeenth centuries. And because the authors I discuss were all reading not only Sidney and Spenser but also, to a large extent, one another, we can understand their work as an ongoing discussion of the nature of sovereignty.[8]

Each chapter of *Erotic Subjects* examines how particular authors use scenarios of erotic subjugation and suffering to ponder questions about sovereignty peculiar to their own moments in English history. Yet, as I argue, early modern erotic literature is not merely topical. Rather, the persistent reappearance of erotic violence as a figure for political union allows these writers to explore power and desire in structural, not just practical or immediate, terms. It is this theoretical component of erotic literature that allows it to speak to political questions that emerge well after its initial moment of production—including questions still central to our contemporary debates about the relationship between gender, sexuality, and power.

The chronological order of my chapters would seem to suggest a developmental narrative from the monarchalism of Sidney to the republicanism of Milton—and thus a move from the unfathomable attachments of personal monarchy to a more restrained constitutionalism. Instead of telling such a teleological story, however, I argue that the persistent use of erotic discourse from the reign of Elizabeth I to that of Charles II challenges easy definitions of naïve royalism and rational republicanism, sycophantic service and principled resistance.[9] Given that the first recorded use of the term "royalist" was in 1643, following the outbreak of the first civil war, simple distinctions between royalist and republican ideologies are inadequate to describe many of the writers I discuss.[10] For all but the most radical apologists for the sort of Continental-style absolutism long critiqued by legal theorists like John Fortescue, support for monarchy generally meant support for an ancient constitution in which king, lords, and commons all shared in English governance.[11] The texts that I analyze thus supplement histories of sovereignty that stress polemic or

---

8. The publication histories of the *Arcadia* and *The Faerie Queene* indicate their enduring popularity throughout the seventeenth century: the *Arcadia* went through thirteen editions between 1590 and 1674; *The Faerie Queene* went through four editions between 1590 and 1679, with multiple printings of each.

9. I thus emphasize the political dimensions of the changes that Tilmouth has seen in seventeenth-century moral philosophy, which recognized that the forces of passion and self-interest played a greater role in determining human action than had been allowed by Aristotelian or Augustinian theory (*Passion's Triumph*).

10. *OED*, 2d ed., s.v. "royalist."

11. For distinctions between monarchalism and absolutism, see Burgess, *Politics* and *Absolute Monarchy*; and Greenberg, *Radical Face*.

progress, for they describe a more hesitant series of negotiations, a political land-scape in which conflicts were as likely to be within individual subjects as between ideological factions.

In chapter 1, I discuss the political questions with which early modern literature engages, and I describe the theoretical frameworks through which I read this litera-ture. I begin by situating debates over obedience and resistance within a history of English theories of mixed rule, which supposed that the submission of sovereign and subject to one another was the basis of good government. I then tell the story of how sixteenth- and seventeenth-century writers, drawing on the discourses of hagiography and courtship, came to understand pain and sacrifice as central components of both erotic pleasure and moral power. As I argue, the late sixteenth century is a crucial juncture in the history of political thought, as well as the history of love. Early modern studies of erotic subjugation and suffering depart strikingly from medieval and early sixteenth-century analogies between conjugal and polit-ical bonds. In those earlier models, marriage signified a union of mutual service and restraint in contrast to the selfish passions of adultery. The relation between hus-band and wife thus exemplified the reciprocal duties of sovereign and subject. In the late sixteenth century, the private emotion of erotic love begins to compete with the public institution of marriage as the central analogue for political union.[12] I am especially interested in how representations of courtship, seduction, and desire, which we might see as offering the prehistory of both marital and political con-tracts, expose irrationality and ambivalence as invariable aspects of political affilia-tion, rather than irregularities to be avoided. I conclude this chapter by proposing that, given the early modern period's habitual correlation of political and sexual affect and behavior, recent theoretical studies of gender and sexuality can give us new insights into sixteenth- and seventeenth-century political history. At the same time, attention to the queer moments of erotic fantasy and identification in early modern texts can compel us to reassess our own contemporary mythologies of love, courtship, marriage, and power.

My second chapter focuses on Philip Sidney, whose use of romance frameworks to explore the concept of sovereignty would shape literary forms and political discourse for the century to come. This chapter reads Sidney's *Arcadia* as exploring the position of "forward Protestants" like himself who opposed many of Elizabeth's

---

12. This is not to say, of course, that conjugal or contractual language disappeared altogether from English discourse. English monarchs from Elizabeth I on continued to claim that they were married to England, and as Victoria Kahn has shown, the marriage contract persisted as both a central political analogy and a site of ideological conflict throughout the seven-teenth century (*Wayward Contracts*). Moreover, as Dolan astutely demonstrates, competing definitions of marriage itself as a relationship of hierarchy, fusion, and contract meant that conjugal ideology created as many conflicts as it solved (*Marriage and Violence*). However, much of the literature that I examine is as interested in the shifting and often inexplicable passions that, at least notionally, lead to companionate bonds as in the contractual or hier-archical character of those bonds once they are established.

policies even as they depended on her power.[13] Rewriting political theory in terms of sexual desire and violence, Sidney examines the dilemmas of oppositional subjects through portraits of women who endure everything from disfigurement to death rather than betray their lovers. Like John Foxe's martyrs, these women redefine heroism even as they force their persecutors either to reform or to destroy themselves in the pursuit of power. Consequently, the hagiographic structure of the *Arcadia* shows that dominance and submission, like masculinity and femininity, are positions that may be occupied by either prince or subject.

Chapter 3 reads Spenser's *Faerie Queene* as a study of the dangers and limitations of the hagiographic politics recommended by Sidney. Writing in a period of increasingly pronounced absolutist discourse—one that Patrick Collinson has called the "nasty nineties"—Spenser questions whether subjects are psychologically capable of practicing the principled resistance that Sidney advocates.[14] In contrast to the more optimistic politics of the *Arcadia*, Spenser explores a Petrarchan erotics of subjection in which it is hard to tell the difference between beloved sovereign and sadistic tyrant. By blurring the lines between rape and seduction, Spenser suggests that love is no longer a sign of sovereign virtue but may be produced by the subject's own self-serving fantasies. The 1596 edition of *The Faerie Queene* thus explores the grim possibility that, because individual motives and desires are always conflicted and often indiscernible, subjects may willfully confuse the internal force of their own perverse passions with the external compulsion of the ruler and therefore find themselves colluding with tyranny.

Whereas Spenser is concerned with the collapse of spiritual resolve, Shakespeare's *The Rape of Lucrece* and *Pericles* consider the problem of physical defeat. Is a subject still complicit with tyranny when he or she has been overcome? In chapter 4, I argue that both *Lucrece* and *Pericles* understand this problem in terms of rape. Because rape may leave such physical marks as pregnancy or disease, the violated woman poses the contradiction of a pure mind in a polluted body. Shakespeare's meditations on physical impurity explore in sexual terms the Tacitean proposition that a corrupt political world may contaminate even the most virtuous of subjects, regardless of their intentions—a pessimistic stance that characterized much late Elizabethan and early Jacobean thought. The individual agency that both Sidney and Spenser take for granted itself becomes a problem, since the virtuous subject is held responsible for resisting tyranny that cannot be stopped. By concluding with descriptions of armed popular revolts, these works move beyond the individual and aristocratic focus of Sidney and Spenser to imagine a world of such overwhelming corruption that organized rebellion may be the only antidote to tyranny.

13. I borrow this phrase from Worden, who uses it to describe Sidney and other members of Elizabeth's Council who urged the queen to head an international Protestant League that would aggressively combat Catholic power (*Sound of Virtue*, xxii, 32). Collinson offers a detailed discussion of the relation between religious conviction and political practice ("Puritans, Men of Business, and Elizabethan Parliaments").

14. Collinson, "Religious Satire in the 1590s," 170.

Like Shakespeare, Mary Wroth is concerned with the practical limits of resistance theory, but she returns to an Elizabethan attention to the psychological dimensions of these limits. Yet, as I argue in chapter 5, Wroth's *Urania* offers a more perverse view of power than the Sidneian or Spenserian romances to which it alludes. For Wroth, it is not that subjects are too weak or self-deceiving to fight tyranny. Rather, by representing love in Petrarchan terms that are consciously masochistic, the *Urania* warns that subjects may put up with tyranny because they actually find enjoyment in abjection. As a member of the Sidney–Herbert circle who opposed many of James I's policies, Wroth warns of the dangerous private and public effects of such obsessive devotion. But she also acknowledges the allure of erotic martyrdom—a stance that emerges in her relentless portraits of women betrayed, degraded, and tortured by men they love.

In chapter 6, I turn to a genre that has often been understood as celebrating exactly the sort of voluntary enslavement that writers like Wroth examined: the Caroline masque. This chapter suggests that the politics of court entertainments look very different when we read them in terms of the erotic tradition I have been tracing. To this end, I examine several masques of the 1630s: Jonson's *Chloridia*, Townshend's *Tempe Restored*, Carew's *Coelum Britannicum*, and Davenant's *Salmacida Spolia*. It is usual to read these spectacles as promoting a theory of monarchal absolutism. I maintain instead that these masques function as a form of counsel for both Charles I and his elite subjects. On the one hand, they remind Charles of the Elizabethan principle that kings rule with the consent of their people. On the other, these masques' Petrarchan view of love warns subjects that the affection that should distinguish king from tyrant may just as easily convert loyal service into helpless slavery.

In chapter 7, I consider what happens to Sidneian ideals of resistance after the civil wars and regicide illustrated their logical extreme. Here, I propose a new reading of Margaret Cavendish's fiction, one grounded in the ancient constitutionalism to which both Cavendish and her husband, the Duke of Newcastle, subscribed. Cavendish's romances struggle to find common ground between the extremes of absolutism and republicanism by turning to the Elizabethan discourse of love: this model insists that monarchs' power is limited by subjects' affections even as it acknowledges love's latent violence. However, by imagining only compromised, even degrading, erotic unions, Cavendish acknowledges that the overwhelming—Petrarchan—desires of sovereign and subject alike may vitiate any possibility of mixed rule. Because the allure of power can be irresistible, the subjects who should restore justice may equally imperil it.

My final chapter argues that Milton's conception of republican virtue looks very different in light of his self-acknowledged debt to "our sage and serious Poet *Spencer*," whom he calls "a better teacher than *Scotus* or *Aquinas*."[15] Milton inherits

---

15. *Areopagitica*, in *Complete Prose Works of John Milton*, 2:516 (hereinafter abbreviated as *CP*).

Spenser's doubt in the human ability to recognize, much less control, self-destructive and perverse impulses. As Milton's divorce tracts acknowledge, and as *Paradise Lost* illustrates, the need for others may really express a narcissistic wish for mastery and coherence that threatens not only conjugal harmony but also the formation of any state grounded on ideals of public service, debate, and compromise. In making Eve's submission the model by which Adam regains his proper relation to God, *Paradise Lost* also situates such feminine humility as a model for political subjects who wish to restore godly rule, which requires chaste leaders who welcome aid and counsel. This Christian republican ideal of humility modulates the classical republican ideal of hard masculinity into a more androgynous *imitatio Christi*. *Paradise Lost* accordingly treats feminine chastity, service, and submission as signs of self-discipline, which for Milton is the truest, and most difficult, form of human authority.

In my conclusion, I propose that reading the history of sexuality together with the history of politics may change our understanding of both. By moving across a wide range of genres, political positions, and historical moments, this book as a whole shows how attentiveness to the erotic aspects of subjection can complicate and expand what we think of as political history. Awareness of love's sadomasochistic potential is hardly new to the early modern period. Numerous Greek and medieval romances depict passion in obsessive and excruciating terms that strongly influence the writers I study. But early modern erotic literature is unique in that it sees human desire, in all of its glorious perversity, as the source of political order, not its enemy. By reading these texts through the lenses of contemporary feminist and queer theory, I uncover intersections and tensions between past and present theories of sexuality as a central component of public power. Ultimately, I hope that *Erotic Subjects* will give us new ways to look at the particular texts I examine and the larger story they tell about the desires that drive political engagement—both then and now.

CHAPTER 1

༄

Erotic Subjects in English History

The analogy between conjugal and political bonds is at least as ancient as Aristotle's *Politics*, and in England it had long been used to describe the balance of royal authority, common law, and parliamentary counsel.[1] In the sixteenth century, political obligation was increasingly understood not only in the contractual terms of marriage but also in the affective terms of love. It is therefore unsurprising that early modern literary works that appear to be primarily concerned with courtship and seduction are in fact fraught with reflections on political obligation and loyalty. This attention to the sexual dimension of politics both connects early modern England to a venerable tradition of medieval political thought and signifies a shift in conceptions of obedience and resistance. In the pages below, I trace some of the significant developments and influences in sixteenth- and seventeenth-century English thought. I then discuss the historiographic and theoretical frameworks that shape my analysis of the period's literary representations of power, gender, and sexual desire.

Medieval ancient constitutionalism saw the relation between ruler and ruled in terms of a marriage contract. This union was most potently symbolized in the coronation ceremony at the moment that the king put St. Edward's ring on his "marrying finger," or the fourth finger of his right hand. When he accepted this token of marriage to the realm, the king vowed to uphold the laws, customs, and religion of England in exchange for his subject's service and obedience.[2] Authority and submission were mutually sustaining, so the ruler who abused his power risked

---

1. Aristotle describes marriage as the original political association (*Politics*, 1.2).
2. Greenberg *Radical Face*, 1–35, 45–53. For further discussion of ancient constitutionalism in sixteenth- and seventeenth-century England, see Pocock, *Ancient Constitution*; and Burgess, *Politics*.

losing it altogether. And this view of contractual obligation was not just a metaphor: as Linda Levy Peck has observed, the principle that a legitimate king will submit to law and counsel was repeatedly invoked in the thirteenth through fifteenth centuries to limit royal power and depose five monarchs.[3]

Mixed government, like its conjugal analogue, was based on the conviction that human beings inevitably want things that are bad for them.[4] This propensity was particularly dangerous in the king, who was in a unique position to indulge his destructive passions. For the good of both himself and his subjects, the king had to be bridled by common law and parliamentary counsel. But the belief that subjects must restrain royal will did not challenge divine right theories of kingship. Rather, sacral and limited ideas of monarchy reinforced one another. In Sir John Fortescue's influential formula, the English ruler's submission to the political community paradoxically enhanced his power. According to Fortescue, England's status as a *dominium politicum et regale*, in which government is "administered by the wisdom and counsel of many," made it superior to Continental countries where monarchs ruled with *dominium regale*, or absolute royal power.[5] The ability to do evil, like the ability to fall ill, signifies weakness and impotence. Given a king's natural human weakness, only law and counsel can keep him from sinning. Because they lack these restraints, Fortescue argues, the absolute monarchs of the Continent may easily fall victim to their own passions and so "cannot be deemed free, being fettered with such heavy bonds of impotence." By contrast, the political king of England submits to law and counsel and thereby achieves a *character angelicus* of divine perfection and immortality.[6] Unlike his absolutist peers, the political king "is free and powerful" for he "is able to defend his own people against enemies alien and native, and also their goods and property, not only against the rapine of their neighbours and fellow-citizens, but against his own oppression and plunder, even though his own passions and necessities struggle for the contrary. For who can be freer and more powerful than he who is able to vanquish not only others but also himself? The king ruling his people politically can and always does do this."[7]

This belief that a ruler's submission enhances his power influenced many Tudor political theorists, who tended to judge monarchs based on their proximity to the

---

3. Peck, "Kingship, Counsel and Law in Early Stuart Britain," 81.

4. The idea of natural human depravity has roots in religious, political, and philosophical writing. Bushnell, for instance, discusses the Platonic origins of the belief that the king's power put him in danger of becoming the irrepressible, self-indulgent tyrant that all humans secretly wish to be (*Tragedies*, 12–15, 37–79). For an early modern study of the dangerous power of human passion, see Burton, *Anatomy of Melancholy*. See also my discussion in chapter 4 of Augustine's descriptions of original sin in *Citie of God*.

5. Fortescue, "The Governance of England," in *On the Laws and Governance of England*, 86. All further references to Fortescue's work will be to this edition. For the close relation between counsel and free speech in the seventeenth century, see Colclough, *Freedom of Speech*.

6. Fortescue, "In Praise of the Laws of England," 53. For a discussion of the concept of the *character angelicus*, see Kantorowicz, *King's Two Bodies*.

7. Fortescue, "In Praise of the Laws of England," 53.

Fortescuean model of the political king. During the Henrician Reformation, the law's ability to restrain the king's "passions and necessities" came to seem especially urgent. For in order to justify his supremacy over the English church, Henry VIII claimed an imperial power that was above the law. Because the king was the absolute, divinely ordained ruler of both church and state, he argued, the pope had no authority over English subjects. Early Tudor writers like Thomas Elyot, Christopher St. German, and Thomas Starkey opposed this Henrician thesis of sacral monarchy and insisted that without law and counsel the king became a tyrant. In order to prevent such royal degeneration, they argued, the king's imperial power was limited by the assent of the realm as represented in parliament. Indeed, the role of Henry's parliaments in legitimating the break with Rome underscored the importance of this assembly.

Like their predecessors, Henrician writers described the relation between monarch and populace in terms of a marriage between a masculine *imperium* and a feminine *concilium*. Marriage offered a model of a voluntary and reciprocal relation in which the sovereign would secure legitimacy by submitting to law and counsel, while the subject would find security in the ruler's might.[8] By reminding the king that he needed his subjects as much as they needed him, Henrician theorists sought to guard England's ancient constitution from the absolutist implications of the break with Rome. In practice, this belief that the king ruled in concert with his noble subjects reached its zenith during the reign of Edward VI. During this time, Edward's Lord Protectors Edward Seymour, Duke of Somerset, and John Dudley, Duke of Northumberland, both described England as experiencing a species of interregnum that would stabilize the realm until Edward came of age. The political circumstance of a king whose youth made him incapable of ruling alone thus advanced commonwealth ideology as a superior alternative to Henrician royal supremacy.[9]

The Fortescuean maxim that the sovereign must "vanquish not only others but also himself" applied not just to kings but also to subjects who might be tempted to obey illegal or ungodly commands rather than risk persecution. During the reign of Mary I, the Protestant experience of exile and martyrdom amplified medieval theories of dissent into arguments for full-blown resistance—and further shifted the responsibility for just rule from sovereign to subject.[10] For Protestant exiles like John Knox, Christopher Goodman, and John Ponet, resistance entailed psychological, as well as physical, struggle. These writers turned the question of whether to obey a Catholic ruler into a choice between body and soul. Knox, for instance,

8. Elyot, Starkey, and St. German all draw on Sir John Fortescue's claim that the origin of public power lay in the people. For a discussion of these Reformation tracts, see John Guy, "The Henrician Age" and "Models of the State"; and Kelley, "Elizabethan Political Thought."

9. McLaren, *Political Culture*, 80–81, 198–200.

10. Guy, "Models of the State," 126. For a detailed study of sixteenth-century Calvinist resistance theory, see Skinner, *Foundations*, 2:189–238.

charged that those who submitted to Mary were not passive victims, but willful "slaves of Satan, and servantes of iniquitie."[11]

In the eyes of many Marian resistance theorists, female rule epitomized the reciprocal dangers of idolatrous obedience and unbridled appetite encouraged by the institution of kingship itself.[12] Conflating what Knox called the "monstrous regiment of women" with royal tyranny in general, Goodman and Ponet endorsed resistance against any ruler who threatened English law and religion. According to Goodman, tyranny could thrive only if subjects were so "bewitched with Satans false illusions, that they are not able to put difference betwyxte obedience & disobedience" and therefore practiced "unlawfull obedience." In "fearinge man more than God," Goodman charged, Marian subjects became "instrumentes of impietie, and destroyers of their native countrie, which firste were ordayned in Realmes to stande in defence of trewe religion, lawes, and welth of their nation, and to be a shylde (to their power) against their enimies in tyme of warre, and a brydel at home to their Princes in tyme of peace."[13] Those who chose such "unlawfull obedience," even under duress, were as culpable as the tyrant they served—so culpable that, as Ponet darkly warned, in the afterlife "not only the doers, but also the consentors to evill, shall be punished."[14]

Mary I's reign was a watershed in English theories of political psychology, for to many resistance writers it appeared that subjects had supported a monarch bent on destroying either their bodies or their souls. In stressing the equivalence of passive submission and active participation, Marian writers introduced problems that would occupy political theorists for the next century: How does one distinguish between proper obedience and improper slavery? When does reverence become idolatry, discretion cowardice, self-protection self-promotion?

Elizabethan apologists like John Aylmer would see the answer not in a change of government, but in a reaffirmation of the ancient constitutionalist principle of balance and reciprocity—a principle that appeared to have been abandoned in the mid-1550s. Refuting Knox's equation of female rule with tyranny, Aylmer artfully defended Elizabeth I's legitimacy by asserting the limited nature of her office. Aylmer insisted that a queen regnant posed no more danger than a king, since she was subject to the same constitutional limitations. Like her father before her,

11. Knox, *First Blast*, 2, 9, 32.
12. For extended discussions of these texts as they shaped ideas of gender and power in Elizabethan England, see McLaren, 46–78; and Montrose, "Spenser and the Elizabethan Political Imaginary," 907–911.
13. *Superior Powers*, 9, 14, 35–36.
14. *A Shorte Treatise*, 28. For Ponet, this evil was secular, as well as spiritual, for "Next unto God, men ought to love their Countrey, and the whole Common-wealth, before any member of it: as Kings and Princes (be they never so great) are but members" (28). Marian exiles supported rebellion in practice, as well as theory: Ponet returned to England in 1554 to participate in Wyatt's rebellion, and both Knox and Goodman defend the rebellion in print (Knox, 52; Goodman, 221ff.).

Elizabeth was a "mixte ruler" not a "mere monark." In fact, a female ruler might best exemplify the Fortescuean political monarch: Elizabeth's gender, like Edward VI's youth, attested to her natural need for parliament to restrain and guide her. "If the parliament vse their priuileges," Aylmer argued, "the King can ordein nothing without them. If he do: it is his fault in usurping it, and their follye in permitting it." Had Mary's parliaments used their privileges as steadfastly as Henry VIII's assemblies— had they "feared no more the fearcenes of a woman, then they did the displeasure of such a man"—they would "not haue stouped contrary to their othes and allegiaunce to the crowne, againste the preuilege of that house, vppon their marye bones to receiue the Deuels blessinge."[15] Royal usurpation is a result of parliamentary "follye" as much as royal "fault." Fear of a monarch's "fearcenes" or "displeasure" becomes something of a self-fulfilling prophecy: by treating rulers as though they have absolute power, subjects in effect give them that power—and betray their duties to crown and commonwealth in the process.

Aylmer insisted that rather than indulge this irrational, idolatrous fear, subjects must push back against attempts to expand monarchal authority. Like many of his predecessors, Aylmer likened political relations to marriage: "I might neare gather an equall authoritie betwixte the wife and the husbande. For euery man knoweth that in the rule of the chefe, whiche is called Aristocratie (whereunto [Aristotle] likeneth Mariage) there is equalitie and none vsurpeth vpon an other."[16] This marriage is based on contractual exchange, not selfless love. If subjects dutifully serve their prince, Aylmer promises, "You shall finde loue for your obedience, faithe for your truthe, care and study to keepe you, for your redy good will to obey hir."[17] Subjects owe their queen obedience, loyalty, and good will—but not unconditionally. They should expect service and protection in return. In the vision of marriage that Aylmer outlines, love, faith, and loyalty are objects of exchange, not ends in themselves. Subjects can protect their "equalitie" and avoid usurpation only by demanding that their queen live up to her end of the bargain.

Elizabeth herself famously exploited the language of love to describe her relations with her subjects. But whereas constitutionalist writers like Aylmer described subjects' obedience in the contractual terms of marriage, Elizabeth and her courtiers tended to describe it in the selfless terms of romantic devotion.[18] Elizabeth was well aware that her sex upset the traditional analogy aligning sovereign with husband, political nation with wife. The queen and her supporters thus supplemented Aylmer's constitutionalism with the discourse of desire. This attention to the affective dimension of politics helped make female rule comprehensible within

15. Aylmer, *Harborowe*, sig. H4, H2.
16. Aylmer, sig. I3.
17. Aylmer, sig. R2.
18. To be sure, Elizabeth described herself as married to England, but she described this marriage in terms that resembled the selfless devotion of Petrarchan courtship rather than the contractual exchange depicted by Aylmer.

a patriarchal world: like the mistress of courtly romance, Elizabeth's power over her subjects was more erotic than formal. According to this narrative, it was not just parliament or law but also the people's love for their queen that proved that their service was voluntary and therefore distinguished Elizabeth's authority from the "monstrous regiment" of her sister.

The Elizabethan discourse of love did not dispense with the ancient constitutionalist principle of resistance, but artfully translated it into affective terms. "Let tyrants fear," Elizabeth reportedly declared in her famous speech at Tilbury, "I have so behaved myself that under God I have placed my chiefest strength and safeguard in the loyal hearts and good will of my subjects."[19] According to this logic, reliance on subjects' "loyal hearts and good will" both restrains and reaffirms the monarch's authority. And this affective contract works all by itself. Subjects' instinctive hatred for a ruler who hurts them automatically keeps monarchal will in check, even without legal or contractual limits to sovereign power. As a sign of love, submission is internally motivated and so cannot be compelled—and if obedience depends on love, it is not subjects who should fear tyrants but tyrants who should fear subjects.

This assumption that love and force were opposites was strikingly challenged by two discourses that shaped Elizabethan political thought and that would continue to influence English ideas of sovereignty for the century to come: Protestant hagiography and Petrarchan courtship. These seemingly unrelated discourses both challenge distinctions between love and force by stressing the complex relation between pleasure and pain, domination and submission. Protestant hagiography, particularly in the influential work of John Foxe, shares with Petrarchan poetry the conviction that unrewarded suffering is the most reliable evidence of sincere love. But the relations they imagine have very different structures. In hagiographic depictions of suffering for the sake of love, the earthly torturer and the divine love object compete for the subject's obedience; in Petrarchan courtship, the heartless tyrant is the prototype of the beloved.

In Foxean hagiography, the tyrant's cruelty allows the martyr to demonstrate the strength of his or her love for the True Church—a strength that, paradoxically, comes from an acceptance of absolute subjection. As recent scholars have argued, Foxe's attention to pain distinguishes his work from its medieval forbears. Whereas medieval Catholic saints' lives tend to stress the miraculous release from suffering, Foxe emphasizes agonized endurance. It is their suffering that makes Protestant martyrs models of strength and virtue.[20] Foxe urges readers to emulate his "mild

19. "Queen Elizabeth's Armada Speech to the Troops at Tilbury, August 9, 1588," in *Elizabeth I: Collected Works*, 326. For the different manuscript versions and sources of this speech, see the notes to this volume (325). Montrose discusses the debate over the attribution of this speech to Elizabeth (*Subject of Elizabeth*, 148).

20. For these distinctions, see Knott, *Discourses of Martyrdom*; Marotti, *Religious Ideology*, esp. 9–31, 66–94; and Truman, "John Foxe." Monta qualifies this distinction, arguing that Foxe maintains in subtle form hagiographic conventions of the mortification of the flesh and last minute signs of divine approval (*Martyrdom and Literature*, 53–78).

and constant martyrs," declaring them "the true conquerors of the world, by whom we learn true manhood." Unlike the "bloody warriors" whose heroism they surpass, Foxean martyrs conquer not through active combat, but by "offer[ing] their bodies willingly to the rough handling of their tormenters."[21] For Foxe, mildness and constancy, virtues traditionally encouraged in women, are constitutive of "true manhood." The abject, feminized figure of the martyr thus becomes a model to which the virtuous male subject ought to aspire. And even as Foxe's male martyrs embrace a feminine subjectivity, his many female martyrs display "true manhood" through their constant devotion to God.[22] Agony and abjection are signs of a power that reconfigures traditional definitions of heroism and masculinity.[23]

This focus on enduring rather than inflicting pain also reveals the limits of coercive power and thereby challenges conventional ideas of authority and submission. In sixteenth-century England, the hagiographic equation of suffering, virtue, and power had clear constitutional implications. Foxe prominently fuses Protestant demands for godly rule, a humanist emphasis on conciliar guidance, and ancient constitutionalist defenses of English liberty. As Janelle Greenberg points out, Foxe printed with his *Acts and Monuments* the first complete English translation of Chapter 17 of the *Leges Edwardi Confessoris*, which states that a ruler who fails in his duty "loses the very name of a king." He thereby recalls the reciprocal promises made by king and people in the coronation oath and ties Protestant martyrdom to just political resistance against perjurious rulers from William the Conqueror to Mary I.[24] For Foxe, the martyrs' feminized suffering offered bodily evidence that the tyrant had forfeited all claim to legitimate—consensual—rule and thereby released

---

21. Foxe, "The Utility of this Story" (1563), in *Acts and Monuments*, 1:xxv–xxvi.

22. Hickerson points out that of the 358 Tudor martyrs described by Foxe's *Acts and Monuments* forty-eight are women (*Making Women Martyrs*, 7). By contrast, of the 239 Catholics executed for treason between 1535 and 1603, only three were women (Dillon, *Construction of Martyrdom*, 3; and Lake and Questier, "Margaret Clitherow," 87). For insightful discussions of the gender dynamics of martyrdom, see Hickerson; Mary Beth Rose, *Gender and Heroism*; and Coles, *Religion*, 1–12.

23. Schoenfeldt has argued that in the context of Renaissance courtly discourse, submission cannot be gendered exclusively as feminine ("Gender and Conduct," 310–312). While I agree that there were many possibilities of what Schoenfeldt calls "manipulative submission" available to male courtiers, the self-abnegation with which I am concerned in this book is powerful precisely because it evinces sincerity, not manipulation. Such suffering and sacrifice, represented largely by female characters in the literature I examine, challenge conventional understandings of gendered identity and political agency.

24. Greenberg, 61–62, 91–96. Helgerson notes the subversive potential of the officially sanctioned *Acts and Monuments*, arguing that in the writings of Foxe and of John Bale, the equation of martyrdom with truth, exile with corruption, stigmatizes as anti-Christian any regime that exercises its monopoly on institutional violence in matters of religion (*Forms of Nationhood*, 259). Along with constitutional history, Foxe's martyrology follows John Bale and other reformers in arguing that the Roman Catholic Church had corrupted the true, primitive Christianity that Protestant martyrs died defending. For post-Reformation battles over English church history, see Dillon, 28–70.

subjects from their obligation to obey. And reformers were not the only English subjects to notice the power of martyrdom to inspire and justify sedition. Indeed, the connection between religious belief and political resistance became codified under Elizabeth I. Under Mary, Protestants had been executed for heresy; under Elizabeth, Catholics were executed for treason. Those who wished to see England return to Roman Catholicism equally drew on the discourse of victimization to justify the challenges to royal authority posed by recusants, Jesuits, and seminary priests in Tudor and Stuart England.[25]

The fact that suffering and sacrifice were compelling evidence of virtue to both sides of the confessional divide in early modern England indicates the extent to which hagiography helped shape political ideas of loyalty and resistance. We can take the changing fortunes of Foxe's *Acts and Monuments* as just one example of the power of hagiographic narratives to shape public opinion. Whereas in Elizabethan England Foxe's *Acts and Monuments* had by law stood in every English cathedral, by the seventeenth century Foxe's work had become sufficiently associated with political resistance that Archbishop Laud refused to license a new edition in 1637.[26] But by the 1640s, royalists were as likely as parliamentarians to exploit the equation of suffering and virtue, particularly after the execution of Charles I. *Eikon Basilike: The Pourtrature of His Sacred Majestie in his Solitudes and Sufferings* was one of the most popular books of the 1650s. Its depiction of Charles as an innocent victim of parliamentary tyranny did much to encourage resistance to the Cromwellian government and to popularize calls for the restoration of monarchy.[27]

Because tales of martyrdom could be appropriated by opposing political and confessional groups, hagiography could blur the very distinctions between villains and victims that it was meant to sharpen. But this was not the only, or (for my purposes) the most significant, way in which hagiography confuses loyalties and categories in the early modern period. Tales of sacrifice and suffering also carry an erotic charge that complicates the resistance that they should inspire. Richard Rambuss has emphasized the transgressive nature of what he calls "devotional eroticism."[28] The sexual charge of religion as such, Rambuss shows, becomes explicit in fantasies of being raped, broken, and mastered by God—the most notorious expression of such "salvific transgressivity" appears in Donne's Holy Sonnet

---

25. As important recent work on Catholic martyrdom has shown, after England's break with Rome, Catholic and Protestant hagiography shared many of the same tropes and assumptions, even as their authors and audiences struggled to draw distinctions between them. See Dillon; Monta; and Brad Gregory, *Salvation at Stake*. Indeed, as Lake and Questier have shown, struggles over martyrdom could expose rifts between different factions of the same faith as well ("Margaret Clitherow" and "Puritans, Romanists, and the State").

26. Knott, 4.

27. For a detailed study of hagiographic images of Charles I, see Lacey, *Cult of King Charles the Martyr.*

28. Rambuss, *Closet Devotions*, 84.

14.[29] Rambuss does not specifically address hagiography, but I would argue that the spiritual shattering that he describes finds physical expression in the "rough handling" that the Foxean martyr endures. Identification with the suffering martyr may accordingly take the form of masochistic fantasy rather than empathetic outrage. And the sadistic component of martyrdom further complicates the assumption that suffering will provoke resistance. For descriptions of physical torment may authorize identification with the cruel tyrant instead of the agonized victim. In particular, as Mary Ellen Lamb reminds us, the valorization of the female body as a site of heroic patience may mask a voyeuristic structure based on sadistic enjoyment of women's pain.[30] Such identification with masculine power means that both male and female readers may be equally aroused and offended by scenarios of torture. Whether this gratification takes masochistic or sadistic form, it disturbs simple associations between bodily agony and moral authority.

The erotic charge of suffering was even more explicit in the other affective discourse that shaped Elizabethan political thought: Petrarchan courtship.[31] As in Foxean hagiography, in Petrarchan courtship humiliation and pain can be sources of both power and pleasure. Incapable of compelling reciprocal passion, the Petrarchan lover takes a suppliant position before a tyrannical mistress who is indifferent to his pain. Self-abasement becomes evidence of a love that asks nothing of its object. But this abjection is not free of aggression. Particularly in its English form, Petrarchan love has a hostile, even cruel, underside. Because she refuses to satisfy the painful longing she has aroused, the Petrarchan mistress inspires not only love but also frustration and hatred. Limitless devotion begets obsessive demand, which assumes the poetic form of complaint from a lover who is at once aggressive and abject, willful and subservient.[32] Like Foxean hagiography, Petrarchan courtship involves a volatile relation between pleasure and pain, authority and submission. But whereas Foxe equates suffering with resistance, English versions of Petrarchism warn that anguish may equally signify devotion.

The prominence of Foxean hagiography and Petrarchan courtship in late sixteenth-century political discourse registers an important shift in English ideas of the relation between monarch and subject. Most notably, the Elizabethan emphasis on affective bonds as the source of institutional ones acknowledges the perverse

---

29. Rambuss, 58; for more extensive analysis, see 11–101. See also Bersani's defense of the attractions of powerlessness and humiliation, on which Rambuss draws ("Rectum," 211–222). For the homoerotic valences of Foxe's martyrology, see Truman, 49–58.

30. *Gender and Authorship*, 109.

31. I am concerned here with specifically English Petrarchism, which gives complaint and suffering a far greater role than praise or transcendence. Useful studies of the English transformation of Petrarch include Dasenbrock, "Wyatt's Transformation of Petrarch"; Roche, *Petrarch and the English Sonnet Sequences*; Dubrow, *Echoes of Desire*; and William Kennedy, *Site of Petrarchism*, 161–250.

32. For the misogyny and aggression inherent in the Petrarchan blazon, see Vickers's classic essay, "Scattered Women and Scattered Rhymes."

aspects of obedience. In earlier political thought, the ancient constitution authorized noble subjects to resist sovereign tyranny, which could be recognized by the misery it inflicted. In the late sixteenth and seventeenth centuries, writers depict pain itself as a source of pleasure. Once love is understood as a basis of sovereignty, and suffering as an intrinsic part of love, constitutionalist ideas of counsel and reciprocity can no longer fully account for the operations of power.

The sense that sovereignty is innately perverse appears most prominently in depictions of sexual violence. Like its classical and medieval precedents, early modern political literature equates a ruler's inability to govern his sexual appetites with his failure to rule effectively. Accordingly, the assaulted virgin stands in for the vulnerable male political subject. Chastity is as important for men as for women, for it signifies the subordination of aggressive libidinal energies to the common good.[33] In early modern erotic literature, however, the possibility of true chastity—both sexual and political—is always suspect. For the texts I study incorporate a hagiographic logic in which to survive assault is to surrender to tyranny.[34] Rape, defined in early modern law as "when a man hath carnall knowledge of a woman by force, and against her will," is conspicuously absent.[35] In erotic literature, women may be spectacularly brutalized, but they are always rescued or slain prior to the moment of penetration. A consummated rape, by contrast, betokens insufficient resistance and therefore suggests consent, however coerced—even in Shakespeare's *The Rape of Lucrece*, Tarquin gives his victim the choice of secret assent or public shame. In treating sexual assault as a test of virtue, early modern erotic writing locates ultimate authority in feminine chastity rather than masculine force. But it also reveals the inadequacy of simple distinctions between the two, since it imagines violence itself as a form of seduction or testing. The Foxean and Petrarchan models that characterize late-sixteenth-century political discourse thus accentuate the inadequacy of classical views of agency and consent to understanding erotic relations and their political analogues.

33. Numerous scholars have discussed the early modern association between libidinal excess, effeminization, and tyranny. See, for instance, Bushnell, 1–17; Shuger, "*The Rape of Lucretia* and the *Old Arcadia*"; and Rudolph, "Women and Consent."

34. As Truman has argued, in early modern culture "rape was primarily about an attempt at seduction that fails as the narrative ends in violence" and thus "becomes a potent metaphor for the theological struggle of the martyr" (40). See also Bamford, *Sexual Violence*, 25–43.

35. See Coke's comments on Westminster 1, ca. 18, in *The Second Part of the Institutes*, 180. The anonymous *Lawes Resolution of Women's Rights* offers an even more dramatic emphasis on violence, describing rape as "when a woman is enforced violently to sustaine the furie of brutish concupiscence." Citing Bracton, the *Lawes Resolution* goes on to explain that the victim must prove such violent enforcement by supplementing immediate complaint with physical evidence, "shewing her wrong, her garments torne, & sanguine tinctas" (377, 392). Several excellent studies have detected suspicion of female virtue at the heart of such an emphasis on violence; among these, see Garthine Walker, "Rereading Rape"; Catty, *Writing Rape*; Baines, *Representing Rape*; and Gowing, *Common Bodies*, 82–111.

Literature that incorporates these hagiographic and erotic discourses voices the possibility that subjects' own perverse desires and fantasies are a greater threat to English religion and liberty than the king's coercive powers. The fear that subjects would find themselves psychologically unable to resist tyranny, or even drawn to it, saw increasingly prominent expression in the seventeenth century as England confronted a series of authority figures who appeared both arbitrary and corrupt. In the face of early Stuart absolutism, Cromwellian military rule, and Restoration libertinism, English political thinkers increasingly idealized Elizabethan England as a time of justice and harmony. Moreover, as John Watkins has argued, this Eliza-bethanism was not mere nostalgia for a lost era. Rather, it was the very sense of continuity with the past that made Elizabeth a powerful and concrete figure in both royalist and parliamentary polemic.[36] As I maintain throughout this book, the seventeenth-century tendency to look back to Elizabethan models also nurses a habit of understanding power in erotic terms. The ongoing recourse to Foxean and Petrarchan theories of the interplay of love and pain, authority and submission, helped determine how seventeenth-century subjects understood their relation to new kinds of rulers who brazenly repudiated the ancient constitutionalism that English political theorists had long embraced.

Jacobean policies may not have represented as sharp a break with the past as idealized depictions of Elizabethan England claimed, but James I's discourse about sovereign prerogative did deliberately depart from that of Elizabeth. As James VI of Scotland, James had rigorously defended royal absolutism, and he began his Eng-lish reign by announcing that he meant to end the conciliar and parliamentary ini-tiative that had characterized Tudor politics. Asserting a break with this recent past, James insisted in 1603 that "Precedents in the times of minors, of tyrants, or women or simple kings [are] not to be credited."[37] For James, only rulers whose age, gender, imbecility, or corruption makes them naturally inept need follow Fortescue's advice to govern politically. By contrast, real men rule royally.

James's infamous misogyny also significantly revised Elizabethan equations between love and obedience. The "marriage" between Elizabeth and her subjects had left the precise locus of political power ambiguous: as Richard Helgerson has argued, the dissonance between Elizabeth's female body and male office meant that she and the nation could equally play the roles of husband and wife.[38] By con-trast, James I rejected Aylmer's idea of "equall authoritie" between himself and his

36. Watkins, *Representing Elizabeth*. Studies of seventeenth-century Elizabethanism include Wedgwood, *Oliver Cromwell*; Julia M. Walker, ed., *Dissing Elizabeth*; O'Callaghan, *"Shep-heard's Nation"*; and Hageman and Conway, eds., *Resurrecting Elizabeth*.

37. Quoted by Kenyon in "Queen Elizabeth and the Historians," 52. James's absolutism was in part a response to his former tutor, George Buchanan, whose 1579 *De Jure Regni Apud Scotos Dialogus* had defended the revolution against Mary Stuart by insisting that subjects had a share in sovereignty and therefore could rightfully depose an unjust ruler.

38. Helgerson, 297–298.

effeminized subjects. Having asserted in his first speech to the 1604 English parliament that "I am the Husband, and the whole Isle is my lawfull Wife," James would steadfastly demand that subjects not only obey him, but like it. For Elizabeth, the monarch's reliance on subjects' "loyal hearts and good will" ensured just rule. For James, "to the King is due both the affection of the soule and the service of the body of his subjects."[39] The structurally effeminized Jacobean subject could never justly rebel, even in the private realms of thought. Because affection is a duty, it no longer has anything to do with royal behavior—the definition of a good subject is one who loves the sovereign unconditionally. For defenders of parliamentary prerogative, such unquestioned devotion was the foundation of tyranny. As Thomas Wentworth warned in 1610, "if we shall once say that we may not dispute the prerogative, let us be sold for slaves."[40]

Like his father, Charles I rejected constitutionalist theories of "equall authortie," claiming even on the scaffold that "a subject and a sovereign are clean different things."[41] For Charles, the proper political bond required not an ongoing negotiation between ruler and ruled, but a rapturous union in which subjects' desires are absorbed into those of their sovereign—an ecstatic vision spectacularly, if ambivalently, expressed in the court masque. The early Stuarts' attempts to translate absolutist theories into policy, and particularly efforts to raise money by extraparliamentary means, provoked intense debates about the limits of English devotion to the king. While these debates centered on practical and immediate issues—taxes on currants, the Bohemian wars, and clerical attire, for instance—they shared a concern with defining the proper boundary between royal and parliamentary will. Determining this boundary appeared particularly troublesome when Charles decided to rule without parliaments after 1629, thereby eschewing the most widely recognized indication that he governed with the consent of the whole realm. Stuart subjects were faced with the theoretical questions that had occupied their Marian forebears: at what point does proper obedience become cowardly or self-serving? If the monarch refuses to submit to law and counsel, when does submission to his will become collusion with his tyranny?

Parliamentary leaders who challenged Charles's "personal rule" did so by appealing to Elizabethan discourses of love and self-sacrifice. Charles's rejection of counsel endangered his authority more than parliament's, they claimed, and virtuous subjects must risk the king's anger in order to stop him from self-destructing. During the Short Parliament of 1640, the first parliamentary meeting in eleven years, John Pym affirmed that "the king can do no wrong." But he understood this maxim in Fortescuean, not absolutist, terms. For Pym, "A parliament is that to the

39. James I, Speech of March 19, 1604, and Speech of March 21, 1610, both in Kenyon, ed., *Stuart Constitution*, 136, 181.
40. Wentworth, Speech on May 11, 1616, in Foster, ed., *Proceedings in Parliament*, 2:82.
41. King's Speech on the Scaffold, January 30, 1649, in Kenyon, ed., *Stuart Constitution*, 295.

Commonwealth which the soul is to the body, which is only able to apprehend and understand the symptoms of all such diseases which threaten the body politic. It behoves us therefore to keep the faculty of that soul from distempers." By refusing such physic, Pym continued, Charles encouraged grievances that were "as prejudicial to his Majesty as to the Commonwealth." And any "breach of parliaments" only allowed these prejudices to fester, "for it is by this means the great union and love which should be kept and communicated betwixt the king and his subjects is interrupted." Pym's speech draws on the Elizabethan notion that royal power depends on "union and love." In their absence, a king exposes himself as an illegitimate tyrant who may be disobeyed and even deposed. As Pym cautioned, "We know how unfortunate Henry III and other princes have been, by the occasion of such breaking of their laws. I pray God that we never see such times."[42] England, of course, would indeed see times to surpass earlier baronial revolts. But as Pym's regretful tone suggests, parliamentarians saw their stance in conservative, not revolutionary terms. Royalists shared this investment in the past, and it appeared most strikingly in both sides' embrace of the Foxean equation of victimhood with moral authority.

Perhaps the strangest thing about civil war discourse is that each side characterized its position in terms of injury rather than strength, its feelings for its opponents as affection rather hostility. Those in parliament who opposed Charles described themselves as "his Majesties' loving subjects," and the parliamentary apologist Henry Parker professed himself "as zealously addicted to Monarchy, as any man can, without dotage."[43] Parliament claimed to be fighting to restore Charles's power under the ancient constitution until the last year of war, when army leaders finally concluded that Charles had proven himself a "man of blood" from whom they must protect the assaulted nation.[44] The royalist version of this tale of wronged innocence appeared most poignantly in *Eikon Basilike*. Here, Charles insisted that he had fought only "to defend My self so far, as to be able to defend My good Subjects from those mens violence and fraud." He cast his physical defeat as a moral victory, thanking God that "I can not only with patience bear this, as other indignities, but with Charity forgive them."[45] As the popularity of *Eikon Basilike* attested, in the seventeenth century feminine love and sacrifice were far more persuasive signs of virtue than masculine anger or conquest.

Although republican apologists figured the Cromwellian government's sober masculinity as an antidote to the effete Caroline court, the severity with which Cromwell and his army governed contributed to a sense among political thinkers of

42. Pym, Speech of April 17, 1640, in Kenyon, ed., *Stuart Constitution*, 184, 188, 189.
43. "Declaration of Both Houses," June 6, 1642, in Kenyon, ed., *Stuart Constitution*, 227; Parker, *Observations*, 41, 44.
44. Stroud, *Stuart England*, 114.
45. *Eikon Basilike*, 72, 200.

various stripes that one sort of tyrant had merely replaced another. In 1649, parliament abolished the office of monarchy on the grounds that "usually and naturally any one person in such power makes it his interest to encroach upon the just freedom and liberty of the people . . . so they might enslave these kingdoms to their own lust."[46] Yet Cromwell's equally arbitrary rule challenged the claim that monarchy was the problem. The Lord Protector was as likely as his Stuart enemies to dissolve recalcitrant parliaments, and he dismissed legal attempts to curtail his power as naïve appeals to what he sneeringly called "Magna Farta."[47] By the mid-1650s England had grown weary of military rule. Even many republicans felt that their cause had been betrayed. Lucy Hutchinson, for instance, expressed the widely held view that individual quests for power and pleasure had transformed brave and godly soldiers into "tyrant's minions."[48] For all but the most ideologically committed republicans, the return of monarchy seemed the best safeguard against arbitrary power: unlike the office of Protector, that of king was known to English common law and therefore subject to well-recognized restrictions.

But most champions of the Restoration wanted the return of an Elizabeth, not a James or a Charles I. Accordingly, the euphoria with which England welcomed Charles II quickly faded. The new king and his court espoused a libertine philosophy of self-interest that scorned romantic ideals of self-sacrifice and made the government's corruption and ineptitude all the more appalling to those who still subscribed to a Foxean definition of virtue. A sense of repetition and failure pervades the political thought of this older generation of seventeenth-century subjects. The 1650s had seen republican ideals crushed by human realities, and for thinkers like John Milton, the return of Stuart rule evinced England's embarrassing indulgence of a "noxious humour of returning to bondage."[49] Similarly, in the 1660s and 1670s many royalists lost faith in the values of personal loyalty and service that had characterized Elizabethan ideals of monarchy. Roger L'Estrange, for example, lamented that Charles II had surrounded himself by a new generation of shallow wits rather than rewarding those who had suffered exile and poverty on his behalf. The king who takes loyalty for granted, L'Estrange warned, "makes Faith and Honor cheap and ridiculous."[50] And once faith and honor lose value, a political system grounded on personal virtue looks similarly cheap and ridiculous. It was not only historical change but also the gradual extinction of the generation to which both Milton and L'Estrange belonged—a group Elizabethan in attitude, if not in fact—that allowed concepts of rights and interests to replace those of love and sacrifice in theories of political psychology. And with this shift, the conviction that obedience

---

46. "Act Abolishing the Kingship," March 17, 1649, in Kenyon, ed., *Stuart Constitution*, 306.
47. See Hirst's description of Cromwell's behavior, *Authority*, 334.
48. Hutchinson, *Memoirs*, 259.
49. *The Readie and Easie Way*, CP, 7:407.
50. *A Caveat to the Cavaliers*, 28.

is inherently perverse gives way to a more rationalist outlook in which political behavior is more a matter of calculation than of desire.

It is in sixteenth- and seventeenth-century literature that we find the most thorough analysis available of the latent perversity of the erotic politics that I have been tracing. This literature offers us an underappreciated picture of the complexities of early modern political psychology. Throughout this book, I argue that by considering the period from the reign of Elizabeth I to that of Charles II as a whole we can better appreciate the extent to which the operative tropes of late sixteenth-century discourse—Foxean martyrdom and Petrarchan courtship—continued to shape the concepts of sovereignty and obedience in the seventeenth century. I propose that by examining the libidinal investments that both shape and represent shifting structures of authority, we can see that political thought in the early modern period rarely fits modern ideas of politics as driven by ideological mystification or cynical self-interest. In political theory that recognizes the allure of pain and humiliation, obedience and resistance no longer seem to operate according to normative expectations. Instead, power and governance look distinctly queer.

My study of early modern depictions of what Judith Butler has called "the psychic life of power" examines how historically-specific political structures and cultural narratives shape erotic life—and how psychic structures of fantasy and identification shape political and cultural ideals.[51] Throughout, I draw on psychoanalytic vocabularies to describe early modern instances of what we would now call masochism, sadism, narcissism, or ambivalence. Although I use these terms in their Freudian senses, I do so not because I think that they exactly diagnose the behavior that early modern literature describes, but because psychoanalysis offers, to my mind, the richest account of sexuality available. New historicist scholars—most influentially, Stephan J. Greenblatt—have long been skeptical about the value of psychoanalysis, charging that it anachronistically imposes nineteenth- and twentieth-century theories of the bourgeois psyche on a period with vastly different social, familial, and marital structures and ideologies.[52] Recently, however, numerous literary scholars have asserted the value of psychoanalysis to understanding the histories of sexuality and subjectivity in earlier periods.[53] As Carla Freccero has argued, psychoanalysis is itself an historical method because "on the one hand, it argues for an eccentric relation between events and their effects; on the other, it often challenges the empiricism of what qualifies as an event itself." For Freccero, psychoanalytic concepts give us a picture of the subject that, unlike the subject

---

51. *Psychic Life of Power.* See also Jessica Benjamin's analysis of the irrational, perverse nature of power relations in *Bonds of Love.*

52. Greenblatt, "Psychoanalysis and Renaissance Culture," in *Learning to Curse,* 131–145.

53. See, for instance, Gearhart, "New Historicism"; Hanson, *Discovering the Subject*; Trevor and Mazzio, "Introduction"; Traub, *Renaissance of Lesbianism,* 326–354; Trevor, *Poetics of Melancholy*; and Freccero, *Queer/Early/Modern.*

described by much new historicism, is not a straightforward effect of culture and power. The "events" experienced and reported by these "deeply unreliable and riven subjectivities" will necessarily be ambiguous and multivalent.[54] It is this subjective experience of history that I examine here. Precisely because psychic life does not obey the rules of temporal causality or logic, examining the narratives through which early modern sovereignty is conceived helps us to appreciate what I have called the queer nature of political thought in a period when writers habitually conflated the problems of sexuality with those of sovereignty.

By reading erotic literature as part of what Louis Montrose has aptly described as the early modern "political imaginary," the following chapters engage with current historiographical debates.[55] Postrevisionist historians have rejected both whiggish narratives of a liberal teleology and revisionist claims of a royalist consensus.[56] They argue instead that while there was broad agreement that sovereigns had certain inalienable prerogatives and subjects certain inalienable liberties, the precise nature and balance of these were the subject of constant debate. I propose that greater attention to the affective component of authority depicted in the period's literature can expand this postrevisionist awareness of the complex spectrum of shifting political configurations and investments. Public engagement is not limited to the polemics of pamphlets, proclamations, or parliamentary speeches, and literary works that insist on the perverse nature of authority can teach us a good deal about the experience of sixteenth- and seventeenth-century politics.[57] In taking sexualized narratives of rule seriously, I seek to rethink what desire has meant historically, and, inseparably, what power has meant as well.

Equally fundamental to this book is the feminist insight that an analysis of the history of gender also alters our picture of political history.[58] Throughout, I build on previous feminist work to show that we can come to a more nuanced understanding of English history if we accept not only that the personal is political but also that the political is personal. Because the authors that I examine all employ a hagiographic understanding of gender and power, their female characters represent subordinate and vulnerable male political subjects as much as actual women. Like Foxe, writers

---

54. Freccero, 4, 7.

55. Montrose defines the "Elizabethan political imaginary" as the "collective repertoire of representational forms and figures in which beliefs and practices of Tudor political culture were pervasively articulated" ("Spenser and the Elizabethan Political Imaginary," 907). Throughout this book, I use the concept of the political imaginary to examine the overlap between the individual and the social, the psychic, and the political.

56. Useful postrevisionist work includes Greenberg; Hirst; Cust and Hughes, "After Revisionism"; and Burgess, *Politics* and *Absolute Monarchy*. For historiographical debates regarding particular periods, see the chapters below.

57. As Dolan has persuasively put it, representations "are what 'really' happened" as much as recorded events (*Whores of Babylon*, 2).

58. See, for instance, Joan Scott, "Gender: A Useful Category of Historical Analysis"; Pateman, *Sexual Contract*; and Stewart-Steinberg, "Gender, Envy, and the Freudian Social Contract."

from Sidney to Milton encourage both male and female readers to see feminine suffering and sacrifice as more effective forms of political resistance than armed opposition. These works assume a triangulated relation between tyrant, martyr, and reader, a dynamic stance of distance and identification that is the peculiar position of the reader of fiction. We can understand such cross-gendered identification in terms of the humanist tradition of poetics that shaped Renaissance theories of education. As Victoria A. Kahn has shown, "in the minds of early modern writers, it was the shared task of the poet, the forensic orator, and the political orator to create plausible fictions that would engage the listener or spectator in an activity of probable reasoning that would in turn result in an equitable judgment."[59] The politically charged depictions of erotic relations that I examine offer just such "plausible fictions" to urge readers to contemplate the relation between virtuous submission and debased servitude. These scenarios constitute hypothetical dilemmas to which readers—whether actual women or structurally effeminized male subjects—apply ethical and political judgment.[60]

The work of female authors like Wroth and Cavendish shows that questions of sovereignty and obedience were as important to women as to men. Pioneering studies of women's writing have taught us to appreciate the complexity of gender relations in the sixteenth and seventeenth centuries. This early scholarship has opened the way to more recent feminist studies showing that early modern women played a significant part in public debates about religion and governance.[61] Drawing on this important background of feminist criticism, in this book I contend that women's literary work registers a complex experience of power that can usefully supplement our studies of their explicitly political and religious writing. Erotic topics like love and courtship allowed women writers to engage in public debate with their male peers, who were themselves using the language of desire to contemplate the nature of authority. In stressing the distance between gender identity and biological sex, early modern women like Wroth and Cavendish remind us that masculine refusals of vulnerability and claims to natural domination are themselves driven by fantasy. Their writing thus allows us to see that despite official exclusion from political or ecclesiastical office, early modern women were quite conscious of the interplay between sexuality and power.

---

59. *Wayward Contracts*, 17.

60. They thus incorporate the rhetorical exercises of impersonation, the practice of composing a speech for a particular character and circumstance, and *suasoria*, practice speeches offering a mythical or historical character advice regarding an imagined ethical dilemma. See the Elder Seneca, *Declamations*, and Aristotle, *Poetics*, chapter 24.

61. Work on gender and women's writing in the early modern period that has influenced my own thinking includes Amussen, *An Ordered Society*; Jordan, *Renaissance Feminism*; and the essays in *Rewriting the Renaissance*, ed. Ferguson, Quilligan, and Vickers; *Women, 'Race', and Writing*, ed. Hendricks and Parker; and *Women and Literature*, ed. Wilcox. For studies of women's political and religious writing, see Underdown, "Placing Women"; Suzuki, *Subordinate Subjects*; Wiseman, *Women, Writing, and Politics*; Gray, *Women Writers*; and Coles, *Religion*.

Alongside the insights of feminism, those of queer theory allow us to appreciate the elusiveness of clear and rational structures of gendered identity, sexual fantasy and practice, or political loyalty.[62] This book locates affects and identifications that are typically understood as "sexual" at the heart of political thought and behavior. In each of my chapters, I seek to defamiliarize the heteroerotic models to which early modern political discourse so often turns. Although my analysis tends to focus on encounters between men and women, I argue that the cruelty and abjection that define these encounters challenge the assumption that heteroerotic love and marriage are models for "normal," natural unions and hierarchies. I thus draw on two important insights of queer studies. The first is that the concept of heterosexuality, like that of homosexuality, is a fairly recent invention. We therefore can see many of the violent and abject passions and practices represented in early modern literature as part of an exploration of the vicissitudes of identification and desire, of which the gender of the persons involved is only one part.[63] The second is the argument that sexuality as such challenges ideals of human relationships as innately altruistic, redemptive, and reasonable.[64] Once we recognize the ineradicable appeal of violence, abjection, and humiliation, a purely rational, de-eroticized view of politics becomes impossible. I propose that early modern authors were equally conscious of the queerness of both erotic and political behavior, even if they would not have described that awareness in modern terms.

In its attention to the volatility of sexual desire and gendered identity, sixteenth- and seventeenth-century erotic literature explores the contradictions of early modern political psychology. As the following chapters demonstrate, political loyalties at this time were rarely rational or coherent. For English governance was composed of an intricate network of alliances and identifications—ties of kinship and patronage, sociopolitical aspirations, factional allegiances, ideological investments— that attenuated the sovereign–subject dyad. All of the authors that I study were either related to, patronized by, or themselves members of England's political elite, and their status and livelihood often depended on the authorities whom they both supported and criticized. My focus on elite, rather than popular, writers is meant to underscore the fact that it was not only the disenfranchised and marginalized members of the political nation who critiqued English power structures. Even those closest to the centers of power expressed ambivalence and anxiety about the forms

62. As Judith Butler has persuasively argued, because feminist and queer theory both interrogate the meanings and practices associated with gender and sexuality, they cannot be firmly separated ("Against Proper Objects. Introduction," 1–26).

63. Lochrie, *Heterosyncrasies*; Schultz, *Courtly Love*; Bach, *Shakespeare and Renaissance Literature before Heterosexuality*; and Neeley, *Distracted Subjects*. As Breitenberg has shown, the cultural codes in which desire is expressed are typically based on heterosexual models, even if individual practices do not themselves fit that model (*Anxious Masculinity*, 9).

64. See Bersani; Berlant and Warner, "Sex in Public," 547–548, 564–566; and Edelman, *No Future*.

of rule, whether monarchal or republican, that they officially supported. While I do not suggest that we interpret this writing according to biographical frameworks, I do argue that it must be read not only in the context of the period's constitutional debates but also in light of the author's political and familial associations and loyalties. Each chapter traces these affiliations, both for the individual authors on which it focuses and for the connections that we can detect among the authors themselves. Writers with a range of relations to the ruling elite—frustrated courtiers like Sidney, Wroth, Carew, Davenant, and Cavendish; public servants like Spenser and Milton; professional poets like Shakespeare, Jonson, and Townshend—were all reading one another in this period. Scholars have widely recognized Wroth's debts to her uncle Philip Sidney and Milton's admiration for Spenser. But the full import of these connections for Wroth's and Milton's conception of political agency has yet to be explored. Even less attention has been paid to the ways in which the specifically Elizabethan intersection of hagiography and courtship shapes understandings of authority and submission in Shakespeare's poems and plays, Caroline masques, and royalist fiction.

The early modern authors studied in the pages below are skeptical of the human ability to escape the grip of the furious desires and fantasies that render clarity of action so elusive. It is therefore no surprise that they turn to theories of erotic addiction and violence to account for political choices that appear absurd, loyalties that persist despite betrayal, and resistance that proves futile. As the literary works I examine show, political loyalty as well as erotic devotion depends in large part on faith, which may itself turn out to be another name for fantasy. In its demonstration of the power of desire to shape the experience of reality, this literature stresses the interplay among political, gendered, and sexual structures in the early modern period, even as it complicates our understanding of these structures in the present as well as the past.

CHAPTER 2

cᐳ

"She Therein Ruling"

Hagiographic Politics in The Countess of Pembroke's Arcadia

On New Year's Day 1581, Philip Sidney gave Elizabeth I a notoriously provocative gift: a "jewel of gold, being a whip garnished with small diamonds in four rows, and cords of small seed pearle."[1] Scholars have typically interpreted this present in topical, rather than theoretical, terms. In this reading, Sidney's offer of a bejeweled whip marks the end of his part in debates over Elizabeth's proposed marriage to François, Duc d'Anjou. In 1579, Sidney had spoken for the forward Protestant faction of Elizabeth's Privy Council when he wrote Elizabeth a publicly circulated letter opposing the union—a liberty for which John Stubbes had notoriously lost his right hand. Shortly afterward, Sidney withdrew from court. Sidney's readers have generally assumed that he was banished as a result of the letter and that the bejeweled whip signified a witty apology for his earlier act of lèse majesté and a promise to defer to royal authority in the future.[2]

But the supposition that Sidney's gift admits defeat and confirms the queen's authority does not fit the actual status of the Anjou debate in 1581. Nor does it fit the generally accepted theory of government that operated in Elizabethan England. Until 1582, Elizabeth officially kept open the possibility of an Anglo-French alliance that would counter Spanish power. However, at the time of Sidney's gift she gave

---

1. Zouch, *Memoirs*, 332.
2. McCoy, *Rebellion*, 69; Minogue, "Astrophil, Stella, and Queen Virture's Court," 555; and Brennan, *Sidneys*, 84–85. Duncan-Jones challenges the assumption that Sidney's letter occasioned his banishment from court (*Sidney*, 164).

every appearance of bowing to popular and conciliar will. By 1581, the faction that Sidney represented had effectively won the debate over the Anjou engagement, and both Sidney and his queen knew it. A year earlier Elizabeth had all but ended talk of the marriage, explaining in a 1580 letter to Anjou that "the public exercise of the Roman religion sticks so much in [the English people's] hearts, that I shall never consent to your coming among such malcontents . . . I cannot and will not let this negotiation trouble us more."[3] As we have seen, Elizabeth, like many late-sixteenth-century writers, equated her subjects' affections—their "hearts"—with their political consent. In invoking her subjects' unhappiness, Elizabeth's letter implicitly concedes the Fortescuean principle that England was a *dominium politicum et regale* in which the prince's will is constrained by that of the political nation.

In this context, Sidney's bejeweled whip constitutes something of a dare, particularly in light of the English association of whipping with Spanish cruelty: if Elizabeth attempts to rule by force, she aligns herself with the same foreign, Catholic tyranny that characterized her sister Mary's reign.[4] She thus risks losing her claims to legitimate rule and her subjects' willing obedience. As I discussed in the introduction and chapter 1, the ancient constitutionalist model that shaped English views of sovereignty for centuries assumed that the danger of rebellion keeps monarchal will in check. In this view, a prince can best secure authority by submitting to law and counsel. The wars of the fifteenth century had demonstrated how disruptive powerful nobles could be, and Elizabeth herself was quite conscious of the threat that her mighty subjects, Protestant as well as Catholic, continued to pose.[5] Indeed, a conviction of aristocratic prerogative fortified the aggression exemplified by such influential royal servants as Sidney's grandfather, the would-be kingmaker John Dudley, Earl of Northumberland, and Sidney's symbolic heir, Robert Devereaux, Earl of Essex. Monarchs who rejected the counsel of their aristocratic subjects hazarded real challenges to their authority.[6]

But even this constitutionalist framework fails to engage adequately with the erotic and political complexity embodied in Sidney's bejeweled whip. For Sidney's

---

3. Quoted in Pollen, *English Catholics*, 324.

4. As Montrose shows, New Year's gifts were part of a ritual exchange that affirmed subjects' bond with their queen, but they could also express counsel and opposition. Montrose does not mention Sidney's whip, but he observes that during the Armada crisis of 1588, Spanish ships were rumored to have carried whips meant to torture their vanquished enemies (*Subject of Elizabeth*, 119–121, 149–150). As Truman has shown, Foxe depicted the Marian bishop Edmund Bonner as a sadist who enjoyed spectacles of flogging ("John Foxe," 45–46).

5. My own discussion is primarily concerned with the Protestant faction to which Sidney belonged. For a discussion of the challenge posed by English Catholic nobles, see Marotti, *Religious Ideology*, 44–46, 61.

6. For aristocratic challenges to royal authority in the sixteenth century, see McCoy, *Rites*. Brennan traces the Dudleys' and Sidneys' claims of aristocratic prerogative in chapter 1 of *Sidneys*. Greenberg demonstrates the importance of ancient constitutionalism to English rebellions from the medieval period through the Glorious Revolution (*Radical Face*).

costly gift does not threaten aristocratic revolt. More remarkably, it threatens aristocratic martyrdom. The whip neatly encompasses the complex relation of power and
pleasure that Sidney explores in detail throughout *The Countess of Pembroke's
Arcadia*.[7] In Sidney's widely read and imitated romance, resistance takes a strikingly
new form, one that would influence the English literary and political imaginaries for
the century to come.[8] The *Arcadia* examines the possibility that martyrdom may be
a powerful source of political, as well as religious, empowerment. Sidney's view of
politics departs from the conventional assertions of masculine strength exemplified
by his Dudley forbears and by Essex. Instead, Sidney cultivated feminized suffering—what Mary Beth Rose has called "the heroicism of endurance"—as a sign of
moral authority and political influence.[9] When he revised the *Arcadia*, Sidney
added to his original pastoral narrative numerous episodes in which young women
defy foolish or cruel parental figures and endure a range of physical and psychological abuses in order to remain true to the men they love. Because the source of their
resolve is erotic devotion, these female characters also redefine the roots of political
loyalty, transforming the self-interest that inspired traditional aristocratic rebellions
into selfless sacrifice on behalf of another.

Given that depictions of female torture and subjugation are so prominent in
the *Arcadia*, it is surprising that scholars who have studied the political implications of this romance have said so little about these scenes. Centuries of readers,
like the seventeenth-century editor William Dugard, have understood Sidney's
narrative as "shadowing moral and politick results under the plain and easie
emblems of Lovers."[10] Typically, however, analyses of the romance's political

---

7. Throughout this book, the version of the *Arcadia* that I study is the composite text primarily
   edited by Sidsney's sister, Mary Sidney Herbert, Countess of Pembroke. This version was
   first published in 1593, and it would be the text best known to readers until the discovery of
   the manuscript of the "old" *Arcadia* in 1907. This composite text, published as *The Countess
   of Pembroke's Arcadia*, joins the revised three books known as the "new" *Arcadia* to the final
   two books of the "old" one. For the relationship between the various published versions of
   the *Arcadia*, see Alexander, *Writing After Sidney*, xiii–xiv, 10–17, 40–55, 128–140. For discussions of the revisions in the 1593 edition, see Godshalk, "Sidney's Revision," 311–326,
   and Evans's introduction to *The Countess of Pembroke's Arcadia*, 10–14. Hardison argues that
   during the 1580s Sidney's increasingly militant political outlook made him dissatisfied with
   the *Old Arcadia* ("Two Voices," 83–99).

8. For Sidney's afterlife in later literary and political discourse, see Patterson, *Censorship*,
   32–51; Worden, *Sound of Virtue*, 21–22, 65–68; Herman, "Bastard Children"; and Alexander, 56–75, 220–282.

9. *Gender and Heroism*, xii. Lamb similarly emphasizes the emptiness of military heroism in
   contrast to female constancy in the *Arcadia* (*Gender and Authorship*, 106).

10. *Arcadia*, ed. Dugard, n.p. In what is perhaps the earliest political reading of the *Arcadia*,
    Fulke Greville treated Sidney as a counterexample of the corruption of the Jacobean court
    (*Life of Sir Philip Sidney*, 223). Along with McCoy, *Rebellion*, and Worden, *Sound of Virtue*,
    esp. 127–294, instructive political readings of the *Arcadia* include Greenlaw, "Sidney's
    Arcadia"; Sinfield, *Faultlines*, 80–94, 143–214; Jones and Stallybrass, "Politics of *Astrophil
    and Stella*," 53–68; Stillman, "Politics of Sidney's Pastoral"; Tennenhouse, "Sidney and the
    Politics of Courtship"; and Lamb, "Exhibiting Class and Displaying the Body."

penumbrae have limited their focus to its male lovers; female characters, by contrast, have been read in terms either of Sidney's views on women or, by extension, the issue of female rule.[11] Scholars who overlook the political significance of the passionate women in the *Arcadia* tend to identify Sidney's own position with Musidorus' initial condemnation of love as a dangerous indulgence that can "womanize a man" (134).[12] In such a view, women represent the private passions that threaten good government of both self and state. I propose, instead, that "womanization" is central to Sidney's view of political negotiation. It is by inhabiting the powerless position traditionally associated with femininity that male political subjects can resist monarchal authority without raising the specter of anarchy often associated with armed rebellion. In the *Arcadia*, Sidney maintains that by withholding consent and suffering the consequences, subjects can compel rulers to reform.

Before examining the political arguments offered by some of the most famous scenarios of erotic torment in the *Arcadia*, I would like briefly to return to Sidney's bejeweled whip. This gift fuses the erotic and hagiographic elements of Sidney's political vision. Catherine Bates, unique among Sidney scholars, understands the New Year's gift as an emblem of the masochistic urges explored throughout Sidney's oeuvre.[13] Bates argues that Sidney cultivates a castrated, disempowered position, one that challenges Foucault's oft-cited dictum that "power is everywhere; not because it embraces everything, but because it comes from everywhere."[14] Bates' insistence on the prominence of masochism in Sidney's writing is instructive, for it reminds us that submission can be as erotic as domination. But because she understands Sidney's fantasies of pain and subjugation as a rejection of power, rather than a redefinition of it, Bates removes Sidney's work from the political context with which it was quite deeply engaged. In fact, the ascesis and martyrdom evoked by Sidney's whip offer more complex choices than those of dominance and disempowerment. Niklaus Largier has shown that for ascetics, flagellation was a ritual, theatrical practice that encouraged imaginative identification with Christ through a bodily imitation of his passion. Before the "structural bifurcation" that Largier locates around 1700, when whipping became associated with "the danger of libidinous arousal" and ascesis was deemed a cover for perversity, the excruciation of the flesh was a way of "actualizing through performance something that words cannot

---

11. Duncan-Jones (*Sidney*) and Katherine Roberts (*Fair Ladies*) applaud Sidney's presentation of female characters. By contrast, critics who see a structural misogyny in Sidney's work include Sullivan, "Gendering Genealogy"; Susan Frye, *Elizabeth I*; and Lei, "Relational Antifeminism."

12. See McCoy, *Rebellion*, 49–59; Worden, *Sound of Virtue*, 301–306, 320–326; and Marenco, "'Double Plot,'" 292. Even those scholars who defend love, like Mark Rose, do so by minimizing its sexual dimension (*Heroic Love*, 54–55, 67–68).

13. *Masculinity*, 36–37.

14. *History of Sexuality*, 87, 93, 94. See also Bates, *Masculinity*, 1–27.

reach."[15] This ritualistic, theatrical *imitatio Christi* shares the hagiographic structure that I have detailed in Foxe's *Acts and Monuments*, where true power appears in the martyr's ability not only to take pain, but to enjoy it as a sign of rapturous union with the divine. Such unspeakable ecstasy disturbs normative ideas of interest, desire, and authority, all of which assume that a rational calculation of worldly comfort or power motivates most human behavior.

In the *Arcadia*, Sidney describes his female characters' erotic ordeals in the same hagiographic language evoked by the bejeweled whip he presented to Elizabeth. He thereby artfully secularizes a narrative in which bodily torment allows subjects to transcend their earthly limits and transform the meaning of power.[16] And the devout endurance of women in the *Arcadia* is not mere stoicism: the rites of ascesis and martyrdom encourage an excess of feeling, not a studied indifference.[17] The pleasure that Sidney's heroines take in disciplined, absolute devotion makes them immune to physical coercion—and because endurance is a sign of love, what might appear to be a masochistic rejection of power is in fact a redefinition of it. This erotic element of suffering is crucial to Sidney's justification of resistance in the *Arcadia*. As Gilles Deleuze has observed, masochistic fantasy and ritual invert the relationship between crime and punishment, so that "the law now ordains what it was once intended to forbid; guilt absolves instead of leading to atonement, and punishment makes permissive what it was intended to chastise."[18] Such proleptic logic operates in the *Arcadia*, where suffering enables political as well as psychological transgression. Characters who accept physical torment gain a moral authority that retroactively legitimates rebellion against both patriarchal and political hierarchy. By refusing to fight back, the subject forces the sovereign into the role of aggressor and thereby translates resistance into self-defense. It is the sadistic tyrant who ends up in a position of feminized impotence, the limits of his or her power exposed, while the martyr ascends to a position of masculine conquest.

Sidney's treatment of pain and humiliation as sources of both pleasure and empowerment tests the conceptual and experiential boundaries between domination and submission, erotic excess and ascetic discipline. By stressing the attraction and the power of feminine suffering, the *Arcadia* imagines a hagiographic politics

---

15. Largier, *In Praise of the Whip*, 217, 221, 14. Elaine Scarry, by contrast, insists on the inexpressibility of pain (*Body in Pain*).
16. In tracing the connection between love, suffering, and resistance, I expand into the political sphere Lamb's reading of the influence of hagiography on the depiction of female subjectivity in the *Arcadia* (*Gender and Authorship*, 72–114).
17. As Lamb has observed, martyrs' delight in death distinguishes them from stoics' equanimity (*Gender and Authorship*, 102–104). It is in stressing hagiography and ascesis that my own argument departs most prominently from Worden's study of politics in the *Arcadia*, which insists on the Neostoic reading of Sidney's romance popularized by Greville (*Sound of Virtue*, 138–139, 337–339, 364–366).
18. *Masochism*, 102.

that challenges more conventional ideas of authority and resistance.[19] As Sidney shows, sovereignty and subjection are not absolute identities, but provisional, contested roles. The view of political power that Sidney explores in the *Arcadia* would help shape political thought throughout the seventeenth century. Sidney's imagination of a secular, eroticized martyrdom represented resistance as a form of loving counsel and thus helped to disseminate a conception of political action that challenged a binary view of obedience and rebellion.

Sidney began composing the *Arcadia* around 1578 and continued to revise until his death in 1586, a period when questions of foreign policy repeatedly put Elizabeth at odds with the forward Protestants of the Leicester–Sidney circle. Given Sidney's close relationship with the Huguenot theorist Hubert Languet, it is hardly surprising that the *Arcadia* shares the Huguenot belief that violence is the prerogative of the sovereign. Unlike their Marian forebears, who insisted that every true Christian had the duty to oppose ungodly rule, Huguenot resistance theorists limited the rights of resistance to officers of the realm, or subaltern magistrates, and then only against the most blatantly tyrannical and illegitimate of rulers.[20] Sidney was equally uneasy about the implications of rebellion. In associating victimization with moral authority throughout the *Arcadia*, Sidney envisions a form of political opposition that avoids the aggressive, even anarchic, possibilities of armed revolt. Positioning himself as a selfless defender of England rather than an ambitious aggressor, Sidney could justify acts of resistance like his protest against the Anjou marriage or his participation in the forward Protestant faction's agitation for English support of the Dutch revolt against Spain.[21] Fulke Greville described Sidney's disobedience to Elizabeth as "an authentical president to after ages, that howsoever tyrants allow of no scope, stamp or standard, but their own will; yet with Princes there is a latitude for subjects to reserve native and legall freedom, by paying humble tribute in

---

19. Sandy sees the *Arcadia* as an apology for the self-interest inherent in sixteenth-century politic ideology (*Seventeenth-Century English Romance*, 19–26). By contrast, I argue that in Sidney's female characters passion is evidence of unselfish principle, not its opposite.

20. This limited acceptance of resistance was particularly prominent in the 1579 *Vindiciae, Contra Tyrannos*, probably jointly written by Sidney's Huguenot mentors Hubert Languet and Philippe Duplessis-Mornay. See Languet and Mornay, esp. 60–61, 158. Sidney's support for an international Protestant League and his insistence on the aristocratic right to participate in government were influenced by his relationships with Languet and Mornay. For Sidney's religious politics, see Osborne, *Young Philip Sidney*; Levy, "Philip Sidney Reconsidered"; McCoy, *Rebellion*, 11–16, 54, 185–194; Worden, *Sound of Virtue*, 47–59; Duncan-Jones, *Sidney*, 63–85, 263; Norbrook, *Poetry and Politics*, 160; and Stillman, *Poetics of Renaissance Cosmopolitanism*. For the development of Huguenot theory, see Skinner, *Foundations*, 2:239–348.

21. For general discussions of the background and debates of the 1570s and 1580s, see Greenberg, 79–115; McLaren, *Political Culture*, 46–74; and MacCaffrey, "Anjou Match." For specific discussions of Sidney's political allegiances, see Arthur Kinney, "Sir Philip Sidney's Rhetoric"; Montrose, *Subject of Elizabeth*; and Quilligan, *Incest and Agency*, 76–101.

manner, though not in matter, to them."[22] Sidney's insistence on protecting his "native and legall freedom" against the encroachment of sovereign will became the stuff of legend, and throughout the seventeenth century he enjoyed a posthumous reputation as a martyr for English liberty and religion.[23] The myth of Sidney as a self-abnegating hero, one whose humility justified his resistance, would define views of political and moral rectitude for the century to come.

Gendered and sexual identities played a central role in Sidney's hagiographic conception of power. As we have seen, early modern writers drew on conjugal analogies to distinguish absolutist from constitutional rule. The comparison of the prince and subject to husband and wife rather than father and children had important political implications: as Donald R. Kelley has argued, the metaphor of conjugal organization envisioned a voluntary union, distinct from the compulsory bond of patriarchy.[24] This description of politics in nuptial terms structured the thought of English constitutional theorists, among them Sidney's fellow MP, Sir Thomas Smyth, whose 1583 *De Republica Anglorum* describes the complementary relation between king and parliament as a marriage in which "ech obeyeth and commaundeth other, and they two together rule the house."[25] In the *Arcadia*, the marriage of Argalus and Parthenia captures the complexity of the mutuality described by Smyth. They are "a happy couple . . . he ruling, because she would obey, or rather because she would obey, she therein ruling" (501).[26] In this idealized formulation, Sidney takes to its logical extreme the Fortescuean principle that submission is a form of power. Argalus and Parthenia's union suggests that shared governance may transfer power from ruler to ruled: if Parthenia's obedience sustains Argalus' authority, is she not really in charge? The treatment of love as a sign of the self-determination that gives mixed rule meaning was integral to the view of politics formulated by the *Arcadia*.

In the revised *Arcadia*, the episode of Argalus and Parthenia sets a pattern in which love is the basis of judgment and in which self-sacrifice is the mark of virtue.[27] Central to this story is Parthenia's determination to remain loyal to her beloved Argalus in defiance of her mother's command that she marry the wealthy lord

---

22. Greville, *Life*, 69.
23. According to Greville, Sidney's apparent defiance was really self-defense, for he shared a widespread fear that if Anjou married Elizabeth he would "steal change of Religion" in England by "lift[ing] up Monarchie above her ancient legall Circles, by banishing all free spirits, and faithfull Patriots . . . till the *Ideas* of native freedom should be utterly forgotten" (*Life*, 53). As Hager has observed, Greville's *Life* is modeled on the structures of Foxean hagiography and deployed as political propaganda ("Fabrication," 17–18).
24. "Elizabethan Political Thought," 51.
25. Smyth, *De Republica Anglorum*, 13.
26. *The Countess of Pembroke's Arcadia*, ed. Evans. All future references will be cited parenthetically.
27. As Clare Kinney has argued, Argalus and Parthenia are the standard for all other lovers in the *Arcadia* ("Court Spectacle," 37).

Demagoras. Before meeting Argalus, Parthenia had agreed to marry Demagoras "not because she liked her choice but because her obedient mind had not yet taken upon it to make choice" (88). Parthenia's unthinking obedience is the opposite of choice, even if that obedience is uncoerced. "Liking" one's choice is synonymous with making a choice, for it signifies the liberty that gives consent meaning. Accordingly, when Parthenia meets Argalus before the arranged marriage can take place, her spontaneous passion clarifies the difference between voluntary and coerced subjection. "Before her word could tie her to Demagoras," the narrator explains, "her heart hath vowed her to Argalus with so grateful a receipt in mutual affection that if she desired above all things to have Argalus, Argalus feared nothing but to miss Parthenia. And now Parthenia had learned both liking and misliking, loving and loathing, and out of passion began to take the authority of judgment" (88–89). Parthenia's "word" means little if her heart is not in it. The "vow" of "mutual affection" in this new relationship is clearly superior to the formal agreement that would "tie" her to Demagoras. The two things that should be opposed—passion and judgment—in fact legitimate one another. Parthenia's affective reactions to the two men allow her to know her own mind and thus to reclaim the authority she had unwittingly relinquished. Her behavior establishes a pattern that will reappear in the erotic choices of Philoclea and Pamela, both of whom cite passion as a justification for disobedience.[28] In all of these cases, active choice, not passive compliance, indicates true consent.

Sidney's depiction of affection as a central part of judgment manifests the sixteenth-century shift that Christopher Tilmouth has demonstrated from an "austerely rationalist model of self-government" to alternative traditions that saw the passions as "morally constructive forces to be harnessed, not eliminated."[29] And for Sidney, the passions were not only "morally constructive forces": they were politically important as well, for they were the mark of the liberty of conscience that distinguished good government from tyranny. As Susanne Woods has argued, the *Arcadia* depicts freedom, the right to participate in maintaining public order, as the prerequisite of individual and state virtue.[30] Sidney shows that because passion cannot be coerced through external means, it is what differentiates blind obedience from considered loyalty, subject from slave. In the *Arcadia*, the distinction between pleasure and self-interest is central to Sidney's imagination of politically constructive passions. Unlike the self-sacrificial ideal that Parthenia embodies, Demagoras "lov[es] nobody but himself, and, for his own delight's sake, Parthenia" (88). His

28. See, for instance, Philoclea's change from a past in which she "had obediently lived under her parents' behests, without framing out of her own will the forechoosing of any thing" to a rebellious commitment to Zelmane (238) and Pamela's decision to elope with Musidorus on the grounds that "my parents deal so cruelly with me, it is time for me to trust something to my own judgement" (249).

29. Tilmouth, *Passion's Triumph*, 1.

30. Woods, "Freedom and Tyranny," 165–175.

desires are entirely self-serving, so he does not care whether they are sincerely reciprocated. By contrast, Parthenia's love for Argalus is completely selfless, as she demonstrates through her willingness to endure torture and humiliation rather than betray her affections. As this ultimately tragic love story suggests, happiness depends on a mutual relinquishment of the delight that Demagoras craves in favor of the pain that Parthenia accepts.

In terms of sixteenth-century ideas of proper filial and feminine behavior, Parthenia's stubborn passion should put her in the wrong: the "authority of judgment" she claims effectively usurps a prerogative that does not belong to her as a daughter. Yet her mother's brutal attempts to force Parthenia to marry Demagoras end up giving Parthenia the moral high ground. In light of Sidney's association of violence with viciousness, suffering with virtue, Parthenia's mother's brutality transforms Parthenia from rebellious child to innocent victim. Parthenia's mother tries "all ways which a witty and hard-hearted mother could use upon so humble a daughter in whom the only resisting power was love. But the more she assaulted, the more she taught Parthenia to defend; and the more Parthenia defended, the more she made her mother obstinate in the assault" (89). Parthenia's humble recalcitrance reveals the limits of her mother's authority. Her mother's behavior suggests a traditional view of power, in which violence compels submission—a view that assumes that people value physical comfort more than anything else. But because Parthenia cares more for Argalus than for herself, bodily pain cannot sway her.

As Knott has noted of Foxean martyrs, the ability to endure, and even embrace, pain puts martyrs in a position of control in that it makes their persecutors helpless to coerce them.[31] Parthenia's willingness to die similarly gives her the upper hand: her death would mean the defeat of her mother's endeavor to "have her will and shew her authority in matching [Parthenia] with Demagorus" (89). Since she is defending her love rather than her life, "to Parthenia malice sooner ceased than her unchanged position" (89). Her mother, by contrast, must stop short of killing Parthenia if she wants to achieve her end. According to the hagiographic logic that structures this scenario, Parthenia's death would signify her mother's failure to "shew her authority." For Sidney, assault and defense entail a battle of wills, not bodies.

Like Foxe, Sidney shows that feminine endurance can be a greater sign of heroism than masculine conquest. Even as Parthenia's mother uses "all extremities possible" on her daughter, she sends Argalus on increasingly dangerous quests in hopes of killing him off. Both Argalus and Parthenia remain so faithful that "it was hard to judge whether he in doing or she in suffering shewed greater constancy of affection" (89). According to conventional ideas of power, Argalus' superhuman feats should indicate greater heroism and therefore greater love. The more complex value system of the *Arcadia*, however, inverts this hierarchy. Argalus' "doing"

31. Knott, *Discourses of Martyrdom*, 8–10.

depends on the same physical combat that Parthenia's mother treats as the test of power. Argalus inflicts as much pain as he risks, and so must protect his own life to demonstrate his devotion. By contrast, because death would be the ultimate sign of constancy for Parthenia, her "suffering" shifts the very meaning of victory. Once Parthenia's mother recognizes the limits of physical coercion, she "took such a spiteful grief at it that her heart brake withal, and she died" (89). This death illustrates the hagiographic principle that tyrants ultimately fight only themselves, putting in romance terms Languet and Mornay's insistence that true martyrs are inevitably victorious. "If you want to wrest the weapons from their hands," they advise tyrants, "it is enough if you simply do not strike them. For because they do not inflict, but sustain, blows, they immediately throw down their shields when you sheathe your sword."[32] In this reflexive view of power, the martyr's endurance turns the tyrant's assaults into self-destruction.

With her mother out of the way, Parthenia poses what might have seemed a real threat to gender and social order in the sixteenth century: she is a woman who takes her erotic destiny entirely into her own hands. Sidney's narrative proleptically defends the virtue of such erotic freedom, however, by subjecting Parthenia to even more misery before she can unite with Argalus. When Demagoras recognizes that "now Parthenia was her own she would never be his," he seizes her and "with unmerciful force (her weak arms in vain resisting) rubbed all over her face a most horrible poison, the effect whereof was such that never leper looked more ugly than she did" (90).[33] Structurally, Demagoras' attack allows Argalus and Parthenia to show the depths of their love through mutual self-sacrifice. For his part, Argalus proves that his feelings for Parthenia go beyond physical desire. Sidney cannot emphasize Parthenia's deformity enough: the poor woman herself insists that she is "so disfigured . . . Greece hath nothing so ugly to behold" (104). But this seemingly gratuitous attention to Parthenia's ugliness confirms Argalus' sincerity. Between "truth of love . . . virtuous constancy, and even a delight to be constant, faith given, and [Parthenia's] inward worthiness shining through the foulest mists," Argalus learns to "delight in horrible foulness" (90–91). For her part, Parthenia swears that she will never "match Argalus to such a Parthenia" and runs away in hopes that he will marry someone who is "fit for both your honour and satisfaction" (92). It is only after Parthenia magically regains her former beauty, and after Argalus has reiterated his selfless devotion, that the two are wed. After her beauty is restored, Parthenia returns to Argalus "to make . . . trial of whether he would quickly forget

---

32. Languet and Mornay, 56.

33. These descriptions of Parthenia's disfigurement echo Henry Sidney's reaction when he returned from abroad to find his wife "as foul a lady as the small-pox could make her, which she did take by continual attendance of her Majesty's most precious person" (quoted in Duncan-Jones, *Sidney*, 4). Kay argues that Mary Sidney's fate must have seemed the most personal of discomforts brought on by the Sidney family's service to Elizabeth ("Sidney, His Mother, and Queen Elizabth," 20, 28).

his true Parthenia or no" (106). Claiming to be a Corinthian stranger who happens to look just like Argalus' lost love, she tells Argalus that on her deathbed the real Parthenia sent her to him, "by the authority of love commanding you, that the affection you bare her you should turn to me, assuring you that nothing can please her soul more than to see you and me matched together" (104–105). When Argalus chooses to remain true to Parthenia even after he believes her to be dead—a faith that can have no earthly reward—Parthenia reveals her identity and they are finally married.

But this romance turns to tragedy later in the *Arcadia*, and the end of Argalus and Parthenia's story stresses the destructive potential of the self-interest that both have heretofore avoided. When we first reencounter the now-married couple in Book III, their trials have given way to a symbiotic bliss. As the antimetabolic structure of Sidney's description attests, mutual self-abnegation has all but erased the boundaries between them. Argalus and Parthenia are "a happy couple: he joying in her, she joying in herself, but in herself, because she enjoyed him: both increasing their riches by giving to each other . . . where desire never wanted satisfaction, nor satisfaction ever bred satiety; he ruling, because she would obey, or rather because she would obey, she therein ruling" (501). As I have noted, the final formulation insists on the paradoxical relation between relinquishment and enrichment, rule and obedience. This mutuality appears particularly urgent in the context of the rebellions of the Helots and Amphialus, which surround Sidney's accounts of Argalus and Parthenia. Unfortunately, the balance that this "happy couple" exemplifies is disrupted by another civil war, that between the Amphialan rebels and the Basilian forces. This war is not merely an intrusion of public demands on Argalus and Parthenia's private desires. Rather, because the fighting has erupted out of the self-serving impulses of its key figures (Basilius, Amphialus, and Cecropia), it suggests the danger that self-promotion poses to both self and state. When Argalus submits to Basilius' command that he challenge Amphialus, he cites not civic duty, but personal honor. As a "man in whom honour could not be rocked asleep by affection," Argalus must make a choice between serving himself and serving Parthenia (502). Although he repeatedly claims that "honour" is the source of his decision, this "honour" occupies an ambiguous ground between morality and personal glory—an ambiguity that only deepens if we remember that the name "Argalus," as Claire Preston has pointed out, is cognate with the Italian *orgoglioso*, or prideful.[34]

Parthenia recognizes that when Argalus chooses his own honor over his love for her, he endangers them both. Because their lives are so intertwined, if Argalus hurts himself he also hurts her. "Kneeling down without regard who either heard her speech or saw her demeanor," Parthenia insists that "then it was time for you to follow those adventures when you adventured nobody but yourself, and were

34. Preston, "Medicine of Cherries," 105.

nobody's but your own. But now pardon me, that now, or never, I claim mine own. Mine you are, and without me you can undertake no danger: and will you endanger Parthenia? Parthenia shall be in the battle of your fight: Parthenia shall smart in your pain, and your blood must be bled by Parthenia" (502–503). Parthenia's appeal emphasizes that the mutual obligation she and Argalus have undertaken entails submission to one another. Argalus, however, is so "carried away by the tyranny of honour" that he insists on a separation of wills, and a hierarchy between them, that has never before been part of their relationship (503). His answer is not really a response, but an assertion of the priority of his own desires: "Dear Parthenia . . . this is the first time that ever you resisted my will. I thank you for it; but persevere not in it" (503). Even as he acknowledges that Parthenia has his own interests at heart, Argalus rejects the formula of reciprocal rule and obedience and shifts to a vocabulary of command and resistance.

Parthenia's response, or lack of one, suggests a similar choice of self over other. Unlike before, when she refused Argalus' proposal because she thought that what he wanted and what was good for him were two different things, Parthenia here falls silent, "as it were thunder-stricken with amazement; for true love made obedience stand up against all other passions" (503). The love that fortified judgment in the case of her betrothal to Demagoras here inhibits Parthenia's impulse—one might say her duty—to oppose Argalus in order to save him. Her fear of losing his love makes her obedient rather than outspoken. We see the consequences of such self-protecting obedience in Argalus' battle with Amphialus, where he is killed when his unchecked pride keeps him from surrendering in the face of certain defeat. In response, Parthenia makes manifest the entanglement of her life with Argalus' when she battles Amphialus disguised as the Knight of the Tomb. Here, her actions make literal her earlier claim that "Parthenia shall smart in your pain, and your blood must be bled by Parthenia." In permitting Argalus to ignore the interdependence of their fortunes, Parthenia has destroyed herself. The love that should have led her to oppose Argalus' will, even if it meant his displeasure, has instead turned into a force of self-destruction.

Read in the structure of Sidney's hagiographic politics, Parthenia's death follows from a momentary faltering of the courage that enabled her to withstand her mother and abandon Argalus rather than permit him to marry her disfigured self. This loss of strength and agency appears most poignantly in the Petrarchan blazon that describes her death:

> For her exceeding fair eyes having with continual weeping gotten a little redness about them; her roundly sweetly swelling lips a little trembling, as though they kissed their neighbour death; in her cheeks the whiteness striving by little and little to get upon the rosiness of them; her neck, a neck indeed of alabaster, displaying the wound, which with most dainty blood laboured to drown his own beauties, so as here as a river of purest red, there an island of perfectest white, each giving lustre to the other . . . though these things to a grossly conceiving sense might seem disgraces, yet indeed were they but apparelling

beauty in a new fashion which, all-looked-upon through the spectacles of pity, did even increase the lines of her natural fairness. (528)

Like rose-colored glasses, "spectacles of pity" transform how we see reality. Weeping, fear, death, and pain lose their disgrace and become sights worthy of admiration. In making Parthenia literally bleed as a result of Argalus' thralldom to the "tyranny of honour," Sidney stresses the inversion of gender roles that desire makes possible. For the "tyrant honour" that Argalus craves could also signify the chastity that in *Astrophil and Stella* keeps Stella from Astrophil, as we see when Stella insists that "Tyran honour doth thus use thee; / Stella's selfe might not refuse thee" or when Astrophil laments that it is "by honour's cruell might, / I am from you, light of my life, mis-led."[35] The tyranny of honor, in both the *Arcadia* and *Astrophil and Stella*, bespeaks an effeminate fear of worldly opinion as opposed to a masculine devotion to love alone. As we shall see in the behavior of Pyrocles, Musidorus, Zelmane, and the Arcadian princesses, a willingness to forgo reputation and happiness in order to remain true to love revalues Musidorus' charge that love may "womanize" a man. It turns out that the willingness to be "womanized"—hurt, degraded, humiliated—is the surest evidence of a masculine spirit, while an excessive concern with personal strength and honor reveals weakness and impotence.

Argalus and Parthenia's story provides a pattern for the romance's main plot of Pyrocles and Musidorus' courtship of Philoclea and Pamela. Like Parthenia, these princesses choose passion over obedience, and they endure suffering that renders their rebellions virtuous. The princess Zelmane, who exists in the romance only as a memory, is central to developing this culture of erotic sacrifice. Zelmane had fallen in love with Pyrocles and disguised herself as a page in order to become his servant, only to die in despair of requital. Zelmane's history of erotic service and martyrdom provides the background for the romance of Philoclea and Pyrocles— indeed, she might be described as a third party to it. Pyrocles is initially attracted to Philoclea because she looks so much like Zelmane, and he himself takes Zelmane's name in his Amazonian disguise. As Zelmane's prominence suggests, the ideal love to which Pyrocles and Philoclea aspire requires them both to be "like" Zelmane, and not just in name or appearance: both must imitate her self-abnegating passion. Similarly, Musidorus and Pamela, who are far more resistant to love and the vulner- ability that it brings, both learn to accept powerlessness and humiliation, Musidorus through his disguise as a lowly shepherd and Pamela through her submission to physical torture.

Scholars who have read the *Arcadia* through the lens of queer theory have noted how the romance's scenes of cross-dressing and play with same-sex desire under- mine readings that assume essential sexual identity and natural heterosexuality.

---

35. *Astrophil and Stella*, Eighth Song (95–96) and sonnet 91 (1–2), in *Poems*, ed. Ringler.

This work has drawn largely on Judith Butler's observation that gender is not a permanent identity or locus of agency, but a series of provisional, temporal itera- tions.[36] The ease with which Arcadian characters can slip into roles that contradict their biological sex and heteronormative expectations suggests that, as Kathryn Schwarz puts it, in the *Arcadia*, "whatever the sexual relations of bodies, eroticism is a contract among roles."[37] The performative, mimetic nature of gender is central to the equation of suffering with power for which Zelmane is a synecdochal figure. As many critics have noted, Pyrocles' position as both subject and object of desire allows him to occupy a range of gendered identities and to arouse desires that challenge heteronormative assumptions.[38] Indeed, the *Arcadia* continues to call Pyrocles "Zelmane" and to assign "her" feminine pronouns even after "she" has revealed "herself" as Pyrocles. Such a decision indicates that gender is, in Schwarz's formulation, an effect of speech: "when all we have is narrative, a shift in gender reference not only describes a sex change but is one."[39] What has gone unre- marked, however, is that the performative nature of Pyrocles' identity suggests the theatrical and mimetic nature of political as well as gender hierarchy. Like the original Zelmane, the ambiguously gendered Pyrocles transforms "natural" posi- tions of feminized submission or masculine dominance into a series of what Judith Butler would call "citational practices" whose reiteration reveals the fantasmatic quality of the "original" it both constructs and imitates.[40] The provisional nature of gender and desire in Sidney's fiction is as important for the history of politics as for that of gender and sexuality—indeed, it shows the inseparability of these histories.

In the narrative that Pyrocles recounts to Philoclea, the original Zelmane's performance of feminized weakness and self-sacrifice is the source of both her attraction and her power. As Pyrocles explains, Zelmane disguised herself as the page Daiphantus in order to be close to him; distraught over the tyranny of her father and despairing of requital from Pyrocles, she dies of love. The orig- inal Zelmane exemplifies a love that is entirely unselfish, and Pyrocles both desires a second Zelmane and takes on her identity. He consequently pursues the same sort of idealized union initially embodied by Argalus and Parthenia, one in which mutual unselfishness guarantees that service will not turn into enslavement.

The *Arcadia* repeatedly invokes the charge that Zelmane has behaved unchastely in pursuing Pyrocles and living with him for two months as a page, but Zelmane's self-sacrifice excuses her immodest behavior. As Pyrocles explains, Zelmane's

---

36. *Gender Trouble*, 3–44, and *Bodies that Matter*, 27–140.

37. Schwarz, *Tough Love*, 182.

38. See Jardine, "Still Harping," 28–29; Orgel, *Impersonations*, 78–82; Levin, "Female–Female Desire"; and Bates, *Masculinity*, 89–135.

39. *Tough Love*, 185.

40. Butler, *Bodies that Matter*, 108–109.

"unconsulting affection . . . had made borrow so much of her natural modesty as to leave her more-decent raiments, and . . . had apparelled herself like a page; with pitiful cruelty cutting off her golden hair, leaving nothing but the short curls to cover that noble head" (359). Like Pyrocles' own feminine disguise, Zelmane's masculine performance leads her to give up the tokens of power and virtue thought proper to her sex. By cutting her hair, that symbol of the ravishing power of female beauty, Zelmane in effect castrates herself. But this refusal of dominance is also empowering, for it authorizes her to pursue Pyrocles. In her role as Daiphantus, Zelmane "well showed there is no service like his that serves because he loves. For though born of prince's blood, brought up with tenderest education, unapt to service (because a woman) and full of thoughts (because in a strange estate) yet love enjoined such diligence that no apprentice—no, no bondslave could ever be by fear more ready at all commandments than that young princess was" (360). Even when she falls deathly ill at the news of her tyrannical father's almost certain demise, Pyrocles recalls, Daiphantus "would needs conquer the delicacy of her constitution and force herself to wait on me" (364). Zelmane's selfless, even masochistic, service here evinces the virtue of her desires—particularly in contrast to her tyrannical father Plexirtus, whose "violence of ambition" makes him a force of cunning and evil, or her lascivious aunt Andromeda, whose sexual demands Pyrocles and Musidorus have just barely escaped (361). Zelmane is utterly without personal aspiration, so her rebellion against traditional social and gendered norms inspires admiration rather than censure.

Zelmane's selflessness, in fact, constitutes a claim on those she serves. As Zelmane reminds Pyrocles, "For your sake myself have become of a princess, a page, and for your sake have put off the apparel of a woman, and (if you judge not more mercifully) the modesty" (365). Because she has done everything for him, Zelmane now deserves to command Pyrocles. Having revealed her identity on her deathbed, Zelmane dramatically invokes her selfless love to extract both affective and practical compensation. As Pyrocles recalls,

> "And I pray you," said she, "even by these dying eyes of mine (which are only sorry to die because they shall lose your sight), and by these polled locks of mine (which while they were long were the ornament of my sex; now in their short curls, the testimony of my servitude), and by the service I have done you (which, God knows, hath been full of love), think of me after my death with kindness, though you cannot with love." (367)

As her parenthetical remarks remind him, Zelmane has despoiled herself of gender, life, status, and power for Pyrocles. Zelmane's "dying eyes," "polled locks," and past "service" are evidence of Pyrocles' debt to her. If he wants to avoid the charge of tyranny, he must think of her with "kindness." This means not only feeling generosity and compassion but also identifying with her misery as though it is his own: Pyrocles can prove his worth only by imitating, indeed desiring, Zelmane's pain.[41] As he tells Philoclea, "her words and her manner, with the lively consider-ation of her love, so pierced me, that though I had divers griefs before, yet me-thought I never felt till then how much sorrow enfeebleth all resolution: for I could not choose but yield to the weakness of abundant weeping, in truth with such grief that I could willingly at that time have changed lives with her" (366). The spectacle of Zelmane's undeserved demise is as "piercing" as Cupid's arrows, driving Pyrocles to the emotional excess of the flagellant or the martyr. Here, helplessness signifies moral worth. If Pyrocles could "choose" not to yield, he would prove himself a heartless tyrant.

Zelmane herself knows that her weakness and misery place her in a position of authority over the healthy and virile Pyrocles. As Pyrocles recalls, "when she saw my tears, 'O God!' said she, 'How largely am I recompensed for my losses! Why then,' said she, 'I may take boldness to make some requests unto you'" (366). Zel-mane's requests end up being no small matter. Besides asking Pyrocles to use her adopted name of Daiphantus and to bury her anonymously in his own country of Macedon, she requires him to ally himself with Plexirtus, a promise that ends up placing both Pyrocles and Musidorus in the life-threatening situations in which we find them at the opening of the *Arcadia*. Zelmane's dying wish that Pyrocles risk death in order to save her father implies that true pity will inspire imitation of its suffering object. Just as she has given up everything to serve him, Pyrocles has to show that he values his memory of Zelmane more than his own life. Sidney borrows this mimetic logic from Foxe's *Acts and Monuments*, where good and evil readers define themselves through their responses to the suffering they witness. "Yet let us yield thus much unto their commemoration," Foxe exhorts, "to glorify the Lord in his saintes, and imitate their death (as much as we may) with like constancy, or their lives at the least with like innocency."[42] The best way to honor martyrs is to be as much like them as possible.

This mimetic structure is crucial to the circulation of desire in the *Arcadia*. In imitating Zelmane's self-abnegation, Pyrocles comes to love her. We first hear mention of Zelmane in reference to Philoclea, whose portrait, Musidorus notes, "resembling her [Pyrocles] had once loved, might perhaps awake again that sleeping passion" (130). And in his own account to Musidorus, Pyrocles traces "the fatal overthrow of all my liberty" to the moment he saw the portrait of Philoclea, "who much resembling (though I must say much surpassing) the lady Zelmane whom so well I loved, there were mine eyes infected" (140). Since his relation with the living Zelmane contained no such passion, this memory of Zelmane as Pyrocles' lost love is clearly a rewriting of history, but that makes it no less true. History, as we see here,

---

41. Kalstone notes a similar self-consciousness in *Astrophil and Stella* ("Sir Philip Sidney"). A more cynical version of this dynamic is suggested by Lanham's claim that the speaker of *Astrophil and Stella* performs sacrifice and suffering for the express purpose of being rewarded ("Pure and Impure Persuasion").

42. Foxe, 1:xxvii.

emerges through memory, which is itself shaped by desire and fantasy. Pyrocles' love affair with the dead Zelmane stresses this imaginary dimension of the past and therefore, as Schwarz has succinctly put it, "the limited relevance of empirical facts."[43] The repeated suggestion that Pyrocles loved the original Zelmane indicates that the pity that earlier pierced him has taken on the same eroticized quality that we saw in the description of the dying Parthenia. Stressing the ambiguous relation between fantasy and reality, memory and event, Pyrocles himself later admits to Philoclea that "something there was which, when I saw a picture of yours, brought again her figure into my remembrance, and made my heart as apt to receive the wound, as the power of your beauty with unresistible force to pierce" (367). Philoclea's likeness to the "figure" of Zelmane reminds Pyrocles of the last time that he was "pierced," a projection of past onto future that equates the effects of suffering with those of beauty. In his relation to Philoclea, Pyrocles imitates the vulnerability of the original Zelmane: he is ready to be "wounded" by a "beauty with unresistible force to pierce." Yet since it was not Zelmane's beauty, but her love and her misery that pierced Pyrocles, he also seeks to appropriate the power of erotic martyrdom for himself in order to arouse Philoclea's desire.

Philoclea's love for Pyrocles-as-Zelmane emerges from this mimetic structure. Like her more aggressive rivals for Zelmane's affection, Philoclea's devotion signifies not mere servility, but a blend of aggression and compliance: "so that as Zelmane did often eye her, she would often eye Zelmane; and as Zelmane's eyes would deliver a submissive but vehement desire in their look, she, though as yet she had not the desire in her, yet should her eyes answer in like piercing kindness of a look" (239). As in Pyrocles' posthumous affection for the original Zelmane, desire here is a form of imitation and performance that tests the boundaries between subject and object, domination and submission, penetration and yielding. And although Philoclea can only imagine her attraction to Zelmane as one of the "unpossible desires [that] are punished in the desire itself," she nonetheless resolves to accept it (243). In part, Philoclea bases her decision on imitation of Gynecia's pursuit of the same "unpossible" object, reasoning that "either she sees a possibility in that which I think impossible, or else impossible loves need not misbecome me" (243). In part, Philoclea bases her choice on her admiration for Zelmane, who, Philoclea observes, appears to "love me with like ardour" (244). Philoclea's final resolution stresses the ability of love to turn subjugation into a form of pleasure that defies rational analysis. "Away then all vain examinations of why and how," Philoclea determines before vowing, "O my Zelmane, govern and direct me, for I am wholly given over unto thee" (244). This decision to be governed and directed is not a simple loss of power. By giving herself wholly to Zelmane, Philoclea pursues the same ecstatic sacrifice of personal will achieved by the ascetic or the masochist, one that brings an unspeakable—"unpossible"—pleasure that defies normative accounts of submission.

43. *Tough Love*, 181.

Musidorus and Pamela, both of whom are far prouder than Pyrocles and Philoclea, similarly learn to relinquish their pride and power in favor of love. Musidorus,
who initially believed that "all the heavens cannot bring me to such a thralldom" as
Pyrocles endures, is willing to divest himself of status and power in order to court
Pamela. And Pamela cites Musidorus' self-subjugation as the impetus for her own
feelings, asking, "can I without the detestable stain of ungratefulness abstain from
loving him who . . . is content so to abase himself as to become Dametas' servant for
my sake?" (247). To slight Musidorus' sacrifice would not so much "stain" Pamela's
reputation as uncover a latent corruption. Musidorus' "content" abasement, then,
actually gives him a degree of influence over Pamela insofar as it requires her
gratitude. As in Argalus and Parthenia's romance or the strange triangle between
Zelmane, Pyrocles, and Philoclea, abasement and empowerment are hard to tell
apart here. In these rather queer relations of mimesis and desire, Sidney envisions a
form of authority based on the ability to choose subjugation and suffering over
comfort and self-interest.

Sidney's transformation of resistance into victimization culminates in the protracted captivity episode that is at the center of the revised *Arcadia*. Here, Cecropia
abducts and tortures Pamela and Philoclea, hoping to secure the succession for her
son Amphialus by compelling one of them to marry him.[44] Typically, these episodes
are read as evidence either of Sidney's profeminist argument for women's virtue or
of his misogynist enjoyment of female vulnerability; those critics who discuss
the political aspects of the captivity episode see it primarily in terms of Pamela's
representation of actual sixteenth-century women like Mary Stuart, Jane Grey, or
Elizabeth I. Bringing together these feminist and topical readings, I propose that the
scenes of the princesses' torture work to develop the political hagiography that I
have been tracing. The captivity episode stresses the erotic dimension of the secular
martyrdom exemplified by Parthenia and Zelmane, for Cecropia comes to enjoy
the very act of inflicting pain, the princesses the agony that evinces their loyalty.
Whereas McCoy has argued that the princesses' virtue "remains essentially passive," Sidney's attention to the power of martyrdom in fact collapses distinctions
between activity and passivity, resistance and suffering.[45] The battle of wills between
Cecropia and her royal nieces has far more influence on the narrative than the martial battles raging in the civil war that surrounds them, a distinction which suggests
that true authority resides in a psychological, rather than physical, realm.

Cecropia, acting as a proxy for Amphialus, can imagine authority only in terms
of physical domination. Her aggression prominently contrasts with the mode of

---

44. Mark Rose argues that the princesses' ordeals demonstrate female virtue (39). Scholars
who stress the antifeminist aspects of the episodes include Susan Frye (135–143); Sullivan
(14); and Shaver, "Woman's Place." For topical readings, see Worden (*Sound of Virtue*, 176);
Duncan-Jones (*Sidney*, 6, 20); and Susan Frye (139).

45. *Rebellion*, 206.

courtship practiced by Pyrocles and Musidorus, in which self-abasement is evidence of sincerity and thus a claim to reciprocity. Sidney draws on the classical equation between rape and tyranny to stress the sexual charge of private ambition, as well as its ability to invert gender hierarchies. As Rebecca Bushnell has observed, the tyrant's inability to control his own desires transforms rape from a demonstration of his power to subjugate others into a revelation of his loss of self-rule— masculine domination of others becomes feminine submission to one's own appetites.[46] But Cecropia's position in the *Arcadia* suggests that the positions of gender and power figured by rape are even more complex. When Philoclea refuses to marry Amphialus, Cecropia suggests rape as a remedy. She insists that because women are aroused by virile displays of force, rape is itself a form of seduction, refusal an extension of foreplay. Philoclea, she claims, "refuseth but to endear the obtaining" (534). "Think she would not strive," Cecropia advises her son, "but that she means to try thy force; and my Amphialus, know thyself a man, and show thyself a man; and, believe me upon my word, a woman is a woman" (534). According to Cecropia's logic, to know and show oneself a "man" is to use overwhelming force—masculine self-knowledge requires the performance of violence. Ironically, however, her suggestion that male force arouses female desire redefines rape as seduction. As a result, Cecropia unknowingly reiterates the centrality of female consent. Male force, that is, succeeds only insofar as it arouses desire. Cecropia's attempt to mystify rape articulates the hagiographic view of sexual assault that I described above in chapter 1. The violence that Cecropia recommends is incapable of compelling the will, so a woman who can endure masculine violence can also defeat it.

When Cecropia attempts to coerce the princesses into submitting to Amphialus, she appropriates the masculine tactic of physical violence, in effect stepping into the role of rapist. Initially, she mimics the rituals of courtship: "for a while [Cecropia] attempted all means of eloquent praying and flattering persuasion, mingling sometimes gifts, sometimes threatenings, as she had cause to hope that either open force or undermining would best win the castle of their resolution" (550). Cecropia's determination to "win the castle of their resolution" means that she wants psychological, not physical, submission. Like that of Parthenia's mother, Cecropia's tumescent fury situates her as the victim of her own sadistic lust for power, "swelling the more she was stopped, and growing hot with her own doings," until "at length abominable rage carried her to absolute tyrannies" (551). Unable to persuade the recalcitrant Philoclea to marry Amphialus, Cecropia takes "a rod in her hand" and begins "to scourge that most beautiful body" (551). In a dynamic typical of hagiography, Cecropia's aggression only strengthens Philoclea's resolve, for "with silence and patience (like a fair gorgeous armour, hammered upon by an ill-favoured smith) [Philoclea] abode their pitiless dealing with her" (552). As

46. *Tragedies of Tyrants*, 20–36.

Sidney's simile suggests, Cecropia unwittingly beats Philoclea into shape, forging her identity as a martyr: the agony that Philoclea's body sustains becomes as it were the armor of a soul that cannot be touched. As Philoclea warns Cecropia, these beatings only reveal Amphialus' illegitimate claim to her affections and thereby make her "every day further-off minded from becoming his wife who useth me like a slave" (552). Her comparison between wife and slave employs the nuptial analogies used by constitutionalists like Smyth to differentiate between political unions based on reciprocal submission and those based on unilateral force. But it also emphasizes that passive resistance forces sovereign figures to choose between violence and compromise. The martyr thereby refuses to endorse the tyrant's deceptive conflation of consent and coercion, courtship and rape, in the first place.

Pamela's ordeal depicts more explicitly the possibility that victimization may become a form of power. Cecropia takes pleasure in violence itself, turning it from means to end, "her heart growing not only to desire the fruit of punishing them, but even to delight in the punishing them" (553). Yet Pamela disrupts the link between Cecropia's pleasure and her power. "I know thy power is not unlimited," Pamela warns, taking a page straight from Foxe, "Thou mayest well wreck this silly body, but me thou canst never overthrow . . . both my life and death shall triumph with honour, laying shame upon thy detestable tyranny" (553–554). Pamela's own endurance turns Cecropia's sadism into a form of service, "for when reason taught [Pamela] there was no resistance—for to just resistance first her heart was inclined—then with so heavenly a quietness and so graceful a calmness did she suffer the divers kinds of torments they used to her, that while they vexed her fair body, it seemed that she rather directed than obeyed the vexation" (553). Pamela has in effect made Cecropia an instrument for revealing her own strength, thus inverting their positions. Pamela's contest with Cecropia is more effective than Musidorus' fight with Amphialus, which ends in an exhausted draw and, in putting the lovesick Amphialus out of commission, ironically allows Cecropia the freedom to brutalize the very women Musidorus sought to save.[47] Unlike Musidorus, Pamela succeeds in "conquering their doing with her suffering" because her affliction is limited only by death, which would itself signal her persecutors' defeat. Traditionally masculine "doing" depends on the weaknesses or failures of one's opponent (a dynamic brought to a parodic pitch in Dametas' battle with Clinias). Feminized "suffering"—the ability to endure—turns other's actions into reactions to the martyr's recalcitrance. While resistance and suffering initially appear to be opposed, the "heavenly" quietness and "graceful" calmness with which Pamela responds to Cecropia suggests that her endurance is in fact a divinely sanctioned form of opposition. This sense of heavenly approval appears

---

47. As Clare Kinney argues, it is Philoclea's violation that forces Amphialus to confront the injuries he has inflicted upon Arcadia ("Courtly Spectacle," 46–48).

in Pamela's lengthy defense of providence, which echoes the translation that Sidney began of Mornay's *A Woorke concerning the trewnesse of the Christian Religion.*[48]

But Pamela's endurance must not be confused with the traditional stoicism that Mornay endorsed. It is not her suppression of desire, but her passion for Musidorus that assures Pamela's victory. And Pamela does not just endure her pain: she enjoys enduring it. Even as Cecropia flies into ever greater fits of rage, "Pamela remained almost as much content with trial in herself what virtue could do, as grieved with the misery wherein she found herself plunged" (554). In large part, this content-ment derives from the fantasy of an audience to appreciate and emulate her choice of virtue over comfort. Martyrs need spectators. Without witnesses, the martyr's own witnessing of virtue fails to expose tyranny. In the absence of a human audi-ence, the *Arcadia* appeals to natural objects to indicate the proper response to Philoclea's torture: "The sun drew clouds up to hide his face from so pitiful a sight, and the very stone walls did yield drops of sweat for agony of such a mistress" (552). This turn to pathetic fallacy reminds us of the fantastic dimension of both love and martyrdom. This dimension also appears in Pamela's projection of agonized identi-fication onto Musidorus, which allows her to experience her torment as theatrical spectacle. It is when she imagines Musidorus' reaction to her ordeal that Pamela experiences the greatest pain, "for then she would think with herself how grievously Musidorus would take this her misery; and she, that wept not for herself, wept yet Musidorus' tears which he would weep for her. For gentle love did easlier yield to lamentation than the constancy of virtue would else admit" (554). Pamela's empa-thy attributes to Musidorus the same assaulted constancy that manifests the virtue of that love. In imagining herself in Musidorus' place, Pamela also takes a masochis-tic enjoyment in his pain, so that her agonized endurance becomes a form of power, her sympathy a sign of virtue.

Sidney's vision of suffering as a sign of honorable political, as well as religious, resis-tance would influence English discourse for centuries to come—so much so that in *Eikon Basilike* Charles I would quote Pamela's prayers as evidence of his own wronged virtue. It is therefore fitting that Philisides, the most explicit representa-tive of Sidney himself in the *Arcadia*, offers the romance's most explicit endorse-ment of disobedience. Philisides' Ister Bank fable puts in political terms the rhetoric of victimization figured in Parthenia's disfigurement and suicide, Zelmane's death, and the princesses' abuse. The fable, which initially appeared in the First Eclogues of the "old" *Arcadia*, is part of the celebration of Thyrsis and Kala's marriage in the Third Eclogues of the *Countess of Pembroke's Arcadia*. This relocation juxtaposes Philisides' song of political resistance with Pamela's actual and Philoclea's intended

48. For the full treatise, the translation of which was completed by Arthur Golding, see *Prose Works*, 3:185–307.

elopements, a structure that emphasizes the political significance of the princesses' willingness to suffer for what they love.[49] The Ister Bank fable challenges the assumption that any earthly hierarchy is inviolable, for it suggests that even beasts can rightfully resist their "natural" subordination to humanity if they are abused.

As Robert Stillman has pointed out, the Ister Bank fable engages in debates about the limits of sovereignty by translating the story of the Israelites' request for a king into a beast fable.[50] Whereas absolutist theorists like James VI of Scotland (the future James I of England) cited this episode from I Samuel as evidence that subjects must obey even the most tyrannical of rulers, resistance writers drew the opposite lesson. As Languet and Mornay put it, "Samuel does not teach that the power of the king is absolute; on the contrary, he wants to warn the people not to bestow unlimited power on the dissolute impotence of a man."[51] Sidney makes this political genealogy clear in his introduction to the eclogue. According to Philisides, the song he "sang unto my sheep lest stray they should" was one that "old Lanquet had me taught." (705). This description of the fable as one of Languet's "old true tales" recalls the Huguenot tendency to ground the right to resist ungodly commands in antiquarian research (705). Most prominently, Hotman's *Francogallia*, which would influence Theodore Beza along with Languet, studied the ancient constitution of Gaul and found a world of equality imagined in the fable's assertion that originally "the beasts with courage clad / Like senators a harmless empire had" (706).[52] This turn to an idealized past makes resistance a conservative rather than revolutionary force and places the tyrant himself in the role of disrupting custom and tradition.

49. Alexander argues that changes in the order of the eclogues was probably not Sidney's own doing, but represented the reading of his first editor the Countess of Pembroke (22–23, 233).

50. See Stillman, "Politics of Sidney's Pastoral"; and Skretkowitz, "Continuity of Rebellion," 15–17.

51. Languet and Mornay, 129. Languet and Mornay also list I Samuel, among other biblical tracts, as an argument for the elective nature of kingship (68–69). See also James VI and I, *The Trew Law of Free Monarchies*, in *Political Writings*, 67–70; Beza, *Rights of Magistrates*, in *Constitutionalism and Resistance*, ed. Franklin, 116–117; and Goodman, *Superior Powers*, 49–51.

52. See, for instance, the first chapter of *Francogallia*, "On the Constitution of Gaul before it was reduced to a province by the Romans": "Gaul was divided into *civitates*, most of which were governed with the advice of the nobles and were called free, while the rest had kings. But there was one institution to be found in all of them. At a certain time each year they held a public council of the people in which anything that seemed to bear on the general welfare of the commonwealth was settled. . . . [kings] did not have boundless, absolute, unchecked power but were bound by settled law, so that they were no less under the people's power and authority than the people were under theirs. These kingships, indeed, seemed to be nothing but magistracies for life" (*Rights of Magistrates*, 53, 55). See also Pocock's discussion of Hotman's antiquarian researches (*Ancient Constitution*, 15–23).

Philisides warns of the perils of such innovation in his description of Jove's response to the beasts' request for a king:

> Jove wisely said (for wisdom wisely says)
> "O beasts, take heed what you of me desire.
> Rulers will think all things made them to please,
> And soon forget the swink due to their hire." (706)

Jove's advice reiterates the Huguenot principle that rulers receive their power from the people. The emphasis here, as in I Samuel, is on the subjects' "desire" and "will," and the beasts' creation of this being further underscores the popular source of kingship. The new king, man, initially treats the beasts as equals, but his kindness turns out to be nothing but a ploy to win their trust. In Philisides' fable, once man's "seat so rooted he had found, / That they now skill'd not how from him to wend," he becomes spectacularly abusive, moving from mere greed to gratuitous sadism:

> Yet first but whool, or feathers off he tear'd;
> And when they were well us'd to be abused,
> For hungry throat their flesh with teeth he bruised:
> At length for gluttontaste he did them kill:
> At last for sport their silly lives did spill. (706)

As in Cecropia's torment of the princesses, violence here becomes not merely a means of satisfying appetite, but an end unto itself. As the king's motivations shift from hunger to gluttony to sport, the desire for power grows increasingly insatiable, the exercise of power increasingly dissatisfying. Moreover, the beasts are reduced entirely to instrumental and expendable bodies: they become not coherent subjects, but wool, meat, and feathers. Yet, as the internal rhyme of "us'd" and "abused" stresses, the beasts themselves consent to such treatment, as do the abused subjects they represent. Indeed, it is the failure of the tyrant fully to efface their potential agency that marks his behavior as tyranny and not the natural order that we might normally see in the use of animal bodies for human pleasure.

As this dynamic suggests, the beasts' obedience only assures their destruction. This voluntary enslavement, however, also indicates that the source of power is ultimately in those who are dominated. Accordingly, Philisides ends his fable with another warning, this one for both king and subjects:

> But yet, O man, rage not beyond thy need:
> Deem it not glory to swell in tyranny.
> Thou fearest death: think they are loath to die.
> A plaint of guiltless hurt doth pierce the sky.
> And you poor beasts in patience bide your hell,
> Or know your strengths, and then you shall do well. (708)

The raging and swelling of tyrants recalls the impotent fury of Parthenia's mother and Cecropia. Likewise, the animals' "plaint of guiltless hurt" evokes the spectacular suffering of martyrs, which exposes injustice and thus threatens its persistence. As the *Arcadia*'s tales of feminine suffering have shown, to bide one's hell and know one's strengths may not be opposites. Weakness and self-sacrifice, as the *Arcadia* has suggested, can justify resistance. The "guiltless hurt" to which the beasts have been subject reveals human tyranny, so its description may also be a form of protest.

Sidney died fighting the Spanish at Zutphen before he could complete his revisions, so the only ending we have to his romance is that of the "old" *Arcadia*, which Mary Sidney appended to the text she published in 1593. As numerous critics have noted, the original conclusion still fits both the theme and the structure of the *Countess of Pembroke's Arcadia*.[53] The "old" *Arcadia* is optimistic about the ability of unyielding love to reform bad rulers, and the scenarios of female suffering that Sidney adds to his revised version make resistance even more sympathetic. The oracular prediction that instigated the action of the story, and which Sidney retains in his revision, suggests that the union of the two couples was itself ordered by providence. The princesses' imperviousness to pain marks the limits of any external power over them, and their obstinate passion thwarts Cecropia, undoes Amphialus, and places Pyrocles in a position where he can rescue them. When Basilius comes to his senses in various ways at the end of Book V, he quickly pardons the couples and permits their marriages, "remembering the oracle (which now indeed was accomplished not as before he had imagined) considering all had fallen out by the highest providence, and withal weighing in all these matters his own fault had been the greatest" (846). Recognizing the error of opposing divine will and authentic love, Basilius reforms. The lovers' resistance to unreasonable constraint and force has worked as a form of counsel, alerting the ruler to his mistakes even as it has perfected the designs of providence.

Such a vision of resistance as reform would inflect political discourse long after Sidney's death, as would his emphasis on internal rather than external strength.[54] But although later writers took Sidney as their hero, they became increasingly skeptical of the possibility that subjects would indeed "know their strengths" well enough to insist on reform. As his ability to imagine disobedient but virtuous heroines indicates, in the years during which Sidney was producing his *Arcadia* there was still

53. Mark Rose, 40–41; and Arthur Kinney, "Sir Philip Sidney's Rhetoric," 52–54. On incompletion, or *aposioperis*, as Sidney's signature trope, see Alexander, 1, 36.
54. We can trace Sidney's influence on seventeenth-century political thought in various ways: through the legend circulated by Greville's *Life*; through his links to Essex and Algernon Sidney (Pooley, "Algernon Sidney and Sir Philip Sidney," 56–64; and Skretkowitz); and through such seventeenth-century imitations as Francis Quarles' *Argalus and Parthenia* and Charles I's *Eikon Basilike*.

some hope that resistance could encourage reform. While the fates of Parthenia and Zelmane warn us of the costs of such self-abnegation, Sidney nonetheless held it up as a model of power. It would be for Spenser, Shakespeare, and their seventeenth-century successors to explore the dangers and limitations of Sidney's association of suffering with moral authority and political power.

CHAPTER 3

✦

"Who Can Loue the Worker of Her Smart?"

Tyrannous Seduction in The Faerie Queene

ike Sidney's *Arcadia*, Spenser's *Faerie Queene* ponders the intricate relationship of authority and submission through images of assaulted female virtue. But whereas Sidney is confident in the ability of the virtuous subject to stand up to unjust monarchal demands and thereby effect reform, Spenser is less optimistic about the possibility of such principled resistance. For Sidney, characters who lose control of their emotions are weak at best (like Amphialus) and demonic at worst (like Cecropia). For Spenser, they are simply human. As the allegorical mode of *The Faerie Queene* stresses, even the most virtuous of beings are constantly battling desires that are so intense that they feel like foreign, external attacks. In Spenser's Faerie Land it is hard to distinguish between innocent and depraved desires, blissful harmony and self-destructive enthrallment—between the natural fecundity of the Garden of Adonis and the sterile luxury of the Bower of Bliss, for instance. And because political and sexual subjects can never fully comprehend their own darker impulses, they can never be sure that they are resisting them. Accordingly, the martyrdom that Sidney saw as the source of both moral and political authority may give way to a perverse pleasure in abjection. By exploring the possibility that one may mistake one's own motives and thereby fail to differentiate external force from internal consent, Spenser tests the limits of the hagiographic politics that Sidney endorses.

In the 1596 version of *The Faerie Queene*, the elusiveness of chastity and friendship are closely tied to the ultimate failure of justice. Following Aristotle, Cicero, and Thomas Elyot, Spenser proposes that friendship offers a model of mutually binding political allegiance based on love, the "roote" "of honor and all vertue" (II. Proem.2).[1] As Laurie Shannon has argued, the discourse of friendship saturated early modern culture, offering a utopian model of political engagement in which mutual submission of king and councilor protected the commonwealth from the potential excesses of royal will.[2] Like Sidney, Spenser takes friendship as a model of government, privileging the "blessed and stable connexion of sondrie willes, makinge of two parsones one in having and suffringe" that Thomas Elyot had placed at the center of a reformed commonwealth.[3] However, Spenser also depicts the inaccessibility of such a union. In particular, he examines the less savory side of the affection in which friendship is rooted by turning from the classical models on which Shannon focuses, which argued that true friendship was possible only between those who were equal in rank and gender, to early modern depictions of marriage as, in Edmund Tilney's words, "the flower of friendship."[4]

As the disturbing erotic unions depicted in the Books of Chastity and Friendship demonstrate, the ideal of a "blessed and stable connexion of sondrie willes" is difficult to sustain in practice. For marriage, like friendship, is grounded on chastity. Spenser designates chastity the "fairest vertue, farre aboue the rest" because it represents the more general ability to control one's destructive and unruly impulses (III.Proem.1). Yet because this chastity must not only resist temptation but also withstand assault, it invites increasingly severe proofs that become pleasurable insofar as they attest to the mastery of both internal and external pressures. As we have seen in Sidney's scenes of torture, the pursuit of chastity may thus shade into what Freud calls "the moral type of masochism," in which the threat of punishment that should deter excessive desire is itself eroticized.[5] Moreover, since voluntary suffering is the most persuasive evidence of love of other over self, only a corresponding sacrifice on the part of the beloved distinguishes the relation between friends who are "one in having and suffringe" from that between master and slave. Amity and abuse, liberty and tyranny, are not opposites, but on a continuum. And because one's perception of his or her position on that continuum is mediated by trust, desire, and fantasy, any assessment of the nature of the relation between self and other is necessarily contingent and provisional. Suspicion and betrayal are thus endemic to the discourse of affection that circulated in the Elizabethan court where, as Colin Clout sardonically comments, "all the walls and windows there are

---

1. *The Faerie Queene*, 718. All future references to *The Faerie Queene* will be cited parenthetically. See also Aristotle, *Politics*, 3.14–18; Cicero, *De amicitia*, chapters 7 and 21; Elyot, *Governour*, 2.11.

2. *Sovereign Amity*, 1–53, 125–155.

3. *Governour*, sig. 120v.

4. See Tilney's *Flower of Friendshippe*. On the reinvention of marriage as friendship by sixteenth-century humanists and Protestant reformers, see Luxon, *Single Imperfection*, 23–55.

5. "Economic Problem in Masochism," in *General Psychological Theory*, 190–201, esp. 196–200.

writ, / All full of loue, and loue, and loue my deare, / And all their talke and studie is of it."[6] Spenser explores the contradictions of such a focus on voluntary submission in *The Faerie Queene*, where scenes of female subjugation manifest the potential perversions of the equation between love, virtue, and sacrifice.

In particular, Books III, IV, and V examine the hagiographic proposition that physical or psychological agony is the most reliable index of inner worth. Particularly as it appears in narratives of sexual violence, this proposition is implicitly allegorical in its assumption that what appears to be an external battle between female virtue and male will is in reality an internal choice between death and dishonor, physical survival and spiritual integrity. By making such allegory explicit, *The Faerie Queene* treats the female body as an emblem of the female mind and so paradoxically locates ultimate authority in female consent rather than male strength. This seeming valorization of female power, however, also implies that the mere fact of erotic relation is evidence of its consensual nature and thus comes close to denying the possibility of rape. By making erotic choice so ambiguous, *The Faerie Queene* suggests that it may be impossible to resist tyranny, since the very threat of physical force excuses and obscures moral weakness to the point that compulsion and consent become indistinguishable, especially to one's own self.

As readers have often noted, the allegory of Book V is distinct from the rest of *The Faerie Queene* in both its transparent topicality and its inexorable bloodiness. These two features are typically seen as working together to break from the private, feminine concerns of Books III and IV. The poem signals its return to public, masculine issues not just by resuming a linear narrative focused on a single hero but also by its attention to real events and unflinching defense of violence as the root of justice.[7] Striking as these shifts in content, structure, and tone are, however, they do not signify a rejection of the sexual and psychological concerns of Spenser's middle books, but rather demonstrate their specifically political applications. In the context of Elizabethan conflations of love and politics, the extended meditation on female virtue and consent that occupies Books III and IV can be understood as providing a theoretical framework for the more historically specific concerns of Book V. This Book, then, does not just make the obvious move of representing countries like the Netherlands, France, and Ireland as women. By treating the sexual virtue of these figures with the same suspicion that he treats that of his more conventional female characters, Spenser reveals the complexities of both domestic and international political responsibility. With their manifold ambivalences, perversions, and fantasies, the erotic relations in *The Faerie Queen* allow Spenser to study

---

6. *Colin Clouts Come Home Again*, in *The Shorter Poems*, 776–778. All references to Spenser's poetry, excepting *The Faerie Queene*, will be to this edition, hereinafter cited parenthetically by line number.

7. Critics who have read Book V as a rejection of feminine content, form, and influence include Quilligan, *Milton's Spenser*, 203; Stanton, "Reading Spenser's *Faerie Queene*"; Eggert, "Genre and the Repeal of Queenship"; and Bowman, "Gender, Conquest, and Justice."

the intricate nature of political action and allegiance and, more particularly, to reflect on the difficulty of reforming royal policies that endanger religion and commonwealth.

In his depictions of ravished damsels, Spenser takes up the concerns expressed by the Huguenot theorists whose works so influenced his Dudley and Sidney patrons.[8] Étienne de la Boétie, the earliest of these writers, describes his *Discourse of Voluntary Servitude* as seeking "to understand how it happens that so many men, so many villages, so many cities, so many nations, sometimes suffer under a single tyrant who has no other power than the power they give him; who is able to harm them only to the extent to which they have the willingness to bear with him; who could do them absolutely no injury unless they preferred to put up with him rather than contradict him."[9] Or, as Hubert Languet and Philippe du Plessis-Mornay even more dramatically put the question two decades later, "what could be more in conflict with nature than for a people to put itself in fetters and shackles; for it to promise a prince that it would put its own jugular against the point of a knife, and for it to turn its own hand violently against itself—for that is what this clearly amounts to?"[10] In posing these questions, Continental tracts ponder not only the tension between political and spiritual obligations but also the psychological testing that such conflict produces. While they differ as to the proper form and extent of resistance, Huguenot writers invariably see what la Boétie called the "obstinate willingness to submit" as the root of tyranny.[11] According to this view, confrontation with a bad ruler creates an internal contest between the imperative to defend the true faith and the subject's desire for pleasure, security, wealth, or power. The tyrant rules only because his subjects have chosen earth over heaven. It is this conflict that Spenser dramatizes in the erotic contests that pervade the middle books of *The Faerie Queene*. Unlike his aristocratic patrons, however, Spenser shows little faith in the power of resistance. For *The Faerie Queene* is unable to shake the suspicion that even the best-meaning subjects will eventually be compromised by their own perverse desires.

Because the Books of Chastity and Friendship focus on female characters and erotic unions, critics have traditionally treated them as diversions from the poem's larger religious and political concerns. Following a logic that sees state politics as the province of men, such work has tended to describe these Books as either

---

8. For Spenser's relation to Leicester, see Carey and Carroll, "Spenser's Reflections"; and Oram, *Edmund Spenser*, 17, 23. Heffner has traced Spenser's celebration of Essex ("Essex and Book Five"). Norbrook notes the Leicester–Sidney circle's connections with Hotman, Beza, Languet, and Mornay, all of whom were familiar with La Boétie (*Poetry and Politics*, 160).

9. *Discourse of Voluntary Servitude*, 42.

10. Languet and Mornay, 140.

11. La Boétie, 50.

meditations on proper sexual roles or as topical allegories about female rule.[12] This work has crucially elucidated the gendered structures and biases of Spenserian poetry, Renaissance culture, and even modern-day academia. But what has not yet been noted is the extent to which female characters in *The Faerie Queene* represent not only actual women but also political subjects—a structure that has important implications for understanding the geopolitical arguments of Book V as well. As we have seen, in sixteenth-century England, gender was embedded in an analogical web that aligned the feminine with the subordinate and inferior position in a venerable series of linked hierarchies: man/woman, husband/wife, head/body, king/subject, Christ/Church. The prevalence of such identifications between man and woman, ruler and ruled, involved an allegorical mode of reading heterosexual relations that was both political and psychological, opening a series of equivalences that Spenser could exploit. In picturing abstract ideas as concrete and thus gendered beings, allegory almost inevitably draws us into conflicting identifications generated by eroticized notions of domination and submission. In Gordon Teskey's analysis of the violence inherent in the allegorical impulse, Aristotelian metaphysics solves the relation of matter to form by imagining it as a type of sexual congress in which shapeless, chaotic matter longs for the penetrating, ordering imposition of form. Such metaphysical gendering has political as well as philosophical implications. For, as Teskey argues, the individual bodies in the agora, or public gathering place, are always on the verge of being transformed into an undifferentiated body politic to be imprinted with ideology. Though biologically male, political subjects are allegorically female insofar as they can be penetrated by princely terror, deceit, and mystification.[13] In *The Faerie Queene*, the explicit fusion of political, historic, and psychological allegory means that while female characters certainly evoke real women, including Elizabeth I, they equally allow Spenser to consider issues of hierarchy and consent that have implications for contemporary debates about the proper relation between sovereign and subject.

Spenser's pessimistic view of the possibilities of loyal resistance was typical of what John Guy has described as the "second reign" of Elizabeth.[14] In the late 1580s,

---

12. Illuminating studies of the gender dynamics of *The Faerie Queene* can be found in Berger, "Squeezing the Text"; Silberman, *Transforming Desire*; Cavanagh, *Wanton Eyes*; Roche, *Kindly Flame*; and Lewis, *Allegory of Love*. As Quilligan has argued, Spenser's dispersal of Elizabeth over a number of dramatis personae responds to intractable political and sexual facts (*Milton's Spenser*). For readings that analyze contemporary anxieties regarding Elizabeth's gender, see Montrose, "Spenser and the Elizabethan Political Imaginary"; Susan Frye, *Elizabeth*, 135–143; and Berry, *Of Chastity and Power*, 153–165.

13. Teskey, *Allegory and Violence*, 14–147. Numerous readers of allegory have attributed to it both political and psychological dimensions. See especially Lewis, 60–61; Angus Fletcher, *Allegory*; Berger, *Allegorical Temper*; and Escobedo, "Will, Personification, and Character." For the challenge that allegory poses to textual interpretation, see Quilligan, *Language of Allegory*; and Anderson, *Reading the Allegorical Intertext*.

14. Guy, "The 1590s." Guy and Elton treat as a watermark in increasing absolutism the judges' decision in Cawdrey's Case of 1591 that the queen could create ecclesiastical commissions

England saw the appointment of Archbishop John Whitgift, the execution of Mary Stuart, and the deaths of such staunchly Protestant courtiers and councilors as Sidney, his uncles Robert Dudley, Earl of Leicester, and Ambrose Dudley, Earl of Warwick, and his father-in-law, Francis Walsingham. In the wake of these events, the official discourse of the Elizabethan regime also shifted toward absolutist definitions of sovereignty and away from theories of mixed polity based on participation, counsel, and consent. For Spenser, as for many adherents of the "forward Protestant" circle newly centered around Essex, this move away from mid-century conciliar theories generated anxiety about the status of the nobility and the future of Protestantism.[15] Accordingly, the work that Spenser completed between arriving in London in 1589 with the first three Books of *The Faerie Queene* and the publication of the second installment in 1596 mourns the not so distant past when the Sidneys, the Dudleys, and Walsingham actively participated in the formation of Elizabethan policy. These poems herald Spenser's allegiance to a group who drew the queen's suspicion for their investment in the international Protestant cause and commitment to aristocratic participation in government. In celebrating the "noble race" of the Dudleys in *The Ruines of Time*, Spenser also commemorates a line of overmighty subjects who were at once long-standing servants to the crown and threats to it. Their loss is both cause and symptom of the corruption and sycophancy that Spenser laments in *Colin Clouts Come Home Again*, the pastoral satire published in 1595.[16] Spenser is blunt about his aversion to what many perceived as a *regnum Cecilanum* that stymied debate in favor of unilateral decree in *Prosopopoia, or Mother Hubbard's Tale*; *The Ruines of Time*; *The Teares of the Muses*; and the Proem to Book IV of *The Faerie Queene*.[17] This antipathy to Burghley was likely exacerbated by Spenser's relationship with Essex, the patron whom Spenser praises in his 1596 *Prothalamion* as "Great *Englands* glory and the Worlds wide wonder" (146) and who would pay for Spenser's funeral three years later. Essex, the primary rival of Burghley and his son, Robert Cecil, was an aggressive spokesperson for the rights of noble subjects vis-à-vis the monarch. His rebellion and execution in 1601 were

by her prerogative (Guy, "The 1590s," 11–12; and Elton, ed., *Tudor Constitution*, 225–226, 231). Baker sees Whitgift's active suppression of the "Puritan" movement after his accession as Archbishop in 1583 as a move toward stifling dissent ("Historical Contexts: Britain and Europe," 45–46).

15. For debate on the propriety of associating Spenser with "republican" politics, see Wilson-Okamura, "Republicanism"; and Hadfield, "Reply to David Scott Wilson-Okamura."

16. As Hammer argues, after the deaths of the these men, Burghley acquired an unprecedented share of influence: he was Lord Treasurer, Master of the Court of Wards, and acting Secretary of State; Burghley's ascendancy inhibited the earlier sense of balance in Elizabethan politics in general and the Privy Council in particular ("Patronage at Court," 65–86).

17. Guy argues that there was no such thing as a reign of Burghley and his son Robert Cecil, and that the pejorative term *regnum Cecilanum* irritated Burghley. But regardless of actual facts, the perception that Burghley prevented dialogue in favor of unilateral royal will fomented widespread criticism ("The 1590s," 6).

acute signs of the fissure between royal authority and aristocratic liberty that Elizabethan discourses of mutual service and affection sought to mend.

Beginning with the revised ending of Book III, the 1596 edition of *The Faerie Queene* registers more subtly such concerns about the absolutist tone of the "nasty nineties."[18] Whereas the 1590 Book of Chastity ends with Scudamour and Amoret merging into a hermaphroditic figure of mutual desire and devotion, the 1596 version replaces this scene of conjugal bliss with a protracted narrative of Scudamour's despair and suspicion and Amoret's continued misery.[19] In replacing a seamless union with a series of erotic tests that culminate in a flashback to an originary rape, the later edition also replaces parity and consent with hierarchy and conquest. Throughout Books III and IV, Amoret endures astonishing humiliation and pain in order to remain loyal to Scudamour. But after all this, the end of Book IV reveals that the husband for whom she has suffered was in fact the first of her assailants.[20] The poem's narrative reordering of these events, along with their placement in the Book of Friendship, suggests that Scudamour's forceful courtship can be sanctioned only retroactively through the lens of Amoret's subsequent loyalty to him. Without this devotion, Scudamour's initial abduction and chronic petulance and distrust would situate him as the prototypical tyrant described by Thomas Smyth: "a tyraunt they name him, who by force commeth to the Monarchy against the will of the people, and regardeth not the wealth of his communes but the aduancement of him selfe, his faction, & kindred."[21] Amoret's ability to resist a series of potential rapists raises the suspicion that she might also have resisted Scudamour if she had really wanted to. The chastity she embodies conspicuously blurs the very distinctions it should clarify between the physical violation of rape and the internal compulsion of ravishment; between her narrative role as abducted, tortured woman and her allegorical role as representative of married love; between conquest and consent, abjection and loyalty. The actual brutality of Amoret's experiences complicates the allegorical significance they should produce, and thus troubles the idealized picture of devotion that her chastity should perpetuate.

The patent disproportion between Amoret's fidelity and Scudamour's desert in the 1596 versions of Books III and IV suggests that the friendship they purportedly exemplify may be little more than a fantasy that has made Amoret complicit in her own abuse. In preceding the revelation of Amoret's abduction with repeated demonstrations of her fidelity, Spenser puts in erotic terms la Boétie's theory that

18. Collinson, "Ecclesiastical Vitriol," 170.

19. Stephens argues that the exclusion of the hermaphrodite in 1596 revives and extends Spenser's disapproval of the violent Petrarchism represented by Busirane ("Amoret's Evasion"). I emphasize the political implications of this disapproval.

20. Fowler, "The Failure of Moral Philosophy," 56–57. Oram notes the change in Scudamour's character from the impatient lover of Book III to the emblem of failed friendship in Book IV (*Edmund Spenser*, 226–228).

21. *De Republica Anglorum*, 6.

tyranny requires the consent of the subject. For la Boétie, "it is therefore the inhabitants themselves who permit, or, rather, bring about, their own subjection, since by ceasing to submit they would put an end to their servitude."[22] Rather than the volition that we would expect, unwavering loyalty to a ruler may evince a willful thralldom to delusion, for subjects "are not so often betrayed by others, as misled by themselves," and the cunning autarch will take advantage of this instinct: "tyrants, in order to strengthen their power, have made every effort to train their people not only in obedience and servility toward themselves, but also in adoration."[23] Such a relationship is the opposite of true friendship, which never "takes root except through mutual respect."[24] Spenser's depiction of Amoret makes the similar argument that authority is in the hands of the subject, rather than the ruler, for the sincerity of Amoret's devotion to Scudamour only indulges his consistently brutish behavior. And the origins of this union further trouble its significance. The conspicuous difference between narrative and real time, the inversion of beginning and ending in Spenser's story, encourages readers to go back and reevaluate the nature of the "friendship" between Amoret and Scudamour. It also casts doubt on the sexual innocence of the endangered damsels who embody foreign nations in Book V. The staging of such disillusion is crucial to Spenser's project of examining the irrational grounds of obedience. In apprehending the distance between idealized narratives of mutual devotion and actual structures of unilateral sacrifice, the reader of *The Faerie Queene* may come to confront his or her own complicity with the failures and injustices of late sixteenth-century political practice.

While Spenser has certainly never fit Karl Marx's account of him as "Elizabeth's arse-kissing poet," in the 1590 *Faerie Queene* he does draw a firmer line between force and consent, ravisher and husband, tyrannous and godly prince, than he would in 1596.[25] In the first installment of *The Faerie Queene*, written in the 1580s, the virtue of Amoret's devotion is unquestionable, even if its potential costs emerge in the extremity of her torture. Here, the descriptions of Amoret prior to her ordeal at the end of Book III focus on the difference between her ravishment by Busirane and her consensual love with Scudamour, a Sidneian distinction that imagines the possibility of virtuous resistance. By the middle of the following decade, however, Spenser saw fit not only to continue Amoret's ordeals beyond Britomart's initial rescue but also to begin them with her abduction by Scudamour. These revisions signal an ambivalent view of the erotic narratives of sovereignty that Spenser supposedly celebrates—erotic attachment in the 1596 version may evince a masochistic enjoyment of powerlessness rather than consent to a legitimate order.

22. La Boétie, 46.
23. La Boétie, 54, 70.
24. La Boétie, 77.
25. "Elizabeths Arschküssende Poet Spenser," in *Ethnological Notebooks*, 305.

In his Letter to Raleigh, which was appended to the 1590 text but omitted from the 1596 edition, Spenser situates the rescue of Amoret as the central event in the Book of Chastity in terms that emphasize the mutual devotion of Amoret and Scudamour:

> a vile Enchaunter called Busirane had in hand a most faire Lady called Amoretta, whom he kept in most grieuous torment, because she would not yield him the pleasure of her body. Whereupon Sir Scudamour the lover of that Lady presently tooke on him that aduenture. But being vnable to performe it by reason of the hard Enchauntments, after long sorrow, in the end met with Britomartis, who succoured him, and reskewed his love. (718)

Like the other central battles between Red Crosse and the Dragon or Guyon and Acrasia, this early draft of Amoret's ordeal imagines the momentary triumph of the titular virtue of the book in which it occurs. This case diverges from the usual pattern only insofar as Britomart replaces both Scudamour as the damsel's hero and Arthur as the embodiment of the grace that supplements heroic action. Nonetheless, the disparity between choice and compulsion, the "vile Enchanter" Busirane and the rightful "lover" Scudamour is clear. Moreover, even Busirane seems to recognize the value of Amoret's free consent. Surely he could overcome and penetrate her if it were only the "pleasure of her body" that he wanted. What he really wants is for her to "yield" her will, without which any sexual victory would be incomplete.

In the 1590 edition of the poem, Spenser reiterates Amoret's active choice of Scudamour midway through Book III when he describes her rejection of the many Faerie knights whom she has ravished with her beauty. The lines' proximity to the picture of the Garden of Adonis appears to promise similar harmonious fecundity to the union they describe:

> But she to none of them her loue did cast,
> Save to the noble knight Sir *Scudamore*,
> To whom her louing hart she linked fast
> In faithfull loue, t'abide for euermore,
> And for his dearest sake endured sore,
> Sore trouble of an hainous enimy;
> Who her would forced haue to haue forlore
> Her former love, and stedfast loialty,
> As ye may elsewhere read that ruefull history. (III.vi.53)

In both this summary and that of the Letter, Amoret's sincere devotion to Scudamour is unquestionable. The active verbs of the above lines create the impression that Amoret has selected Scudamour among many possible suitors, and her ability to withstand Busirane's violence proves the sincerity of her choice. As an emblem of inviolable chastity, Amoret must "endure sore / Sore trouble of an hainous enemy" to show her faith to her beloved. Yet the sadism of such a test is deflected by the pluperfect subjunctive tense of Busirane's actions (he "her would forced haue to haue forlore / Her former love"), which allows us to anticipate Amoret's trial with the confidence of her victory and the triumph of justice that it signifies.

Even in the 1590 text, however, the distinction between rapist and husband, tyrant and king, force and consent, threatens to give way at the very moment when it should be most apparent. At the conclusion of Book III, these boundaries initially appear to be intact. As Britomart enters the House of Busirane, she confronts first a series of tapestries depicting Ovidian myths of divine ravishment, then a golden idol of Cupid. Both prepare us for the juxtaposition of abuse and idolatry with which the Legend of Chastity concludes. Kimberly Anne Coles has rightly pointed out that Spenser's adaptation of Ovid in Busirane's tapestries describes the oppression of humanity by the gods in feminized terms.[26] By foreshadowing Amoret's ordeal with picture after picture equating subjugation with effeminizing penetration, Spenser invites his readers to identify with the tormented woman that we confront in the next room and, moreover, to avoid the weakness and idolatry that perpetuate such exploitation. Busirane's very name situates him as a symbol of dangerous tyranny opposed to Scudamour's protective "shield of love": Thomas P. Roche traces Busirane to the famously cruel Egyptian king Busiris, who was himself identified with the oppressive Pharaoh of Exodus.[27] But, it turns out, Busirane is not Amoret's original tormenter. He may have "drawne forth" Amoret's "trembling hart," but the "wide orifice" from which this quivering organ has been extracted also exposes the "deadly dart" of Amoret's painful devotion to Scudamour (III.xii.21).[28] As in the Ovidian and Petrarchan traditions that Busirane embodies, love here appears as an invasive force, at once the most involuntary and incoercible of emotions.

Amoret's position in the Masque of Cupid further underscores the ambivalence of the passion that assures her fidelity: she is surrounded by such unsavory aspects of love as Doubt, Fear, Cruelty, Fury, Shame, Poverty, and Death. Busirane's grisly literalization of Petrarchan sensibility is accentuated by his misguided attempt to woo Amoret by writing love lyrics in her blood, at which point the narrator asks a seemingly simple question: "Ah who can loue the worker of her smart?" (III.xii.31).[29] The obvious answer should be "nobody," but Amoret's devotion to Scudamour—and Busirane's obsession with Amoret—render such a

26. Coles, "Elizabeth I, Spenser, and Chaste Productions," 50. By contrast, Benson argues that readers' distance from Florimell's ordeals permits their enjoyment ("The Action of Grace," 87–89).

27. Roche, *Kindly Flame*, 81–82.

28. See Berger for this convergence of Scudamour and Busirane (*Revisionary Play*, 184).

29. For the fusion of literary and psychic dynamics in this scene, see Roche, *Kindly Flame*, 74–78.

vision of love naïve. In a logic made familiar by the Petrarchan sonnet, embracing the source of one's pain is the only sure sign of erotic sincerity. The cruelty that Busirane represents is not the antitype of the narratives of chaste devotion that characterized Elizabethan courtship. It is their grotesque fundament. And far from staying contained in the House of Busirane, anxiety about the potential abuses and misreadings of erotic fantasies provides a structural principle that allows the later books of *The Faerie Queene* to interrogate the Elizabethan idealization of the sovereign–subject relation.

Whereas the 1590 *Faerie Queene* reunites Amoret with an equally devoted Scudamour, the 1596 revision replaces the lovers' hermaphroditic rapture with continued separation and disproportionate suffering. Unlike Amoret, who has borne "seuen moneths" of "bitter smart," Scudamour can barely last two days: because the women took longer than anticipated, his "expectation to despaire did turne" and he has left (IV.i.4; III.xii.45). Having commenced on a note of disappointment, the Book of Friendship turns to an account of Amoret's abduction from her wedding, the details of which further question the "love" and "friendship" between the bride and groom:

> For from the time that Scudamour her bought
> In perilous fight, she never joyed day;
> A perilous fight when he with force her brought
> From twentie knights, that did him all assay:
> Yet fairely well he did them all dismay,
> And with great glorie both the Shield of Love
> And eke the lady selfe he brought away;
> Whom having wedded as did him behove,
> A new unknowen mischiefe did from him remove. (IV.i.2)

In contrast to Book III, where he stresses Amoret's agency, here Spenser situates Amoret as the passive object of Scudamour's conquest, not an active partner in the union. Scudamour "bought," "brought," and "brought away" Amoret, and while his single-handed victory over the twenty knights who guarded her may establish his military prowess, his expertise as a lover goes tellingly unremarked. The "unknowen mischiefe" of Busirane's abduction again aligns the two men, for Amoret is "remove[d]" in a way that differs little from her removal from the Temple of Venus. The marriage that Scudamour was "behove[d]" to make—along with his youth and nobility—may be the primary difference between him and Busirane.

Significantly, this second of Amoret's abductions has occurred in the context of the same "Mask of Love" that we witnessed at the conclusion of Book III. The discrepancy between what initially appeared to be a voyeuristic glimpse of sadism and its socially acceptable, even desirable, presence at the wedding again presses us to reevaluate Busirane, Scudamour, and the cultural narrative they represent. Here, Busirane's grisly spectacle is redefined as courtly entertainment:

> For that same vile enchauntor Busyran
> The very selfe same day that she was wedded,
> Amidst the brydale feast, whilest every man,
> Surcharg'd with wine, were heedlesse and ill headded,
> All bent on mirth before the bride was bedded.
> Brought in that Mask of Love, which late was showen
> And there the ladie ill of friends bestedded,
> By way of sport, as oft in maskes is knowen
> Conveyed quite away to living wight unknowen. (IV.i.3)

Performed amid the drunken mirth in which "every man"—presumably including Amoret's new husband—shares, the court masque becomes a vehicle of ravishment.[30] As in the previous stanza, Amoret is the passive object, not the active participant, in the struggles for her affection. Busirane, like Archimago, Duessa, and Acrasia, is an "enchauntor." And like the spells these other figures weave, the wedding masque embodies the idolatry and delusion on which political and spiritual tyranny depend, for it carries its spectators away from themselves into a glamorous and pacifying world of pleasure. That Busirane was able to ravish Amoret "quite away" because such behavior "oft in masques is knowen" literalizes the assault of Elizabethan entertainments. As the word "masque," which comprises the double meaning of spectacle and disguise, indicates, these performances sought both to display official ideology and to obscure real inequities. Busirane's intoxicated audience, unable to distinguish illusion from reality, fails to notice that what should be happening merely "by way of sport" has become serious, as the disconcerting echo of "way" and "away" suggests.

In conflating visual and sexual captivity, Spenser expresses misgivings about the political implications of spectacle that are similar to those voiced by la Boétie:

> Truly it is a marvelous thing that they let themselves be caught so quickly at the slightest tickling of their fancy. Plays, farces, spectacles, gladiators, strange beasts, medals, pictures, and other such opiates, these were for ancient peoples the bait toward slavery, the price of their liberty, the instruments of tyranny. By these practices and enticement the ancient dictators so successfully lulled their subjects under the yoke, that the stupefied peoples, fascinated by the pastimes and vain pleasures flashed before their eyes, learned subservience as naively, but not so creditably, as little children learn to read by looking at bright picture books.[31]

30. In this way, it offers a politically inflected instance of Eggert's argument that in *The Faerie Queene* "the narrative event of rape itself is a metaphoric maneuver, a substitute action foisted on the narrative in order to conceal or evade a rapturous mode of poetic operation" ("Rape and Rapture," 3).
31. La Boétie, 65.

In la Boétie's analysis, if passive enjoyment of resplendent images supplants active interpretation of difficult concepts, then adults regress to the state of impressionable children. In such a context, it is no wonder that Amoret is "ill of friends bestedded." Everyone else is so "bent on mirth" and distracted by what la Boétie would call the opiates—"*drogueries*"—of Busirane's show that they fail to grasp its implications.[32] Amoret's ravishment epitomizes their own.

Perhaps the most telling critique of Amoret's unshakable devotion occurs in her confrontation with the monster Lust. This episode intimates that her passion for Scudamour has carried her away against her conscious intent—even such an avatar of chastity as Amoret may be subject to irrational internal coercion. This possibility reminds us that given the inevitable ambiguity of human motivation, perfect innocence is unimaginable. It thus troubles distinctions between the altruistic love that sustains private and public order and the self-serving lust that destroys it. Amoret's loyalty is echoed by her fellow prisoner Aemylia, who tells her that "nothing could my fixed mind remoue" from her passion for the lower-born Amyas, for whom she was willing "Both sire, and friends, and all for euer to forgo" (IV.vii.16). The terms in which Aemylia describes her devotion recall the narrator's earlier assurance that Busirane's "thousand charmes" could not "remoue" Amoret's "steadfast hart," so that the wisdom of her fidelity here is treated with greater skepticism (III.xii.31). Certainly, Aemylia's situation differs from that of Amoret: the former has repudiated her family, friends, and social sphere in favor of a forbidden suitor, while the latter seeks her lawful husband. Nonetheless, both women—like Sidney's passionate heroines—willingly relinquish self-interest in favor of love.

It is no accident that both Amoret and Aemylia end up in Lust's cave, for the depths of their passion makes them vulnerable to the advances of a monster who "with his shamefull lust doth [women] first deflowre, / And afterwards themselves doth cruelly devour" (IV.vii.12). Lust's autoerotic sexuality, however, emphasizes that such desire may be directed as much to narcissistic fantasy as to any objective reality.[33] Lust appears as a swollen, hairy monster made up of both male and female genitalia—a caricature of the 1590 Book III's "faire *Hermaphrodite*" (III.xiii.46).[34] As his propensity to self-gratification indicates, his objects are only an extension of his ego:

> And spredding ouer all the flore alone,
> [He] Gan dight him selfe vnto his wonted sinne;
> Which ended, then his bloudy banket should begin. (IV.vii.20)

32. For the French text, see *The Will to Bondage*, 93.

33. Freud, of course, argues that all desire may be essentially narcissistic in "On Narcissism: An Introduction," in *General Psychological Theory*, 56–82, esp. 68–72.

34. For the bisexual nature of Lust's features, see Oram, "Elizabethan Fact," 42.

Lust's onanism suggests his isolation from any external relationship or reality: others are necessary only insofar as can be incorporated into fantasy. Even the "bloudy banket" of penetrating another body is mediated by self-regard, as shown by Lust's inability to distinguish between the virginal damsels and the aged Hag who takes their place. While such narcissism may seem the opposite of Amoret's devotion to Scudamour, her inability to escape Lust implies that both are similarly dedicated to an image rather than a reality.

The difficulty that even the most virtuous of persons have escaping the clutches of passion emerges in Amoret's flight from Lust and Timias' botched attempt to rescue her. Timias cannot defeat Lust because, like the monster, he is a refraction of the same narcissistic erasure of reality that Amoret embodies in her self-sacrificial devotion. Timias and Amoret's excessive idealizations are inversions of Belphoebe's preternatural self-sufficiency and Scudamour's paranoid jealousy: each trusts in absolutist notions of love and virtue that fails to take account of context or contingency.[35] This limitless devotion recalls Spenser's description of Raleigh, the historical model for Timias, in *Colin Clout*: "And there that shepheard of the Ocean is, / That spends his wit in loues consuming smart" (428–429). Imprisoned when the queen discovered his clandestine marriage to Elizabeth Throckmorton, Raleigh is a living example of the dangers of a regime in which the caprices of monarchal will go unchecked. Like Timias and Amoret, both of whose lovers cast them off for perceived disloyalty, Raleigh could only respond to Elizabeth's fury with continued expressions of devout obedience. The relations of Raleigh and Elizabeth, Amoret and Scudamour, and Timias and Belphoebe are all inherently imbalanced, and the overlap of Spenser's historical and moral allegories cautions that the ideal of self-subjugation can easily consume reality.[36]

The extent to which Amoret's reason may have been overwhelmed by her passion is further indicated in the staining of her garments with Lust's blood when Timias wounds him: "A streame of coleblacke bloud thence gusht amaine, / That all her silken garments did with bloud bestaine" (IV.vii.27). This description recalls the black blood of Error in Book I, associating Amoret's love for Scudamour with the same delusion and idolatry that the faithful must battle in the name of spiritual, as well as national, integrity. Amoret's excessive suffering for the less-than-ideal Scudamour may signal the same misprision that John Knox describes in his invective against loyalty to Mary Tudor. "An idol I call that," explains Knox, "which hath the forme and apparance, but lacketh the vertue and strength, which the name and proportion do resemble and promise." English subjects, Knox insists, must not suffer such self-created tyranny, for it is their

---

35. Scudamour's jealousy connects him both to the figure of Lechery in the parade of the Seven Deadly Sins, who has "whally eyes (the signe of gelosy)" (I.iv.24), and to Malbecco, who precedes Scudamour's entrance in Book III.

36. Oram argues that rather than merely praising the figures he portrays, Spenser uses his allegorical portraits to analyze the larger problems they evoke ("Elizabethan Fact," 37–38).

duty to "retreate that, which unadvisedlie and by ignorance they have pronounced."[37] Once the tyrant reveals himself as such, disenchanted subjects must
depose him, however sincere their initial consent. But Spenser emphasizes how
complex and difficult such resistance is, for it entails struggle not just with external tyranny, but with erotic desires and fantasies that one may keep secret even
from oneself. We see as much in the injuries that Amoret receives when Timias
attempts to disentangle her from Lust's grip: "For of that Carle she sorey bruz'd
had beene, / Als of his owne rash hand one wound was to be seene" (IV.vii.35).
If we understand Lust, Timias, and Amoret as different versions of the same
problem, the cuts and bruises that Amoret sustains mark the self-destructive
nature of the emotion these characters embody. Their idolatrous devotion—
expressed in Amoret's obsession with chastity and Timias' adoration of Belphoebe—is a form of narcissism, the projection of one's idealized self onto an
external object.[38]

The difficulty of distinguishing between ideal and reality, internal and external
coercion, is perhaps most manifest in our final vision of Amoret and Scudamour.
Here, we learn of Scudamour's quest "to winne me honour by some noble gest,"
which takes the form of boldly seizing Amoret, along with the Shield of Love that
marks his identity, from the Temple of Venus (IV.x.4). This adventure is filtered
through Scudamour's own memories; we get no objective account of Amoret's
response. Although his story reveals that their union originated in conquest
rather than mutual agreement, Scudamour's narrative is inflected by early modern ideas of sexuality. These views, like the Lust episode, conflate feminine consent with masculine force to suggest that it is disturbingly difficult to locate the
precise line between rape and ravishment, tyranny and kingship.[39] Scudamour's
invasion of the Temple of Venus does not portray an actual, physical rape of
Amoret's body, but instead pictures her otherwise ineffable will in physical terms.
As Jonathan Sawday has shown, in the Renaissance Anatomia was depicted as a

---

37. *The First Blast*, 27, 49.

38. For Freud, overestimation is a "sure indication of a narcissistic feature in object-choice" ("On Narcissism," 72).

39. Because distinctions between rape and ravishment break down in Renaissance legal and poetic practice, to draw any sharp distinction between them would be to simplify some-thing that *The Faerie Queene* leaves ambivalent. Legally, the term "rape" signified forcible penetration followed by emission (1 West. ca 13 and 18 Eliz ca 16). "Ravishment," on the other hand, could mean either abduction—physically carrying a woman away against her will (2 Hen 7 ca 2)—or seduction—figuratively being carried away by one's own desires. See Coke's summary of 1 Westminster ca. 13 and Westminster 2 ca. 34 in *The Second Part of the Institutes*, 180–182, 433–435; and chapters on "Rape" and "Ravishment," *The Third Part of the Institutes*, 60–61. See also the anonymous *The Lawes Resolution on Women's Rights*, 376–379, 395–396. Analyses of the troubling ambiguity of the concept of rape in the early modern period include Catty, *Writing Rape*; and Baines, *Representing Rape*. I further discuss the conceptual and political implications of the conflations of rape, ravishment, and seduc-tion outlined by Catty, Baines, and others in chapter 4, below.

woman whose iconographic tools of mirror and knife would reveal the inner person.[40] Spenser's attention to anatomy in *The Faerie Queene* suggests precisely such a relation between body and mind. Much as Book III figures psychic vulnerability as an arrow penetrating Amoret's heart, Book IV struggles to reconcile Amoret's initial resistance with her subsequent loyalty by examining contemporary views about the female body. Sixteenth-century culture was well versed in the questionable wisdom about female desire popularized by authors like Ovid, who viewed resistance as mere flirtation: "They terme it force, such force comes welcome still, / What pleaseth them they grant against their will."[41] In the sixteenth century, the distinction between rape, abduction, and seduction hinged on finding out the truth about a woman's will, but that truth was unknowable in any objective sense. Medical and anatomical tracts addressed this impasse by insisting that the mechanics of reproduction inevitably betray what a woman "really" wants: the female genitals are allegories of the female psyche.

Given the contemporary understanding of the individual body as both microcosm of and analogy for the state, Scudamour's aggressive style of courtship has clear political significance. Scudamour abducts his future wife from a "temple faire and auncient, / Which of great mother *Venus* bare the name" (IV.10.5). The Temple of Venus evokes early modern descriptions of both the female reproductive organs and the body politic, drawing an implicit connection between the violation of one and the conquest of the other. As Helkiah Crooke put it, "The whole body is the Epitome of the world, containing therein whatsoeuer is in the large vniuerse; Seede is the Epitomy of the body, hauing in it the power and immediate possibility of all the parts."[42] Elizabeth's maidenhead figured the security and integrity of the male political nation, and Spenser further articulates this conflation of the vulnerable female body and the body politic in the figures of Belge, Flourdelis, and Irena in Book V. In the context of her role as the younger and frailer twin of Belphoebe— one of Spenser's designated representatives of Elizabeth—Amoret's abduction betokens a similar threat to an English state whose head was a Virgin Queen. The terms in which Scudamour describes the tellingly named Temple of Venus are hardly reassuring, however, for they transform its defensive architecture into an anatomy of feminine arousal:

---

40. *Body Emblazoned*, 183. Both Sawday and Harvey note that Helkiah Crooke used *The Faerie Queene* as a model for his *Mikrokosmographia*, but they focus on his use of the tour of Alma's Castle in Book II (Sawday, *Body Emblazoned*, 163–170; and Harvey, "Helkiah Crooke's Incorporation of Spenser," 295–314). For the medical view of love as a physiological disease, see Dawson, *Lovesickness and Gender*.

41. *Ars amoratia*, 1.673.

42. *Mikrokosmographia*, 197. Elyot justifies his authorship of the health manual *The Castell of Health* by arguing that "if they will call him a Phisition, which is studious about the weale of his countrey, I vouchsafe they so name me, for during my life, I will in that affection always continue" (sig. Aii–v).

And it was seated in an Island strong,
Abounding all with delices most rare,
And wall'd by nature gainst inuaders wrong,
That none mote haue accesse, nor inward fare,
But by one way, that passage did prepare.

. . .

And for defence thereof, on th'other end
There reared was a castle faire and strong,
That warded all which in or out did wend,
And flancked both the bridges sides along,
Gainst all that would it faine to force or wrong.

. . .

Before that Castle was an open plaine,
And in the midst thereof a piller placed;
On which this shield, of many sought in vaine,
The shield of Loue, whose guerdon me hath graced,
Was hangd on high with golden ribbands laced;
And in the marble stone was written this,
With golden letters goodly well enchanced,
Blessed the man that well can vse his blis:
Whose euer be the shield, faire Amoret be his. (IV.x.6–8)

Scudamour's account of a delectable place, "wall'd by nature gainst inuaders wrong" to which "none mote haue accesse, nor inward fare, / But by one way," envisions Amoret's psyche as reproductive architecture. Amoret's virtue cannot be corrupted by "force or wrong." It succumbs only to authentic passion. Only by penetrating the labial fortress that emblematizes Amoret's incorruptible virtue can suitors access the vaginal bridge that links the outer world with the inner sanctum of her reproductive womb. Having captured the hymeneal shield of love from the twenty knights who guard it, Scudamour easily goes on to defeat the medieval figures of Doubt, Delay, and Danger within. Scudamour's continued triumphs over what initially seemed "invincible" virtue parses the shield's legend to mean that physical coercion may stimulate psychic compliance: "Whose euer be the shield, faire Amoret be his."

In contrast to the assailants that follow him, Scudamour has no problem ravishing Amoret. His report of the ease with which he achieves his goal incorporates the anatomical principle that a woman may become aroused in spite of her conscious intentions. Spenser's allegory resembles strikingly such early modern treatises on female anatomy as Thomas Vicary's 1586 *The English-Mans Treasure*, Crooke's 1615 *Mikrokosmographia*, and the anonymous 1698 *Aristotle's Master Piece*, all of which offer remarkably consistent descriptions of the correlation between arousal, penetration, and conception. Crooke describes the hymen as "the entrance, the piller, or locke, or flowere of virginity" and imagines it in the center of

> The last dissimilar part of the wombe . . . in Latin *pudendem muliere,* that is, the woman's
> modesty of some Vulva, as it were a vallis a valley, or valua a Flood-gate, because it is
> diuided into two parts by a cleft, which like Flood gates or leafedoores are easily opened
> or shut as need be . . . in the middle of this trench is placed the orifice of the necke, and
> this is the fissure that admitteth the yard, and is a part thought too obscoene to look
> vpon.[43]

Crooke's shifting metaphors of entrance, pillar, lock, flower, valley, floodgates, leaf-
doors, and trench situate the "part thought too obscoene to look vpon" in a network
of natural, civic, domestic, and military shelters, which collectively prevent undue
incursions. His attention to "an instinct of lust or desire, not inordinate such as by
sinne is super-induced by man, but natural residing in the exquisite sense of the
obscoene parts" anticipates the description in *Aristotle's Master Piece* of the active
role in intercourse of the vaginal passage.[44] As this popular medical text has it,
"Whilst the passage is related with Spirit and Vital Blood, it becomes more strait for
embracing the *Penis.*"[45] In these accounts, erotic union requires both male and
female erection, a simultaneous arousal that indicates mutual consent. At the same
time, these anatomical tracts complicate the nature of that consent by attributing it
as much to instinct and fantasy as to reason. Crooke describes sexual excitement as
"a sting or rage of pleasure, as whereby we are transported for a time as it were out
of our selues." But such arousal is not simply physical, for "this part or member is
not erected without the help of the imagination."[46]

The palimpsest of architectural, anatomical, and allegorical levels of meaning in
the Temple of Venus recapitulates the ambivalent agency of the Lust episode. This
indeterminacy decidedly undercuts the idealized vision of Scudamour and Amoret
in the 1590 *Faerie Queene.* In terms of the anatomical operations pictured here,
Scudamour and Amoret are both reduced to their genitalia. And insofar as such
anatomical allegories carry a political charge, they characterize the union between
sovereign and subject as simultaneously coercive and voluntary. Although Amoret
remains a "virgin wife" throughout the poem, Scudamour's description of "leading"
Amoret from the Temple of Venus indicates that she does not leave freely:

> She often prayd, and often me besought,
> Sometime with tender teares to let her goe,
> Sometime with witching smyles: but yet for nought,
> That ever she to me could say or doe,
> Could she her wished freedome fro me wooe;

43. Crooke, 235–238.
44. Crooke, 200.
45. *Aristotle's Master Piece,* 85.
46. Crooke, 200, 247.

> But forth I led her through the Temple gate,
> By which I hardly past with much adoe:
> But that same Ladie which me friended late
> In entrance, did me also friend in my retrate. (IV.x.57–58)

Even if we take Amoret's "witching smyles," or Venus' apparent approval, as hints that this resistance is more flirtatious than earnest, the distinction does not matter to Scudamour. We might compare Scudamour to the speaker of *Amoretti* 67, whose surrender gives his "gentle deare" space to consent to be "fyrmely tyde" "with her owne goodwill" (7; 12). By contrast, Scudamour will not take no for an answer. He has already "queld" the objections of Womanhood with "terror" at the sight of his Gorgonian shield (IV.x.55), and nothing that Amoret can say or do will allow her to win her "wished freedom."[47]

Scudamour's story of the abduction provides both the commencement and the conclusion to the history of his union with Amoret, but such violence cannot be assimilated into a romantic picture of marriage as a relation of mutual regard and complimentary authority—the flower of friendship. Scudamour's tale is followed by the merging of the Thames and the Medway in the subsequent canto, a marriage that seems to restore the hermaphroditic union of the 1590 version. In the context of the anxiety felt by Spenser and his patrons about the increasingly imperial language of rule, however, a more apt figure for the body politic might be the forced conjunction of Love and Hate by Concord that Scudamour confronts at the entrance to the Temple of Venus. Here, the "inuiolable bands" that sustain peace must suppress originary Hate—or egoism—in favor of his younger sibling Love— or altruism (IV.x.32–33, 35). Far from an ideal merging, Spenser's portrait of *discordia concors* requires discipline, repression, and self-delusion—the willful confusion of "paines and perlous ieopardie" with "true harts consent" that is the stuff of the Elizabethan sonnet (IV.x.28, 26). This mystification affirms the necessity of consent at the same time that it suggests the ambivalent status of even voluntary loyalty. As the discrepancy between Amoret's allegorical and narrative roles reminds us, idealizing fictions of chastity and friendship may so enthrall subjects that the reciprocal self-discipline of mixed rule gives way to the irrational servility and egotism of absolute monarchy—a blurring of boundaries that signals not a perfect merging of wills, but the ecstatic engulfment of one by another.

Spenser's disturbing depictions of female assault and desire in Books III and IV are allegorical versions of the Huguenot claim that the real root of injustice is the victim's consent, not the tyrant's superior force.[48] Read in light of the connection

---

47. For an alternate reading of this scene, see Roche, *Kindly Flame*, 129–133.
48. As I discuss in chapter 4, the classical examples of both the connection between rape and tyranny and the suspicion of female complicity are Livy's *History* and Augustine's commentary on it. Languet and Mornay themselves evoke this connection by designating the

between sexual and political purity—one embodied in the virgin figure of Astrea, the goddess of Justice whom Artegall should represent—the chivalric battles that occupy the final three cantos of Book V exhibit a more complex psychological study than has usually been acknowledged. Kenneth Borris argues that the Burbon episode "marks a transition from the Arthurian plane of ideal resolutions to the compromises of human history."[49] These concessions are especially prominent in the Book of Justice, but I would extend Boris' claim to suggest that they have been present throughout *The Faerie Queene*. In particular, the latter half of Book V demonstrates the difficulty of distinguishing proper obedience or necessary compromise from cowardice or self-service. Here, suspicion of female virtue underlies the depictions of Belge, Flourdelis, and Irena, all of whom are complicit in their own oppression to varying degrees. And lest we understand such lapses of virtue as purely feminine or foreign phenomena, Spenser not only treats Burbon as an emblem of failed Protestant conviction but also suggests that even such avatars of English chivalry as Artegall have the tendency to choose private desire over public duty. Because the threat that Spain poses to the Low Countries, France, and Ireland is equally a threat to England, Spenser's eroticization of foreign conflict also has a domestic application. Following the Huguenot premise that rulers who fail to defend coreligionists under assault are, in the words of the *Vindiciae Contra Tyrannos*, "most deservedly and rightfully entitled tyrants," such lesser magistrates as Sidney, Leicester, Walsingham, and Essex saw it as their duty to oppose Elizabeth for her and England's own good.[50] As we have seen, Spenser's career and writing indicate that he endorsed a similar theory of resistance. We can understand the study of political psychology in Book V as warning that English subjects who fail to resist unjust policies, to "sip from the cup of bitterness with their brothers," as the *Vindiciae* put it, may be perpetuating their own demise.[51]

Evoking the same ambiguity we saw in Amoret's union with Scudamour, *The Faerie Queene* initially depicts Belge as a helpless widow oppressed by Geryoneo, "a strong Tyrant, who inuaded has / Her land, and slaine her children ruefully alas" (V.x.6). Critics have tended to accept this initial description of Belge's innocence at face value, but Spenser quickly qualifies his picture of blameless

---

"author" of the *Vindiciae* "Stephanus Junius Brutus." This pseudonym connects the tract to both Lucius Junius Brutus, who liberated Rome from the Tarquins, and Marcus Junius Brutus, Caesar's assassin, thus collapsing the rebellions that began and ended the Roman republic.

49. *Spenser's Poetics of Prophecy*, 62. See also Anderson's argument that Book V demonstrates the elusiveness of ideal justice in the real world of geopolitical conflict ("Knight of Justice," 65–77).

50. Languet and Mornay, 185. For Spenser's relation to the internationalist politics of the "forward Protestant" party centered on Leicester and Essex, see Tobias Gregory, "On the Politics of *The Faerie Queene*," 386–389; and Ellis, *Tudor Frontiers*.

51. Languet and Mornay, 180.

victimization.[52] Certainly, Geryoneo may have taken advantage of Belge's weakened state when he "Himselfe and seruice to her offered, / Her to defend against all forrein foes" (V.x.12). But this deceptively chivalric proposal is nonetheless just that—a proposal. It is not the act of "huge power and great oppresion" that the poem initially described (V.x.9). In the theoretical context in which Books III and IV situate courtship, such offers can always be refused, even if that refusal leads to death. But Belge does not hesitate to accept Geryoneo's proposal: "glad" of his offer, she "Him entertayn'd, and did her champion chose" (V.x.12). Geryoneo seems initially to uphold his end of the bargain, "long" acting as her champion "with carefull diligence / The better to confirme her fearelesse confidence" (V.x.12). And, we learn, once his seeming kindness has persuaded her of his honorable intentions, Belge "did at last commit / All to his hand, and gaue him soueraine powre / To doe, what euer he thought good or fit" (V.x.13). The active verbs here indicate voluntary submission, not helpless enslavement.

Spenser's description of Belge emphasizes the weakness and complicity of the southern Netherlands in permitting Spanish power to keep a stronghold, a choice that has endangered not only the northern provinces but also the larger cause of international Protestantism. In the universe of *The Faerie Queene*, Belge's "fearelesse confidence" in the possibility of Catholic benevolence can only be a form of self-deceit. Her acceptance of a dubious champion to protect her "wealth and happinesse" is consistent with early modern descriptions of the Netherlands as willing to tolerate all religions in order to maintain the trade and commerce that brought economic strength (V.x.11). Condemning this choice of worldly gain over spiritual conviction, men like the early seventeenth-century Reformed minister Bartens complained of the largely Protestant city of Amsterdam that "The whore on the Y can be bought with anybody's money: She serves Pope and heathen, Moor and Turk, She bothers about neither God nor the dear fatherland, She is concerned with profit alone, profit alone! Profit alone."[53] As a result of Belge's self-serving acceptance of Catholic protection, Geryoneo not only imposes "new lawes and orders new" but also "forced it, the honour that is dew / To God, to doe vnto his Idole most vntrew" (V.x.27).[54] By giving in to Geryoneo's demand to worship an "Idole most vntrew," the Dutch have put worldly profit above spiritual reward. They

---

52. See, for instance, Tobias Gregory's claim that Belge, unlike Flourdelis, is "represented as a wholly innocent victim" (373) and Bowman's argument that Belge, Flourdelis, and Irena are all so "deprived of agency" that they are not persons, but real estate. Bowman discusses Belge's relinquishment of authority to Geryoneo, but she makes little of the suspicion this act casts on Belge's innocence (168–170). Silberman emphasizes the extent to which the manipulation of sexual ideology for political ends is troubled by the conflation of actual women and the male political nation that they figure in the Britomart–Radigund episode of Book V ("*The Faerie Queene*, Book V," 1–16).

53. Quoted in Marshall, *Locke*, 154.

54. For background of the Dutch revolt, see Israel, *Dutch Republic*, and van Nierop, "Alva's Throne." As Stump shows, in 1569 it was rumored that if Catholic Englishmen rose against Elizabeth, Spain would have backed them using Alva's forces in the Netherlands ("Historical

have thus abandoned the struggle that defines the true Christian, who, according to the *Vindiciae*, should "be crucified themselves, rather than crucify Christ anew, as the apostles say."[55]

Arthur's defeat of Geryoneo, his Seneschal, and his Idol is meant to teach that "Iustice, though her dome she doe prolong, / Yet at the last she will her owne cause right" (V.xi.1). As numerous scholars have pointed out, this is a rather idealized take on Leicester's mission to the Netherlands, not least because the Dutch and Spanish were at war until 1648. By waiting for the divine intervention that these lines seem to describe, subjects like "sad *Belge*" "suff[er]" wrongs they should oppose (V.xi.1). In the opening of Canto xi, Spenser briefly steps back from the narrative to spell out the more general application of Belge's situation:

> It often fals in course of common life,
> That right long time is ouerborne of wrong,
> Through auarice, or powre, or guile, or strife,
> That weakens her, and makes her party strong. (V.xi.1)

Belge's situation is not exceptional, but something that "often falls in course of common life." Moreover, this happens not simply through raw "powre" but also through "auarice," "or guile," "or strife." These options all blur boundaries between right and wrong, victimization and complicity, as is suggested in the indeterminate feminine pronouns of line 4. Similarly, the *Vindiciae* takes Geryoneo's triple body itself as an emblem of the popular consent that sustains sovereign power:

> Why, I ask, are kings said to have innumerable eyes and ears, far-reaching hands and very swift feet? Is it because they are like Argos, Geryonys, Midas, and those others told of in legend? Not at all. Rather, it is clearly because the whole people, whose concern this is, lends its eyes, its ears, its strength and faculties to the king for the use of the common-wealth. If the people deserts the king, he who once seemed sharp-eyed and sharp-eared, mighty and active, will begin to go blind and deaf, and will suddenly fall down. He who once triumphed in spendour, will in an instant become vile to all. . . . So since the king exists through the people and on account of the people, he cannot remain standing with-out the people.[56]

As it turns out, Arthur has really been fighting against Belge insofar as her consent has given Geryoneo his power.

When the narrative turns from Arthur to Artegall, the poem expresses an increased sense of the difficulty of pinpointing where the compromise necessary to

---

Allegory," 96). For England's investment in aiding the Dutch, see Carey and Carroll, 40–43, and Tobias Gregory, 367–370.

55. Languet and Mornay, 61.
56. Languet and Mornay, 76.

worldly action ends and self-serving acceptance of corrupt—irreligious—rule begins. Artegall's experiences in Book V disrupt the fantasy of Protestant ascendancy to show that the human tendency toward ease and ambition undermine the desire for justice. The Book concludes with reflections on the conversion of Henri IV, which split English religious conviction from political security, and the colonial situation in Ireland, in which obedience to the queen was at odds with both the religious and political convictions of the forward Protestant party with whom Spenser allied himself.[57] The interlaced structure of these events confounds any attempt firmly to distinguish the temporizing Burbon from the aggressive Artegall, for both are susceptible to seduction—the original meaning of which was to lure a soldier away from his post.

By the middle of Book V, Artegall has already been so enticed. His charge from the beginning has been "to succour a distressed Dame, / Whom a strong tyrant did vnjustly thrall" (V.i.3). But Artegall has failed in that duty, first because of the months-long delay in Radigone, then because he "continu'd" in Mercilla's court for a while, "Both doing and receiuing courtesies" (V.x.5). As he journeys from Mercilla's court to renew his "first quest" of rescuing Irena, Artegall encounters Sir Sergis, possibly a figure for Henry Sidney, former Lord Deputy of Ireland (V.xi.36). Like his sons Philip and Robert, Henry Sidney was a key adherent of the views of Leicester and Walsingham, which linked the Catholic menace in the Low Countries, France, and Ireland. While this identification of Sergis with Sidney is neither stable nor certain, it makes sense in terms of the rebuke that such a steadfastly loyal adherent of Leicester might make to one who had lapsed in his duty as Artegall has.[58] As a result of Artegall's dallying, Irena, "presuming on th'appointed tyde" at which Artegall promised to meet her to defend her honor,

> Did thither come, where she afrayd of nought,
> By guilefull treason and by subtill slight
> Surprized was, and to *Grantorto* brought,
> Who her imprisond hath, and her life often sought. (V.xi.39)

Like Belge, Irena is overconfident, "afrayd of nought." But here the misplaced sense of security is founded on belief in Artegall's chivalry: he has promised to defend Irena "as [he] were a Knight" (V.xi.39). Without such protection, Irena, like Belge, seems unable to resist the "guilefull treason" and "subtill slight" that leads to her imprisonment.

While Irena is partly at fault here for her lack of vigilance, her physical vulnerability is a result of Artegall's own sacrifice of integrity to passion. As Artegall himself

---

57. See Carey and Carroll, 39. Both Dutch and Huguenot thinkers saw their causes linked to one another and to the larger need for a Protestant league to counterbalance Spanish power; see Franklin, ed., *Constitutionalism and Resistance*, 45, 139.

58. For Henry Sidney's loyalty to Leicester, see Carey and Carroll, 310–338.

initially acknowledges, his delay has placed Irena in this imperiled position. But his quick shift from self-blame to self-defense suggests the difficulty of acknowledging one's own weaknesses, much less rectifying them:

> Too much am I to blame for that faire Maide,
> That haue her drawne to all this troublous strife,
> Through promise to afford her timely aide,
> Which by default I haue not yet defraide.
> But witnesse vnto me, ye heauens, that know
> How cleare I am from blame of this vpbraide:
> For ye into like thraldome me did throw,
> And kept from complishing the faith, which I did owe. (V.xi.41)

Artegall's echo here of his own charge to Terpine that "faulty men . . . / lay on heauen the guilt of their own crimes" challenges not only this particular excuse but also the providential perspective of Spenser's earlier assertion that "at the last [Justice] will her owne cause right" (V.iv.28 and xi.1). As *The Faerie Queene* insists, human agency, not divine providence, is responsible for creating justice. Even Radigund admits that it was "not [her] valour, but [Artegall's] own brave mind" that "Subjected" him to her "vnequall might" (V.v.32). However, the narrator's own unstable account of Artegall's fall indicates how hard it is to admit internal weakness: "So was he ouercome, not ouercome, / But to her yeelded of his own accord" (V.v.17). The narrator here initially offers what is undoubtedly Artegall's own view, that he has been "ouercome," but then quickly corrects himself. Yet even as the poem insists on the difference between being "ouercome" by superior might and being undone by one's own desire or pity, the clumsy shift in perspectives is itself delayed by the line break. This pause emphasizes the difficulty of separating human responsibility from providential design, internal from external assaults on virtue.[59]

The resonances between the situations of Belge, Irena, and Artegall become explicit in that of Burbon, whose appearance further delays Artegall's quest to rescue Irena. Burbon is "in daungerous distress" of a "rude rout" that "sought with lawless powre to oppresse" him. In the meantime, Flourdelis has been "left all succorless," the prisoner of the "rakehell bands" that dominate the king (V.xi.44). As the ambiguity of the verb "assay" suggests, the crowd's assault is also a test of Burbon's faith,

---

59. Stump argues that the Radigund episode follows the same course of events as Elizabeth's struggles with Mary Stuart through the 1570s, with Artegall's imprisonment suggesting Mary's seduction of leading courtiers, and that Artegall's submission indicates how easily humility and submissiveness can lapse into self-humiliation and servility ("Historical Allegory," 94, and "Cross-Dressing," 107, 115). See also Williams, *Spenser's World of Glass*, 134, and Suzuki, "Scapegoating Radigund," 107. As Hadfield notes, Radigund is more like the single, childless Elizabeth than the maternal Mary, and this suggests that Spenser may be critiquing excessive acquiescence to Elizabethan policy ("Judging Elizabeth," 62).

one that he has failed. Yet even here the extent of Burbon's agency is unclear. The claim that the rout has "forced" Burbon to abandon his shield suggests that he had no choice, but the modifier "quite" reveals an excessive acquiescence to their demands. And even if "forced," Burbon has forsaken his faith in order to save his "doubtfull life"—a mortal life of dubious duration and value in comparison to the eternal life of his soul. What he experiences as compulsion is in fact choice, for Burbon has failed to follow the examples of incorruptible faith left by Protestant martyrs. Burbon's choice of political expediency over religious commitment appears especially cowardly in light of Artegall and Talus' easy defeat of the rout, who run from them "like Squirrels" (V.xi.59). But England's own self-interest required similar compromise. As both Elizabeth and Essex remained loyal to Henri after his conversion, Artegall defends Burbon as the lesser of two evils, even after he has proven a perfidious Catholic.[60]

Burbon's faithlessness is matched by that of Flourdelis. The infidelity of the French subjects that she represents is of indeterminate origin, and Burbon is unable to "read aright" whether she is "withheld from me by wrongfull might, / Or with her owne good will" (V.xi.49). Here, as with Belge, Artegall, and Burbon himself, force and consent blur into one another: Grantorto's "wrongfull might" and Flourdelis' "owne good will" are in dialogue, not opposition. Burbon acknowledges that Grantorto has "Entyced" Flourdelis "With golden giftes and many a guilefull word." His rhetorical question—"O who may not with gifts and words be tempted?"—deems gifts and words invariably irresistible, even as its erratic meter and feminine ending attributes succumbing to such temptation to an effete lack of control (V. xi.50). As with Spenser's earlier question, "Who can loue the worker of her smart?", what would seem to be the logical answer is not the true one. A good Protestant reader would reply that no one should be tempted with gifts and words. But Burbon, who himself has been lured from his faith by the promise of worldly gain, implicitly suggests that everyone is subject to such seduction. Moreover, Burbon's shift from Grantorto's "guilefull words" to Flourdelis' "guilefull" consent, stressed in the grumbling that "ever guyle in wemen was inuented," makes Flourdelis herself not victim but oppressor (V.xi.50). Burbon here acknowledges the symbiotic relationship between the tyrant and the corrupt subjects who, as Hotman put it, betray the ruler by flattering him.[61] He verges on exculpating Grantorto along with himself by designating Flourdelis the promiscuous temptress of both.

As with Belge, force follows seduction. This narrative pattern suggests that even a momentary failure of resistance may so weaken subjects and states that they

---

60. For contemporary perceptions of Henri's conversion, see Prescott, "Henri IV and Spenser's Burbon," 195. We may detect a connection between Belge and Flourdelis in light of Prescott's attention to the link between *The Faerie Queene* and the anonymous 1593 tract *The Flower de Luce*, which envisions France as a dying mother urging her children to fight the Catholic League.

61. *Francogallia*, in Franklin, ed. *Constitutionalism and Resistance*, 68.

become helpless to resist more open acts of violence. Having tempted Flourdelis, Grantorto "hath this troupe of villains sent, / By open force to fetch her quite away" (V.xi.51). The "open force" here contrasts with the gifts and words of the previous stanza, situating both as a form of compulsion. Burbon himself is help-less to rescue Flourdelis from the "vnequall might" of the "multitude." This de-scription strains the poem's allegory almost to the breaking point. Recalling the image of Amoret devoured by her own lust, Paris appears as a damsel assaulted by her own inhabitants, who have "forced" Burbon "to forgoe th'attempt remedi-lesse" (V.xi.51). The inchoate desires and corrupt allegiances of the Catholic masses appear as the uncontrolled greed and lust that divide Flourdelis from her proper mate.

As Artegall's reaction to Burbon's story suggests, however, the problem is less Flourdelis' inconstancy than Burbon's own. In response to Artegall's simple ques-tion, "But why haue ye . . . forborne / Your owne good shield in dangerous dismay?" Burbon "blush[es] halfe for shame" and promises to answer, "Least ye therefore mote happily me blame, / And deeme it doen of will, that through inforcement came" (V.xi.52). He states the problem over which the middle books of *The Faerie Queene* obsess, which is that of distinguishing "will" from "inforce-ment." Burbon insists that he has only "layd aside" his "bloudie scutchin" "of late" in hopes of regaining Flourdelis' love (V.xi.54). Artegall initially responds with sympathy: "Certres Sir knight, / Hard is the case, the which ye doe complaine" (V.xi.55). But, in a move that recalls the poem's earlier self-emendation regarding Artegall's own surrender to Radigund, the Knight of Justice quickly corrects himself:

> Yet not so hard (for nought so hard may light,
> That it to such a streight mote you constraine)
> As to abandon, that which doth containe
> Your honours stile, that is your warlike shield.
> All perill ought be lesse, and lesse all paine
> Then losse of fame in disauentrous field;
> Dye rather, then doe ought, that mote dishonour yield. (V.xi.55)

In attempting to secure power or safety, Burbon has failed to accept the martyrdom that would be the true sign of virtue. "Perill," "paine," and even death are "lesse" than honor. Artegall's own past attests to how easy it is to tell oneself that "To tem-porize is not from truth to swerve" (V.xi.56). But Artegall now rejects such a flex-ible and expedient vision of political and religious action, mercilessly demanding a standard that he himself has not been able to meet.

The distinction between honor and expediency, truth and self-delusion, breaks down further in Spenser's description of Flourdelis' response to being rescued from the Parisian throngs. Rather than express the relief or gratitude usual among damsels in distress, Flourdelis appears "halfe dismayed . . . in doubtfull plight, / As neither glad nor sorie for their sight" (V.xi.60). As the pun on "halfe dismayed" suggests, Flourdelis' promiscuous loyalties have left the true state of both her body and her feelings as uncertain as Burbon's. And Burbon's own "greedie great desyre" for such a fickle maid suggests his own corruption, even as the poem's emphasis on his greed further likens him to both Flourdelis and Grantorto. Rather than support Artegall as he rebukes Flourdelis for her infidelity, Burbon takes advantage of the shock this scolding induces. As she stands "amazed," Burbon

> . . . her againe assayd,
> And clasping twixt his armes, her vp did reare
> Vpon his steede, whiles she no whit gainesyd,
> So bore her quite away, nor well nor ill apayd. (V.xi.61)

Like Scudamour, Burbon gives his beloved no opportunity to consent, indicating that he has as much potential as Grantorto to become a tyrant.

In the final Canto of Book V, Spenser suggests that the countenancing of tyranny—whether that of the Catholic Church or the rabble and rulers who follow it—is a result of the "Sacred hunger of ambitious mindes," which overcomes "dread of God," "lawes of men," and "bands of nature" (V.xii.1). This "hunger" to promote oneself transforms passive acceptance of tyranny to active transgression of divine, civil, and natural laws. Temporizing subjects are not just helpless victims. They are determined partners in crime who cannot be restrained from "outrage" or "doing wrong" (V.xii.1). Because there is "No faith so firme, no trust can be so strong, / No loue so lasting then, that may endure long," all are subject to such vice (V.xii.1). As a result of his "impotent desire" "to raine" (V.xii.1), Burbon has become as bad as Geryoneo or Grantorto:

> Witnesse may *Burbon* be, whom all the bands,
> Which may a Knight assure, had surely bound,
> Vntill the loue of Lordship and of lands
> Made him become most faithless and vnsound:
> And witnesse be *Gerioneo* found,
> Who for like cause faire *Belge* did oppresse,
> And right and wrong most cruelly confound:
> And so be now *Grantorto*, who no lesse
> Then all the rest burst out to all outragiousnesse. (V.xii.2)

This alignment of tyrants makes Burbon the oppressor of Flourdelis, whom he is helpless to rescue from either the masses or Grantorto. Failure to discipline oneself encourages collaboration with the corrupt desires of others.

As numerous readers have noted, Irena is the most helpless and passive of Spenser's distressed damsels, and this passivity is usually read as mystifying colonization as rescue, rebellion as submission, by erasing the claims of both the native

Irish and the Old English.[62] Richard McCabe has suggested that since Irena is presented as Ireland's "true Liege and Princesse naturall" (V.xii.24) and no Englishman
would have acknowledged Irish sovereignty, Irena is really a pseudonym for Glori-
anna.[63] Anne Fogarty, meanwhile, argues that Irena is Spenser's representative of
the New English in Ireland, but not the only one: Irenus, the spokesman for brutal
colonial measures in *The View of the State of Ireland*, is her masculine counterpart.[64]
These seemingly conflicting interpretations of Ireland as both queen and subjects
are resolved when we recall the sixteenth-century association between Elizabeth's
virginal integrity, England's insular geography, and the security of the English subjects who are literally contained in the island and figuratively protected by the body
of their queen.[65] And since Irenus is also the voice of Spenser-as-colonizer, we can
understand Irena's degradation and misery as enunciating that felt by male public
servants like Spenser, whose subordinate positions rendered them helpless to introduce the extreme measures they desired. By imagining such colonists in Irena's
abject condition, Spenser appeals to the same chivalric structure that demanded
the rescue of Belge and Flourdelis. Moreover, as Book I's frequent descriptions of
Una in similar terms suggests, these individual romance rescues are all part of a
larger battle on behalf of the true church or Bride of Christ.[66] In placing himself in
the feminine position of needing rescue, Spenser like Sidney implicitly accepts the
monarchomach premise that private citizens could not actively oppose sovereign
commands, even if those commands endangered religion and commonwealth alike.
Instead, subjects could only flee or become martyrs, like Irena, ready "to receiue the
doome of her decay" (V.xii.12). Yet as Beza also argued, private persons do have the
right to "appeal to the legitimate magistrates so that, if possible, the public enemy
may be repulsed by public authority and common consent."[67] Spenser's allegory
constitutes such an appeal to magistrates like Essex, who condoned an aggressive
Irish policy and drew up a "Memorial against Invasion" in 1595 urging Elizabeth to
stop the Tyrone rebellion.[68]

62. See Bowman, 168–169, 174; McCabe, "Spenser and Political Violence"; and Carroll, "The
   Critics," 184. Spenser emphasizes Irena's pathetic state before Artegall arrives: she "Lookt
   vp with eyes full sad and hart full sore; / Weening her lifes last howre then neare to bee, /
   Sith no redemption nigh she did nor heare nor see" (V.xii.3).

63. McCabe, 121.

64. Fogarty, "Narrative Strategy," 75–108.

65. See Stallybrass, "Body Enclosed"; and King, *Elizabeth I*. On the pictorial representations of
   the Catholic menace as an assault on Elizabeth's virgin integrity, see Montrose, *Subject of
   Elizabeth*, 132–163.

66. McCabe has also noted this apocalyptic strain in *The Faerie Queene* (112).

67. *Right of Magistrates*, 107.

68. For Essex's position, see Heffner. The connection between Henri and Artegall that Prescott
   has observed—they are both Herculean heroes—is also shared by Essex, whom Spenser's
   Prothalamion claims "late through all Spaine did thunder / And Hercules two pillars
   standing neere, / Did make to quake and feare" (147–149). This poem's confidence "That

Yet what I am reading as Spenser's self-representation as a damsel in distress is colored by the ambiguity of Amoret, Belge, Burbon, Flourdelis, and Artegall. Consequently, his allegory also represents a potential uneasiness with such help-lessness. These apparent narratives of ravishment and oppression question exactly how one can distinguish consent from force, necessary compromise from self-serving expediency. Ann Rosalind Jones and Peter Stallybrass have noted the English association of the unisex Irish mantle with resistance to "civilizing" pro-jects, the collapse of gender boundaries, the accessibility of a prostitute's body, and the concealment of illegitimate pregnancy. According to this argument, the English "fantasy of degenerate masculinity" was projected not onto the native Irish them-selves, whose extreme measure of resistance made them alarmingly, excessively masculine, but onto the Old English. Such effeminate promiscuity was not yet imagined as "infecting" New English colonizers, but the Old English stood as a troubling warning of its possibility.[69] In Book V of *The Faerie Queene*, Spenser's meditations on the allure of tyrannous power register his anxiety about the ability of such New English administrators as himself to prevent not only the attacks of Catholic forces and Irish rebels but also the more insidious assaults of their own desires for power and prestige. Particularly because lower-level officials like Spenser were the beneficiaries of court appointment, the helpless femininity of Irena attests to an uneasy awareness that men who profit from Elizabethan policies they oppose are implicitly sanctioning those policies. They thus share the position of Artegall, who is "called . . . away / To Faerie Court" before he can reform Ireland entirely. The "heauinesse" in which Artegall leaves Irena may reflect the position of those New English officials who felt powerless to enact the aggressive religious reform and colonial policies they deemed necessary. Worse, it may register anxiety about the lack of resolve of even powerful magistrates like Essex.

As Spenser uneasily shows, it is hard to tell just where such obedience shades into self-service and to what extent loyalty to the Faerie Court endangers not only Irena but all of Faerie Land. But Spenser still imagines that resistance is possible, if sub-jects only have the stomach for it. As we shall see, for Shakespeare, the problem is somewhat different. As *The Rape of Lucrece* and *Pericles* warn, the danger is not just that subjects may deceive themselves, but that they may be genuinely helpless to resist injustice. In these studies of sexual assault, Shakespeare struggles with both the practical options and the ethical status of erotic and political subjects for whom principled opposition is futile, invisible, or impossible.

---

through thy [Essex's] prowesse and victorious armes, / Thy country may be freed from for-
raine harmes" (154–155) envisions the sort of reform that Artegall and Burbon have failed
to enact. For the significance of Catholic worship and Spanish power in Ireland, see Haigh,
Catholics Writing, 118–154.

69. Jones and Stallybrass, "Sexualization of Ireland."

CHAPTER 4

༦ᢣᢦ

"Accessory Yieldings"

Consent without Agency in The Rape *of Lucrece and* Pericles

Unlike Sidney and Spenser, both of whom suggest that the virtuous individual can reform government, Shakespeare depicts the problem of tyranny as more systemic and therefore less tractable. This difference is clear in Shakespeare's use of the analogy between rape and tyranny in *The Rape of Lucrece* and *Pericles*, two works that examine the physical and psychological consequences of sexual assault. Sidney and Spenser portray truly virtuous women as inviolable, and thus endorse a hagiographic logic that is skeptical about the possibility of rape. As Karen Bamford has argued, saints' tales deny the reality of rape by suggesting that if a woman can "freely" choose death instead of sex then assault is really seduction.[1] As we have seen, this hagiographic logic is not limited to medieval Catholic texts but also shapes early modern Protestant politics. Shakespeare explores the limits of such logic by representing situations in which women are helpless to withstand their assailants but nonetheless suffer physical effects of sexual activity like pregnancy and disease. These corporeal remainders of sex manifest the more abstract shame and stigma that surround rape, the sense that woman are somehow tainted by sex, even if they have had no choice about it.

Hagiographic views of female virtue evoke the Roman concept of *stuprum*, the pollution assumed to follow from any form of illicit sex, whether consensual or not. In *Lucrece* and *Pericles*, Shakespeare gives *stuprum* political meaning, suggesting that

---

1. Bamford, *Sexual Violence*, 33. See also Helms, "Eloquence Rewarded"; Gossett, "Introduction," 71–72, 113; and Kelly, *Performing Virginity*, 42–61.

subjects who endure a tyrannous regime share in its corruption.[2] The female body that can be contaminated against its will—penetrated, impregnated, infected—figures a body politic that may be similarly compromised by abusive and violent rule. *Lucrece* and *Pericles* thus explore problems that they are tellingly unable to solve. What is the nature of individual responsibility when individual resistance is futile, if not impossible? Without the ability to resist, what does consent mean?

The sense that rape defiles its victim emerges in part from an idealization of female passivity, a view inscribed in English statutes that treated rape as a crime against family property.[3] Feminist studies of early modern representations of rape have argued that in a culture that eroticizes male force and female submission, it becomes hard to tell the difference between rape and consensual sex.[4] In particular, as Garthine Walker's study of early modern rape trials has shown, violent behavior had no place in the ideal of women as silent and obedient. Rape survivors risked appearing disorderly and unfeminine if they represented themselves as aggressively fighting their assailants. Consequently, in their testimony many women depict themselves as passive objects of brutal male lust, denying themselves agency in an attempt to remove any trace of accountability. But because this position is hard to distinguish from the submissiveness expected of women in conventional—consensual—sex, the suspicion of female compliance remains.[5] Indeed, as Miranda Chaytor has argued, the increasing focus on female consent in sixteenth- and seventeenth-century rape law made the victim's moral status, not the act of assault, central to determining whether rape had occurred. Chaytor has seen early modern rape victims' reluctance to describe the sexual act itself in their testimony as evidence of a sexual culture in which "the opposite of innocence is knowledge, complicity, guilt."[6] By this logic, to have been raped is to lose one's innocence and thus to be complicit in the sinful knowledge attached to sexual activity. This logic is inscribed in both the biblical use of "knowledge" as a euphemism for intercourse and the legal term used to describe sex from Henry de Bracton to Matthew Hale: "carnal knowledge." The pervasive belief that women were tarnished by any illicit sexual activity helps explain why so many rapists escaped public prosecution and why so many

2. For a discussion of the Roman concept of *stuprum*, see Westrup, *Introduction to Early Roman Law*; and Donaldson, *Rapes of Lucrece*, 22–24. *Stuprum* carries the sense of "transferred pollution" described by Mary Douglas. In Douglas' account, pollution rules create a sharp line between pure and defiled bodies that no appeal to motive or intention can modify (*Purity and Danger*, 130–140).

3. For a history of English law concerning rape as a property crime, see Burks, "Women's Complicity with Their Rapists," 759–779.

4. See Bashar, "Rape in England," 28–42; Porter, "Rape," 216–236; Chaytor, "Narratives of Rape," 378–407; and Kelly.

5. Garthine Walker, "Rereading Rape," 6–18. See also MacKinnon's analysis of the physical similarity between forced and consensual sex ("An Agenda for Theory").

6. Chaytor, 398–399. See also Gowing, *Common Bodies*, 82–110.

women married their rapists, who were often the only men who would take them in their deflowered state.[7] It is, paradoxically, the belief in women's agency that means that they, like the allegorical beasts in Sidney's Ister Bank fable, cannot be considered completely innocent victims. Unlike, say, a stolen purse or cow, they have wills of their own and therefore the potential to resist their attackers.

The gendered language of sexual assault provides Shakespeare a powerful idiom for analyzing political consent precisely because it depicts agency in such confused and paradoxical terms.[8] By taking the cultural logic of seduction to extremes politically, *Lucrece* and *Pericles* demonstrate the limitations of the individual choice that Sidney and Spenser take for granted. As Shakespeare's works show, good subjects, like good women, cannot actively resist their superiors—even abusive ones—without raising the specter of anarchy. And if resistance is unthinkable, then consent is the only option, and so no longer a sign of the difference between prince and tyrant.

In particular, the uncertain parameters of female sexual agency allow Shakespeare to explore the ethical and practical implications of the Neostoic worldview that became prominent in late Elizabethan and early Stuart England. Many historians have argued that this blend of Senecan, Tacitean, and Machiavellian thought challenged the Ciceronian belief in the power of counsel to reform corrupt states. Instead, Neostoic thinkers expressed doubt in the efficacy of individual virtue, even as they warned that popular rebellion bred the horrors of civil war.[9] As Henry Savile noted in the Preface to his 1591 translation of Tacitus, however bad a tyrant might be, his abuses were better than "the calamities that follow civill warres, where lawes lye a sleepe, and all things are judged by the sworde." In the history of Galba, for instance, so many Romans are "outraged and slain" in the anarchic power-grab that follows the revolt against Nero that "in Senate a grave & honourable counsellor openlie protested, that in short time there would be great cause to wish Nero again, as beeing more tolerable one tirannie then manie."[10] In a Neostoic world where subjects must choose between the Aristotelian extremes of tyranny and anarchy, "one tirannie and manie," male subjects occupy the same compromised and vulnerable position as women. The hagiographic politics recommended by Sidney have no power to effect reform, since martyrdom requires an audience willing to acknowledge tyranny as such. When corruption and self-interest pervade every aspect of public life,

7. As Burks shows, men often abducted heiresses in order to force parents to consent to marriages that they otherwise would never have allowed. By tarnishing a woman's reputation, hopeful "suitors" forced parents to consider whether any other, more socially desirable, match was possible (764–766).

8. For connections between seventeenth-century theories of rape and political, social, and legal structures, see Herrup, *House in Gross Disorder*; and Rudolph, "Women and Consent."

9. For the political significance of Neostoicism—also described by scholars as "the new humanism," "the discourse of the court," and "politic ideology"—see Burgess, *Politics*, 52–62; Salmon, "Seneca and Tacitus," 169–188; Smuts, "Court-Centered Politics"; Peltonen, *Classical Humanism*, 124–145; and Sandy, "Stoicism."

10. *The Ende of Nero and the Beginning of Galba*, sig. 3v, 13.

the abuse of virtue is either shrouded in secrecy or met with indifference. And in a state that cannot be rehabilitated, subjects are left with the stark choice of quietly accepting tyranny or destroying all order and stability.

But this disenchantment with humanist ideals of counsel and reform did not breed resignation in all English subjects, and Shakespeare had ties to two of the most outspoken groups of aristocrats opposing court corruption: the Essex circle and then the Sidney–Herbert circle.[11] In the 1590s, Essex was at the center of a group of courtiers who refused to accept that their only options were to accommodate themselves to the servility and dissimulation of court politics or withdraw from public life altogether. As we have seen, although he inherited Sidney's mantle as champion of English Protestantism, Essex's view of resistance had far more in common with the aristocratic militarism of medieval and early Tudor magnates than with the political hagiography that Sidney endorsed. For Essex and his circle, pervasive court corruption only made honorable action all the more urgent. In this version of Neostoicism, the real lesson of Tacitus' histories is that, as Savile put it, "a good Prince governed by evill ministers is as dangerous as if hee were evill himselfe." The sycophancy and self-interest that characterized Nero's Rome were what produced the "miseries of a torn and bleeding state" riven by civil war.[12] It was up to noble subjects, supported by a virtuous populace, to rescue both sovereign and state from the effects of such vice. Indeed, the purpose of Essex's attempted coup in 1601 was not to seize power for himself. He hoped rather to force an audience with Elizabeth, from whom he believed himself unjustly barred by his enemies, so as to set forth his and the nation's grievances and persuade her to call a parliament to ensure the succession of James Stuart. In order to succeed, Essex depended on his popularity with the City and the puritan clergy. His friends infamously sought to rile up the former with a performance of *Richard II*. Meanwhile, the latter had gathered at Essex House on the eve of the revolt to preach the right of a noble magnate to lead a fight against tyranny. Unable to secure sufficient noble or popular support, however, Essex failed, and he was executed for treason.[13]

11. Although his relation to Essex is not as direct as that of Spenser, Shakespeare was tied to Essex's circle through his sometime patron, Henry Wriothesley, the Earl of Southampton, the dedicatee of both *Venus and Adonis* and *The Rape of Lucrece*. Southampton was a strong proponent of anti-absolutist ideas of government and one of the "hardliners" in the Essex circle who argued against those who urged Essex to reconcile with the queen. Southampton was condemned to die for his part in the 1601 revolt and spent two years in prison before he was pardoned by James I in 1603. See Akrigg, *Shakespeare and the Earl of Southampton*; and Duncan-Jones, *Ungentle Shakespeare*, 54–104. For a detailed account of the politics of Essex and his circle, see Hammer, *Polarisation of Elizabethan Politics*.

12. Tacitus, sig. 3v.

13. While the plan to stage *Richard II* on the eve of Essex's revolt is the most notorious connection between Shakespeare and the rebellious Earl, *Henry V* specifically compares Essex's 1599 Irish expedition to Henry V's triumph at Agincourt. For details of the Essex revolt, see McCoy, *Rites*, 6–8, 98–101; and James, *Society, Politics, and Culture*, 416–466, esp. 446–459.

Essex's death marked the end of an era of aristocratic militarism, but it did not mean the end of opposition to royal policy. Following the accession of James I, members of the Sidney and Herbert families often led challenges to monarchal policies. This group of courtiers embraced the same conviction in the importance of aristocratic counsel that Philip Sidney had endorsed. The Sidney–Herbert party aligned itself with the courts of Anne of Denmark and Prince Henry and challenged the power of the Howard faction. Like James I, the Howards favored peace with Spain and union with Scotland and insisted that royal prerogative trumped parliamentary authority—practical and ideological stances that the Sidney–Herbert group opposed. One of the most powerful members of this group was William Herbert, the Earl of Pembroke, one of Shakespeare's patrons and a dedicatee of the posthumous First Folio.[14]

Andrew Hadfield has argued that *Lucrece* foreshadows the Essex rebellion and reveals Shakespeare's interest in republicanism, while later plays reveal Shakespeare's acceptance of monarchal government.[15] Hadfield's attention to the importance of republican theory in the late sixteenth century offers a useful corrective to revisionist claims that there was almost perfect political consensus before the 1640s. But the similarity between the endings of *Lucrece* and *Pericles* compels us to reexamine the belief that Shakespeare turned from republicanism to monarchalism. Within such a narrative of developing conservatism, it is hard to explain why a later "monarchist" play like *Pericles* would end with the same sort of armed popular revolt as an earlier "republican" poem like *Lucrece*—particularly when both revolts are specifically contrasted with the hypocrisy and cowardice that has allowed tyranny to flourish. I would argue instead that while the historical situations of *Lucrece* and *Pericles* help us understand the differences between their depictions of rape and tyranny, these works are not about supporting a "monarchal" or "republican" ideology. Rather, they are concerned with what Kevin Sharpe has called the "crisis of counsel," a crisis that many saw as a threat to England's unique status as a *dominium regale et politicum*.[16] In *Lucrece* and *Pericles*, it is difficult to tell honorable public servants from self-serving courtiers who enable tyranny. Forced compliance collapses into what Lucrece calls "accessory yieldings." And such a lack of distinction begs

14. Heinemann has demonstrated that many of the patrons of Elizabethan and Jacobean drama inclined to militant Protestantism supporting a strongly anti-Spanish, anti-Catholic policy in opposition to the more conservative Howard faction ("Political Drama," 172–173). Duncan-Jones argues that Shakespeare's company likely received royal patronage in 1603 through the intervention of Pembroke, who was then Lord Chamberlain (*Ungentle Shakespeare*, 172–174).

15. Hadfield, *Shakespeare and Renaissance Politics*, 111–137, esp. 119–120, 183. See also Hadfield, "Tarquin's Everlasting Banishment."

16. See Sharpe, "Introduction," 37–42. Strier argues that Shakespeare's later plays endorse Marian theories of resistance (*Resistant Structures*, 165–202).

the question of where proper submission to the sovereign ends and collusion with tyranny begins. Accordingly, in both works, suffering itself does not prompt reform: insurgent subjects depose the abusive tyrant.

This is not to say, of course, that either *Lucrece* or *Pericles* is a manifesto of revolt, or even a cautious endorsement of the sentiments of Essex and his circle. As James Shapiro notes, Shakespeare was well aware of the punishments visited on outspoken playwrights, and he was the only major dramatist of the 1590s who managed to avoid confrontation with the Elizabethan authorities.[17] Rather than encourage a particular course of action, these works ponder a question to which there is no good answer: what can sexual or political subjects do when the only means of protecting both life and integrity is the violent revolt that was so widely condemned in Elizabethan and Jacobean England as to be virtually unthinkable?[18] Unable to advocate fully any of the available responses to tyranny—obedience, self-destruction, or rebellion—*Lucrece* and *Pericles* offer a melancholic look at the situation of the early modern political subjects who, like early modern English women, lived lives defined by vulnerability and compromise.

Livy's account of Lucretia's death is, of course, the *locus classicus* for the venerable association of rape with tyranny. His *History of Rome* is therefore central to an ideology in which inner virtue and outer action are perfectly in sync. The Renaissance inherited from Livy's *History* a tradition in which the choice of death over dishonor was an unambiguous sign of the inner discipline and courage that made Rome great. The Roman republic itself was founded in response to Lucretia's suicide, which set the pattern of uncompromising virtue that later Romans like Brutus, Cato, Antony, and Seneca would follow. Since the Roman identity epitomized by stoic suicide is so overwhelmingly masculine, it seems counterintuitive to say that the original type of Roman *virtus* is a woman. But Lucretia's femininity is in fact central to her exemplary status. As a woman, Lucretia cannot hope to overcome Tarquin physically, and this bodily weakness forces her to choose between dying with honor or surviving with ignominy. So Lucretia models Roman *virtus* because, like later Christian martyrs, she shows the strength of her virtuous mind to resist the temptation to escape pain and death. Lucretia's actions, in Livy's account, give us a clear picture of her soul. Her ruthless virtue famously inspires Brutus to lead a revolt against the Tarquins, driving out lustful kings and replacing them with chaste consuls. Lucretia and Brutus constitute alternate models of political agency: self-destruction and outright rebellion. Implicit in both models is the assumption

---

17. Shapiro, *Year in the Life of Shakespeare*, 126.
18. While Protestant resistance theory is my primary focus, Catholic resistance theory was equally prominent, and it took form in the numerous plots to assassinate Elizabeth and the Gunpowder Plot in 1605. See Marotti, *Religious Ideology*; and Haigh, *Catholics Writing*, 47–53.

that the political subject always has a choice about whether to accept or oppose tyranny. For the Romans, this possibility of choice means that submission, however coerced, is invariably a sign of consent.

Early Christian writers, who were more concerned with suicide's spiritual effects than with its political force, challenged this strictly political reading of Lucretia's rape and suicide. The most influential of these writers, of course, was St. Augustine, who condemned suicide as strongly as the Romans commended it. Augustine's *Citie of God* treats Lucretia not as a model of Roman courage, but rather as an example of the complex, obscure nature of human motivation and sexual desire. In order to convince women not to follow Lucretia's example, Augustine insists on the distinction between bodily and spiritual states. Because chastity inheres in the mind, not the body, he assures women, "anothers lust cannot pollute thee; if it doe, it is not anothers but thine owne."[19] Accordingly, Lucretia's shame may bespeak complicity. "What if it were so," Augustine asks, "which none could know but her-selfe, that though Tarquinius son offered her force, yet she her self gaue a lustfull consent, & after did so greeue at that, that she held it worthy to be punished with death" (30). Consent here is not entirely a matter of conscious choice. Rather, as the etymology of the word suggests, volition and passion may be hard to tell apart— *consentire* can mean both to think together and to feel together.

The suggestion that physical force can produce "lustfull consent" follows from Augustine's mechanistic view of arousal. According to this theory, the *pudenda*, or shameful parts, were "taken from the wills rule, and given to lusts" as punishment for Adam and Eve's disobedience (494). Augustine took the male experiences of erection and impotence as the model for the relation between the will and the body more generally, noting that "the motion [of the penis] will be sometimes importunate, against the will, and sometimes immoveable when it is desired" (491). Accordingly, "justly is man ashamed of this lust, and justly are those members (which lust moves or suppresses against our will, as it lusteth) called shamefull" (493). Like Amoret in Lust's clutches, we (or, at least, Augustine) are helpless before these lustful motions, no matter how we fight them. This assumption that even the most virtuous of persons may be aroused against his or her conscious will may explain the "fascination with female sexual shame" that Jocelyn Catty has identified in early modern depictions of rape.[20] In the early modern period, Augustine's mechanical view of arousal informed a larger cultural skepticism about female virtue, one that appears in Juan

---

19. *Citie of God*, 28. All future references will be cited parenthetically.
20. *Writing Rape*, 57. Augustine argues that if Lucretia was in fact not corrupted by Tarquin's act, then her suicide evinces an equally damnable pride (*Citie of God*, 1.18). Augustine goes on to proposes that rape may be a divine punishment for women who take pride in their chastity, insisting that even women who "never had their hearts puffed uppe with the good of this chastity, (and yet had their bodies thus abused by the enemie) had (notwithstanding) some infirmity lurking within them which if they had escaped, this humiliation by the warres fury might have increased unto a fastidious pride" (*Citie of God*, 1.27).

Luis Vives' commentary to his sixteenth-century translation of *Citie of God*. Vives is even more strident than Augustine in judging Lucretia's virtue ambiguous at best, "For who can tell," he asks, "whether she gave consent by the touch of some incited pleasure?" (30). Vives' question demonstrates that even as Augustine's condemnation of Lucretia's suicide challenges the Roman equation of bodily and spiritual states, his reflexive view of lust makes the distinction between them unavailable by any empirical means. As a result, Augustinian analyses of Lucretia's rape tend unwittingly to confirm the classical principle that to yield is to consent.

In bringing together classical and Augustinian readings of Lucretia's rape and suicide, Shakespeare's *The Rape of Lucrece* deploys a cultural suspicion of female virtue in order to consider the nature of political agency. As scholars have pointed out, Shakespeare's *Lucrece* participates in a history that saw connections between the republican institutions of Rome and the ancient constitution of England.[21] Central to this history is an ancient constitutionalist view that the power of the English monarch, unlike that of his Continental peers, depended on the counsel and consent of his subjects. As we have seen, this constitutionalist model makes English subjects responsible for either containing or deposing an abusive ruler.[22] By implication, those who submit to a tyrant's violence are as culpable as those who serve him willingly. As a model for the Roman populace, Lucrece appears to accept such a view of responsibility, declaring herself "mistress of my fate" (1069). The burdens and limitations of such agency are the subject of Shakespeare's meditation on political consent and resistance.

Feminist critics of Shakespeare's *Lucrece* have pointed out that studies that focus on the political allegory of rape often overlook the patriarchal ideology that rape serves. As Stephanie Jed has argued, the "republican rape topos"—a narrative structure in which rape is the necessary prologue to liberation—displaces attention from the injury of the raped woman to the honor of her male survivors.[23] In an effort to correct this erasure of sexual politics, feminist scholarship has examined the gendered ideology of rape itself. While this work has disagreed as to whether Lucrece is a victim or a hero, it has tended to agree that her rigid views of honor and consent emerge from a culture that requires women to be chaste, silent, and obedient.[24]

---

21. See Hadfield, "Tarquin's Everlasting Banishment," 77–80, 96–98, and *Shakespeare and Renaissance Politics*, 111–137; and Arnold, *Third Citizen*, 20, 68–69. Although Hadfield and Arnold differ as to Shakespeare's opinion of representative government, both see his Roman plays and poems as weighing the same questions as his history plays. Dubrow argues that Lucrece herself divides individual suffering from political history (*Captive Victors*, 156).

22. Shakespeare's history plays draw on Holinshed's *Chronicles*, which was a key source of parliamentary history (Arnold, *Third Citizen*, 21).

23. Jed, *Chaste Thinking*, 1–11.

24. See Donaldson for an overview of responses to Lucretia's story over the centuries. Feminist readings of the poem include Belsey, "Expropriation and Consent"; Vickers, "Shakespeare's *Lucrece*"; Quay, "Construction of Rape"; Breitenberg, *Anxious Masculinity*, 97–127; and Coppélia Kahn, *Roman Shakespeare*, 27–45.

As Jane O. Newman has argued, this demand for female passivity necessarily represses a countertradition of female vengeance, which threatens male claims to natural dominance. In such a context, Lucrece's suicide—violence directed against herself—is the only legitimate expression of female agency.[25]

What has been less remarked is that Lucrece's vulnerable position may also register that of the male political subject who cannot legitimately rebel against his ruler. A feminist understanding of sexual assault thus also enables a more nuanced analysis of political power in Shakespeare's poem. By taking the potentially contradictory demands for chastity and passivity to extremes politically, Lucrece reveals that a rigid view of virtue may disrupt the very gendered and political hierarchies it appears to sustain. In a world where coercion and consent are so easily conflated, only violence against one's self or one's oppressor can prevent the corruption that makes subjects as responsible as the sovereign for unjust rule. So when Lucrece insists that she is "mistress of [her] fate," or when Brutus argues that Lucrece "mistook the matter so / To slay herself, that should have slain her foe," both assume an absolute power of resistance that threatens to disrupt a political order that requires a more ambiguous view of agency (1069, 1826–1827). Significantly, Lucrece ends not with reform or redemption of tyranny, but with an armed popular revolt that replaces kings with consuls. By concluding with this rejection not only of tyranny, but of monarchy more generally, the poem suggests that widespread rebellion against traditional authority and hierarchy may be the only way to restore justice. In fact, popular violence can restructure government entirely. Shakespeare's poem thus makes the extraordinary suggestion that subjects of all ranks are in the position of deciding whether to accept a poor ruler. Consequently, the failure actively to resist tyranny bespeaks a quiet collusion with the abuse of power. But by simultaneously emphasizing the self-destructive nature of active rebellion, Lucrece also reveals a reluctance fully to sanction such a concept of agency.

The prose Argument that precedes the poem proper seems to endorse the same vision of consent and agency that appears in classical versions of Lucrece's story. The Argument stresses the involvement of Lucrece's male relatives, especially her husband, with the Tarquins. It also implicitly contrasts Lucrece's uncompromising behavior with the initial weakness of the men who should protect her. Both of Shakespeare's main classical sources, Livy's History and Ovid's Fasti, note Collatine's kinship with the tyrant whose son rapes his wife, a relation that leads to his eventual expulsion from republican Rome.[26] Shakespeare's own version places as much emphasis on Collatine's close personal relationship to the Tarquins as on the

---

25. Jane Newman, "Philomela," 305–307, 326. See also Coppélia Kahn, "The Rape in Shakespeare's Lucrece"; Bromley, "Lucrece's Re-Creation"; and Maus, "Language and Violence," 73.

26. Livy, 197–199, 223–225; Ovid, Fasti, 111. See also Painter's version in The Palace of Pleasure, 5.

blood relation between them. As the nephew of Tarquinus Superbus, Collatine is a member of the Tarquins' inner circle: Shakespeare's Tarquin himself calls Lucrece's husband "my kinsman, my dear friend" (237). And this close personal relation is also a political alliance. By abetting the Tarquins' usurped rule, Collatine shares both its benefits and its blame.

The Argument accentuates Collatine's intimacy with the Tarquins and his support of their pursuit of power. Critics have widely seen Collatine's boast about Lucrece's chastity as the motivation of Tarquin's crime, recognizing his participation in a patriarchal structure that makes women rapable.[27] But, much as the rape is an extreme expression of a larger habit of tyranny, so Collatine's participation in the men's bragging contest is evidence of his collusion with the Tarquinian regime. The Argument makes this connection clear by situating Collatine's boast in a clause that follows a more general description of political appetite:

> Lucius Tarquinius (surnamed Superbus for his excessive pride), after he had caused his own father-in-law Servius Tullius to be cruelly murdered, and, contrary to the Roman laws and customs, not requiring or staying for the people's suffrages had possessed himself of the kingdom, went accompanied with his sons and other noblemen of Rome to besiege Ardea, during which siege the principle men of the army meeting one evening at the tent of Sextus Tarquinius, the King's son, in their discourses after supper everyone commended the virtues of his own wife, among whom Collatinus extolled the incomparable chastity of his wife, Lucretia.

I want to stress that this is a single sentence, one whose breathless, intricate accumulation of details registers the conceptual connections between the siege, the contest, and the men who participate in both. We have two competing main actions here: the attack on Ardea and the bragging contest that is grammatically subordinate to it. Yet because it is the contest that will lead to the rape that is main action of the poem, what appears incidental from a political and grammatical standpoint proves to be central from an historical view. The delayed main verb suggests that the siege of Ardea is just one more act of tyranny, contextualized as it is by Superbus' seizure of Rome without the benefit of law, custom, or popular consent. As Shakespeare's sources show, Superbus attacks the wealthy Rutuli in hopes of amassing enough money to pacify the restive Roman populace, a motive that suggests that their "suffrages" are both necessary and for sale.[28] And Superbus does not act alone,

27. Critics who blame Collatine for inciting Tarquin include Belsey, 317; Vickers, "Shakespeare's Lucrece," 95; and Fineman, "Temporality of Rape."
28. Livy notes that the purpose of the attack on the wealthy Rutuli is to "appease with booty the feelings of the common people" (197); Painter claims that the Tarquins need money to replenish their own coffers, which have been depleted "by reason of [Superbus'] sumptuous buildinges" (5).

but goes to Ardea "accompanied with his sons and other noblemen" who support the Tarquins' illegal rule and violent attempt to expand it. As one of the "principle men of the army," Collatine is one of these supporters—an active accomplice in the Tarquins' seizure of power, not its helpless victim. His insider status is manifest in his presence in Sextus Tarquinius' tent for supper and conversation. Collatine represents the same failure of counsel that so many were concerned about in the 1590s, and his exposure of Lucrece to Tarquin's lust exemplifies the danger this failure poses to the people of Rome.

The popular consent with which the Argument ends would appear to be the opposite of the tyranny with which it begins, and this turn from passivity to activity is inspired by Lucrece's martyrdom. Unlike her husband and the other "principle men of the army," Lucrece refuses to uphold the Tarquins' tyranny. As an example of uncompromising virtue, Lucrece's suicide reminds the Roman noblemen and populace that their choice of safety over honor has upheld the Tarquins' power. Unable to overcome Tarquin herself, Lucrece exhibits her agency through a suicide that inspires her male audience to take revenge on her behalf. The morning after the rape, she calls all of the men to her and, the Argument explains,

> She, first taking an oath of them for her revenge, revealed the actor and whole manner of his dealing, and withal suddenly stabbed herself. Which done, with one consent they all vowed to root out the whole hated family of the Tarquins, and, bearing the dead body to Rome, Brutus acquainted the people with the doer and manner of the vile deed, with a bitter invective against the tyranny of the King; wherewith the people were so moved that with one consent and a general acclamation the Tarquins were all exiled and the state government changed from kings to consuls.

Again, the grammar of these sentences is telling. The first is simple and heavy with verbs, emphasizing Lucrece's purposeful action. Her suicide represents an uncompromising form of agency that manifests itself through self-destruction. Having refused the men's assurance that "Her body's stain her mind untainted clears," Lucrece acts out her conviction that one cannot submit to a tyrant and remain virtuous (1710). The second sentence is nearly three times as long, piling clause upon clause until the revolution it describes is complete. The "one consent" with which both nobleman and people drive out the Tarquins and change the form of government does not so much signify a shift from forced subjection to voluntary, communal rule as a recuperation of agency and a rejection of the passivity that their previous tolerance indicated. For despite the emphasis on the hatred that both nobility and people have long borne their oppressors, the revolt indicates that it has been these subjects' compliance that has upheld the Tarquins' power all along. This connection appears in the collapse of active and passive obedience, explicit and implicit consent, the "people's suffrages" of the Argument's first sentence and the "one consent" of the last. The Romans' former willingness to "suffer" a tyrant becomes a virtual election of that tyrant—a slippage built into the etymology of "suffrages"—so that their success in expelling the Tarquins reveals their former complicity.[29]

This equation of passive acquiescence with active choice structures Shakespeare's depiction of Lucrece's rape. The ease with which Tarquin passes through the locked doors that should protect Lucrece's chamber revises a common metaphor of sexual assault. As Walker has demonstrated, women's testimony in early modern rape trials often figured sex in metaphors of broken locks and chamber doors.[30] This testimony displaced the violation of female bodies onto the rupture of the physical barriers between the rapist and his victim. In Shakespeare's poem, however, Tarquin does not actually break the locks. They open on their own in response to his forceful desires:

> The locks between her chamber and his will
> Each one by him enforc'd, retires his ward;
> But as they open they all rate his ill,
> Which drives the creeping thief to some regard. (302–305)

Joel Fineman has suggested that the presence of these barriers makes Lucrece (paradoxically) responsible for her violation by virtue of the "energetic and energizing resistance" she offers to it. In the structure of desire imagined by the poem, Fineman argues, "Lucrece is asking for her rape because 'no,' as 'no,' means 'yes.'"[31] I want to suggest that the poem is even more ambiguous than Fineman allows, for the description of the locks suggest that Lucrece's initial "no" may mean neither "no" nor "yes," insofar as meaning is knowable only through action. Once "enforced," the locks are not passively broken; rather, each "retires his ward." This resignation of the control or guardianship signified by "ward" is in the active voice, suggesting some form of agency on the part of the locks. And active verbs reappear in the following line, where the locks "open" (rather than "are opened"), even if they complain about it. In subsequent stanzas, doors and locks are repeatedly described as "yielding": "each unwilling portal yields him way" (309) and the "yielding latch" which "Hath barred him from the blessed thing he sought" eventually opens on its own (339–340). This emphasis on yielding incorporates a cultural logic that so blurs ideas of female sexual activity and passivity that "no" and "yes" cease to have meaning as rhetorical acts. Like the people's "suffrages" in the Argument, the locks yield because they have no choice.

Although the poem insists on the insurgent, irrepressible nature of Tarquin's passion, one cannot help but be struck by how much talking precedes the rape

---

29. *OED*, 2d ed., s.v. "suffrage."
30. Garthine Walker, 14.
31. Fineman, 40–43.

itself: 402 lines, in fact. This debate between Tarquin and Lucrece is characterized by the same confusion of force and consent, activity and passivity, that appeared in the description of the locks. Initially, Tarquin promises Lucrece that "if thou yield, I rest thy secret friend" (326). In pledging to "rest" as Lucrece's "secret friend," Tarquin suggests not only that her compliance will secure his friendship and the benefits it can bring but also that he will be at peace only if she succumbs to him. Like that of his "dear friend" Collatine, Lucrece's submission to his power will signify an affective as well as political bond. Tarquin's dependence on Lucrece's consent appears further in his later, more insistent command that she "Yield to my love. If not, enforced hate / Instead of love's coy touch shall rudely tear thee" (668–669). Here, the curt imperative "yield to my love" is undercut by the conditional sentence that follows. The clumsy, violent embraces to which Tarquin will be reduced, like the "enforced hate" that will take him over, suggest that it is only Lucrece's submission that allows for an orderly, seemingly natural show of authority. Lucrece here becomes the primary agent to whom Tarquin can only react.

While Tarquin's promise of violence is ultimately unsuccessful, his threat to Lucrece's honor leads her to offer a strategic consent—one not unlike Brutus' strategic appearance of stupidity—that appears to affirm his power over her. Like that of the "principle men of the army," Lucrece's cooperation, however coerced, establishes an implicit league between herself and Tarquin. In the aftermath of the rape, the poem describes Tarquin and Lucrece in strikingly similar terms that stress the affinity of the tyrant and those who obey him. Like the speaker of Shakespeare's Sonnet 129, Tarquin sees himself as corrupted by his own sated lust. Tarquin imagines his body as a "fair temple," now "defaced," that should protect the soul inside. In this analogy, his physical corruption makes his spirit a "spotted princess." The poem describes this contamination of the soul by the body as involuntary on Tarquin's part, a result of the anarchy of his passions. Tarquin's agency, it appears, is as ambiguous as Lucrece's. His soul

> . . . says her subjects with foul insurrection
> Have batter'd down her consecrated wall,
> And by their mortal fault brought in subjection
> Her immortality, and made her thrall
> To living death and pain perpetual,
>   Which in her prescience she controlled still,
>   But her foresight could not forestall their will. (719–728)

Lucrece describes her own soul's condition in uncomfortably similar terms. Her metaphors of military invasion suggest that the violation of her body has given Tarquin access to her soul, whose

> . . . house is sack'd, her quiet interrupted,
> Her mansion batter'd by the enemy,

> Her sacred temple spotted, spoil'd, corrupted,
> Grossly engirt with daring infamy. (1170–1173)

Both Tarquin and Lucrece have been battered and spotted, and they share the "scar that will, despite of cure, remain" (732). The poem's emphasis on their affinity evokes the humanist principle that resistance may be as valuable to the tyrant as to his subjects, for Lucrece's yielding has permitted Tarquin's pollution, as well as her own. But this view of resistance as counsel assumes a ruler who will reform or a populace strong enough to band together with the "one consent" of the Argument. Alone and vulnerable, Lucrece's opposition would have been futile, for it could only have resulted in a loss of her good name. In such a context, her choice to "take all patiently" makes her Tarquin's "accessory"—ornament, supplement, and accomplice were all contemporary meanings of this term (1641, 1658).[32] Because patience and passivity signify assent here, only a violent assertion of agency can sever Lucrece's ties to Tarquin.

Lucrece herself is convinced that public self-sacrifice alone can break this league. In contemplating suicide, Lucrece understands her act as ending the alliance with Tarquin that would be physically present in the "bastard graft" that the rape may have produced. Her determination that "This bastard graft shall never come to growth" evokes the medical commonplace that conception is impossible without consent (1062). In this view, the mechanics of reproduction inevitably betray what a woman "really" wants. According to Thomas Vicary, for instance, conception required the ejaculation of both male and female seed, and so was a collaborative effort in which "eche of them worketh in the other, and suffereth in the other, [to] engender Embreon."[33] Since ejaculation required arousal, pregnancy signified that the woman's body had been aroused against her will. Such thralldom to bodily sensations situates consent somewhere between conscious choice and passive reflex.[34] By introducing the possibility that the rape has produced a child, a suspicion notably absent from his sources, Shakespeare evokes this early modern medical commonplace and thereby accentuates the difficulty of defining resistance.

For Lucrece, the possibility that the rape will produce a child turns a single act of tyranny into an ongoing secret alliance between herself and Collatine. Even if she never truly consented to Tarquin's demands, Lucrece is certain that if she allows

---

32. *OED*, 2d ed., s.v. "accessory."

33. Vicary, *The English-Man's Treasure*, 55.

34. This view endured for several centuries. Michael Dalton's 1681 *The Country Justice* asserts that "if the woman at the time of the supposed rape, doe conceive with childe, by the ravisher, this is no rape, for a woman cannot conceive with child, except she do consent" (248), and Giles Jacob's 1772 *New Law-Dictionary* notes that "formerly it was adjudged not to be a *rape* to force a woman, *who conceived at the time*; because *if she had not consented, she could not have conceived*: Tho' this opinion hath been since questioned, by reason *the previous violence is no way extenuated by such a subsequent consent*" (n.p.).

herself or Tarquin's child to live, she will be an accomplice in cuckolding Collatine. Instead, she promises that

> "He shall not boast, who did thy stock pollute,
> That thou art doting father of his fruit
> Nor shall he smile at thee in secret thought,
> Nor laugh with his companions at thy state." (1063–1066)

Lucrece's determination that Tarquin must not "smile ... in secret thought" at Collatine forces her to reveal Tarquin's crime and thereby to publicize the impurity that she assumes has followed it. Her belief that concealing Tarquin's crime would only compound her own guilt evokes the classical association of tyranny not only with rape, but with secrecy. As Hadfield has argued, Lucrece's publication of Tarquin's crime insists on the openness that was associated with republican government. Similarly, Markku Peltonen notes that decades later Thomas Scott's *Vox Populi* would take Tarquinius Superbus as his example of the tyrant who rules through a secret "chamber-Councell" rather than follow the principle that "publique persons should do publique actions in publique."[35] Lucrece's image of Tarquin boasting, smiling, and laughing at Collatine's expense registers the fear that the finite pleasure that Tarquin found in the rape itself will be infinitely extended by its concealment, which itself signifies a power over Collatine's experience of reality. In urging her hand to "Kill both thyself and her for yielding so," Lucrece refuses to be complicit with such an abuse of power (1036).

Lucrece's suicide manifests an agency that achieves its highest form in self-destruction—she can prove that she is "mistress" of her "fate" only by taking from others the capacity to shape her will through violence. Yet when Lucrece actually describes the rape to her male auditors, she curiously stresses the ambiguity of her violation. In the poem's earlier, presumably objective, account of the event, Tarquin literally silences Lucrece: using her nightgown, he "Entombs her outcry in her lips' sweet fold" and "pens her piteous clamours in her head" (679, 681). In Lucrece's own, more faithfully Livian description of the rape, however, it is unclear whether it is Tarquin's physical force or his threat of dishonor that keeps her from crying out or fighting back. For rather than focus on Tarquin's violence, she stresses the choice he gives her between chastity and reputation. In Lucrece's version of the events, Tarquin crept into her chamber

> "And softly cried, 'Awake, thou Roman dame,
> And entertain my love, else lasting shame
>   On thee and thine this night I will inflict,
>   If thou my love's desire do contradict.

35. Hadfield, "Tarquin's Everlasting Banishment," 84–85, 94; Peltonen, 238.

> "'For some hard-favour'd groom of thine,' quoth he,
> 'Unless thou yoke thy liking to my will,
> I'll murther straight, and then I'll slaughter thee,
> And swear I found you where you did fulfill
> The loathsome act of lust and so did kill
> The lechers in their deed. This act will be
> My fame, and thy perpetual infamy." (1628–1638)

Lucrece's account makes clear that Tarquin's threat is dangerous precisely because he has the power to shape not only her earthly life, but her eternal reputation as well. If she contradicts his desire—literally, if she speaks against it—she will sacrifice forever the ability to speak the truth. Tarquin's power over what people think gives him power over what Lucrece can do.

In this light, to succumb to Tarquin is necessary in order to defeat him. If Tarquin kills Lucrece he controls public discourse about her, and the Romans will be helpless to recognize or resist the full extent of his tyranny. This depiction not of struggle but of its impossibility complicates Lucrece's perception of her violation, making her both innocent and guilty:

> "Mine enemy was strong, my poor self weak
> (And far the weaker with so strong a fear)
> My bloody judge forbod my tongue to speak;
> No rightful plea might plead for justice there." (1646–1649)

Lucrece's lack of physical strength here signifies her political vulnerability. In forbidding Lucrece to speak through threats to her honor rather than to her body, Tarquin demands that Lucrece discipline herself. Shakespeare transforms the external battle between Tarquin and Lucrece to an internal one between Lucrece's chastity and her reputation, a change that accentuates the psychological struggle faced by subjects under tyranny. When "no rightful plea might plead for justice," subjects not only cannot resist a tyrant. They also cannot represent themselves as resisting, and therefore have no way of revealing the coercive rule under which they exist. Individual resistance is worse than futile. It is invisible.

Lucrece's need to represent herself as resisting, to make her opposition visible, makes her suicide a rejection of Tarquin's offer to "rest [her] secret friend." In death, she recaptures the possibility of resistance that Tarquin's threat of eternal shame denied her. Asserting that it is Tarquin "That guides this hand to give this wound to me," Lucrece represents herself as resisting the rape—of choosing death over violation—and thereby recuperates the agency that Tarquin's threat denied her (1722). Significantly, Lucrece adopts the same discourse of martyrdom described by Sidney to emphasize that her suffering should inspire further resistance. Her demand that the men "Be suddenly revenged on my foe— / Thine, mine, his own" draws the same identification between herself and the Roman body politic that has shaped the poem's representation of agency (1684–1685). Insisting that "sparing justice feeds iniquity," Lucrece demands that her auditors adhere to a militant definition of justice in which there is no middle ground for compromise. Her plea to her kinsmen that they "Suppose thou dost defend me / From what is past" requires an imaginative equation of rape and suicide, past and present. A prior act of violence can only be represented in its repetition. And if Lucrece "is" Rome, indeed, "is" all of the men around her, then by defending her they also defend their own future. Unlike Lucrece, they have a chance to destroy Tarquin before he destroys them.[36]

Lucrece's self-sacrifice makes the Tarquins' tyranny undeniable, and Collatine and Brutus offer alternate models of responding to this revelation. Whereas Collatine wails at the injustice, Brutus insists that this passive mourning only gives into the tyranny that has occasioned it. Throwing off the "shallow habit" of stupidity "Wherein deep policy did him disguise," Brutus insists on the folly of Lucrece's self-destruction and the political dangers of passive suffering (1814–1815). Instead, he encourages active resistance:

> "Why, Collatine, is woe the cure for woe?
> Do wounds help wounds, or grief help grievous deeds?
> Is it revenge to give thyself a blow
> For his foul act by whom thy fair wife bleeds?
> Such childish humour from weak minds proceeds;
>   Thy wretched wife mistook the matter so
>   To slay herself, that should have slain her foe." (1821–1827)

This is an extraordinary call to rebellion. Insisting that it is not only legitimate but obligatory to slay one's foe, Brutus both denies the relevance of Lucrece's bodily weakness and makes anything but outright rebellion a sign of moral frailty. According to Brutus, grief constitutes an aggression against the self that would be better turned outward:

> "Courageous Roman, do not steep thy heart
> In such relenting dew of lamentations,
> But kneel with me, and help to bear thy part
> To rouse our Roman gods with invocations
> That they will suffer these abominations
>   (Since Rome herself in them doth stand disgraced)
>   By our strong arms from forth her fair streets chased." (1828–1834)

---

36. Several critics have noted that the ending of Lucrece's story may create a more just order, but that that order nonetheless requires the continued subordination of women. See Jane Newman, 317; Quay, 9; and Arnold, 115.

Brutus' speech expresses the same sentiment as Essex's oft-quoted words to Thomas Egerton defending aristocratic rebellion: "Cannot Princes erre? Can they not wrong their Subjects? Is any earthly power or authority infinite? Pardon me, pardon me, my good Lord, I can never subscribe to these principles."[37] Moreover, Brutus asserts the divine sanction of this revolt by insisting that it will not succeed without the gods' permission. He reverses the traditional idea that people must "suffer" what the gods send them, so often invoked to defend royal prerogative and to profess the sinfulness of rebellion. But by inverting the syntax of the plea, Brutus also acknowledges that the reestablishment of justice may fail. The lines begin with the prayer that the gods will "suffer these abominations," a disturbing sentiment that is allowed to persist for a full line by Brutus' interruption equating Lucrece with Rome "herself." It is only in the final line of the stanza that he completes the prayer for what the gods will allow, which turns out to be a syntactically disjoined hope that they will permit "these abominations" to be "By our strong arms from forth her fair streets chased." The delayed verb here registers the difficulty of justice and the uncertainty of success. Under such conditions, resistance may appear less attractive, more risky, than Lucrece's "accessory yieldings," which at least offer to secure life and peace.[38]

Yet it is not the gods alone who must "suffer" the Tarquins to be chased out of the city. The aristocratic rebels also need the support of the cowed populace. In order to get this backing, "They did conclude to bear dead Lucrece thence, / To show her bleeding body thorough Rome, / And so to publish Tarquin's foul offence" (1850–1852). As we have seen, to "publish" a tyrant's offence is to oppose it, so this move from private secrecy to public revelation of Lucrece's bleeding body—a mirror for the Roman body politic—is itself a form of rebellion. In response to this spectacle, "The Romans plausibly did give consent / To Tarquin's everlasting banishment." As in the Argument with which the poem began, this "consent" appears to differentiate republican from imperial rule, but the Romans' action is made ambiguous by the adverb that modifies it. 'Plausibly' to consent is to give consent that either shows itself by applause or in such a way that seems itself to deserve such commendation.[39] While this final couplet seems to illustrate a moral and political conviction that has otherwise appeared only in Lucrece's Roman suicide, the ambiguity of this adverb registers the same uncertainty about the nature of political agency that occupies *Lucrece* as a whole. For it is unclear who really deserves credit—applause—for Tarquin's banishment, the noblemen or the people.

---

37. Camden, *Annales*, 494. For more detailed discussions of Essex's resistance to royal claims of absolute prerogative, see McCoy, *Rites*, 79–102; and Hammer, *Polarisation of Elizabethan Politics*.
38. In Lucan's *Pharsalia*, as McCoy notes, civil war is the only possible way of preventing tyranny, which inevitably accompanies peace (*Rites*, 114–116).
39. *OED*, 2d ed., s.v. "plausible."

And, more problematically, it is therefore unclear whether republicanism has restored the possibility of agency or only perpetuated the elusiveness of that concept.

However equivocal its conclusion, *Lucrece* follows a familiar revolutionary trajectory, one in which the refusal to suffer tyranny produces a more just political system. As does *Lucrece*, *Pericles* questions the wisdom of the silent endurance recommended by some strains of Neostoicism, warning that such patience may signify consent and therefore legitimate tyranny. But *Pericles* is hardly revolutionary. Like all of Shakespeare's romances, *Pericles* seeks to restore an idealized past and therefore is conservative in the strictest sense of the word. This conservatism, however, should not be equated with support for absolute monarchal power, as opposed to the republican narrative of *Lucrece*. As Shakespeare and his contemporaries knew, a turn to the past could signify a critique of the present or an appeal to the feudal values of aristocratic resistance. In the 1590s, as Margot Heinemann has shown, history plays had been a crucial vehicle for presenting the chronicles of Holinshed, Stowe, and Foxe, and for publicly pondering the history of the English government. After the rebellion and execution of Essex in 1601, however, no English history at all could be published or performed without special authorization from the Privy Council.[40] The Shakespearean romances that came to the stage in the decades that followed can be seen as picking up where the histories left off, as they share a similar interest in the origins and extent of royal authority.[41] As Simon Palfrey has argued, in the early seventeenth century chivalry was associated with the superior Elizabethan past increasingly symbolized by Philip Sidney and deliberately evoked in the neo-feudal Protestantism of Prince Henry and Princess Elizabeth. Consequently, romance became a useful forum for voicing political critique and pan-European grievances.[42]

As does *Lucrece*, *Pericles* considers these issues through meditations on endangered female virtue. In particular, the play figures the difference between subjects

---

40. Heinemann, 175–176, 182, 189.

41. Unlike most other plays of the period, *Pericles* existed simultaneously as drama and prose: in addition to Gower's *Confessio* and Lawrence Twine's *The Patterne of Painefull Adventures* (entered in the Stationer's Register in 1574 and published in 1594 and 1607), George Wilkins published his own prose version in 1608, the same year that *Pericles* was first performed. See Gossett, "Introduction," 1–54, for the textual and editorial history of *Pericles*. For a more general discussion of the relationship between Shakespeare's printed poetry and his drama, see Cheney, "Poetry and Theater," 222–254.

42. Palfrey, *Late Shakespeare*, 37, 46. Cohen emphasizes the "irreducibly political character of gender relations" in what he calls "prerevolutionary" drama ("Prerevolutionary Drama," 123, 132). Heinemann argues that the nobility's desire to retain economic and political power often translated into an ideological commitment to the individual liberties and heroics offered by radical Protestantism and the ancient constitution (172). On Shakespeare's commitment to these values in the romances, see Strier, 199–201. Strong traces Prince Henry's revival of the aggressive Protestant policy associated with Sidney and Elizabethan England (*Henry, Prince of Wales*, 141–158).

who enable tyranny and those who seek to reform it by contrasting the corruption of Antiochus' daughter with the innocence of Marina. Antiochus' daughter, *Pericles* makes clear, is a willing partner in her father's incestuous desires, however much she may have been coerced initially. By comparison, Marina miraculously escapes the murder that her foster parents, Cleon and Dionyza, have arranged, then manages to preserve her virginity despite being captured by pirates and sold to a brothel. The distinction between good and bad women, however, is not completely stable. *Pericles* presents Marina as helpless to resist her potential rapists physically, and she maintains her honor not through her own power but because of the men's mercy. Like Lucrece's suspected pregnancy, Marina's potential to be infected by one of the brothel's syphilitic customers suggests that she may be made part of an economy of prostitution regardless of her own intentions. And even though her captors eventually allow Marina to earn her keep through the honest means of teaching, the fruits of her labor nonetheless go toward sustaining a house of sin. The possibility that even virtuous subjects are implicated in the corruption that surrounds them reappears at the play's end when Pericles betroths Marina to Lysimachus, the governor of Myteline and one of the brothel customers that she earlier resisted. This collapse of prostitution, honest employment, and marriage troubles any neat distinction between the cynical corruption of Antiochus' daughter and the earnest integrity of Marina—or between the analogous political positions of sycophantic courtier and honest councilor.

Pericles makes few topical or local references, so historicist scholars have generally agreed with Steven Mullaney's influential assessment of this play as a "tale of universal significance uncontaminated by historical or cultural contexts."[43] More recently, however, critics have understood *Pericles* as contemplating many of the same political questions that occupy Shakespeare's other late plays.[44] The presence of Gower as choral narrator would seem to take *Pericles* from the political Jacobean present to the romantic medieval past, making it just the sort of inconsequential, "mouldy" tale that Ben Jonson famously mocked.[45] But Gower's prominence, in fact, proclaims the affinity of *Pericles* with Shakespeare's history plays and accordingly with the feudal past and noble rights that those plays investigate.[46] As a figure

---

43. Mullaney, *Place of the Stage*, 148. See also Cohen, Introduction to *Pericles*, 2713.
44. See, for instance, Palfrey, 57–78; Zurcher, "Stoicism," 917–924; and Jordan, *Shakespeare's Monarchies*, 35–67.
45. As Hillman shows, Gower is the most sustained literary allusion in the Shakespeare canon ("Larger Debt of Pericles," 427–428). Along with Gower's *Confessio Amantis*, scholars have noted the influence of North's and Thucydides' accounts of Pericles, Wilkins's own translation of *The History of Justine* (1606), and Sidney's *Arcadia*. See Tompkins, "Why Pericles?", 315–324; and Gossett, "Introduction," 72–73.
46. For Watt, Gower's own version of these tales of female violation and sacrifice are about deposition, not republicanism (*Amoral Gower*, 125–126). Bergeron argues that Gower's presence alerts us to double significance of *Pericles* as both ancient story and current reality (*Shakespeare's Romances*, 118).

for the medieval past, Gower locates *Pericles* within ongoing debates about the relation of royal prerogative to ancient liberties and common law. For Shakespeare, Gower was himself a figure for the "Englishness" that seemed to many observers to be under assault by the swarms of Scots taking over the court and by James' desire to unite England and Scotland.[47] Perhaps more significantly, the manuscript and print history of Gower's *Confessio Amantis* was shaped by the deposition of Richard II—an act of noble rebellion that would be cited as a precedent for resisting tyranny in 1642.[48] Given these associations with English custom and law, it is no surprise that in the plays' opening lines Gower stresses the antiquity of his story. Having informed us that he has risen from "ashes ancient" in order "To sing a song that old was sung," Gower connects this story to both the popular customs of merry old England and to the moral education of the nobility: this tale has been both "sung at festivals, / On ember eves and holy ales" and "read for restoratives" by "lords and ladies" (1.0.1–2, 4–7). Gower then concludes his prologue by pronouncing that "*Et bonum quo antiquius eo melius*" (1.0.10).[49] The principle that "the older a good is, the better" evokes contemporary arguments that saw the antiquity of the common law and ancient constitution as evidence for their superiority over monarchal will. Indeed, this principle would be embraced by the parliamentary polemicist William Prynne decades later in the maxim that "THE OLD IS BETTER."[50]

In equating antiquity with authority, Shakespeare evokes the constitutional conservatism to which opponents of absolutism would increasingly appeal. From the accession of James I through the last year of the English civil wars, aristocratic and parliamentary opponents of Stuart policy formulated their grievances not as appeals for change, but as defenses against royal assaults on the ancient constitution. In the first parliament of James I's reign, for instance, the Commons depicted their particular grievances over matters like wardship and purveyance as cause for a more general uneasiness with the perceived growth of royal power. "What cause we

47. As Gossett notes, in *Henry V* Gower the Englishman joins Fluellen the Welshman, Jamy the Scotsman, and Macmorris the Irishman in defending the British Isles against the French ("Introduction," 121). In *Eastward Ho!* (1605) Jonson, George Chapman, and Marston satirize the influx of Scots to the Jacobean court.
48. McCoy, *Rites*, esp. 1–4. As Watt shows, the political context of Gower's writing is inscribed in the two principle forms of the *Confessio*, both of which continued to be copied until the late fifteenth century: the "Ricardian" text, which praises Richard II, and the "Lancastrian" text, which celebrates Henry IV. Gower's romance allowed for competing political interpretations throughout the fifteenth century as the Wars of the Roses kept alive questions about the source and extent of sovereign power (11–12).
49. Scholars have long debated the extent of collaboration between Shakespeare and George Wilson on *Pericles*. While I do not wish to erase Wilkins's contribution, I follow all seventeenth-century quartos in referring to Shakespeare as primary author of *Pericles*. For a recent discussion of the authorship of *Pericles*, see Newcomb, "Sources of Romance," 21–46.
50. From *Independency Examined*, 2. The capitals are Prynne's own.

your poor Commons have to watch over our privileges is manifest in itself to all men," the 1604 Commons Apology stated, for "The prerogatives of princes may easily and do daily grow; the privileges of the subject are for the most part at an everlasting stand. They may be by good providence and care preserved, but being once lost are not recovered but with much disquiet."[51] The more that James I and Charles I asserted royal prerogative, the more MPs, lawyers, and powerful nobles accused them of betraying English law and custom. The argument that monarchal absolutism was innovative was of a piece with the historical work undertaken by the Society of Antiquaries, whose study of the English past were commonly seen as buttressing the parliament's claim that the privileges they sought to "preserve" were hardly new but "at an everlasting stand." This appeal to history allowed opponents of absolutism to frame their behavior as defensive and thus to participate in the same rhetoric of victimization that Sidney had translated into secular and popular discourse. And the challenge that history posed to monarchal power was not lost on the Stuarts. As Henry Spelman wrote, James "took a little mislike" to the Society's meetings and ended them in 1614; Charles I would close down Cotton's library altogether in 1629.[52]

At the time that *Pericles* was being composed and performed, debates over James I's attempt to unite England with Scotland made the English past a political battleground. Because royal attempts to assert the affinity of the two kingdoms stood on the claim that both derived from the Norman conquest, many feared that union would signify that England was a conquered nation whose laws and parliaments would have no force to curb royal will. Supporters of the union—including James I, who traced his descent from William the Conqueror—did not deny this absolutist interpretation. They argued that 1066 represented a sharp break with the Saxon past and its laws, which became subject to royal will.[53] According to James, this history meant that the king made the laws and therefore was above them. For that reason, while "a good king will frame all his actions to be according to the Law . . . hee is not bound thereto but of his own good will."[54]

This contest between will and law appears in *Pericles* in the gendered and sexual terms that would have been familiar to Jacobean audiences. In departing from his

51. In Kenyon, ed., *Stuart Constitution*, 32. For the ideological significance of the Apology, see Colclough, *Freedom of Speech*, 143–149.

52. Quoted in Greenberg, *Radical Face*, 102. See also Sharpe, *Sir Robert Cotton*; and Parry, *Trophies of Time*.

53. Greenberg outlines the constitutional implications of James' proposed union (116–133). See also Peltonen, 190–194, 219. Rhodes aligns Shakespeare's drama with unionist views ("Shakespeare and King James," 50). Margaret Healy reads the ending of *Pericles* as a critique of James' proposals for union and his attempts to ally England with Spain ("Pericles and the Pox," 94–95).

54. *The Trew Law of Free Monarchies*, in *Political Writings*, 75.

sources' depictions of the incestuous relationship between Antiochus and his daughter, Shakespeare imagines consent apart from agency. In all previous versions of the story Antiochus' daughter is unequivocally raped, a helpless victim of the unruly libido that signifies her father's tyranny. This political analogy occupies Gower throughout Book 7 of the *Confessio*, which adapts Livy's tales of Lucretia and Virginia. Similarly, in Twine's version Antiochus "violently forced" his daughter into sexual relations with him. Wilkins's prose romance is more ambiguous, but still emphasizes Antiochus' brutality and its connection to his political tyranny. Like that of Tarquin, Antiochus' "love" is a sinister, devouring force. According to Wilkins, when Antiochus first attempts his daughter's honor, "much perswasion, though to little reason, he used, as, that he was her father, whome shee was bound to obey, he was a King that had power to commaund, he was in love, and his love was resistlesse, and if resistlesse, therefore pittilesse, either to youth, blood, or beauty: In briefe, he was a tyrant and would execute his will." The daughter struggles to withstand her father and is devastated when she fails: "so fast came the wet from the sentinells of her ransackt cittie, that it is improper to say they dropped and rayned downe teares, but rather, that with great flouds they powred out water." Yet once the initial rape occurs, there is a strange ellipses during which rape becomes seduction: "So with these and such like perswasions prevailing with his daughter, they long continued in these foule and unjust imbracements, till at last, the custome of sinne made it accompted no sinne."[55] As in *The Faerie Queene*, compliance retroactively turns force into to persuasion.

Shakespeare's version of the story transforms Antiochus' daughter from the reluctant participant of the prose sources to an active partner. Even the initial moment of force is absent in Shakespeare's Gower's description of Antiochus' "female heir,"

> With whom the father liking took
> And her to incest did provoke.
> Bad child, worse father, to entice his own
> To evil should be done by none. (1.0.22, 25–28)

Here, the daughter has not been raped, which would imply a lack of choice. She has been "provoke[d]" to incest, "entice[d]" to evil. But these verbs register the ambiguous nature of the daughter's agency. As its Latin etymon, *provocare*, indicates, to "provoke" is to call forth. In its most familiar sense, this is a calling away from objective, dispassionate thought in favor of arousal, stimulation, or vexation. If we understand the daughter's provocation in this sense, she appears to have been led—or called—away from her better self by the emotions stirred by Antiochus' advances.

55. *The Painfull Adventures of Pericles Prince of Tyre*, 10–11, 13.

But in the early modern period "provoke" also had the sense of appeal, supplication, and invitation, the rousing of action rather than emotion. In this sense, the daughter's participation in incest may have been genuinely consensual, a product of cool calculation rather than confused passion. "Entice" similarly collapses activity and passivity, emotion and reason. To "entice" has been traced to the Latin *intitiare*, "to set on fire." This root suggests the same irrationality and loss of control that appears in the first sense of provoke. However, "entice" could also mean to attract by promising pleasure or advantage, a definition that, like the second sense of "provoke," allows for more dispassionate reckoning.[56] The focus is not on Antiochus' evil lust, but on his daughter's responsibility for satisfying it. And we cannot know the source of her consent: helpless passion or rational interest.

Feminist work on the relationship between Antiochus and his daughter has understood it in terms of the play's larger attempt to resolve male anxieties about female sexuality and power.[57] In light of contemporary analogies between political, familial, and conjugal relationships, the anxieties that feminist analysis has uncovered also have important implications for debates over the proper behavior of the virtuous subject. Constance Jordan has observed that the Jacobean conflation of the roles of wife and child, tending to infantilize the wife and alienate the child, jeopardizes their respective rights. In analogical terms, incest signifies an unnatural political power that abuses those it should protect.[58] I would add that by suggesting that Antiochus' incestuous union originated in seduction rather than rape, Shakespeare underscores the place of the subject in sustaining relations of power. By equating acquiescence and consent, *Pericles* emphasizes the danger that abuse will become custom once it is accepted. The play thereby incorporates the doctrine of prescription so important to antiquarian arguments for the ancient constitution and the common law. According to this doctrine, acquiescence, not permission, legitimates a given state of things. As long as one resists an encroachment on one's property, one retains the right to it. Medieval and early modern thinkers extended this doctrine to constitutional thought, arguing that because the English nobility had consistently rejected Norman attempts to do away with the Saxon laws, those laws had endured until the present.[59] *Pericles* shifts focus away from Antiochus and onto those who permit his tyranny by making the daughter a willing partner in her father's lust.

56. *OED*, 2d ed., s.v. "provoke" and "entice."

57. See, for instance, Adelman, *Suffocating Mothers*, 193–238; Barber and Wheeler, *Whole Journey*, 310–328; and Coppélia Kahn, *Man's Estate*, 193–225.

58. Jordan, *Shakespeare's Monarchies*, 39–42. This awareness of the incestuous implications of political language was not limited to Shakespeare. As Loughlin notes, Thomas Campion's dedication to *Lord Hay's Masque* shows how James' fashioning of the state in both sexual and familial terms inevitably results in a series of potentially disruptive and incongruous erotic relations (*Hymeneutics*, 50–51).

59. Greenberg, 19–26, 66–78.

Like *Lucrece*, *Pericles* places female sexual endangerment within a structure of male complicity and corruption. By interweaving political and sexual narratives, *Pericles* accentuates Marina's superiority not only to Antiochus' daughter but also to a series of male politicians—including her father—who selfishly refuse to challenge, and therefore to cure, the tyranny that confronts them. At the play's opening, for instance, Pericles' decides to conceal Antiochus' incest in order to protect his own life. "Who has a book of all that monarchs do," he opines, "He's more secure to keep it shut than shown. . . . Kings are earth's gods; in vice their law's their will; / And, if Jove stray, who dares say Jove doth ill?" (95–96, 104–105). Pericles' willingness to treat incest as part of the *arcana imperii* helps to perpetuate Antiochus' tyranny, for such concealment prevents his subjects from accurately assessing their political situation.[60] Ironically, the collusive secrecy that Pericles sees as his only protection is in fact the source of his endangerment, for Antiochus orders him killed so that he cannot "trumpet forth my infamy" (1.1.146). Pericles' would-be murderer, Thaliard, should be the opposite of our hero. But corrupt courtier and innocent prince merge in their willingness to conceal—and thereby support— Antiochus' tyranny. Upon arriving in Tyre to complete his murderous mission, Thaliard describes his relationship to Antiochus in terms that recall Pericles' own desire to keep the book of royal secrets firmly shut: "Well, I perceive he was a wise fellow and had good discretion that, being bid to ask what he would of the king, desired he might know none of his secrets. Now do I see he had some reason for't: for, if a king bid a man be a villain, he's bound by the indenture of his oath to be one" (1.3.3–8). In accepting such helplessness, both Pericles and Thaliard sustain the very authority that they experience as irresistible.[61]

The most prominent and sustained critique of absolutist demands for unquestioning obedience appears in the ordeals of Marina, which in seventeenth-century publications of *Pericles* were included on the title page along with those of her father.[62] Several critics have noted the connections between Marina's stories and classical and medieval accounts of the saint in the brothel, and this affinity sets her in a hagiographic context that, as we have seen, was highly politicized in the seventeenth century.[63] Unlike the mythical virgins she evokes, however, Marina does not have a simple choice between life and chastity, for the play makes clear that she may

---

60. Critics who have lamented Pericles' conspiratory silence include Jordan (*Shakespeare's Monarchies*, 48) and Palfrey (59–60).

61. In the story of Demetrius to which Thaliard refers, the king's name is Lysimachus, an allusion that connects Marina's future husband to Antiochus.

62. Until 1630, the full title of the published play text was *The late and much admired play, called Pericles Prince of Tyre: with the true relation of the whole history, adventures, and fortunes of the said prince: as also, the no lesse strange, and worthy accidents, in the birth and life, of his daughter Marina.*

63. See, for instance, Bamford, 33; Helms; and Gossett, "Introduction," 71–72, 113.

be forcibly violated. And the resulting physical contamination would make her indistinguishable from the other prostitutes. The initial exchange between the Bawd, the Pander, and Boult emphasizes that the inhabitants of the brothel are literally wasting away: the "poor three" prostitutes that remain alive are "as good as rotten" with "continual action," "so pitifully sodden" that "a strong wind will blow [them] to pieces" (4.2.6–8). Disease pervades Myteline, circulating from prostitute to client and back. Even as the Pander laments that "the poor Transylvanian is dead that lay with the little baggage," the Bawd suggests a foreign source of this infection. Monsieur Veroles—whose very name means "pox" (*vérole*) in French—has, according to the Bawd, "brought his disease hither; here he does but repair it" (4.2.20–21, 102–103). As opposed to the "restorative" nature of virtue and counsel, the self-indulgence that fuels the brothel's economy has so entrenched disease that it is impossible to isolate its origin. All are equally contaminated and contaminating.

The depiction of Monsieur Veroles as the origin of the disease that the prostitutes help circulate accentuates the political and religious significance that the pox would have had for a seventeenth-century audience. As Margaret Healy points out, there are no references to syphilis in the versions of the story by Gower, Twine, or Wilkins, and so the dramatic version's obsessive detailing of this disease's pervasiveness and danger invites an unidealized reading of the politics that occupy *Pericles* as a whole.[64] Healy shows that even as Erasmus dispersed images of syphilitic priests throughout his work to foreground what he saw as the corruption and decay of the Catholic Church, Lutheran reformers like Foxe, John Bale, and William Turner appropriated the image of the diseased body for the Protestant cause. In these sixteenth-century polemics, Rome was both rapist and harlot, threatening to overpower the virgin state of England. Shortly before the first performance of *Pericles*, Dekker's *The Whore of Babylon* adapted these Reformation images in order to expose the "blody stratagems, of that Purple whore of Roome" in the reign of Elizabeth I. As Healy suggests, while the play has topical resonance with the courtships of Philip II of Spain and François, Duc d'Anjou, for the hand of England's Virgin Queen, its real thrust "was undoubtedly to persuade Jacobean spectators that the forces of Antichrist continued to pose a threat to the English Protestant church and to encourage a more militant stance against Rome."[65] In similarly depicting syphilis as a foreign disease that permeates the body politic of Myteline, *Pericles* warns against the corrosive potential of James I's plan to secure peace with a Catholic nation like Spain through marital alliance. It thus resonates with a long-standing association of parliamentary debate with English national strength, Catholic-style absolutism with servile weakness.

64. Margaret Healy, 95.
65. Margaret Healy, 101–103.

In Myteline, the economy of the brothel literalizes the exchange of poison for profit that Antiochus made in ordering Thaliard to kill Pericles: "Thaliard, behold, here's poison and here's gold: / We hate the Prince of Tyre, and thou must kill him" (1.1.155–156).[66] Antiochus' accidental equation of poison and gold, destruction and advancement, anticipates the brothel's endless circulation of money and disease. A pun on courtier and courtesan was widely available in the early modern period: *cortegiana* was the feminine form of the *cortigiano* that Castiglione taught ambitious men to emulate. As this pun suggests, the court may be little different from the brothel in its meretricious flattery and ruthless pursuit of advancement. Although Marina refuses to emulate Thaliard in becoming a "creature of sale," the success of her resistance depends not on her own strength, but on Lysimachus' willingness to be persuaded (4.5.83). When he initially arrives on stage, Lysimachus' appearance and behavior show that he is as corrupt and ungoverned as the body politic he leads. The Bawd greets his entrance with "Here comes the Lord Lysimachus disguised," at once emphasizing and mocking the governor's attempt to camouflage his true nature—an effort that aligns him with Cleon's, Dionyza's, and Antiochus' abuses of their subjects' trust and thereby casts doubt on his virtue as a ruler (4.5.24). In response to Marina's repeated refusals to satisfy his lust, Lysimachus first offers bribes, then threats. In his promise that "my / authority shall not see thee, or else look friendly upon / thee," Lysimachus recalls Tarquin's own offers of secret complicity, as well as the secrecy of Antiochus (4.5.93–95).[67] Like Lucrece, Marina responds by warning against such misuse of power by stressing the larger political implications of Lysimachus' willingness to put himself above the law. "If you were born to honour," Marina pleads, "show it now; / If put upon you, make the judgement good / That thought you worthy of it" (4.5.96–98). Lysimachus' assault on Marina signifies his larger failure to govern—rather than stopping the corruption of prostitution, he has encouraged it. Moreover, while Marina is eventually able to persuade him to reform, Lysimachus does not go so far as to shut down the brothel in which she is entrapped. And although Marina is able to escape "the way of womankind" by becoming a teacher, the money she earns still sustains the brothel: "her gain / She gives the cursed bawd" (5.0.10–11).

Numerous critics have been unhappy with the conclusion of *Pericles*, where Pericles promises his daughter's hand to Lysimachus in marriage and therefore

---

66. Harris demonstrates the prominence of infectious disease as a metaphor for foreign trade (*Sick Economies*, 29–51).

67. In Wilkins's prose version, Lysimachus' turn to physical coercion recalls that of Antiochus. When Marina refuses his initial advances, he "beganne to be more rough with her, urging her that he was the Governour, whose authoritie could wincke at those blemishes, her selfe, and that sinnefull house could cast uppon her, or his displeasure punish at his owne pleasure" (88–89).

forces Marina to marry a potential rapist—and a syphilitic one to boot.[68] Here, the ambiguous relation of wife to prostitute points to the analogously obscure relation of loyal subject to corrupt sycophant.[69] Within eleven lines, the play moves from Pericles' promise to Lysimachus that "you shall prevail, were it to woo my daughter" to Gower's announcement that Lysimachus "is promised to be wived / To fair Marina" (5.1.247, 5.2.10–11). Marina is conspicuously mute in these transactions, and she speaks only one more line for the rest of the play: "My heart / Leaps to be gone into my mother's bosom" (5.3.44–45). Marina's uncharacteristic silence about her feelings for Lysimachus may well signify her quiet endurance of a situation that she cannot resist without disobeying legitimate paternal authority. Marriage, in this reading, is another form of prostitution, hidden under the language of companionship, consent, and love. Marina's position thus resonates with Julia Rudolph's description of women in the seventeenth century more generally: she is "both free and unfree: she is envisioned consenting to marriage, but her choice is constrained and her subordination necessary."[70] This constrained freedom uncannily describes the position of the political subject as well.

The Epilogue of *Pericles* confirms the ambivalent status of obedience. Like *Lucrece*, *Pericles* ends with armed revolt. Yet unlike the revolution of *Lucrece*, which involves both nobility and people in changing the system by which Rome is governed, that of *Pericles* is a purely popular act that destroys Marina's would-be murderers, Cleon and Dionyza, without addressing the absolutist system that enabled their abuse. As Gower informs us:

> For wicked Cleon and his wife, when fame
> Had spread his cursed deed to th'honoured name
> Of Pericles, to rage the city turn,
> That him and his they in his palace burn.
> The gods for murder seemed so content
> To punish, although not done, but meant.

68. The Victorian editor F. G. Fleay, for instance, blames this incongruous union on Wilkins's corruption of the text, insisting that Shakespeare "would not have married Marina to a man whose acquaintance she had made in a public brothel" (quoted in Skeele, *Thwarting the Wayward Seas*, 27). Margaret Healy links Marina's marriage to the Renaissance emblem "Nupta contagioso," which depicted a king binding his daughter to a syphilitic son-in-law, and to the Erasmian colloquy "The Unequal Match," in which two participants discuss the marriage between a beautiful virgin and a syphilitic nobleman (98–101).

69. A more optimistic reading would be that the marriage may effect a physical, as well as moral, cure of Lysimachus. Syphilis was first identified as an incurable disease in 1876, and because its symptoms were often invisible for years, many believed that it could be cured through intercourse with a healthy virgin. See Hayden, *Pox*, 28–47; Arrizabalaga, Henderson, and French, *Great Pox*; and Margaret Healy, 123–151.

70. Rudolph, 170.

So on your patience evermore attending,
New joy wait on you. Here our play has ending. (Epilogue, 11–18)

Dionyza and Cleon have demonstrated their tyranny as much in their willingness to trick their people as in their attempted murder of Marina. Like Tarquin's plea for Lucrece's secrecy, their deceit signifies a coercion of the will in that it acquires consent under false pretences. Gower quickly draws allegorical meaning from this rebellion, treating the citizens as the instruments of the same gods who ostensibly destroyed Antiochus and his daughter. However, the abrupt and formulaic couplet that concludes the epilogue feels rushed, and the feminine line ending undermines any sense of closure. The possibility lingers that, far from bringing a happy romance conclusion, the aftermath of rebellion may be as bad as the tyranny it was meant to check.

As at the close of *Lucrece*, we are left with a rather bleak picture of the political and sexual subject's options: helpless acquiescence or dangerous resistance. Both of these choices are tainted by the accusation of self-interest that *Pericles* so consistently equates with prostitution. Amelia Zurcher Sandy has tied this anxiety to Neostoicism, arguing that *Pericles* makes death the only means of escaping suspicion of self-service.[71] As we next shall see, this condemnation of selfishness persists in Wroth's *Urania*, but Wroth stresses the danger of equating self-sacrifice with virtue. As Wroth shows, the desire to eschew all possible charges of self-interest, which offered such a strong rhetorical defense of resistance for Sidney, may lead women to pursue lovers who hurt them—and, analogously, may encourage subjects not just to accept but even to adore abusive tyrants.

71. "Stoicism," 920–922.

CHAPTER 5

✧

"Love, Thou Dost Master Me"

Political Masochism in Mary Wroth's Urania

Mary Wroth's *The Countess of Montgomery's Urania* reconsiders the political hagiography recommended by her uncle Philip Sidney in light of later Jacobean and early Caroline debates over the proper balance between royal and parliamentary prerogative. Wroth's skepticism about the possibility of resistance runs even deeper than that of Spenser or Shakespeare. In the *Urania*, characters endure abuse not out of moral weakness or physical helplessness, but because suffering provides moral and erotic gratification. Throughout both the 1621 *Urania* and its manuscript continuation, Wroth considers the possibility that political subjects will so enjoy the moral and erotic authority associated with victimization that they will remain loyal to their sovereign not in spite of his abuse, but because of it. In Wroth's hands political martyrdom—submission to the punishments of an unjust ruler—fails to function as effective protest. Instead, it becomes a form of political masochism in which subjects come to enjoy pain and to love the person inflicting it.

Wroth's frequent use of Sidneian political language directs us to read the *Urania* as a part of Stuart political debates, but until recently this direction has been largely overlooked. As the first English woman to publish an original prose romance and sonnet sequence, and the first English woman to have written a pastoral tragicomedy, Wroth has understandably attracted decades of feminist scholarship focusing primarily on the gender dynamics of her work. It has been customary to read the *Urania* as a semiautobiographical meditation on women's writing, gender inequality, and romantic disappointment. Such interpretations of the *Urania* have offered crucial insight into the means by which seventeenth-century English women registered and negotiated the patriarchal structures that surrounded them, even as they have helped to make the gendered dimension of literary production as such unavoidable.[1] However, attention to what is often treated as Wroth's nascent feminism has also had the less salutary effect of circumscribing her work to an almost exclusive focus on the status of women. By interpreting the well-documented topical references of the *Urania* according to a logic that limits female autobiography to romantic or gendered concerns, early feminist scholarship tended to magnify Wroth's female marginalization in order to show how she resisted it. As a result, such work has often, ironically, denied Wroth a voice in the larger political debates of early seventeenth-century England.

But feminism's nuanced understanding of the dynamics of power and desire can also offer vital insight into Wroth's analysis of Stuart political tensions. This potential is manifested in several recent studies of the *Urania* that have understood it as a meditation on the nature of governance.[2] What has not yet been remarked, however, is how the extremity of submission in this romance becomes a satire on that very demand. In this chapter, I argue that by stressing the masochist elements of female desire, Wroth insists on the irrationality of the political bonds for which love was one of the period's most common analogues. For in the *Urania*, she shows that the erotic impulse that notionally binds woman to man, subject to sovereign, is filled with perversity and ambivalence that transform the meaning of the submission that love should produce.

As a member of a circle of courtiers who both depended on royal favor and challenged royal policy, Wroth's fascination with the predicament of erotic thralldom allows her to evaluate the widening fissure in seventeenth-century England between royal claims to discretionary authority and a communitarian view of sovereignty emphasizing counsel and consent. What records we have depict Wroth, the most widely read member of the Sidney–Herbert circle in Jacobean England, as alert to a range of foreign and domestic events, and her work registers a transitional moment in English literary and political history between the forward Protestantism on which her uncle Philip Sidney staked his political career and the radical republicanism for which her nephew Algernon Sidney lost his life.[3] During this time, as we have seen, defenders of Stuart absolutism appealed to gendered hierarchies as a

---

1. See, for instance, Waller, "Gender Construction"; Swift, "Female Identity"; Naomi Miller, *Changing the Subject*; Fienberg, "Mary Wroth's Poetics of the Self"; and Clare Kinney, "Female Authorship."

2. Masten's influential essay claims that Wroth's work stages a withdrawal from the public sphere ("Circulation, Gender, and Subjectivity"). However, a number of critics have urged us to consider Wroth's participation in contemporary intellectual and political debates. See, for instance, Josephine Roberts, "Introduction," xlix; Beilin, "Role of the Political Subject"; Brennan, *Sidneys*, 134–135; Hackett, *Women and Romance Fiction*; Cavanagh, *Cherished Torment*; Clarke, *Politics of Early Modern Women's Writing*; Andrea, "Gendered Authorship"; and Rosalind Smith, *Sonnets and the English Woman Writer*, 88–118.

3. As Hannay notes, Wroth showed interest in the affairs in Flushing, where her father was governor, and she was a source of international news for other female courtiers. Anne Clifford's diary records that at Queen Anne's funeral in 1619 she talked with Wroth, "who

means of naturalizing the domination of ruler over implicitly feminized subjects. Doubly subordinate as both woman and subject, Wroth was well aware of the limitations of the aristocratic resistance that had been practiced by the men to whom she was tied by blood and kinship—most notably, Leicester, Sidney, and Essex.[4] In particular, the relentless scenes of feminine anguish, humiliation, and torture in the *Urania* warn that idealized equations of love and suffering may create subjects who not only endure but actually enjoy their own abuse.[5] Such an awareness of the masochistic potential of subjection makes politics as usual impossible. As the *Urania* demonstrates, both egoistic passions and narcissistic identifications can easily be turned around on the subject and transformed into their opposites. These sexual dynamics alter not only the meaning of gender identity but also conventional understandings of consent, submission, and authority.[6] As the idealism of Part One of the *Urania* gives way to the disappointment of Part Two, Wroth's characters relinquish romanticized notions of absolute devotion in favor of a more tempered vision of compromise. Yet this vision, like the romance itself, remains incomplete, suggesting that dreams of rule based on rational calculations of public good or self-interest may be similarly difficult to realize, mediated as they are by inchoate fantasies and desires.

As I argued in chapter 1, terms like "royalist" and "republican" are inappropriate to thinkers of Wroth's generation, most of whom supported monarchy as a system but also opposed Continental-style absolutism.[7] Rather than advocate any exclusively radical or reactionary program, the *Urania* turns to romance to ponder the limitations and contradictions of constitutionalist ideas of counsel and prerogative. In the early

---

brought news from beyond the sea" ("The Countess of Pembroke as Mentor to Mary Wroth," 25). See also Hay's suggestion that Wroth may have been a useful ally to Sir Michael Everarde in his 1612 quarrel with Sir John Throckmorton (*Life of Robert Sidney*, 133–134); and Josephine Roberts's observation that Wroth's correspondence with Dudley Carleton and intimacy with William Herbert gave her access to political reports ("Introduction," lxv).

4. In addition to her blood ties to Leicester and Sidney, Wroth was related to Essex through his marriage to Frances Walsingham Sidney after Philip Sidney's death.

5. Sandy has described self-abnegation as an antidote to self-interest in Wroth's work (*Seventeenth-Century Romance*, 26–59). I would modify this claim a bit to argue that read in political as well as moral terms, the *Urania* demonstrates the danger of self-sacrifice to both self and state.

6. I am thinking here of Freud's definition of "feminine masochism" as based on specifically male fantasies of "being pinioned, bound, beaten painfully, whipped, in some way mishandled, forced to obey unconditionally, defiled, degraded"; moreover, "in cases in which the masochistic phantasies have undergone specifically rich elaboration" the male subject "is placed in a situation characteristic of womanhood, *i.e.* they mean that he is being castrated, is playing the passive part in coitus, or is giving birth." These fantasies depend on an association of suffering as such with a particular fantasy of femininity. See "Economic Problem of Masochism," in *General Psychological Theory*, esp. 192–195, 198–201.

7. Donagan has shown that it was almost impossible to tell which sides would be taken in the 1640s from the positions of the 1620s and 1630s ("Casuistry and Allegiance," 89–111).

seventeenth century, as Derek Hirst has argued, potentially conflicting theories of monarchy as both absolute and limited coexisted, so that it was possible for the early modern mind "to conceive of both a sovereign king and a sovereign common law, or absolute royal prerogative and absolute rights to property."[8] As long-standing members of the court whose livelihood often depended on the princes whom they both served and opposed, the Sidney, Dudley, and Herbert families to whom Wroth was intimately connected were well aware of the ambivalent and conflicting allegiances and identities that such a dual definition of sovereignty generated.

In opposition to the privileges and powers claimed by outspoken aristocrats, James I was himself quite keen to promote royal absolutism. Accordingly, while he appropriated Elizabethan accounts of affection as the basis of public stability, James repudiated the ambiguous gendered hierarchies that Elizabeth had exploited. Instead, his conjugal language unequivocally effeminized his subjects as a means of defending monarchal prerogative. As we have seen, James habitually described himself as the husband of the English nation. But lest we imagine that this marriage implies anything like political parity, we might remember the advice on marriage that James famously offered Prince Henry in his 1598 *Basilicon Doron*: "It is your office to command, and hers to obey; but yet with such a sweet harmonie, as shee should be as ready to obey, as ye to command; as willing to follow, as ye to go before; your loue being wholly knit vnto her, and all her affections louingly bent to follow your will."[9] Like the good wife, the decisively feminized Jacobean subject evinces virtue by taking pleasure in obedience itself. The "sweet harmony" that James envisions presupposes a subject who is "ready" and "willing" to bend not just actions but "affections" to the will of the ruler. Yet even as it requires the subject to experience the king's desire as his or her own, James's formulation also promises that the sovereign will "knit" his love entirely to his subjects. James thereby situates the selfless love of the ruler as a safeguard against the possibility that, in contorting their own wills to that of the sovereign, subjects will fail to perceive—or even cooperate in—their own abuse. Like political theorists from Aristotle to Jean Bodin, James locates the difference between *rex* and *tyrannos* in the former's willingness to place his duty to his people over love of himself, the good of the commonwealth over the pursuit his own desires.[10] He thus differentiates himself from tyrants like Spenser's Geryoneo and Grantorto, or Shakespeare's Tarquin, by insisting that a real king seeks more than bodily compliance. He wants to love and be loved.

8. *Authority*, 42, 87.

9. *Political Writings*, 42.

10. In the *Ethics*, Aristotle argues that "the tyrant regards his own interest, but the king regards that of his subjects" (8.10). Bodin echoes this sentiment in arguing that "a king conformeth himselfe unto the lawes of nature, which the tyrant at his pleasure treadeth under foot ... the one of them refereth all of his actions to the good of the Commonweale, and safetie of his subjects; whereas the other respecteth nothing more than his owne particular profit, revenge, or pleasure" (212).

James's formulation of an affinity between the affections and duties of sovereign and subject, man and wife, was accentuated by the full title of his widely disseminated defense of absolutism, *The Trew Law of Free Monarchies: Or, the Reciprock and Mutuall Duetie Betwixt A Free King, and His Naturall Subjects.* In making the monarch "free" of any but self-imposed obligations to rule for the good of his people, James's theory dispenses with the necessity of counsel. Because the free king has no limitations on his will, subjects are incapable not only of resisting his desires but also of evaluating or questioning them at all, as the king's desires have become indistinguishable from their own. The ease with which kings may become tyrannical, lovers abusive, under such a model is expressed in the corrupt intrigues imagined no less in Shakespeare's *Lucrece* and *Pericles* than in Jonson's *Sejanus* or *Catiline*, all of which depict the potentially disastrous implications of the absolutist theories to which James clung.

As Janelle Greenberg has argued, ideological debates over the scope of royal authority were rooted in fiscal questions. In the early seventeenth century, questions as to the legality of specific royal policies—particularly attempts to raise money by extraparliamentary means—brought to the fore long-standing questions about the proper boundaries between the king's prerogative and the subject's consent as represented in parliament.[11] In an attempt to stave off both ballooning deficits and increasing tensions, James's Secretary of State, Robert Cecil, Earl of Salisbury, proposed the Great Contract in 1610. According to the terms of this settlement between king and parliament, James would relinquish his feudal rights to wardship and purveyance in return for a fixed income.[12] This solution failed, however, and (with the exception of the short-lived and unproductive "Addled Parliament" of 1614) James ruled without parliament from 1611 to 1621, and without a secretary after Salisbury's death in 1612.[13] During this time, there was a real

11. See Greenberg, *Radical Face*, 157; and Keir, *Constitutional History*, 71–75, 134–136, 177. Notestein claims that from its first session in 1604 parliament, and particularly the House of Commons, embraced a common law argument for balanced sovereignty (*Winning of the Initiative* and *The House of Commons*). Tyacke and Munden respond to Notestein by arguing that members of the Lower House, including Mary Wroth's future father-in-law, were working on behalf of Cecil, not seizing initiative for themselves (Tyacke, "Wroth, Cecil, and the Parliamentary Session of 1604," 120–125; and Munden, "King, Commons, and Reform," 43–72). Colclough examines the historiographic significance of Jacobean parliamentary conflicts (*Freedom of Speech*, 120–195).

12. Alan G. R. Smith argues that the failure of the Great Contract was due as much to mutual distrust between king and parliament as to disagreement over its specific terms ("Crown, Parliament and the Great Contract," 111–127).

13. James dissolved the Addled Parliament after bitter disputes over impositions, the controversial taxes on imports and exports levied by royal decree rather than parliamentary vote (Kenyon, *Stuart England*, 77–79). Thrush explores the practical and theoretical implications of James's loathing of parliament, and particularly the House of Commons ("Personal Rule of James I," 84–102).

question as to whether parliament would ever meet again and a genuine fear that England would follow the Continental trend toward absolutism.[14]

Tellingly, observers typically described James's dismissive attitude toward his parliaments and subjects in the same affective terms to which he himself appealed. For instance, a 1607 report of the Venetian Ambassador, Nicolo Molin, emphasized not James's absolutist rhetoric but his failure to offer the demonstrations of love that had made Elizabeth so popular. As Molin put it,

> He does not caress the people nor make them that good cheer the late Queen did, whereby she won their loves: for the English adore their Sovereigns, and if the King passed through the same street a hundred times a day the people would still run to see him; they like their King to show pleasure at their devotion, as the late Queen knew well how to do; but this King manifests no taste for them but rather contempt and dislike. The result is he is despised and almost hated.[15]

Molin's report imagines affection as a reciprocal, mimetic process. By showing "contempt and dislike," James has alienated his subjects. James's refusal to treat his subjects with affection not only decreased his popularity but also underscored just how central the fantasy of mutual love was to the workings of government. The 1604 Common's Apology, to take just one example, drew on the timeworn formula that equated love with supply in advising James that

> The voice of the people in things of their knowledge is said to be as the voice of God. And if your Majesty shall vouchsafe at your best pleasure and leisure to enter into gracious consideration of our petitions for ease of these burdens under which your whole people have of long time mourned, hoping for relief by your Majesty, then you may be assured to be possessor of their hearts for ever, and if of their hearts, then of all they can do or have.[16]

By refusing to "caress the people" or "show pleasure at their devotion," James forfeits his claims to supply, or "all they can do or have."

Wroth's *Urania* acknowledges that indifference and betrayal may indeed make sovereigns "despised and almost hated." However, she also reminds her readers that

---

14. Hirst argues that widespread awareness of Continental absolutism hardened the beliefs that the common law and parliamentary privilege must be protected (*Authority*, 33–42, 52–59). The States-General of France, for instance, was dissolved in 1614 and did not reconvene until 1789.

15. Ashton, *James I*, 10. Watkins argues that such early Stuart historians as William Camden, Robert Naunton, and Greville adapted historiographic and literary forms that furthered the sense that the Stuarts had betrayed the constitutionalist rule of the Elizabethan era (56–86).

16. Kenyon, ed., *Stuart Constitution*, 35.

the beloved's coldness and cruelty may actually increase affection, or at least testify to the lover's own selfless virtue—precisely the dynamic that Sidney had traced in *Astrophil and Stella* and that she herself details in *Pamphilia to Amphilanthus*, the sonnet sequence she appended to the first part of the *Urania*. Wroth's work creates a picture of the same heroic but ineffective erotic and political suffering as that imagined by Philip Sidney's friend and first biographer, Fulke Greville. In *A Letter to an Honorable Lady*, Greville inverts the typical relation of vehicle and tenor by making politics a metaphor for unrequited love. Greville's *Letter* urges his ostensible addressee to consider her position in light of "the opinions of worthie men, borne under Tyrants, and bound to obay, though they could not please: the comparison holdinge in some affinitie betweene a wives subjection to a husband, and a subjects obedience to his sovereign."[17] The Lady's problem is that her husband is an inveterate adulterer. Evoking the Aristotelian association between unbridled appetite and tyrannous rule, the *Letter* treats the husband's "change of delights, and delight in change" as the mark of his corruption. Greville stresses the futility of active opposition and urges the Lady instead to "weigh what follie it is for a Subject under a Prince, or a wife under the yoke of a husband, to strive alone, with the strange corporations of power? Since in obedience we need overcome but one (our selfe I meane) where in these other contentions, we must serve many masters, worshippe equalls, flatter inferiors, and trust in strangers."[18] By turning politics into a figure for love, Greville's *Letter* discreetly condemns royal absolutism for reducing subjects to helpless, feminized positions in which anger and self-assertion are forbidden. And even as Greville insists on the futility of resistance, the rhetorical situation of the *Letter* contradicts its fictional one. The very act of writing a letter lamenting the corrosive effects of "affected absoluteness" rejects the silent suffering Greville ostensibly counsels.[19]

Greville's *Letter* is concerned more with the reaction of those who might read this "private" correspondence than with the predicament of his much-abused addressee. The *Letter*, like the hagiographies I have discussed above, assumes not a dyadic agon between victim and villain, but a triangulated relation between ruler, subject, and observer. Wroth's *Urania* employs similarly triangulated structures in its depictions of women who have been betrayed and abused by fickle and cruel lovers. Any of her female characters could be Greville's Honourable Lady—or the political subject whose trials this Lady shares. The question of how a woman might properly respond to an unfaithful lover offers Wroth a forum for considering the position of oppositional subjects in the latter decades of James I's reign, when the insularity of his Council and effective absence of parliament meant that challenges

17. *Letter*, in *Prose Works of Fulke Greville*, 154.
18. *Letter*, 147, 164–165.
19. *Letter*, 140.

to monarchal policy were increasingly indirect and futile. For Sidney and Spenser, confrontation with injustice is conceivable, if only in the fictional space of chivalric romance. For Wroth, the erotics of suffering have so vitiated even the fantasy world of romance that injustice itself becomes desirable as a means of proving the virtue of its victim.

Part One of the *Urania* was likely written during the latter years of the decade in which James ruled substantially alone, Part Two during increasingly contentious debates over the source and extent of parliamentary authority that would lead to the personal rule of Charles I from 1629 to 1640.[20] It is unsurprising, then, that the *Urania* is deeply engaged with questions of rule as it struggles to postulate a viable alternative to the obsession and idolatry inherent in absolutist rhetoric. In one particularly bizarre episode in Part Two of the *Urania*, for instance, the aptly named King Demonarus, overcome by lust for his daughter, "commaunded his wyfe to hold her while hee tooke his full pleasure of her" (2.311). The wife refuses, and she and her daughter fight Demonarus to the death. This surreal perversion of Jacobean patriarchal discourse literalizes classical metaphors of tyrannical appetite, and Wroth thereby asks readers to reconsider the proposition that the king-husband-father deserves absolute obedience. The episode, with its titillating possibility of an incestuous ménage à trois, may provoke both fascination with the erotics of power and revulsion at its logical conclusion.

Wroth's skepticism about absolutist discourse was shared by the many of her circle of friends and relations. Indeed, the frontispiece of the *Urania* advertises Wroth's familial and affective loyalties to persons who were strong proponents of counsel and parliament and thereby accentuates the network of alliances from which the romance emerged.[21] As Michael G. Brennan has argued, the deaths of Philip Sidney's daughter, Elizabeth, Countess of Rutland, and Wroth's brother, William Sidney, cast Wroth as a figure of central importance to an intimate group of writers who hoped to bolster their own literary and political careers by preserving

20. Brennan has demonstrated that the circumstances under which the *Urania* was published in 1621 connect it not only to the 1621 edition of the *Arcadia* but also to George Wither's *Motto*, which had been condemned as a seditious work by the Privy Council, resulting in the imprisonment of its sellers, John Marriott and John Grismand. Marriott and Grismand entered the *Urania* into the Stationers' Register on July 13, 1621, only three days after their release from prison for their involvement in the publication of Wither's *Motto* (*Sidneys*, 135–136). For Wroth's connections with Wither and other writers who consciously drew on a Sidneian and Spenserian heritage as a means of expressing opposition to royal policy, see Salzman, *Reading 1621*, 113–117; and Rosalind Smith, 99–101. For the debates surrounding the 1621 parliament, see Keir, 185–186; Sharpe, *Criticism*, 17; O'Farrell, "William Herbert," 97–102; Lake, "Thomas Scott and the Spanish Match," 814–820; and Thompson, *Debate on Freedom of Speech*.

21. For a detailed analysis of the frontispiece as an illustration of Wroth's larger project of finding a space for female agency within the kinship networks of the Sidneys, see Quilligan, *Incest and Agency*, 168–191.

Sidney's memory.[22] The frontispiece bears this out, for it identifies Wroth as "Daughter to the right Noble Robert Earle of Leicester, And Neece to the ever famous and renowned Sir Phillips Sidney, knight. And to the most exelent Lady Mary Countesse of Pembroke late deceased" (1.cxxi). Wroth's father, Robert Sidney, First Earl of Leicester, owed to James I and Anne of Denmark the political ascent he enjoyed after decades of frustration under Elizabeth, but he was also an ardent supporter of Frederick and Elizabeth of Bohemia who frowned upon the king's pacifist stance in the Thirty Years War. Robert Sidney's decision to marry his eldest daughter to the son of Robert Wroth, Sr., a former Marian exile and one of the most outspoken members of the Lower House, is consistent with the political opinions recorded in his commonplace book. In addition to his frustration with specific Jacobean policies, Robert Sidney also expressed a general skepticism about monarchy and a belief in the principles of subjects' rights and mixed government.[23] Moreover, as the frontispiece reminds us, Wroth took as a literary model her uncle Philip Sidney's *The Countess of Pembroke's Arcadia*, which, as Paul Salzman has observed, was "saturated" with Sidney's critique of Elizabethan policy and deployed in seventeenth-century protest against James I. The homage Wroth paid him in her title thus had noticeable political implications.[24] Finally, Wroth's aunt, Mary Sidney Herbert, the Countess of Pembroke, was known in seventeenth-century England not only for editing Philip Sidney's partially revised *Arcadia* but also for her politically inflected translations of biblical, classical, and Continental literature.[25]

In addition to the older Elizabethan relatives named in the frontispiece, the Jacobean generation of which Wroth was part was deeply engaged in contemporary political discussions. Most prominently, Wroth's famous affair with her cousin William Herbert, Earl of Pembroke, bespeaks her closeness to incipient proponents of parliamentary participation in the government of England. Pembroke, a favorite of Anne of Denmark, sustained a sizable faction in the House of Commons and sought to counter Somerset's, and later Buckingham's, influence on James. During the years when Wroth was writing the *Urania* and bearing Pembroke's illegitimate children, Pembroke's "interest" in parliament repeatedly urged English involvement in the Thirty Years War and stridently opposed a match between Charles Stuart and the Spanish Infanta, even though James insisted that foreign policy was entirely at his discretion. His brother, Philip Herbert, Earl of Montgomery—the husband of the dedicatee of the *Urania*, Susan Herbert—was a favorite of James and served as

---

22. "Ben Jonson and Lady Mary Wroth," 76–78.
23. Shepherd shows that the commonplace books of Robert Sidney demonstrate a preference for mixed monarchy ("Political Commonplace Books of Sir Robert Sidney," 210–228). Hay discusses his rise in fortune under James and support of the Bohemian cause (210-217). Hannay has read the *Urania* in the context of the correspondence between Wroth and her father, Robert Sidney ("Lady Mary Wroth in the Correspondence of Robert Sidney").
24. Salzman, 64–69.
25. Hannay emphasizes Mary Sidney Herbert's political interests (*Philip's Phoenix*).

Charles I's Lord Chamberlain but fought for parliament in the civil wars.[26] Wroth's brother, Robert Sidney, Second Earl of Leicester, retired to his library during the civil wars to avoid fighting, but his son Algernon Sidney enthusiastically defended the parliamentary cause and was posthumously celebrated as a martyr to republican principles.[27]

Wroth's intimacy with such proponents of counsel and parliament, of course, does not bespeak a simple rejection of monarchy as such. Her work instead demonstrates that the cultural mindset that defended the institution of monarchy while debating specific policies was as practical as it was ideological. Robert Wroth's death in 1614 left Mary Wroth heavily in debt, and her financial predicament worsened when her son died and the estate reverted to his uncles. For much of her life, Wroth depended on royal warrants of protection from creditors, so the sovereign prerogative that the Stuarts propounded was essential to her livelihood. In 1622, for instance, Wroth wrote a letter to James I's advisor, Sir Edward Conway, begging him to "procure mee the kings hand once again" to defer collection of her debts.[28] Wroth's request for the king's "hand," or favor, inverts the gender roles of courtly rhetoric in order to claim her subservience as a reminder of James's obligation. Figuring James as a mistress to be courted, Wroth appropriates the role of the enamored vassal. By conflating James's real political power with metaphoric erotic sway, however, she also places herself in the position of the potential husband, her king in that of the wife who will lovingly obey her spouse's will.

Wroth's use of the discourse of love in her letter to James reveals the instability of both gendered and political identities and hierarchies. She thus marshals the same logic that structures the *Urania*, where abjection can signify an irresistible, if troubling, form of power. In the *Urania*, however, scenarios of helpless devotion have more than an immediate end. In their very repetitiveness, Wroth's depictions of physical and psychological agony constitute hypothetical situations through which readers can test ethical and political principles. While Part One of the *Urania* focuses on the danger of self-enthrallment to idealized equations of love, loyalty, and suffering, Part Two pictures unions that depend less on idealized sacrifice than on mutual concession. The *Urania* proposes that erotic and political tyranny can be avoided only by relinquishing the fantasies that sustain it—which, as the text demonstrates, is an impossible task. Ultimately, Wroth suggests that the balanced

26. For William and Philip Herbert's political actions during the reigns of James I and Charles I, see O'Farrell; and Brennan, *Literary Patronage*. See also Thomas Herbert's *Vox Secunda Populi*, which praises Philip Herbert as both "true to King and country" and the champion of the Commons.

27. Jonathan Scott, *Algernon Sidney*. For the activities of Wroth's brother, Robert, and his son, Algernon, after the outbreak of the civil wars, see Brennan, *Sidneys*, 147–169. For Wroth's life in her later years, see Hannay, *Mary Sidney, Lady Wroth*, 274–308.

28. Quoted in *Poems of Lady Mary Wroth*, ed. Roberts, 243.

sovereignty urged by the Sidney–Herbert circle may itself be a fantasy, the elusiveness of which emerges in the fragmented, incomplete narrative of the *Urania*.

The first episode of the *Urania* employs the discourse of martyrdom to offer an interpretive rubric for the erotic suffering that fills the romance. And from this opening moment Wroth also underscores the masochistic potential of hagiographic equations of virtue, power, and suffering. The title situates Urania—the name for the muse of heavenly contemplation—as the central character, and I suggest that we take Wroth's own emphasis seriously.[29] Pamphilia, who is typically identified with Wroth herself, certainly takes up more narrative space than any other character, particularly in Part Two. But it is Urania whose choices and arguments are consistently presented as the most reasonable and rewarding, and it is through the lens of her own initial scene of reading that Wroth prepares us to react to the stories that follow. The political valence of Urania's guidance becomes explicit in Part Two of the romance, when her husband describes her in terms of her conciliar role: "Butt then how did her counsell ravish our eares, more Judiciall, more exquisite then the whole great counsells of the greatest Monarckies!" (2.153). In her first opportunity to offer advice, Urania overhears the knight Perissus bemoaning his dead love Limena. In counsel that emphasizes romance's capacity to instigate action, Urania reminds the lovelorn knight that his sorrow prevents him from avenging the murder he laments:

> "Sir," said she, "having heard some part of your sorrowes, they have not only made me truly pity you, but wonder at you; since if you have lost so great a treasure, you should not lie thus leaving her and your love unrevenged, suffering her murderers to live, while you lie here complaining, and if such perfections be dead in her, why make you not the Phoenix of your deeds live againe, as to new life rais'd out of the revenge you should take on them? then were her end satisfied, and you deservedly accounted worthie of her favour, if shee were so worthie as you say." (1.4)

According to Urania's logic, the acceptance of injustice signals a voluntary effeminization. Rather than passively "suffering" Limena's death, Perissus should avenge it; rather than lying supine on the craggy floor while Limena's murderers go free, Perissus must "raise" both himself and the "Phoenix" of his lately abandoned heroism to new life through revenge. The crime that Perissus has witnessed should inspire indignation and action, not anguished histrionics.

---

29. Several readers note that the *Urania* is named after the absent shepherdess of the *Arcadia*, but they have tended to overlook the significance of Wroth's own Urania to her romance's political argument. See Beilin, *Redeeming Eve*, 216; and Quilligan, "Female Authority," 257–280. Andrea describes Urania as a lone voice of sanity, but nonetheless identifies Pamphilia most with Wroth herself (346). Rosalind Smith argues that Urania should be identified with Mary Sidney, Countess of Pembroke (97–98).

Urania's advice evokes the resistance theory of the Marian exiles. As we have seen, these theorists encouraged identification with the martyrs they describe and, correspondingly, revolt against the tyrants oppressing them. This sentiment is neatly expressed in Foxe's report of the Marian martyr Hugh Latimer's final words to his death mate Nicholas Ridley: "Be of good comfort, master Ridley, and play the man. We shall this day light such a candle, by God's grace, in England, as I trust shall never be put out."[30] As Limena's experience warns us, the fidelity that martyrdom exhibits requires physical evidence of pain in order to be legible. But because it is the surest sign of virtue, agony may itself become desirable. Wroth's incorporation of the discursive fields of hagiography calls attention to three available responses to martyrdom, none of which are mutually exclusive. The first two, sadistic enjoyment and masochistic emulation, depend on an identification with either persecutor or victim. The third, empathetic resistance, retains a distance that prompts witnesses to prevent suffering rather than merely enjoy or endure it. As we have seen, because the reader of romance may identify with both the feminine subject-victim and the masculine ruler-aggressor, the genre's voyeuristic scenes have the potential to create both pleasure, which would uphold power relations, and indignation, which would resist them.[31] Consequently, there is always the danger that the martyrdom that should encourage resistance will give way to masochistic gratification. Perissus' reaction to Limena's story exemplifies just such a mode of misreading.

Perissus' detailed account of Limena's slow and painful death at the hands of her jealous husband is typically read as distinguishing between true love and arranged marriage to reveal the cruelty of the latter.[32] Yet because physical pain alone provides proof of sincere devotion, Limena's torture is peculiarly necessary to this love story.[33] It serves the dual purpose of revealing Philargus' tyranny and confirming Perissus' desert. The centrality of this tale of suffering indicates that the sadomasochistic dynamic that should oppose true love might actually be the driving force of any narrative that equates voluntary suffering with erotic authenticity. Despite her

---

30. Foxe, *Acts and Monuments*, 7:550.

31. Critics of romance disagree as to whether such scenes register pleasure in or resistance to female subjection. Lucas (*Writing for Women*) and Krontiras (*Oppositional Voices*) argue that female readers of romance practice an "oppositional" or "resistant" reading that allows women to enjoy the escape it provides from their quotidian limitations. Hackett suggests that romance's appeal to women might inhere in the "erotic sainthood" that evinces female heroism ("Sex and Violence" and *Women and Romance Fiction*, 10–11, 32). Relihan and Stanivukovic argue that voyeuristic pleasure is unavailable to female readers who do not adopt a male-identified position ("Introduction," 5).

32. See Josephine Roberts, "Controversy Regarding Marriage," 112–113; and Hackett, "Sex and Violence," 104. Beilin reads the connection between Limena's rebellious love and a concurrent popular revolt as Wroth's means of promoting mixed monarchy ("Role of the Political Subject," 10–11).

33. For a discussion of suffering in Greek and early modern romance, see Greenhalgh, "Greek Romance," 15–42.

passion for Perissus, Limena obeys her father's command that she marry the wealthy lord Philargus, and Perissus' portrayal of her distress indicates that the same anguish defines both force and love. Unlike Sidney's Parthenia, for whom passion is opposed to obedience, Wroth's Limena makes obedience itself the most irresistible of passions:

> Shee seeing it was her fathers will, esteeming obedience beyond all passions, how worthily soever, suffered; most dutifully, though unwillingly, said, she would obey; her tongue faintly delivering, what her heart so much detested; loathing almost it selfe, for consenting in shew to that which was most contrarie to it selfe; yet thus it was concluded, and with as much speed as any man would make to an eternall happines. (1.5)

In this characterization, Wroth converts the idealized patriarch—whether king, husband, or father—into a tyrant whose commands force his subjects to betray, and even loathe, themselves. Opposed to Limena's passion is her father's will that she marry, which is grammatically equivalent to his will that she suffer—here used in its dual sense of submitting to another and experiencing pain. The passage enunciates Limena's reluctance through its desperate multiplication of antitheses. The euphuistic tension between obedience and passion, duty and will, public "show" and private self, erases any clear lines between love and force. Finally ending on the ironic note of the "eternal happiness" that marriage purportedly offers, Limena's betrothal is achieved with alacrity in a brief clause that sinks the accomplished fact under the weight of her painful deliberation, making visible the process by which women's wills become identical with those of their husbands.

In Wroth's hands, Limena's forced marriage does not so much threaten her love for Perissus as provide an opportunity for her to demonstrate it. Upon learning of his new wife's devotion to another man, Philargus determines to punish her, initially "with daily whippings, and such other tortures, as pinching with irons," and finally with death (1.88). To her husband's frustration, such treatment does not diminish Limena's loyalty to Perissus. Rather, it allows her to express abstract devotion in the form of physical pain. In response to Philargus' demand that she confess her error, Limena retorts that "threatnings are but meanes to strengthen free and pure hearts against the threatners" and warns that "such revenge will my death have, as though by you I die, I pittie your ensuing overthrow" (1.12, 13). Limena here draws attention to the discrepancy between her physical vulnerability and her inner resolve, the former of which testifies to the latter. She thereby reminds Philargus that, as the Foxean martyr John Philpot reportedly declared to his persecutors, "you have nothing but violence."[34]

Limena's martyrdom illuminates the cruelty not only of forced marriage but also of idealized narratives of devotion. Perissus' initial inaction, moreover, represents

34. Foxe, 7:671.

the ease with which both erotic and political subjects may be lulled into passivity by idealizations of suffering and self-abnegation. We might align Urania's reading of Limena's martyrdom with Foxe's own instructions that his readers imitate his martyrs' resistance. Urania's insistence that erotic violence should provoke action, not gratuitous pity, proves right some seventy pages later, when we discover that Philargus has only staged Limena's death so that he can continue to torture her without worrying about prospective rescuers. Before Limena's secret torment culminates in her death, Perissus and the knight Parselius fortuitously discover what has been happening. Initially, however, Parselius is so transfixed by the titillating vision of sadism that he fails to intervene:

> The Morean Prince staid to behold, and beholding did admire the exquisitnes of that sad beautie, but more then that did the cruelty of the armed man seeme wonderful, for leading her to a pillar which stood on the sand (a fit place that the sea might stil wash away the memorie of such inhumanity) he tied her to it by the haire, which was of greate length, and Sun-like brightnesse. Then pulled hee off a mantle which she wore, leaving her from the girdle upwards al naked, her soft, daintie white hands hee fastened behind her, with a cord about both wrists, in manner of a crosse, as testimony of her cruellest Martyrdome.
>
> When she was thus miserably bound to his unmercifull liking, with whipps hee was about to torment her: but Parselius with this sight was quickly put out of his admiration. (1.84)

Parselius, like Perissus earlier, represents the inept romance reader who falls too easily into sadistic or masochistic identification to retain the distance that will provoke action. Here, Parselius' "admiration" threatens to supersede his capacity for a rational response to the injustice before him. Limena's helpless nudity and "crosse"-like bindings testify to her unfeigned fidelity to Perissus, even as her *imitatio Christi* makes literal the equation of suffering and virtue. Yet Limena's would-be hero is so fascinated by the "wonderful cruelty of the armed man" and the "exquisitness" of her beauty that he nearly shirks his generic—and moral—duty. Fortunately for Limena, Parselius eventually realizes that he should oppose, not enjoy, injustice, and his disenchantment leads to her rescue. Perissus arrives just in time, and together the men subdue Philargus and release Limena.

Having been vanquished, Philargus repents, and his subsequent reconciliation with Perissus and Limena recalls Sidneian structures that depict passive resistance as an anecdote to tyranny. With his last breath Philargus urges Perissus and Limena to marry, reiterating his conjugal authority even as he acknowledges his misuse of it. As a result of his defeat, Philargus confesses, "now are mine eyes open to the injuries done to vertuous Limena . . . before, my eyes were dimme, and eares deafe, seeing and hearing nothing, but base falshoods, being govern'd by so strong and undeserved Jealousie" (1.85). Like the classical tyrant, Philargus has allowed passion to rule him, and his retreat from the eyes of society suggests the same rejection of frank counsel that many identified in James I.[35] Rather than destroying such a ruler's power, subjects' reasoned resistance may restore proper order. Once Philargus recovers his reason, Perissus and Limena are willing to yield to his authority: "He needed not urge them much to what they most coveted, and purposed in their hearts before: yet to give him full satisfaction (though on her side with bashfull and fearefull consenting) they yeelded to him" (1.86). Wills have been united not by the subject's unilateral obedience, but through a salutary resistance to unjust demands.

Once safe, Limena exhibits her own fidelity even as she tests that of Perissus by displaying her lacerated flesh to both of her fascinated rescuers. Her scars are physical tokens of her love, but they also manifest the effects of idealized narratives of erotic martyrdom:

> [The sight of her scars] made newe hurts in the loving heart of Perissus, [who] suffer[ed] more paine for them, then he had done for all those himselfe had received in his former adventures; therefore softly putting the Mantle up againe, and gently covering them, lest yet they might chance to smart, [Perissus] besought her to goe on, longing to have an end of that tragicall historie, and to come againe to their meeting, which was the onely balme could be applied unto his bleeding heart. She joyfull to see this passion, because it was for her, and sorry it was Perissus did sorrow, proceeded. (1.87–88)

The joy that Limena takes in Perissus' empathetic agony again situates suffering as the most effective means of making internal affect legible. But Perissus wants to cover up her wounds so that he can focus on the devotion that they evince, rather than the pain that love has occasioned. His squeamishness exemplifies the tendency to disavow the consequences of narratives of unshakable fidelity. Wroth's relentless attention to these consequences urges her readers to confront the effects of self-sacrificial ideals and the injustice they may support.

If Limena's martyrdom indicates the difficulty of distinguishing between love and masochism, a later episode detailing the humiliation of Nereana, the arrogant Queen of Stalamine, reveals the dangers of both monarchal and popular willfulness. The resolution of this story exemplifies the Aristotelian principle that the best government is a blend of monarchy, aristocracy, and democracy. If not restrained by the others, each of these forms may degenerate into its respective extreme of tyranny, oligarchy, and anarchy.[36] Nereana's failure to control her own pride means that she

---

35. The Commons' Protestation of December 18, 1621, for instance, responded to James's insistence that they avoid meddling in "mysteries of state" with the assertion that "the liberties, franchises, privileges, and jurisdictions of parliament are the ancient and undoubted birthright and inheritance of the subjects of England and that the arduous and urgent affairs concerning the king, state and defence of the realm . . . are proper subjects and matters of debate in parliament" (Rushworth, 1:53). James ripped the Protestation from the Commons' Journal and dissolved the parliament shortly thereafter.

36. *Politics*, 3.7.

is also incapable of controlling her subjects, and her feminine vanity and passion are emblems of the dangers that unbridled royal power may pose to the state as such. It is only after she has been disciplined by a combination of sexual assault, starvation, and imprisonment that Nereana becomes an effective ruler. When Wroth designates such disciplining experiences as "most profitable to Princes," she implies that subjects may benefit both ruler and commonwealth by resisting irrational monarchal commands (1.496). However, the extremity of Nereana's various punishments suggests the potential danger of placing the bulk of power in the hands of the people. By stressing the perversity of Nereana's treatment, the *Urania* demonstrates how easily loyal opposition may shade into deluded anarchy. The story of Nereana illustrates the unsavory potential of popular rule and thereby registers Wroth's anxiety that the theories of mixed government that she and others endorsed may be impossible in practice.

In one particularly disturbing episode, Nereana is subjected to a sexual attack that reveals a prince's thralldom to the adoration he or she demands. Having become lost in the woods as she pursues a knight who has spurned her, Nereana is the epitome of the tyrant driven by unstanched desire. She is soon waylaid by the mad woodsman Alanius, who mistakes her first for his lost love, then for the forest's presiding deity. Acting on these fantasies, Alanius subjects her to a bizarre ritual that demonstrates the ease with which political hierarchies may be inverted by the erotic ideals that should sustain them:

> [He] fully perswaded shee was that Goddesse, whether she would or noe, would worship her, and that he might be sure of her stay, hee tide her to a tree; then to have her in her owne shape out of those vestures, which he imagined made her unwilling to abide with him: hee undress'd her, pulling her haire downe to the full length; cloathes hee left her none, save onely one little petticoate of carnation tafatie; her greene silke stockins hee turn'd, or row'ld a little downe, making them serve for buskins; garlands hee put on her head, and armes, tucking up her smock-sleeves to the elbowes, her necke bare, and a wreath of fine flowers he hung crosse from one shoulder under the other arme, like a belt, to hang her quiver in: a white sticke which he had newly whittled, he put into her hand, instead of a boare speare: then setting her at liberty he kneeled downe, and admired her, when she almost hating her selfe in this estate fled away, but as fast as his sad madnesse would carry him, he pursued her. (1.197–198)

The detailed blazon in which Wroth describes Nereana's humiliating transformation from queen to forest nymph registers how easily myths of royal power may be contradicted by the reality of material conditions.[37] As monarch, Nereana should

---

37. Beilin reads Nereana's humiliation as a satire on discourses of absolutism ("Role of the Political Subject," 15), while Sandy sees it as just punishment for Nereana's self-involvement (*Seventeenth-Century Romance*, 46).

have absolute authority over Alanius. But as a woman, she is physically helpless before this bedraggled maniac. And this vulnerability is not limited to female rulers. The bondage and exposure to which Alanius subjects his imagined goddess antici- pates the ambivalence that Freud has noted with regard to the totemic royal figure who arouses both love and hatred.[38] Alanius' ability to have his way with Nereana reveals that absolutism and anarchy are mutually reinforcing. Both place desire beyond the reach of law.

Alanius' domination of Nereana disproves myths of royal invulnerability at the same time that it warns against excessive popular authority. Subsequently, Nereana is mocked and abandoned by a knight who should help her, then forced to live in a cave subsisting on nuts and berries; once returned to her country, she is imprisoned by her usurping younger sister with her subjects' assent. It is only through the inter- vention of a noble counselor that Nereana finally regains her rightful office. In a more temperate version of Alanius' construction of a sovereign image, the nobleman persuades the people to restore their legitimate ruler. Once they agree, "hee with the rest of the Counsel, fetched Nereana forth, solemnly againe establish'd her, had pardons for all things past, and all was made up with a kind and gratious conclusion" (1.496). The difficulty of finding a true balance between prerogative and participation emerges here in Nereana's grammatical position as object of her Counsel's actions. Even the undoubted royal prerogative of pardon seems not to originate in Nereana's independent agency. Rather, pardon simply appears as some- thing her subjects "had" as a result of her restoration, as though it might be too dangerous to grant her even this benign expression of authority. Nereana's story reaches a "kind and gratious conclusion" not because the queen suppresses rebel- lion and reasserts sovereign prerogative, but through debate in which the monarch herself takes only a small part.

The conclusion of Nereana's story recalls the power structure of the middle ages, when powerful "kingmakers" like Richard Neville, Earl of Warwick, domi- nated royal policy and appointments. Wroth hardly argues for the sort of baro- nial influence that led to the civil wars of the fifteenth century (or even that briefly enjoyed by her great-grandfather John Dudley, Earl of Northumberland, in the mid-sixteenth century). But Nereana's persistent helplessness makes it dif- ficult to distinguish between the triumph of noble counsel exemplified by Nere- ana's restoration and the domination evinced by Alanius, which—like that of Somerset and then Buckingham over James I—reduces royalty to mere parody of itself.

The Nereana episode of the *Urania* thus acknowledges the same inevitability of political struggle that troubled Wroth's immediate family. An entry on "Prerogative" in the Sidney commonplace book begun by Wroth's father and continued by her

38. See *Totem and Taboo.*

brother Robert defines prerogative as an executive power that may be located in different individuals or institutions depending on the organization of a given state. Even in monarchy, the passage states, the royal prerogative is founded not on divine right, but on the "fundamentall Lawes" of the state. Moreover, every monarchy sees a constant struggle between the prince's and people's desires to expand their powers, "no man holding his estate or person secure, while he knows himself subject to the pleasure of any other . . . and hereupon grows the uncertainty of prerogative (where it is not established by the laws, which in all cases is impossible)."[39] In Nereana's metamorphoses from an overbearing tyrant to a helpless prisoner and then to a limited monarch, Wroth indicates the difficulty of finding a genuine and sustainable balance of power between ruler and people when unappeasable human desires defy both legal and customary attempts at compromise. Even more problematically, as Pamphilia's situation demonstrates, such desires are based at least as much on irrational fantasies and identifications as they are on a reasoned and realistic assessment of their object.

Unlike Limena and Nereana, whose ordeals are forced upon them, Pamphilia embraces her emotional subjection to the royal hero Amphilanthus. She becomes a "miserable spectacle" embodying the consequences of the Stuart narratives of asymmetrical obligation expressed in her blissful statement of surrender: "O love, thou dost master me" (1.463, 63).[40] Crucially, the most persistent of Pamphilia's outbursts occur just before and after Amphilanthus' coronation as Holy Roman Emperor. Fourteen pages detailing Pamphilia's sorrows frame two paragraphs describing Amphilanthus' triumph, a structure that suggests the disproportion between imperial power and the subjection it demands. Pamphilia's devotion to a man who is unable to control his own appetite figures the obedience of subjects so fascinated by the allure of power that they are strangely attracted to its abuse. Pamphilia's response to Amphilanthus' infidelity demonstrates that her self-imposed identity as a martyr to love has become its own perverse reward:

> Rather then my lips shall give the least way to discover any fault in him, I wil conceale all though they breake my heart; and if I only could be saved by accusing him, I sooner would be secret and so dye: no, my love will not let me use thee ill; then be it as it is, Ile live forsaken and forlorne, yet silently I will indure this wrong, nor once blame him to any others eare, for deare (alas) he is to me, deare to my eyes, deare to my thoughts, and

39. Quoted in Shepherd, 21. The entry is written in the hand of Wroth's brother but with the annotation "partly out of a paper of my fathers," suggesting continuity in the Sidney family's views of monarchy. For discussions about the attribution of the sentiments expressed in the entry, see Hay, 205–206; and Scott, *Algernon Sidney*, 55.

40. Previous critics have perhaps too easily credited Pamphilia's own self-perception as a constant martyr and thus seen her as a model of female autonomy and resistance. See Quilligan, "Female Authority," 272–273; and Shaver, "New Woman," 76.

dearest to my heart; since he will ravish that poore part of all the joy and sweet content
it ever had, converting it to bitter lasting paine. (1.462–463)

Pamphilia's pride in her own agony takes the equation of love, virtue, and sacrifice
to its logical extreme: she has so entirely bent her will to that of Amphilanthus that
his betrayal itself is a source of pleasure. In an attempt to secure a bond of mutual
obligation, she dwells at length on the concealment, secrecy, and silence that she
endures to protect Amphilanthus' reputation. Because no one else in the romance
thinks that Amphilanthus is anything but a cad, however, Pamphilia's belief that her
loyalty protects him situates her as a deluded, self-dramatizing mess who willfully
embraces her own misery.

Scholars have almost unanimously understood Pamphilia's constancy as a
means of establishing female autonomy. According to this analysis, the more
unfaithful Amphilanthus is, the more Pamphilia's love can be understood not
merely as a response to male desire, but in Maureen Quilligan's words, "an act of
willful self-definition."[41] Pamphilia's ability to remain steadfast in her devotion no
matter how badly she is treated, accordingly, offers evidence of the sort of heroic
self-mastery that Greville's *Letter* advises for women and subjects alike. What these
analyses neglect is the extent to which Pamphilia's constancy may itself signal a
form of uncontrollable perversion. The *Urania*, that is, provides the narrative context
for the abject desire that the appended sonnet sequence, *Pamphilia to Amphilanthus*,
traces in such relentless detail. As this Petrarchan sequence repeatedly reminds
us, Pamphilia has chosen love despite the pain it brings: "my hurt, makes my lost
heart confess / I love, and must: So farewell liberty" (14.13–14). Moreover, she
recognizes not only that "Hope kills the hart, and tirants shed the blood" but also
that such attachment "brings us to the pride / Of our desires the furder downe to
slide" (35.12, 14). Because her torment is itself a source of pleasure and power, it
can no longer be an unproblematic sign of virtue. Rather than merely evading or
inverting structures of domination, Pamphilia's masochism renders them diffuse
and unrecognizable.

The narrative of the *Urania* shows that Pamphilia's passion for Amphilanthus,
like Perissus' empty histrionics, is rooted in her refusal to examine critically the
Petrarchan ideal that suffering is an intrinsic part of true love. Pamphilia's
self-deception appears prominently in an episode in which she rejects as fiction the
very description of eros so inexorably repeated in the *Urania*. During a solitary
walk, Pamphilia reads a story of a woman betrayed by her lover but refuses to credit
its relevance to her own situation:

---

41. *Incest and Agency*, 209. See also Naomi Miller, *Changing the Subject*, 61. Beilin argues, to the
contrary, that Wroth is critical of Pamphilia's misplaced constancy ("Constancy in Mary
Wroth's *Pamphilia to Amphilanthus*," 234).

A booke shee had with her, wherin she read a while, the subject was Love, and the story
she then was reading, the affection of a Lady to a brave Gentleman, who equally loved,
but being a man, it was necessary for him to exceede a woman in all things, so much as
inconstancie was found fit for him to excell her in, hee left her for a new.

"Poore love," said the Queene, "how doth all storyes, and every writer use thee at their
pleasure, apparrelling thee according to their various fancies? canst thou suffer thy selfe to
be thus put in cloathes, nay raggs instead of vertuous habits? punish such Traytors, and
cherrish mee thy loyall subject who will not so much as keepe thy injuries neere me."

Then threw she away the booke, and walked up and downe, her hand on her heart, to
feele if there were but the motion left in the place of that shee had so freely given, which
she found, and as great, and brave an one in the stead of it. (1.317)

Pamphilia's dismissal of "all" stories and "every" writer ironically avoids romance's
unsettling celebration of erotic tyranny by citing conventional polemics against the
genre in which she herself exists. Love, in Pamphilia's analogy, has been transformed
by romance writers into a sovereign who, like Nereana, can be captured and made
over into unlikely images. What Pamphilia cannot admit is that her own thralldom
to love depends on perverse fantasy, even when reading a story that so closely
resembles her own. Her response thus casts truth as treason, loyalty as a willfull
ignorance of the gap between reality and ideal. The intense emotion that accompanies her refusal of self-recognition suggests that belief in a certain view of love has
made Pamphilia helpless to react appropriately to her own betrayal. She can affirm
her identity as a "loyall subject" only to the extent that she is also a miserable one.

In response to Pamphilia's obstinate suffering, Urania casts the misery that Pamphilia so proudly parades as a craven servility that fails to acknowledge the conventional nature of all models of sovereignty. Urania insists that neither Amphilanthus
nor love itself is "such a Deity, as your Idolatry makes him . . . and so deare Cosin it
is our want of curage and judgement makes us his slaves" (1.469–470). In opposition to such idolatry, Urania proposes a theory of political and erotic attachment in
which all human relations are subject to contingency and change:

"Tis pittie," said Urania, "that ever that fruitlesse thing Constancy was taught you as a
vertue, since for vertues sake you will love it, but understand, this vertue hath limits to
hold it in, being a vertue, but thus that it is a vice in them that breake it, but those with
whom it is broken, are by the breach free to leave or choose againe where more staidnes
may be found; besides tis a dangerous thing to hold that opinion, which in time will
prove flat heresie." (1.470)

Urania's assertion that a woman is free to replace an unworthy lover—something
that she herself has done—has important political meaning. This argument for
provisional loyalty rejects absolutist theorists like James I who deem it impious to
sunder analogous affective and political bonds. Both, Urania proposes, must be
subject to review and revision. Rather than mindlessly accepting the absolutist

equation of constancy with virtue, Pamphilia must act according to the "limits" of context and consequences. Urania's account of Pamphilia's constancy as a "fruitless thing," bespeaks the autoerotic sterility of unreciprocated love. Urania insists that Pamphilia devotes herself to Amphilanthus because she idealizes devotion itself. Such circular logic follows the dictates of fantasy, not reason. While passion should regenerate those it inspires, Pamphilia's loyalty lies fallow and decaying. Joining the language of natural change to that of religious recusancy, Urania further warns that such blind faith will eventually prove itself "flat heresie." Erotic idolatry, like popish superstition, promotes a self-flagellating servility that is dangerous to subject and country alike. Tellingly, Pamphilia's response only confirms Urania's characterization of her behavior: "To leave him for being false, would shew my love was not for his sake, but mine owne, that because he loved me, I therefore loved him, but when hee leaves I can doe so to. O no deere Cousen I loved him for himselfe, and would have loved him had hee not loved mee, and will love though he dispise me" (1.470). Pamphilia's insistence that true loyalty is defined precisely by its lack of reward sanctions a narrative of love that replaces mutual compromise and service with unilateral fidelity and sacrifice.

Urania's countermodel of reciprocal obligation prominently rejects Pamphilia's ethos of martyrdom by deflating the lofty ideals that support it. Early in Wroth's romance, Urania is herself betrayed by Parselius. But rather than cling to destructive affection like Pamphilia, she consents to be hurled into a sea that will wash this first love from her memory. Subsequently, she falls in love with and marries Steriamus, the King of Albania, with whom she lives as happily ever after as anyone in the *Urania* is allowed. Significantly, Pamphilia was Steriamus' first love, and his shift of affection to Urania confirms the superiority of her course of action on the level of both narrative and political allegory. Both Urania's behavior and advice, in fact, evoke the same legal and constitutional limits to sovereign power described in the parliamentarian Thomas Hedley's widely disseminated argument that the common law is above both king and parliament. According to Hedley, the common law's adaptability is the source of its superiority, for "as restiness in opinion without great reason is properly pertinacity not constancy, so change of opinion upon good grounds is not levity but rather constancy to goodness and reason."[42] Both Urania's exceptionally happy ending and her place in the romance's title indicate that her moderate view of love and loyalty is more representative of Wroth's own vision of sovereignty than Pamphilia's extravagant defense of unswerving devotion. Nonetheless, Urania's small role in the romance can be read as a structural comment on the difficulty of aligning real events with theoretical ideals. Her views may be central to the *Urania*, but the title character's comparatively minor role in the action warns that it is hard to sustain such balance and restraint in practice.

42. Speech on June 28, 1610, in Foster, ed., *Proceedings in Parliament 1610*, 2:178.

Pamphilia is not only victimized by Amphilanthus' inconstancy but also com-plicit in perpetuating it. We see the possibility that unbending loyalty may be as harmful to others as to oneself when Pamphilia's own affective thralldom leads her to deny the objective grounds of the anger of Antissia, another princess whom Amphilanthus has betrayed. Gwynne Kennedy has observed that women's anger in the early modern period was widely viewed not only as an unreasonable and futile revolt against her proper position in divine, natural, and social hierarchies but also as a challenge to authority and order more generally.[43] In the context of the analogy between gendered and political orders that I have been examining, female anger has decided political significance in Wroth's romance. Because women in early modern discourse were so often figures for subordinates more generally, Antissia's anger in the *Urania* offers Wroth a means for contemplating the proper response to the injustice of authority figures. As Elizabeth Spelman has argued, although subordinate groups are typically described as excessively emotional, their anger is not tolerated. Efficacious, defensible anger is considered the prerogative of those in positions of power, while the anger of subordinate groups is stigmatized as the hysteria and insolence that accompany disobedience and rebellion. Anger, in Spelman's analysis, implies an equality with its object, for "to be angry at him is to make myself, at least on this occasion, his judge—to have, and to express, a standard against which I assess his conduct. If he is in other ways regarded as my superior, when I get angry at him I at least on that occasion am regarding him as no more and no less than my equal. So my anger is in such a case an act of insubordination."[44] Writing in such an ideological context, Wroth registers the difficulty of confronting abuse in a culture that equates submission with virtue by depicting Antissia's anger at Amphilanthus' betrayal as a form of madness.

In the *Urania*, romance ideals have become sufficiently distorted that Amphilanthus can still be described as "the worthiest Knight" even as he deceives, seduces, and abandons a string of innocent women. Antissia's dilemma—she is expected not only to accept Amphilanthus' perfidy but also to pretend that it does not exist—presents both gendered and political hierarchies not as the product of rational choice or legal codes but as a willful embrace of fan-tasy. Antissia is treated as insane for even attempting to name Amphilanthus' injustice, and this disjunction between ideal and reality drives her mad. And although Antissia is eventually cured of her madness, the clumsy, uncontrolled poetry that she writes up until that point registers the impotence of the courtier who can express anger and opposition only indirectly in fiction and poetry. As Jocelyn Catty has pointed out, Antissia therefore risks the same accusations

43. Gwynne Kennedy, *Just Anger*, 3–4.
44. Spelman, "Anger and Insubordination," 266.

of incontinent, insane fury that Sir Edward Denny so famously flung at Wroth herself.[45]

Critics have typically treated Antissia's emotional excess as the embarrassing antitype of Pamphilia's patient discretion.[46] But Wroth takes pains to emphasize Antissia's initial beauty, virtue, sincerity, and charm. She thereby makes Antissia's inability effectively to confront Amphilanthus' duplicity the chief cause of her disintegration. Antissia is the first woman whom Amphilanthus courts in the *Urania*, and he initially makes a very public "shew of love" to her (2.30). Even after he has tired of her, he continues "to like her love, if only that his might be the more prized, wonne from so brave and passionate a Lady" (1.325). The political implications of such erotic cruelty on the part of a man who is also Holy Roman Emperor emerge in the vocabulary with which Antissia describes her predicament. In becoming Amphilanthus' "subject," she exchanges her innate "liberty" for a "bondage" that is all the more inescapable because she herself chooses it (1.321). Moreover, as Antissia recognizes, Amphilanthus' dishonesty and self-indulgence endanger the same romance ideals that he, as the romance's hero, should protect: "How is this change?" she wonders, "Can noblenesse bee, where deceit rules? Can justice be where cousonage governs? can freedome bee, where falsehood lives?" (1.113). As witnesses of Antissia's tortured confrontation with injustice, readers might well ask the same questions. Yet Antissia persists in her love even after this realization, becoming increasingly distraught over the disjunction between the fantasy of Amphilanthus that Pamphilia endorses and the reality of his self-serving duplicity.

Unfortunately, Antissia is largely isolated in her determination to point out the discrepancy between Amphilanthus' expected role as chivalric emperor and his actual behavior. Consequently, when she voices her accurate suspicion that Amphilanthus and Pamphilia have fallen in love, we see how swiftly candor can become madness. As Pamphilia's response illustrates, Tacitean duplicity or masochistic delusion are the only "sane" responses to royal corruption. Pamphilia, whom the *Urania*'s narrator designates "the most silent and discreetly retir'd of any Princess," privately declares that she is "tyranically tortured by love" for Amphilanthus almost immediately upon appearing in the romance, and her solitary suffering is the focus of the *Urania* as a whole (1.61, 62). Yet when Antissia questions her, Pamphilia does not only deny the object and extent of her passion. She also insists that Antissia's jealousy arises from a "troubled imagination" and urges her to "banish that Devill from you, which otherwise will daily increase new mischiefs" (1.95–96). Faced with Pamphilia's denial, Antissia has to accept sophistry as truth and to apologize for her own inquisitiveness, "taking the Princesse in her armes, protesting her

---

45. Catty, *Writing Rape*, 208. Numerous scholars have discussed the heated exchange between Denny and Wroth. See Weidemann, *Theatricality and Identity*, 209; Shannon Miller, "Textual Crimes and Punishment," 385–427; and Rosalind Smith, 88–92. The Denny–Wroth correspondence is available in *Poems of Lady Mary Wroth*.

46. See, for example, Shaver, "New Woman," 66; and Naomi Miller, *Changing the Subject*, 174–177.

life too little, to pay for requitall for this royal freedome she had found in her, and the favour received from her" (1.97).[47] Kennedy has argued that Pamphilia's attitude to Antissia reflects cultural strictures on female anger, which distinguish worthy from unworthy women based on the former's willingness to tolerate injustice.[48] I would add that such a readiness not only to accept but also to embrace mistreatment becomes the mark of the "virtuous" political subject as well.

As subsequent events reveal, however, if such self-abasement is not entirely sincere—based, like Pamphilia's, on a devotion so absolute that it has become part of one's own identity—it may easily become aggression. Antissia's humility does eventually turn to rage, demonstrating the fine line between love and hatred. In response to Amphilanthus' betrayal, "vowing to revenge, and no more to complaine," Antissia persuades the lovesick knight Dolorindus to murder Amphilanthus (1.111, 357–358). But this plot fails, showing that Antissia is helpless to prevent further injustice by rendering Amphilanthus "no longer able to deceive, or betray thyselfe or others" (1.113). Antissia's shame and the nearly universal censure she earns makes real the madness of which Pamphilia earlier accused her, with the result that the truth of Amphilanthus' betrayal is lost in the deranged behavior it produces.

Even if Antissia's story functions as a warning against excessive anger, the alternative represented by Pamphilia is just as bad. Venting her pain at her own betrayal at Amphilanthus' hands, Pamphilia acknowledges that his inconstancy is neither an anomaly nor an illusion, but an inveterate habit revealed by his treatment of Antissia: "once I remember I told him of his change when he left Antissia, he denyed it not, but excused it with having chosen better, and so to chuse was no fault, but it seemes the best is not found, unhappy I, must behold these dayes, and be left, who most unchangeably love him" (1.467). As Pamphilia acknowledges, Amphilanthus' claims of discernment are the cover for an egoistic appetite that will employ any means to satisfy itself. Yet even as she suffers additional betrayals, and even after admitting that Antissia has been subjected to similar mistreatment, Pamphilia characterizes Antissia's madness as a "just revenge and punishment on her" for the attempt to murder Amphilanthus (2.40). Pamphilia's equation of silent suffering with sincere love demonstrates how easily cultural ideals may become perverse practices, with martyrdom shading into masochism and selflessness becoming abjection.[49]

In Part Two of the *Urania*, begun in the early 1620s and never completed, Wroth endeavors to depict a political relation that can divest itself of sadomasochistic

---

47. As Catty has observed, Antissia may actually be a better reader of this situation insofar as she recognizes the destructive potential of Pamphilia's love melancholy (183, 200).

48. Kennedy, 122–131.

49. Lamb argues that the anger of Wroth's text emerges in its suppression (*Gender and Authorship*, 142–143, 185–187).

fantasy. Here, the *Urania* privileges compromised stability over idealized passion. But the romance's visions of moderation and mutuality are themselves erratic and short-lived: although Part One ends with a joyous reunion between Pamphilia and Amphilanthus, Part Two only separates them further. In Part One, Pamphilia vows that she will not change the object of her affection until she can "change [her] selfe, and have new creation and another soule" (1.459). But in the romance's manuscript continuation, she marries Rodomandro, the King of Tartaria, after Amphilanthus has wed the princess of Slavonia. Pamphilia's change in loyalty prominently rejects fantasies of inviolable erotic or political bonds, especially given her *verba de presenti* marriage to Amphilanthus at the beginning of Part Two. Wroth takes pains to affirm that the ceremony is binding even if dubiously legal, for "it was parformed butt nott as an absolute mariage, though as perfect as that, beeing onely an outward serimony of the church; this as absolute beefore God and as fast a tiing, for such a contract can nott bee broken by any lawe whatsoever" (2.45).[50] However "absolute" and "perfect" this marriage may be, neither party honors it for long. Both Amphilanthus and Pamphilia, believing themselves betrayed, precipitously follow Urania's earlier advice that "those with whom [a vow] is broken, are by the breach free to leave or choose againe where more staidnes may be found." In thwarting Pamphilia's desire for eternal union, the *Urania* also eschews the romance genre's conventional monogamy, and Part Two eventually replaces the customary reunion of lovers with a much queerer *ménage à trois* between Pamphilia, Amphilanthus, and Rodomandro. The addition of Rodomandro into the unhappy dyad of Pamphilia and Amphilanthus limits Pamphilia's devotion and, consequently, her pain. An inconsistency in the final pages of the manuscript, however, marks the difficulty of relinquishing normative ideals of perfect affinity, along with the disappointment that attends such compromise: Wroth announces Rodomandro's death, only to have him reappear in perfect health a page later (2.406–407).

In contrast to the overwhelming passion represented by Amphilanthus, Rodomandro offers Pamphilia a more sober model of conjugal affection. In response to his marriage proposal, Pamphilia charges him with a desire to dominate: "as your owne dainty expressions testify, your ambition is to conquer love. Since if I commaund in soveraine po[w]er, you must needs, if you winn mee, bee master of him. Soe I take this as your desire to have sole power over love, to make mee your instrument for itt" (2.271). In the context of her relationship with Amphilanthus, Pamphilia can only conceive of desire as an emotion of conquest and slavery. Rodomandro responds with an assurance of a less ambitious vision of marriage, replacing her notion of idolatry and hierarchy with one of moderation and balance: "Nor seeke I soverainitie over love, as that way to master, butt to bee a meanes for mee, poore mee, to bee accepted and receaved by you" (2.271). Pamphilia's second

---

50. Josephine Roberts discusses the status of *de presenti* contracts in the early seventeenth century ("Controversy Regarding Marriage," 109–132).

marriage is not a picture of blissful fulfillment, but it is freely "accepted." Even this
most constant of women has recognized the need to "limit" her own sacrifices: "For
now Pamphilia against her owne minde (yett nott constrain'd, for non durst attempt
that) had sayd '[aye],' though not in soule contented" (2.274). This reluctant consent is superficially similar to that of Limena (and recalls a number of other women
forced to marry against their wills throughout both parts of the *Urania*). Unlike her
precursors, however, Pamphilia is compelled by a jarring recognition that exclusive
union with Amphilanthus is unattainable, not by external pressures. Given that she
will not be "in soule contented" except with fantasy, her marriage to Rodomandro
is painful, but for different reasons than Limena's. This marriage forces her to sacrifice not only seductive dreams of untroubled monogamy with her first love but also
the masochistic gratification of continued suffering.

Though Pamphilia continues to adore Amphilanthus, her marriage to Rodomandro hardly inhibits this earlier relationship. The three form an unlikely trio
throughout the last third of Part Two, traveling, talking, and hunting together. Such
happiness is possible only because Amphilanthus has recognized that true affection
makes man and woman "youke fellows, noe superior, nor commanding power but
in love betweene united harts" (2.381). Their ability to command one another
through love, importantly, does not signify perfect liberty—they are still "youke
fellows"—but it does imply a relation of parity and reciprocity, not rule and subjection. Significantly, Pamphilia's affection for her husband is as sincere as that she feels
for her lover, even if it is less consuming. Rodomandro is crucial to Pamphilia's
eponymous country's victories over Persia, and he proves a loving husband
throughout Part Two. Not only does she bear Rodomandro a son, confirming the
sexual dimension of their relationship, but the genuine warmth of their union
emerges when Rodomandro comforts Pamphilia after her brother's death: "the
good Cham, did att the first newes bringing, hold her in his armes, buss her, and call
her his deer ducke, and intreat her to bear her brothers loss patiently for his sake"
(2.403). Because it withholds the expected fairytale ending, Wroth's peculiar
replacement of jealous, obsessive monogamy with more fluid and dispersed affective relations challenges naïve notions of the stability or singularity of either love or
sovereignty.

Pamphilia's surrender of her obsession signifies the importance and necessity of
a more nuanced view of sovereign obligation, embodied in her dual roles of woman
and ruler. The ironic detachment that permits balanced rule is expressed in the arch
counsel that the Marquise of Gargadia offers Pamphilia shortly after her second
marriage:

> Husbands are strange things if nott discreetly handled; they will bee in such commaund-
> ing hieght, if they may have their owne swinge, as wee must bee even wreched Vassalls.
> Noe, Madame, Noe, obay your husband with discresion and noe farder, and that will
> make him soe discreete as nott to tirannise. Which els they will doe fiercly (when they
> have the raines, like horses gett the bitt betweene their teeth and runn the full race or

course) of their owne humour, and the wives slavereye. Love itt self is nott to bee commaunded; hee is Emperiall and all soverainly governing. Butt as a Monarchy hath many lawes to be governed by, so is this a part. Therfor heere the lawe binds you only discreetly to respect and love your husband, nott to abound as loveres doe, United wholy butt to Loves sweetest tiranny. (2.281–282)

This description of mutual respect, which even Amphilanthus enthusiastically agrees is the "truthe" about love, evokes arguments for mixed monarchy that envision feminine counsel restraining masculine will. The Marquise's emphasis on discretion—variants of the word appear four times in her brief speech—indicates that the ability to determine the most appropriate course of action is tied to protection of a distinct identity, a separation made visible by her insistent "Noe, Madame, Noe." The above picture of a good marriage is precisely the opposite of the one offered by James I. Rather than fuse her will with that of her husband, the "discrete" wife will detach herself from such an idealized picture of erotic union. Such feminine disenchantment will, in turn, ensure that husbands are sufficiently "discrete" not to tyrannize.[51]

Significantly, "discreete" could also function in the sixteenth and seventeenth centuries as a noun, in which capacity it described a sage councilor or confidential advisor. By so insistently repeating this word, Wroth evokes an image of mixed rule, which depends on disjunction between king and councilor, husband and wife. Without this distance, injustice becomes indiscernible, its alleviation impossible. The speech's equestrian imagery further urges restriction of sovereign discretion. This classical analogy situates counsel and law as the guides of a potentially rebellious horse who, left unbridled, will abduct its rider and trample everything in its path. Dispute, as in the Marquise's speech, does not signify rebellion or revolution. Rather, opposition and debate help protect a lawful, reasonable state against potentially chronic incursions of monarchal will.

Recalling the "limits" that, according to Urania, separate virtuous constancy from vicious obsession, the Marquise urges Pamphilia not to "abound as loveres doe." Like Pamphilia, the wise subject must relinquish the expansive passion of idolatry, the ecstatic pain of masochism, in favor of a steady pursuit of justice. Wroth, however, does not simply replace a fantasy of erotic engulfment with one of sensible restraint. For the Marquise is one of the silliest characters to appear in the romance, and her roseate vision of judicious affective bonds may be conspicuously utopian by design. Even she is unable to separate proper from improper love, since her warning against abundance is troubled by the shifting characterization of love as respectful, all-encompassing, and tyrannical. In placing an argument for moderation

---

51. *OED*, 2d ed., s.v. "discreet." Masten discusses Wroth's pun on discreet/discrete in *Pamphilia to Amphilanthus* as a comment on Pamphilia's autonomy ("Circulation, Gender, and Subjectivity," 82).

in the mouth of such a shallow character, Wroth accentuates the incongruity between idealized narratives of rule—whether absolute or mixed—and the actual experience of power.

As the absence of a conclusion to the *Urania* indicates, Wroth's idea of "discresion" entails not a solution to political conflict, but a series of contingent, and necessarily imperfect, responses to the shifting seventeenth-century political terrain. And Wroth was not alone in her awareness that the allure of political masochism may vitiate attempts to respond to monarchal injustice. The ambivalence that characterizes Part Two of the *Urania* expresses a larger cultural apprehension about the threat that Stuart discourses of absolutism posed to the ancient constitution. Wroth's work suggests that even those families who were closest to the center of power shared the anxiety that cultural idealizations of unending fidelity would lead to just the sort of enslavement that the *Urania* depicts.

Wroth's literary representation of political anxiety, pessimistic as it is, itself constitutes a form of resistance to the blind devotion publicly urged by James I and Charles I. As we shall see, concerns about the dangers of such unswerving allegiance structure even the aesthetic form that modern scholars had most associated with royal absolutism: the Caroline masque. Wroth herself had danced in at least two Jacobean masques, Jonson's *The Masque of Blackness* and *The Masque of Beauty*, and members of the Sidney–Herbert circle continued to participate in these entertainments throughout the 1620s and 1630s. Yet these courtiers, as I have argued, were hardly simpering yes-men who indulged Stuart dreams of divine power. To the contrary, they were vocal about their unease regarding the practical and constitutional implications of certain royal policies. Their involvement in court masques, then, suggests that these festivities were more ideologically complex than they might seem. Rather than idealize royal absolutism, the erotic idioms in which court masques represent the sovereign–subject relation demonstrate the potential humiliation and dissolution of self that absolutism requires of its subjects—even as they acknowledge the appeal of such disempowerment.

CHAPTER 6

✿

"It Is Consent that Makes a Perfect Slave"

Love and Liberty in the Caroline Masque

For many contemporary and modern readers, the Caroline masque depicts pre-cisely the erotic engulfment and political absolutism that Wroth and others feared. Charles I, however, sought to distance himself from such an absolutist image, not to promote it. Like James and Elizabeth I before him, Charles lacked a standing army and a salaried bureaucracy. He therefore had to rely in large measure on his subjects' cooperation, a situation summarized in the oft-repeated common-place that English rulers' greatest source of strength is their people's love, which begets obedience and supply.[1] And Charles needed to preserve this fiction of mutual affection and voluntary service even more than his predecessors had. When he decided to rule without parliaments after 1629, Charles did not just renounce his only legitimate source of passing statutes and levying taxes; he also eschewed the most widely recognized indication that he governed with the consent of the whole realm. Although, as Conrad Russell has established, there was no such thing as "parliament in the seventeenth century," only "irregularly occurring events called Parliaments," these events offered an important symbol of the unity of king and people.[2] By calling a parliament, the king showed that, rather than tyrannically

---

1. See Russell, *Unrevolutionary England*, 89–109, esp. 91; Sharpe, *Personal Rule*, 604–605; Martin Butler, "Ben Jonson," 91–115, esp. 91–92; and Smuts, "Force, Love, and Authority," 32. Goldie describes the symbiotic relationship between local and central government ("Officeholding in Early Modern England").
2. See Russell, 5–8, 12–13, 20.

relying on a small circle of flatterers who would merely affirm his private impulses, he was willing to accept advice and criticism from the *commune concilium regni*.[3] The abrupt dissolution of parliament on March 2, 1629, upset such a narrative of cooperation and seemed to confirm rumors that Charles would emulate the absolutism of Continental monarchs who had done away with representative assemblies altogether.[4] A label pinned to Paul's Cross two months later claimed that Charles had lost the hearts of his people, ominously suggesting that his rule would require forces that he did not have, now that he had dispensed with the traditional forum for securing voluntary support.[5]

Performed, viewed, and read by the subjects on whose compliance the administration of personal government relied, the masques of the 1630s seek to counter this narrative of betrayal and disaffection. These masques' resolute idealization of desire had both practical and ideological functions in the decade during which Charles ruled without parliament. As Charles well knew, without recourse to parliaments, his ability to raise funds and administer government required the aid and participation of aristocratic courtiers, City officials, and country magistrates, many of them the same men who had been his loudest critics in the 1620s.[6] To insist on absolute royal prerogative unfettered by law would have alienated many of the persons whose cooperation allowed the personal rule to function. So rather than celebrate a theory of extralegal monarchal absolutism, as early critics of the masques supposed, Caroline entertainments cultivated the languages of love and marriage to profess that Charles ruled by the laws of the land and the consent of his subjects— or, more accurately, that the affective bond between king and political nation was sufficient protection against royal excess and abuse, even without parliamentary intervention.[7] In Charles' own account, the late parliaments had been led by

3. Colclough analyzes the concepts of counsel and freedom of speech in Stuart parliamentary thought (*Freedom of Speech*, 120–195).

4. On rumors and threats that Charles would permanently dispense with parliament, see Hirst, *Authority*, 36, 41; and Kenyon, ed., *Stuart Constitution*, 28, 52. Historians have disagreed as to the extent to which Charles himself deserves blame for the eruption of war. The literature here is quite copious, but the best recent example of the argument that Charles' mishandling of political crisis led to war and regicide is Cust, *Charles I*. For a defense of Charles' character and political choices, see Kishlansky, "Case of Mistaken Identity."

5. Sharpe, *Personal Rule*, 58.

6. Sharpe, for instance, cites the elevation of such men as Thomas Wentworth, William Noy, and Dudley Digges in the government of the 1630s (*Personal Rule*, xviii, 38, 134, 706–707). Russell notes that many members of Charles' Privy Council persisted in their parliamentary convictions throughout the decade (1–29, esp. 26). See also Cust and Hughes, "After Revisionism," 4–5.

7. Critics who have described Caroline entertainments as absolutist propaganda include Orgel and Strong, *Inigo Jones*; Orgel, *Illusion of Power*; Kogan, *Hieroglyphic King*; and J. Newman, "Inigo Jones." As Martin Butler has argued, the picture of royal absolutism drawn by literary critics is at odds with the limited monarchy described by historians of the period (*Stuart Court Masque*, 8–33).

"turbulent and ill-affected spirits" who hoped to "cast a blindness upon the good affections of our people" in order to alter England's fundamental laws.[8] By thwarting this parliamentary power grab, Charles claimed, his personal rule in fact protected the traditional balance of government by allowing a more immediate relation between king and subjects.

But even as Caroline masques celebrate this union of hearts and minds, they also explore its more unsettling implications. The queerness that characterizes eros also subtends the cool Neoplatonism of Caroline allegory, so the affective idioms that asserted the virtue of Charles' rule also invariably registered the ambivalence it inspired. As Kevin Sharpe has aptly put it, "love was the metaphor, the medium, through which political comment and criticism were articulated in Caroline England."[9] Insofar as they exhibit the sadism and abjection, the obsession and delusion, that haunt eros in the texts I have discussed thus far, Caroline masques work against the king's own agenda, which was to appear a reasonable and balanced monarch who was being assaulted by ambitious members of parliament. As Busirane's masque in *The Faerie Queene* demonstrates to appalling effect, love is not only the tender, spiritualized emotion celebrated on the Whitehall stage but also includes impulses that are predatory, cringing, and delusional. Accordingly, the mutual love that notionally distinguishes *rex* from *tyrannos* may be similarly troubled by the violence, fantasy, and abjection that turn subjects into slaves.

In light of the longer history of royal entertainments, it should be no surprise that Caroline masques would, to borrow Sharpe's terms, deploy the humanist tactic of fusing criticism and compliment. Numerous readers of Tudor progresses, pageants, and tournaments have demonstrated that these forerunners of the Stuart masque provided a forum for public dialogue between monarch and subject. As Richard McCoy argues, the spectacles staged for the Henrician and Edwardian courts advertised aristocratic influence and power even as they glorified prince and country; under Mary I, chivalric pageants worked to contain antagonisms between English and Spanish factions at court. These shows thus performed a "chivalric compromise" in which ambitious nobles could critique and advise the crown at the same time that they affirmed their loyalty. Rather than celebrate royal dominance, as some readers of Tudor chivalry have supposed, Tudor entertainments staged a dialogue between the competing agendas of ruler and ruled.[10] Particularly during the reign of Elizabeth, such courtiers as Leicester, Sidney, and Essex used entertainments as fora in which to urge particular policies on the queen. As Hester Lee-Jeffries has shown, for instance, the culminating pageants in Elizabeth's coronation

---

8. "His Majesty's Declaration to all his Loving Subjects, of the Causes which moved him to Dissolve the last Parliament," March 10, 1629, in Kenyon, ed., *Stuart Constitution*, 71–72.

9. Sharpe, *Criticism*, 39.

10. McCoy, *Rites*, 28–32, 18–20. For more conservative readings of court spectacle, see Yates, *Astraea*, 88–111; and Strong, *Cult of Elizabeth*.

entry insisted on the Protestant and communal nature of English government by advising that the successful ruler would look to Scripture alone for religious guidance and would seek and heed counsel.[11] Several other scholars have read entertainments from throughout Elizabeth's reign in light of what Susan Frye has called a "competition for representation" between queen and courtiers regarding issues like foreign policy, religious affairs, the royal marriage, and the threat posed by Mary Stuart.[12]

When James came to the English throne, he initially followed the Elizabethan custom of holding public tournaments, events that bespoke his court's ties to Elizabethan England.[13] But, as we have seen, James wished to promote monarchal authority, not compromise, and the dialogic form of Elizabethan entertainments, along with the Protestant nationalism associated with their chivalry, held little appeal for him. Court spectacle thus saw significant change in the early seventeenth century. Performances moved indoors, where they were viewed by a much smaller and more elite audience; the neo-medieval chivalry of Tudor masques was replaced by classical set designs and mythological themes; spectacles focused as much on displaying the English monarch's strength to a European audience as on mediating conflicts within the English court; James, unlike Elizabeth, did not participate in courtly performances; and Inigo Jones' introduction of the perspective stage made the king the central spectator, and the only one who saw the masque perfectly.[14] To be sure, Jacobean masques were still capable of registering disagreement and criticism—the most notorious example is Jonson's *Neptune's Triumph for the Return of Albion*, which celebrated the failure of Charles Stuart's projected match with the Spanish Infanta. Nonetheless, the performances staged for the Jacobean court tended to depict the monarch as a distant and absolute force of benevolent authority, not a part of an ongoing conversation.

The Caroline masque sought to represent a more cooperative and loving relationship between monarch and people. Unlike James, Charles danced in his own masques, demonstrating his direct relationship and active involvement with his subjects. Moreover, a number of courtiers who opposed Charles' policies—some of whom would go on to fight for parliament in the civil wars—were prominent participants. Caroline spectacles also depicted gender relations quite differently

11. Lees-Jeffries, "Location as Metaphor," 65–85.
12. Susan Frye, *Elizabeth I*, 62. Along with McCoy's book-length analysis of court ritual (*Rites*), see Collinson, "Religion and Politics in the Progress of 1578"; Heale, "Loyal Catholicism and Lord Montague's Entertainment"; and Heaton, "The Harefield Festivities." The most comprehensive collections of Elizabethan entertainments remain Nichols, *Progresses and Public Processions of Queen Elizabeth*; and Chambers, *Elizabethan Stage*. See also Wilson's shorter critical edition, *Entertainments for Elizabeth I*.
13. See Martin Butler, *Stuart Court Masque*, 73.
14. For these changes, see Orgel, *Illusion of Power*, 10–14; Smuts, "Political Failure of Stuart Cultural Patronage," 183; Prescott, "Stuart Masque"; and Martin Butler, *Stuart Court Masque*, 1, 14, 29, 74.

from their Jacobean predecessors. As Martin Butler has argued, Jacobean masques typically represented the relation between men and women as inherently conflicted, affirming royal, masculine power through the defeat of feminine disobedience. By contrast, Caroline masques depicted the mutual passion and conjugal harmony of Charles and his queen as a model for the relation between king and subject.[15] These changes, I propose, worked to protect Charles from charges of absolutism by harking back to an Elizabethan tradition of compromise and dialogue between sovereign and people. Yet because love itself was understood to include cruel and self-destructive impulses, the eroticism of the Caroline masque could critique, as well as celebrate, sovereign authority.

By reading Caroline masques through the lens of early modern erotic discourse, then, we can appreciate how artfully these entertainments expose the anxieties produced by the subjection they represent. Most prominently, by taking the royal marriage as their paradigmatic allegory for the harmonious union of king and subject, Caroline masques highlighted a central cause of the fear that a self-indulgent king would abuse the trust of the political nation.[16] As the decade of personal rule wore on, Henrietta Maria was increasingly seen as the people's rival, not their representative. Given the long-standing identification of Catholicism with foreignness and arbitrary rule, the queen's religion provided a particular focal point for the fear that in the absence of the constraining influence of parliament, Charles would destroy English Protestantism and liberty.[17] Many were unhappy with the religious concessions granted in the 1625 Anglo-French marriage treaty, and Henrietta Maria only increased distrust by refusing to attend Charles' Protestant coronation ceremony, learn English, or curb her displays of Catholicism.[18] To make matters worse, Henrietta Maria inspired a number of English courtiers to convert to Roman Catholicism, and her marriage to Charles was hailed by Europe's Catholic powers as the best hope for England's return to the old religion.[19] Even the queen consort's name—she was most typically addressed as Mary or Maria—suggested, in Lucy

---

15. *Stuart Court Masque*, 133–143, 151–153.

16. For discussions of the allegorical significance of the royal marriage, see, for instance, Sharpe, *Criticism*, 183–184; Veevers, *Images of Love and Religion*, 4–5, 72–74; and Wikander, *Princes to Act*, 94–147.

17. The queen's brazen Catholicism, and especially the public conversions of members of her court, not only alarmed such English subjects as Pym and Prynne but also antagonized Charles and infuriated Laud. See Veevers, 70–90; Sharpe, *Personal Rule*, 285, 304–306; White, *Henrietta Maria*, 21–24, 30–33; and McRae, "Seditious Libel," 190.

18. While Henrietta Maria's biographers disagree as to the extent of her role in English history, they generally concur in seeing her unpopularity as the combined effect of her stubborn Catholicism and French hauteur. See Veevers; Haynes, *Henrietta Maria*; Oman, *Henrietta Maria*; Wedgwood, *King's Peace*; Bone, *Henrietta Maria*; Dolan, *Whores*, chapter 3; and White. On reactions to the marriage treaty, see Hirst, *Authority*, 137; and Sharpe, *Personal Rule*, 8.

19. Bailey, *Staging the Old Faith*, 17–48, 89–131.

Hutchinson's words, "some kind of fatality" in a country whose luck with Marys had not been good.[20] This hostility grew in proportion to Henrietta Maria's intimacy with and influence upon Charles, which began after the assassination of Buckingham in 1628, increased after the death of Lord Treasurer Weston in 1635, and reached its zenith with Strafford's execution and the outbreak of civil war.[21] By 1640, Charles' devotion to his wife was widely viewed as infidelity to his subjects. Accordingly, the uxoriousness celebrated in the masques evinced not analogical mutuality and moderation in the political arena, but Charles' choice to indulge his private desires rather than perform his public duties.[22]

Contemporary critics of the Caroline masque were well aware that the genre went beyond royal self-deceit to propagate what Lauren Shohet describes as a "politics of awe."[23] Charles' detractors routinely appealed to the masques' own language of desire to charge that these shows would lead English subjects to follow their king in succumbing to the allures of Continental popery and absolutism. William Prynne, for instance, worried that their "effeminate mixt Dancing, lascivious Pictures, wanton Fashions, Face painting," and "lascivious effeminate Musicke" would "seduce" Protestants from the true faith, while Milton would persistently attack "the superficial actings of State" that allow a monarch "to pageant himself up and down in progress among the perpetual bowings and cringings of an abject people, on either side deifying and adoring him for nothing done that can deserve it."[24]

---

20. *Memoirs*, 70. Charles himself, according to Hutchinson, preferred to call Henrietta Maria "Marie" (70), and Ben Jonson consistently addresses the queen as "Mary" in his verses. Henrietta Maria was both revered and reviled for her association with the cult of the Virgin: in *The Popish Royal Favourite* Prynne satirized the comparison between the queen's intercessions for Catholics and the Virgin's intercessions for humanity made by the author of *Maria Triumphans* (Veevers, 94–108). The historical resonances of the queen's name were likewise exploited by civil war pamphlets warning that England would "suffer greater tortures under Queen Mary the Second, than ever the Martyrs did under Queen Mary the First" (quoted in White, 146–147). And a seventeenth-century biography notes that during her first passage to England, Henrietta Maria encountered "the same rough and tempestuous weather which Mary Queen of Scots found when she was wafted over from Calais" (*The History of the Thrice Illustrious Princess*, 28).

21. See Russell, 94–96; White, 11–20, 30, 60–90; and Kenyon, *Stuart England*, 136–140. Martin Butler (*Theatre and Crisis*, 26–35, and *Stuart Court Masque*, 147) and Smuts ("Puritan Followers of Henrietta Maria") emphasize the complexity of Henrietta Maria's allegiances and her appeal for the pro-French, Protestant party at court until the late 1630s.

22. This anxiety would continue to assert itself in both the Long Parliament's order that Charles was "not to entertain any Advice, or Mediation, from the Queen" ("Declaration to the King of Causes and Remedies: February 18, 1642," *Journals of the House of Commons*, 2:443) and the Privy Council's complaints about the amount of time Charles and Henrietta Maria spent together (Sharpe, *Personal Rule*, 171–174). For an analysis of the gendered dimensions of the anxieties about the royal marriage, see Dolan, *Whores*, chapter three.

23. "Localizing Caroline Masques," 78.

24. Prynne's words are quoted by Veevers, 90; Milton, *The Readie and Easie Way, CP*, 7:426). Hausted also censured the masques' spectacles as dangerously "ravishing" (see Orgel and Strong, 51).

Caroline masques, however, do not just labor to produce what Milton calls "a civil kinde of Idolatry."[25] They also scrutinize the pathologies that such idealization inspires. Since it can bring both pleasure and pain, transcendence and humiliation, love offered an ideal vehicle for considering the problems of liberty and consent that vexed many in the decade without parliaments. As Spenser's *Faerie Queene* and Wroth's *Urania* demonstrate, what is experienced as ennobling love may in fact be debasing infatuation. In its political dimension this signifies the erotic enslavement and self-deceit that, according to writers from la Boétie to Milton to Algernon Sidney, is the true prop of tyranny.[26]

Given the centrality of love as both analogy for and basis of political commitment, it is surprising that the Caroline masques' erotic structures and mythologies have attracted little study, with many critics accepting the evaluations of Prynne and Milton and so treating the language of love as propaganda of the crudest order.[27] A number of recent scholars have emphasized the complex and contestatory dimensions of masque design, performance, and publication.[28] This work has shown how court masques staged a conversation between Charles and his influential subjects about both specific questions of policy and more general constitutional questions. I would like to expand on this post-revisionist analysis to show how a theoretical focus on the psychology of love in these entertainments can further illuminate the experience of politics in the Caroline period. In this chapter, I consider the ways in which several masques performed and published in the 1630s examine erotic desire as both a source of and an analogy for political authority and consent in the decade of personal rule. While I recognize that the architectural and performative aspects of Caroline masques were crucial to their meaning, with the dances lasting far longer than the songs and the costumes and scenery undeniably shaping their messages, I focus primarily on masques as they appeared in print for several reasons. First, it is in this format that they reached a wide audience that, as Shohet has established, included politically aware readers from a range of classes,

---

25. *Eikonoklastes, CP*, 3:343.

26. Like such Huguenot and republican theorists, Algernon Sidney attributes tyranny not to force but to deluded consent ("Of Love," in *The Essence of Algernon Sidney's Work on Government*, 271–287, and *Discourses*, 1.3, 5, 11 and 2.8, 11, 19, 25). Silver offers a detailed analysis of Sidney's criticism of royal charisma ("Sidney's *Discourses*").

27. Parry, for instance, sees Charles' adaptation of Henrietta Maria's interest in courtly love as an attempt to replace political debate with a vision of "a benevolent love at the heart of a happy nation," but he does not discuss the darker implications of the masques' erotic idiom (*Golden Age Restor'd*, 189).

28. See, for instance, Norbrook, "Reformation of the Masque"; Martin Butler, *Theatre and Crisis*, 1–9, 35, "Politics and the Masque," "Courtly Negotiations," and *Stuart Court Masque*; Sharpe, *Criticism*, 26–29, 180, 192–196, 291–294; Bevington and Holbrook, "Introduction"; Craig, "Jonson"; Wright, "Civic and Courtly Ceremonies"; and Ravelhofer, "Unstable Movement Codes." Kroll has shown that since the principles of architectural design that Jones implemented were humanistic and Ciceronian, they visually support customary and legal limits on monarchal prerogative (*Restoration Drama*, 122–168).

professions, and ideological stances.[29] Second, the printed versions of masques typically include notes, commentary, and even songs that were not accessible to the audience at Whitehall. The addition of this extra-performative material to printed versions registers an awareness on the part of their authors that masques might speak to this wider audience in a register not appropriate to or available in private performances.[30] This material also indicates that the monarchs for whom masques were notionally written had less control over their content and interpretation than many contemporary and modern critics have assumed. The topical commentary that fills Caroline masques also translates into more general theories of political affect and negotiation. Readers could return to these masques and reread them in light of changing circumstances and not only in their immediate moments, thereby revising the texts' political significance.[31] Like the romances from which they derive and whose perversions they rehearse, these masques reveal that subjection may itself be pleasurable. They thereby situate readers' own insurgent desires and delusions, not the king's coercive powers, as the true threat to English religion and liberty.

The most consistent and discerning critic of the ravishing potential of masques was neither a puritan nor a parliamentarian. He was the person most responsible for defining and perfecting the conventions and structures of these court entertainments: Ben Jonson. Jonson's masques, like his poems and plays, acknowledge the danger that, as his friend John Selden put it, "the flattering language of lord and king" and the "obsequious" deification of monarchy can make men "servile" and politically "idolatrous" and therefore imperil liberty.[32] Yet even as they suggest that

---

29. Shohet, "Masque in/as Print" and "On 1630s Masques." See also Sharpe, *Criticism*, 191–193.

30. Martin Butler notes that while non-courtiers like members of the gentry and Inns of Court had access to masque performance, the venues in which masques were performed could accommodate no more than 1,200 spectators, a physical limitation that enforced a sense of exclusivity. By contrast, James Shirley's *The Triumph of Peace*, which went through three separate impressions of several thousand copies each, may have been the period's most widely read literary text (*Stuart Court Masque*, 34–62, 308–310).

31. As Lesser has shown, literary works could acquire new meanings to fit new situations (*Renaissance Drama and the Politics of Publication*, 81–114).

32. Quoted in Worden, "Ben Jonson," 74. Among Jonson's closest friends were Selden and William Camden, who was his teacher and mentor at Westminster School and to whom Jonson attributes "All that I am in arts, all that I know" (*Epigrams* XIV, 2, in *Complete Poems*; all references to Jonson's lyrics will be to this edition). These men consistently described honest counsel and common law as the source of royal authority. Jonson explicitly anatomizes the relationship between tyranny and flattery in *Sejanus* and *Catiline*, and more subtly locates its origins in private ambition and desire in *Eastward Ho!* (for which he was briefly imprisoned), *Epicoene*, and, most horrifically, *Volpone*. Scholars who have noted Jonson's affinity with Camden and Selden include Martin Butler, "Late Jonson," esp. 170–172; and Worden, "Ben Jonson." For discussions of Camden's politics, see Sharpe, *Criticism*, 17, and *Personal Rule*, 655–657; and Burgess, *Politics*, 159. For Selden's views, see Greenberg, *Radical Face*, 147–151.

the way to avoid such a cycle of delusion and hypocrisy is to examine one's own motivations and desires, Jonson's Caroline entertainments admit the difficulty of doing so. Long before Henrietta Maria made Neoplatonism fashionable, Jonson described the relative value of the masque's poetry and its spectacle by drawing on a philosophic system in which physical beauty, as an emanation of spiritual goodness, enraptures its beholders and so inspires them to pursue the ideal truth of which it is mere copy or advertisement.[33] According to Jonson, the poetic dimension of the masque is its soul, the architecture its body. It is usual to read this definition in the context of Jonson's rivalry with Inigo Jones, but the anxiety that external appearance will supplant interior reality is also part of Jonson's larger view of the poet's intellectual project.[34] The ultimate achievement, for Jonson, is to resist the desire to conflate beauty with goodness and learn to "think life, a thing but lent," as he insists in any number of poems whose subjects are united in their contempt for "spectacles, and shows."[35]

But Jonson knows that this idealized order can break down with disturbing ease, as is evident from the oft-quoted Preface to his 1606 *Hymenaei*:

> It is a noble and just advantage that the things subjected to understanding have of those which are objected to sense that the one sort are but momentary and merely taking, the other impressing and lasting. Else the glory of all these solemnities had perished like a blaze and gone out in the beholders' eyes. So short lived are the bodies of all things in comparison of their souls. (1–7)[36]

Here, the unannounced chiasmus creates a syntactical disorder that briefly tempts us—against all convention and logic—to rate the understanding as "momentary and merely taking" the senses as "impressing and lasting." As if to stress the prevalence of such misprision, Jonson goes on to concede that "bodies ofttimes have the ill luck to be sensually preferred"—we are subject to the allure of the physical and so burden it with a significance that it is too frail and transient to sustain (8). This awareness of misplaced value compels Jonson obsessively to warn his readers against an excessively naïve hermeneutics, begging those "That take'st my book in

33. Veevers describes the sources and politics of Henrietta Maria's Neoplatonism (14–47). For discussions of Renaissance Neoplatonism, see Wind, *Pagan Mysteries*; Cassirer, Kristeller, and Randall, eds., *Renaissance Philosophy of Man*; and Jayne, *Plato in Renaissance England*.

34. Martin Butler ("Late Jonson," 176) and Gordon ("The Intellectual Setting") both describe the ongoing rivalry between Jonson and Jones.

35. *The Forest* III ("To Sir Robert Wroth"), 107, and XIII ("Epistle. To Katherine, Lady Aubigny"), 65. See also *Epigrams* XLV, *The Forest* IV and XII, *Underwoods* LXI, LXX, LXXVII, LXXXIII, and *Miscellaneous Poems* XXIX.

36. From *Ben Jonson: The Complete Masques*. All citations of Jonson's masques will be from this edition, unless otherwise noted.

hand, / To read it well: that is, to understand."[37] And such interpretive rigor has erotic, as well as intellectual, consequences, for it enables readers to examine their own projections and desires before they devote themselves to anything, much as Jonson himself promises Selden to "turn a sharper eye / Upon myself, and ask to whom, and why, / and what I write."[38] Awareness of one's own motives, however difficult to achieve, is the foundation of both private and public virtue.

For Jonson, it is a moral and political duty to resist the human propensity to mistake surface for substance, desire for reality. According to his most notorious indictment of masques, the "Expostulation with Inigo Jones," the Caroline court has failed dismally in this regard.[39] In the "Expostulation," Jonson denigrates not just the "transitory devices" he dismissed in the Preface to *Hymenaei* (18), but the self-serving credulity with which Jones and his fans have accepted "Painting and carpentry" as "the soul of masque" ("Expostulation," 50). For Jonson, this situation reveals not only Jones' own egoism and chicanery, but the pathology of a "money-get, mechanic age" ("Expostulation," 52):

> O shows, shows, mighty shows!
> The eloquence of masques! What need of prose,
> Or verse, or sense to express immortal you?
> You are the spectacles of state! 'Tis true
> Court hieroglyphics, and all arts afford
> In the mere perspective of an inch board!
> You ask no more than certain politic eyes,
> Eyes that can pierce into the mysteries
> Of many colours, read them, and reveal
> Mythology there painted on slit deal! (39–49)

By stubbornly treating such "spectacles of state" as divine "mysteries," the Caroline court has gone beyond the mere folly that Jonson attacks in his satires on dimwits like Sir Cod, Sir Luckless Woo-All, or Fine Lady Would-be, or the naïve misreading of which he admits himself guilty of in his Epistle to Selden.[40] Jonson only emphasizes their folly by stressing that these shows are constructed of "inch boards" and "slit deals," cheap, thin wooden materials meant to last no longer than the performances themselves. The credulity of the "politic eyes"—calculated acceptance of

---

37. Epigram I, 1–2. Jonson expresses such anxiety about misinterpretation, itself almost inevitable in a world devoted to the superficial, in his Dedication of the *Epigrams* to Pembroke and in *Miscellaneous Poems* II, III, VIII, and, perhaps most famously, XIV, which reminds those encountering Shakespeare's First Folio to "look / Not on his picture, but his book" (9–10).

38. *Underwoods* XIV, 23–25.

39. See *Epigrams* XIX, XX, XLVI, and LXII, and *Underwoods* XIV.

40. *Underwoods* XIV.

fictions—is the mark of the parasitic combination of servility and self-promotion that makes impossible the frank, self-sacrificing counsel that benefits both ruler and realm.

The absence of loyal criticism may have seemed especially troubling in the early years of Charles' personal rule, with the recent breakdown of the 1629 parliament and Charles' failed foreign expeditions appearing to expose the king's weakness both at home and abroad. In 1630 the Venetian ambassador at court had described England as "enfeebled" by a "King . . . out of sympathy with his people, unequal to governing by himself and his councils distracted by private interests."[41] In both his masques and his poems dedicated to the king, Jonson tries to correct this destructive confusion of private interest with public duty by praising the monarch for virtues he should cultivate. In *Underwoods* LXIV, "To our Great and Good K[ing] Charles on His Anniversary Day" (1629), for instance, Jonson facetiously wonders

> . . . when had great Britain greater cause
> Than now, to love the sovereign, and the laws?
> When you that reign, are her example grown,
> And what are bounds to her, you make your own? (7–10)

In the context of what many had seen as Charles' recent attacks on English law—the forced loan, the arbitrary imprisonment of the Five Knights who refused to pay it, and the alteration of court records and the original Answer to the Petition of Right—Jonson's compliment must ring either cynical or ironic.[42] The poem to Charles insists that greatness and goodness, sovereignty and law, should be identical. But it also acknowledges that they may not be. The relation between king and mimetic, feminized country should be one of mutual self-restraint, which Charles himself has not yet achieved.[43]

Chloridia, Jonson's last masque performed at court, registers the difficulty of achieving such mutuality by tracing the complex relationship between chastity, desire, and rape. Although critics have generally seen Jonson's final entertainments as the most uncomplicated celebrations of royalty in his oeuvre, Jonson demonstrates the complexities inherent in the erotic vehicles he employs.[44] In *Chloridia,* performed February 22, 1631, Jonson equates the political disruption that Charles attributed to "factious spirits" in the 1629 parliament with erotic degeneracy, political harmony with true affection, but he also makes it difficult to distinguish

---

41. Quoted in Smuts, "Force, Love, and Authority," 33.
42. Burgess discusses in detail the implications of these acts for the common law (*Politics,* 179–211).
43. For the gendered significance and contradictions of Jonson's ethical ideal more generally, see Silver, "Duplicity of Gender."
44. See, for instance, Craig, 177; Kogan, 114; and Martin Butler, "Late Jonson," 176.

rapacious, illicit lust from mutual, married love. Here, the Ovidian epigram with which Jonson begins the printed text, "*Unius tellus ante coloris erat*" ("Till then, the earth was of one color") aligns the accession of Charles with the transforming power of Zephyrus, whose ravishment of the virginal nymph Chloris transformed her to Flora, goddess of the flowers. The compliment seems obvious enough: under Charles, England has similarly blossomed. But the Ovidian myth that Jonson takes as his source renders its celebration of Caroline rule far more ambiguous, not least because earth's foisoning originates in rape. As Flora's monologue in the *Fasti* makes clear, she initially resisted union with Zephyrus. It was only after her stronger assailant pursued, overpowered, and penetrated her that she agreed to marry him and became queen of flowers, delighting in eternal spring.[45]

By situating rape as the origin of marriage, rather than its opposite, the *Fasti* reveals the vexed nature of the consent that notionally distinguishes the two. Although Chloris' initial resistance was futile, her subsequent acceptance was necessary to legitimize Zephyrus' advances. Accordingly, her retroactive consent, like that of Amoret in *The Faerie Queene*, identifies Chloris/Flora as both innocent victim of Zephyrus' desire and guilty partner in it. Neoplatonic philosophy—most famously illustrated in Botticelli's sumptuous *Primavera*—saw the transformation of the terrified, fleeing Chloris into the satisfied, pregnant Flora as an expression of beauty's ability to effect the union of chastity and love.[46] Such conflation of physical rape and spiritual rapture implies that the former is at once felicitous (because it transforms frigidity to fertility) and impossible (because women themselves invariably consent to such violation, if only unconsciously or belatedly). This assumption that women share the blame—or the credit—for even coerced defloration may explain the alternative tradition of regarding Flora as, in the words of E.K. in *The Shepheardes Calendar*, "a notorious whore."[47] According to this legend, the Ovidian myth had been invented to conceal the fact that the Roman celebration of spring, the Floralia, had in reality been funded by a wealthy prostitute.[48]

Since the conceit of *Chloridia* is that England is as fortunate in its union with Charles as was Chloris/Flora in her marriage to Zephyrus, Ovid's troubling synthesis of coercion and consent registers the dilemma of subjects whose acceptance of Caroline policy is both essential and irrelevant. Jonson, in effect, acknowledges these problematic implications of the *Fasti* by banishing Flora herself from the masque. The very title of the masque insists on its distance from the public, notoriously licentious Floralia described in the *Fasti*, and the name "Flora" never appears

---

45. Ovid, *Fasti*, 5.201–212.
46. See Wind, 115–117.
47. For discussion of the problematic ideological association of rape and chastity in the *Fasti*, see Sanchez, "Libertinism and Romance," 443–448.
48. See Held, "Flora, Goddess and Courtesan," 1:201–216, 2:72–74. As Held shows, Renaissance courtesans were frequently painted in the guise of Flora.

at all in the text. Instead, the masque celebrates the innocent, intact Chloris, who has earned her title as goddess of the flowers not by assenting to Zephyrus' demands but by a "general council of the gods" (6). In addition to replacing the pulls of individual desire with the decree of a divine assembly, the masque represents Zephyrus as a "mild," "plump boy," hardly the rapacious deity of Ovidian myth (25–26). Ideally, Charles' governance would be similarly innocent.

Jonson's own foregrounding of the *Fasti*, however, hints that despite the prim change of title, the Chloridia, or "Rites to Chloris and her Nymphs," may actually be the Floralia. In addition to Jonson's textual allusions to his suggestively unwholesome model, Jones' designs for Henrietta Maria's costume align the queen not with Botticelli's frightened, virginal Chloris but with the slyly smiling, pregnant Flora. Henrietta Maria surely would have been aware of this sartorial quotation—the Medici family owned Botticelli's work—and may even have encouraged it, unaware of its residual significances.[49] The precise relation between Chloris, Flora, Henrietta Maria, and the English subject—all potential objects of sovereign will—is as unstable and fluid as that between rape and seduction, coercion and consent. The ambiguous status of Flora's desire explains Ovid's assertion that "a rakish stage fits Flora well; she is not, believe me she is not, to be counted among your buskined goddesses" (5.347–348) and Flora's own sly admission that "nocturnal license befits my revels" (5.366–367). Indeed, the very flowers that Jonson's masque takes as signs of peace and harmony are in the *Fasti* sprung of the blood of such egoistic, furious, rejected, treacherous, self-castrating, and evasive lovers as Narcissus, Crocus, Attics, and Adonis (5.223–228). Much as the revelry of the Caroline masque may be just as decadent as that of the Floralia, the voluntary, chaste love the masque celebrates may be as coercive and compromised as that imagined in the *Fasti*.

In *Chloridia*, Jonson consigns the darker aspects of the conjugal passion he celebrates to the antimasque. Here, Cupid, insulted that the other gods have not included him in their "council" or their "guild," descends to Hell to "make a party 'gainst the gods / And set heaven, earth and hell at odds" (87–88). The Hell described by the Dwarf Postillion in the first antimasque, however, is not a site of loss and agony. Instead, it resembles the festivity and indulgence of the Floralia— or, more recently, the Jacobean masque. According to the Dwarf's report, "Love hath been . . . so entertained by Pluto and Proserpine and all the grandees of the place as it is there perpetual holiday, and a cessation of torment granted and proclaimed forever" (101–104). As a result, Tantalus "is fallen to his fruit," Ixion "is loosed from his wheel and turned dancer," Sisyphus "is grown a master bowler," the furies "are at a game called ninepins or kayles," and Danaus' daughters have "made bonfires" of their tubs (106, 110, 112–113, 116, 120). In short "Never was there such freedom of sport! . . . All is turned triumph there" (121). The combination of

---

49. See Veevers, 128. Sharpe notes that the preface to *Chloridia* suggests the close involvement of Charles and Henrietta Maria in the masques invention (*Criticism*, 186).

courtly and rural pastimes equates the Sunday sports that puritans condemned and that James (and later Charles) encouraged with the festivities at court. Both are meant to distract their participants from looking carefully at their own motives.

Having escaped from Hell, Cupid leads a series of antimasques in which seasonal change—represented here for the first time on an indoor English stage—figured the vicissitudes of desire.[50] The antidote is married chastity, embodied by Juno, by whose "providence" "the enamoured Spring" is "Sent to quench Jealousy, and all those powers / Of Love's rebellious war" (164, 169–170). This victory appears, as Suzanne Gossett has argued, to assert the power of marriage to contain the riotous, infernal impulses embodied by Cupid.[51] Certainly as Chloris, Henrietta Maria represents eros purged of all of its more intense qualities and reduced to a chaste, uncomplicated affection. But as the Ovidian myth that governs *Chloridia* insists, such a clear opposition between rape and marriage, passion and reason, is difficult to draw. Jonson's meditation on the relation between seduction and force, Floris from Chlora, acknowledges that the union between king and subject may be equally compromised, merely sanctioning the irresistible royal will that it should temper.

Jonson's final court masques ironically undermine their own celebration of conjugal love by questioning the distinction between seduction and force, rape and marriage. By contrast, Aurelian Townshend's *Tempe Restored* evokes a Foxean tradition that makes rape itself impossible, insisting instead that virtue cannot be lost without one's own consent. Performed on February 14, 1632, Townshend's masque demonstrates that feminine charm, which can secure psychological contentment, is a far more powerful means of securing obedience and allegiance than masculine force, which can generate only external compliance. *Tempe Restored* develops this argument through the myth of Circe. For writers from Homer to Spenser, this enchantress did not so much transform innocent men into degenerate beasts as make legible the power of animal instincts to overwhelm human reason. In the allegorical and psychological operation that Harry Berger, Jr., has called "specular tautology," this surrender to passion is then projected onto an external, feminine figure who is both embodiment of and scapegoat for the frailty of male virtue.[52] *Tempe Restored* destabilizes traditional stagings of gender to challenge male claims of helpless seduction. Whereas the dancers are listed at the end of the masque, the text itself notes that Circe was "represented by Madam Coniack," a French singer and member of Henrietta Maria's court (98).[53] By underscoring this unprecedented

---

50. For the place of *Chloridia* in the history of theatrical technology, see Orgel and Strong, 423.

51. Gossett, "Women in Masques," 127.

52. "Squeezing the Text," 86

53. *Tempe Restored*, in *Court Masques*, ed. Lindley. All references to non-Jonsonian masques will be to this edition.

appearance of a female singer in a female role, *Tempe Restored* literalized Prynne's association between the sensual powers of women and music, both which can either elevate or corrupt.[54] And because music was a metaphor not only of feminine seduction but also of the king's power to command the affections of his subjects, the masque's insistence that the virtuous constantly guard against their own desires casts suspicion on the royal charisma it ostensibly celebrates.[55] As Circe's final transfer of power to Charles and Henrietta Maria suggests, the royal image propagated by the court masque may be as dangerous and suspect as Circe's magic, for both replace rational consent with enchanted yielding. By making political and erotic subjects responsible for their own seduction and enslavement, *Tempe Restored* grounds sovereignty on their consent, rather than any inherent power of the ruler.

Tempe Restored centers on a young gentleman, the Fugitive Favourite, who was once the thrall of Circe, living with her, as the Argument explains, "in all sensual delights, until, upon some jealousy conceived, she gave him to drink of an enchanted cup, and touching him with her golden wand, transformed him into a lion" (1–4). Immediately before the opening of the masque, Circe, "remembering her former love, [has] retransformed him into his former shape" (5–6). The Favourite finds salvation in Circe's betrayal, which allows him to extricate himself from his own destructive illusions. Having regained his human reason along with his human form, the Favourite has fled to the reassuring presence of Charles, "whose sight frees him from all fear" (8). The Favourite's change of allegiance suggests that the abjection that seemed to have been imposed upon him was really his own choice, for Circe has no power to compel his return. As the masque repeatedly affirms, those who obey Circe are "voluntary beasts" and "willing servants"—men who choose to behave as animals (13, 115). The gendered structure here is important: the male Favourite submits while the female Circe dominates. This inversion of traditional gender roles underscores the psychological, affective dimension of sovereignty with less ambiguity than do the Ovidian figures of ravishing Zephyrus and helpless Chloris. By making the Favourite a victim of his own desires, Townshend locates the source of authority firmly in the subject. To submit to a corrupt ruler is to enslave oneself to one's own passions. This state of erotic addiction may be experienced as involuntary but is in actuality freely chosen, and therefore always revocable.

---

54. Sharpe, *Criticism*, 229. McManus has argued that it was the stricture on public aristocratic speech (which demanded male, as well as female, silence) that created the possibility of female masque performance, which initially consisted only of dancing (*Women on the Renaissance Stage*, 1–59, 202–213). Some female roles in Townshend's masque were also played by cross-dressed professional male actors. As Tomlinson has observed, the consequent juxtaposition of "real" with "artificial" women gave the audience a chance to compare naturalistic and illusionistic performances of gender ("Theatrical Vibrancy," 187).

55. See Lindley's discussion of early modern anxieties about music's persuasive power ("Politics of Music," 273–295).

The Favourite's first lines acknowledge his own responsibility for his erstwhile servitude. As he flees Circe, he ponders the problem of voluntary subjugation:

> Was I a lion, that am now afraid?
> I fear no danger; nor I fear no death
> But to be retransformed into a beast;
> Which while I was, although I must confess
> I was the bravest (what else could she do less
> That saw me subject to no base desire?)
> Yet was there in me a Promethean fire
> That made me covet to be man again,
> Governed by reason, and not ruled by sense.
> Therefore I shun this place of residence,
> And fly to virtue; in whose awful sight
> She dares not come but in a mask, and crouch
> As low as I did for my liberty. (63–70)

The Favourite's fear of spiritual decay rather than physical distress is itself evidence of his regeneration. When he was a lion, he felt no such anxiety. Yet even as a beast, there persisted within him a "Promethean fire" that strained against his creaturely shell. His struggle to be "governed by reason, and not ruled by sense" constitutes a rather Spenserian psychomachia, not a battle against the external figure of Circe. The Allegory that concludes the printed version of *Tempe Restored* informs us that the Favourite represents "an incontinent man, that striving with his affections is at last, by the power of reason, persuaded to fly from those sensual desires which formerly corrupted his judgment" (295–297). The fear that he might be "retransformed into a beast" indicates not Circe's power, but his own potential weakness, an incomplete regeneration enunciated in the inconsistency of his rhymes. The Favourite must flee Circe because she tempts him to relinquish his hard-won control over his own self-destructive passions.

Unfortunately, the place of refuge to which the Favourite runs may offer only illusory protection from desires that are at once egoistic and abject. The "awful sight" of the Caroline court to which Favourite flees should be the opposite of the Circean luxury whose allure he dreads, but the terms in which he compares the two undermine this distinction. In an irony that would not have been lost on attentive readers or viewers, the Favourite vows to "shun this place of residence" while standing in the midst of Whitehall. Moreover, his assurance that Circe cannot approach his royal sanctuary "but in a mask" reminds us of the dangerous seduction of court entertainment itself. *Tempe Restored* has permitted Circe and the sinister, corrupting delights she represents to appear at the center of English government.

As the Favourite ultimately realizes, the indulgence that disguises itself as pleasure has no force beyond that which he gives it. What saves this young gentleman is not the king's power, but the Favourite's ability to resist his own illusions and desires:

> 'Tis not her rod, her philtres nor her herbs
> (Though strong in magic) that can bound men's minds,
> And make them prisoners where there is no wall:
> It is consent that makes a perfect slave,
> And sloth that binds us to lust's easy trades,
> Wherein we serve out our youth's 'prenticeship,
> Thinking at last Love should enfranchise us,
> Whom we have never either served or known:
> 'He finds no help, that uses not his own.' (80–88)

The consent that enables tyranny need not be active, conscious choice. It may be a form of laziness ("sloth"), a devotion to pleasure that corrodes liberty. Such erotic addiction is often misidentified as Love, making it seem desirable and legitimate, when it is in fact an egoistic servility. "Lust's easy trades" exchange pleasure for virtue, comfort for self-respect. However, the proverb that concludes the Favourite's speech undermines his confidence in the power of independent judgment. The scare quotes around the phrase "He finds no help, that uses not his own" in the printed text remind us that this statement of self-reliance and self-determination is itself a commonplace. The line emphasizes the gap between knowing what one should do and actually doing it.[56]

The antimasque confirms the Favourite's claims of choice and agency by depicting Circe as an impotent victim of her own urges rather than a truly threatening force. Heartbroken and furious over her Favourite's escape, Circe commands her attendants to "Bring me some physic, though that bring no health, / And feign me pleasures, since I find none true" (113–114). An archetypal tyrant, Circe is ruled by will rather than reason. Her power therefore rests on the readiness of her servants to sustain her delusions—which her nymphs immediately do by assuring her that the Favourite's departure was motivated by his own "ingratitude" and "fickle mind," charges frequently leveled at Charles' own detractors (103, 109).

Tempe Restored concludes by acknowledging that Circe's charms may be of the same order as the royal charisma that Caroline masques described as the source of English harmony. In the celebration of Henrietta Maria's Divine Beauty, which initiates the masque proper, the Highest Sphere of heaven enthuses that the queen's presence "will amaze / And send the senses all one way" (216–217). Charles, whom the masque makes the embodiment of Heroic Virtue, joins Henrietta Maria. According to the Chorus, those who behold the rulers are "ravished with delight,"

---

56. For an alternate reading of *Tempe Restored* as "unequivocally rationalist," see Martin Butler, *Stuart Court Masque*, 158–159.

helpless before a monarchal magnetism that is disconcertingly similar to Circean charm (244). This ability to ravish and subdue beholders aligns the influence of royalty with that of earthly attraction and stresses the disorienting, stupefying powers of both. Indeed, the masque's Allegory confirms that "desire cannot be moved without appearance of beauty, either true or false" (307–308). Beauty is equally fascinating whether it is real or apparent, virtuous or vicious. As a result, love and lust, masque and antimasque, Charles and Circe, cannot be definitively separated.

When Circe banishes Pallas Athena from the masque with a curt "Man-maid, begone!" she further emphasizes how easily desire can blur ethical and political categories (268). Given Townshend's connections with the Earl of Holland's circle, which urged greater intervention on behalf of the Protestant forces in the Thirty Years War, the dismissal of the goddess of war and wisdom by an incarnation of sensual delight may comment on the masque's own effects.[57] Circe and Pallas embody the difference between Charles, whose military expeditions at Cadiz, Ile de Rhe, and La Rochelle had been humiliating disasters, and Gustavus Adolphus of Sweden, whose invasion of Germany in 1630 and defeat of Catholic forces at Breitenfeld in 1631 had only increased pressure on Charles to enter the European conflict.[58] Townshend's own elegy on Gustavus' death, likely written later in 1632, states that the Swedish king's prowess was such that "Minerva may withowt hir gorgon com / To beare his sheld, the shield of Christendom."[59] The banishment of this martial goddess in *Tempe Restored* may represent Charles' desire to exile the figure of Gustavus, with whom he was often unfavorably compared, with similar ease—indeed, in October 1632, the king would codify his distaste for Protestant alliance by prohibiting corontos, most of which were filled with news of Gustavus' triumphs.[60]

57. Sharpe notes that Holland may have been the one to introduce Townshend to Henrietta Maria (*Criticism*, 154–155). Britland proposes that Townshend may have shared Holland's interests and notes the large number of child dancers in *Tempe Restored* who were from firmly Protestant families (*Drama*, 90, 96–101). On Holland and his circle, see Sharpe, *Personal Rule*, 164–165, 740–742; and Martin Butler, "Politics and the Masque," 62–63.

58. See Kenyon, *Stuart England*, 123.

59. The poem is reproduced by G. C. Moore Smith, "Aurelian Townshend," 422–427; 422–423 (no line numbers). All references to this poem will quote the version in Moore's article, itself a transcription of the manuscript version in St. John's College, Cambridge (MS. S.23, article 44). I have silently changed 'u' and 'v' to conform to modern spellings.

60. Hirst, *Authority*, 176; and Sharpe, *Personal Rule*, 646. In his elegy, Townshend himself laments that no ruler comparable to Gustavus exists:

Prinses ambitius of renoune shall still
Strive for his spures to helpe them up the hill.
His gloryus gauntlettes shall unquestioned lye
Till handes are found fitt for a monarchie.

After silencing Pallas, Circe does not assent to Jove and Cupid's demand that she herself depart until she has named the "matchless pair" of rulers her "heir," thus reiterating the affinity between her court and theirs (273–276). The morality of Circe's legacy is dubious. What has she to give, if not the power to bewitch? This gift appears even more disturbing when we remember that Jupiter, who represents divine authority, and Cupid, who represents the desire that has undone both Circe and her minions, both claim credit for Circe's relinquishment of power. Rather than resolve this indeterminacy, *Tempe Restored* simply concludes with the debate between imperial and erotic authority, the irresistible will of Jupiter and the ravishing arrows of Cupid. This choice, however, turns out not to be a choice at all. Like love and lust, imperial and erotic forms of authority are not opposites but exist, more treacherously, on a continuum. As the Allegory tells us, the impulse represented by Circe is not inevitably vicious, but "signifies desire in general, the which hath power on all living creatures, and being mixed of the divine and sensible, hath diverse effects, leading some to virtue and others to vice. She is described as a queen, having in her service and subjection the nymphs, which participate of divinity, figuring the virtues, and the brute beasts, denoting the vices" (298–303). Given the ambivalent, unstable nature of desire, *Tempe Restored* admonishes, the unquestioning devotion that Charles encouraged risked transforming his subjects into the same "perfect slave[s]" that follow Circe.

Carew's *Coelum Britannicum* shifts focus from courtship to chivalry, but it depicts Charles' conquests as moral rather than military. Charles' pacific heroism distinguishes Caroline England not only from the rest of Europe but also from its Elizabethan past.[61] But like those of Jonson and Townshend, Carew's entertainment can be understood as something of a metamasque, examining, as Jennifer Chibnall puts it, the process of constructing Caroline mythology.[62] *Coelum Britannicum* celebrates Charles' well-known reform of court manners, one esteemed even by such critics as Lucy Hutchinson, by imagining that his example has inspired the gods to amend their promiscuous habits.[63] In recognition of this change, "CARLOMARIA" will replace the constellations in the English skies. This astral inscription of the idealized royal union will supplant records of divine lust and jealousy. Unfortunately, as the masque goes on to demonstrate, such a turn from the past is also a dismantling of the "ancient constellations" of the military victories that Charles' personal morality has replaced (405). In erasing the Elizabethan past, England may be abandoning its religion and liberty in favor of an indolent and irresponsible peace, if not Catholicism and tyranny. Performed February 18, 1634, *Coelum Britannicum* follows a

61. Peacock discusses the translation of Prince Henry's chivalric, military image into the portrayal of Charles as a "hero of the inner life" in court masques and portraiture of the 1630s ("Image of Charles I as a Roman Emperor," 55).

62. Chibnall, "Function of the Caroline Masque," 85.

63. Hutchinson, 67.

series of domestic and international events that in 1632 and 1633 had converged to create the impression of a crisis in English identity. With the death of Gustavus on November 16, 1632, followed by that of Frederick of Bohemia less than two weeks later, the international Protestant cause lost its best hopes for success. Charles' refusal to intervene and continued dialogue with Spain drew renewed complaints that he was failing to protect England from the ever-present menace of Rome.[64] Fear that England was abandoning its mythologized Elizabethan role as champion of Protestantism was exacerbated by the construction of Henrietta Maria's Capuchin chapel at Somerset House; the appointment of Laud as Archbishop of Canterbury; the reissue of the Book of Sports; the printing of the Scottish Prayer Book; and the reopening of negotiations between England and Rome, which would culminate in the arrival of the Papal envoy Gregorio Panzani in December 1634.[65]

Anxieties about a possible break from England's chivalric Protestantism emerge in the debate between the two central figures of *Coelum Britannicum*, Mercury and Momus. Scholars typically see these characters as opposites, with Mercury representing the obsequious flattery of the masque and Momus the clumsy criticism of the antimasque.[66] Rather than see these characters as figuring the court and its critics, however, we should understand them as illustrating two different ideas of what the court should be. Together, Mercury and Momus recapitulate the dilemma explored in Carew's poem, "In Answer of an Elegiacal Letter, upon the Death of the King of Sweden, from Aurelian Townshend, Inviting Me to Write on the Subject." Here, Carew rejects Townshend's invitation, replying that the "subjects proper to our clime" are "Tourneys, masques, theaters" (95–97). These, according to Carew, "better become / Our halcyon days" than the "mighty" actions of Sweden's "Victorious king," which would require a far "loftier pitch" than Carew's "lyric feet" can manage.[67]

In *Coelum Britannicum*, Mercury embodies the persona that Carew takes in the "Answer"—glib, placid, delighted that Charles' policies have made the "thunder" of European "carapins" helpless to "Drown the sweet airs of our tuned violins" ("Answer," 99–100). But there is an inescapable irony that the same author who slighted temperance in "Mediocrity in Love Rejected" and described oral sex in extraordinary detail in "A Rapture" should also announce that Charles' "exemplar

---

64. Sharpe, *Personal Rule*, 72–75; Kenyon, *Stuart England*, 123.

65. The details and significance of these events are discussed in detail by Veevers, 84–88, 135–136; Leah Marcus, *Politics of Mirth*, 1–23, 175; and Atherton and Sanders, "Introducing the 1630s," 6–8.

66. Sharpe sees Momus as a figure for Carew, satirically debunking the court's flattering vision of itself (*Criticism*, 235–243), while Adamson understands him as a figure for an outmoded knightly belligerence that Charles' more genteel brand of chivalry had replaced ("Chivalry and Political Culture," 171–175). Kogan treats Mercury's triumphant vision as Carew's earnest celebration of court values (128–134).

67. "In Answer of an Elegiacal Letter," 9, 15, 6, in *Ben Jonson and the Cavalier Poets*, ed. Maclean. All references to Carew's lyrics will be to this edition.

life" has "transfused a zealous heat / Of imitation through your virtuous court" (*CB*, 52–54). As Lucy Hutchinson would later observe, Charles' reforms did not compel courtiers to "abandon their debaucheries," only to "retire into corners to practise them."[68] A court poet like Carew, whom one contemporary account had helping to cover up an affair between Henrietta Maria and Henry Jermyn, would only have called attention to the fact that courtiers like William Davenant, John Suckling, and George Goring were notorious drunks, playboys, and gamblers. As a fictional alter ego for Carew's cavalier persona, Mercury calls attention to the superficiality of the reforms he extols. Mercury has a similar reputation for complicity in Jovian misdeeds—we might remember, for instance, that he distracted Argus so that Jupiter could seduce poor Io. By his own admission, in former times Mercury would have come to court only "to whisper amorous tales / Of wanton love into the glowing ear / Of some choice beauty," and Momus reminds him of his familiar role as "god of petty larceny" (*CB*, 46–48, 109). Such a conflation of seduction and theft places the masque audience as targets of Mercurial deceit, rather than witnesses of true reform.

Momus, to the contrary, personifies the more sober, critical poetic voice that Carew takes in "To Saxham," "To My Friend G.N., from Wrest," or "To My Worthy Friend Master George Sandys, On His Translations of the Psalms." All of these lyrics express a Jonsonian preference for those who "delight / Rather to be in act, than seem in sight" ("G.N.," 31–32) and a sober recognition that it would be better to seek "one thorn" from "the dry leafless trunk on Golgotha" than "all the flourishing wreaths by laureates worn" ("Sandys," 34–36). Momus' choice of truth over promotion links him to the values of an Elizabethan past in which the duty of the counselor was, in Elizabeth's words to Burghley, "that without respect of my private will you will give me that counsel which you think best."[69] The most celebrated emblem of this lost era of counsel and chivalry was Philip Sidney. As J. G. A. Adamson has shown, Sidney is linked with *Coelum Britannicum* in two ways. First, much of Carew's text is a free translation of Giordano Bruno's *Spaccio de la Bestia Trionfante*, which was dedicated to Sidney. Second, Momus wears a porcupine, which was the Sidney family emblem, on his head.[70] Gustavus had been to the Caroline Protestant cause what Sidney had been to that of the Elizabethan age, so Carew's equation of the critic of the gods with the exemplar of militant, chivalric English Protestantism may celebrate the same values that he facetiously rejects in "An Answer."[71] In this poem, Carew equates Gustavus' militarism with sixteenth-century romance:

68. Hutchinson, 67. For further discussions of the decidedly unchaste behavior of the Caroline court, see White, 19, 49; Poynting, "Henrietta Maria's Notorious Whores"; and Tomlinson, "Henrietta Maria and the Threat of the Actress."

69. Read, *Mr. Secretary Cecil*, 119.

70. Adamson, 172.

71. For the reputation of Gustavus, see Hirst, *Authority*, 86; Sharpe, *Personal Rule*, 79; and Holbrook, "Jacobean Masques," 70.

His actions were too mighty to be raised
Higher by verse; let him in prose be praised,
In modest, faithful story, which his deeds
Shall turn to poems. When the next age reads
Of Frankfort, Leipzig, Würzburg, of the Rhine,
The Lech, the Danube, Tilly, Wallenstein,
Bavaria, Pappenheim, Lützen-field, where he
Gained after death a posthume victory,
They'll think his acts things rather feigned than done,
Like our romances of the Knight o'the Sun. (15–24)

This lengthy list of battles constitutes the elegy that Carew ostensibly refuses to write, and its prosaic nature only highlights the power of deeds that need no poetic adornment. In light of this poem's association of prose with a chivalric past that has no place in the present, Momus' prose in *Coelum Britannicum* distinguishes the true heroism whose death he laments from the false ideals of Mercury's easy lyricism. In contrast to Mercury's—or Carew's—slick praise, the rough honesty of a Sidney or an Essex, a Leicester or a Burghley, may be more proper to courtiers.

As we discover, the dismantling of the age-old constellations and replacement of them with the mere word "CARLOMARIA" signifies in *Coelum Britannicum* not only a chastening of the Jove's "incests, rapes, adulteries" and Juno's "revengeful fury" but also a destruction of England's past chivalric ethos (66, 68). Along with the astral records of Jove's "loose strumpets and their spurious race," Mercury has "improvidently" banished "some innocent and some generous constellations, that might have been reserved for noble uses" (71, 381, 372–373). Momus' first example is "the Scales and Swords to adorn the statue of Justice, since she resides here on earth only in picture and effigy" (374–375). This not only indicates that Charles and his queen have displaced the virgin Astraea, a well-recognized symbol for Elizabeth. It also suggests a loss of the justice that is connected to a military strength that Charles cannot claim. The subsequent examples are similarly martial. The "Eagle" who bears Jove's thunder would have "been a fit present for the Germans, in regard their bird hath mewed most of her feathers lately" (375–377). And "Perseus on his Pegasus, brandishing his sword, the Dragon yawning on his back under the horse's feet, with Python's dart through his throat," would have "been a divine St George for this nation" (379–381). With their loss of Gustavus, the German forces in the Thirty Years' War sorely needed some divine intervention that might inspire England to emulate the bravery of Perseus, whose destruction of the sea-monster offered a type of the same St. George whom Charles had transformed from a Spenserian crusader against Catholicism into an emblem of private moral victory.

In describing the renovation of England's Star Chamber, Momus insists that the mementos of England's former glory have real effects. Pompously speaking in the royal "we," Momus notes that past monarchs have "observed a very commendable practice . . . of perpetuating the memory of their famous enterprises, sieges, battles victories, in picture, sculpture, tapestry, embroideries, and other manufactures" (386, 388–390). One prominent example is the tapestry "wherein the naval victory of '88 is to the eternal glory of this nation exactly delineated" (394–395). Charles, however, "after mature deliberation and long debate, held first in our own inscrutable bosom and afterwards communicated with our Privy Council" has decided that it is "meet to our omnipotency, for causes to ourself best known, to unfurnish and disarray our foresaid Star Chamber of all those ancient constellations which have for so many ages been sufficiently notorious" (401–406). In privately determining to break with the heroism of the English past, here represented by the 1588 destruction of the Spanish Armada, Momus' Charles has likewise repudiated the frank counsel and public debate of earlier eras. In place of these "ancient constellations"—the Armada hangings bought by James I in 1616, which Charles had removed from Whitehall and stored in Oatlands—Charles will admit "such persons only as shall be qualified with exemplar virtue and eminent desert" (407–408). As Adamson has argued, Momus here censures Charles' replacement of individual and collective displays of martial valor with the central, triumphant figure of the king, and his redefinition of virtue as private loyalty and morality, rather than public heroism.[72]

The subsequent antimasques demonstrate that while Charles hopes that perfect loyalty will replace the heroism of past eras, such sincere and selfless devotion cannot be found. For although Momus has invited "any person whatsoever that conceiveth him or her self to be really endued with any heroical virtue or transcendent merit worth so high a calling and dignity" to apply for service in Caroline government court, not a single fitting candidate appears. Instead, there is a succession of corrupt claimants to virtue. Plutus, "Which feeble virtue seldom can resist, / Stronger than towers of brass, or chastity," confuses virtue with the very riches that corrode it (499–500). The puritanical Poenia signifies "unnatural stupidity / That knows nor joy nor sorrow" (608–609). Tiche attracts only "the lazy sluggard" who "licks the easy hand that feeds his sloth" (698–700). And Hedone is characterized by "fierce appetite" that "oft strangles thee / And cuts thy slender thread" (770–771). The quality that all of these aspirants share is their rejection of the active, self-sacrificing heroism that characterized the Protestant heroes and public servants of the increasingly idealized Elizabethan age. By attempting to reduce public virtue to private temperance and royal service, Charles has emptied England of its national glory and strength. As a result, his court is vulnerable to effete, egoistic parasites from within and resentful, bitter puritans from without. Neither are capable of restoring England's ancient magnificence.

The masque proper, which begins only after seven antimasques and 832 lines, celebrates just this ancient chivalric past and urges the king to emulate it. The final

---

72. Adamson, 172–173.

dance is led by masquers "richly attired like ancient heroes" and "a troop of young lords and noblemen's sons" "apparelled after the old British fashion" (895, 897–899). Their performance is followed by an assurance to Henrietta Maria that the chivalry of England's Golden Age will also return:

> We bring Prince Arthur, or the brave
> St George himself (great Queen) to you,
> You'll soon discern him; and we have
> A Guy, a Bevis, or some true
> Round-Table knight as ever fought
> For lady, to each beauty brought. (967–972)

Charles was himself an enthusiastic supporter of the Order of the Garter, whose patron was the same St. George that Spenser took as the model for his Redcrosse.[73] But the athletic entertainments of the Elizabethan era have been replaced by courtly dances like the one being performed. In *Coelum Britannicum*, these figures of knightly prowess never even appear, suggesting the emptiness of this promise of a heroic future. The effort and strength of bygone days turn out to be as much an illusion as the giant mountain that rose and then descended below the stage, giving, as the text reports, "great cause of admiration, but especially how so huge a machine, and of that great height, should come from under the stage, which was but six foot high" (910–912). The private desire that replaces chivalric conquest is equally a product of cunning and illusion, making England's former greatness the stuff of romance.

Davenant's *Salmacida Spolia* (1640), the last masque ever presented at court, makes a final, somewhat desperate attempt to cast Charles' relationship with his subjects as one of love and mutuality even as it reveals the hollowness of this claim. This masque represents Charles as Philogenes, the Lover of his People, whose ability to compromise and forgive will dispel the conflicts threatening England. As numerous scholars have noted, on February 12, 1640, three weeks after the masque's first performance and nine days before its second, Charles issued writs for the first parliament to meet in eleven years. Davenant's emphasis on conciliation was a plea for trust and the supply it would engender. Indeed, as Martin Butler has shown, the appeals for cooperation by Lord Keeper Finch at the opening of the Short Parliament in April sound like a paraphrase of *Salmacida Spolia*.[74] Yet Davenant's masque

---

73. As Martin Butler observes, readers and spectators of *Coelum Brittanicum* would likely have caught this Spenserian allusion (*Stuart Court Masque*, 315).

74. Martin Butler suggests that the unusual repetition of performances and the large number of dancers known to oppose Charles' policies signaled Charles' desire to reach the widest audience he could ("Politics and the Masque," 65, 68–71, and *Stuart Court Masque*, 333–348). Sharpe argues that *Salmacida Spolia* urges moderation and compromise (*Criticism*, 251–255, 264).

also makes explicit the subtext of the decade's earlier entertainments, which warned that love may be a form of force, not its opposite.[75] This depiction of love as inseparable from coercion had appeared in Davenant's earlier work. Here he warns that a king who saw his English subjects as extensions of himself might abuse his people's wholehearted trust in royal motives and policies.[76]

The extent to which appeals for love in *Salmacida Spolia* may signal hostility is reflected in the masque's title. As the folio's preface tells us, this title alludes to the adage "Salmacida spolia sine sanguine sine sudore, potius quam / Cadmia victoria, ubi ipsos victores pernicies opprimit" ["Salmacian spoils, achieved without bloodshed or sweat, rather than a Cadmian victory in which destruction falls upon the victors themselves"] (59–60).[77] The first line of the proverb refers to the fountain of Salmacis, which enticed barbarians attacking Halicarnassus; having imbibed its waters, the barbarians' "fierce and cruel natures were reduced of their own accord to the sweetness of Grecian customs" (75–77). The next line evokes a more compromised victory, "gotten with great damage and slaughter of the Thebans, for few of them returned alive into their city" (87–89). "The allusion," according to the printed version of the masque, "is that his Majesty, out of his mercy and clemency approving the first proverb, seeks by all means to reduce tempestuous and turbulent natures into a sweet calm of civil concord" (90–92).

But as the source of the Salmacian pool's ability to mollify those who drink its waters indicates, coercion and conciliation may not be true opposites. In the *Metamorphoses*, Ovid explains why "the fountaine of Salmacis diffamed is of yore, / Why with his waters overstrong it weakeneth men so sore / That whoso bathes him there commes thence a perfect man no more" (4.347–349). The fountain acquired such enfeebling properties after the lovelorn nymph Salmacis attacked the unsuspecting Hermaphroditus as he swam in its waters. Even more than the Ovidian stories of Chloris-Flora or the Fortunate Favourite, the tale of Salmacis and Hermaphroditus suggests that resistance may be insufficient against desire. "Maugre all his wrestling

75. Wikander points out that Davenant's plays critically scrutinize the self-absorption of couples in love (96–99). Kroll argues that Davenant's satiric picture of Platonic love emphasizes the limits of royal prerogative (93–121). As Shohet observes, Davenant's Inns of Court entertainment *Triumphs of the Prince d'Amour*, which was performed for Henrietta Maria and the Bohemian princes Charles Louis and Rupert, suggests that in cases of uncertain succession, power reverts to subjects ("On Late-1630s Masques," 240). Veevers argues that Davenant, like Jonson, appeared to have trouble adjusting to Henrietta Maria's version of Neoplatonism (53), while Bailey suggests that Davenant's conversion to Catholicism in the 1650s was a result of political calculation rather than religious conviction (136–140).

76. According to Secretary Windebanke, calling a parliament would prove an advantage to Charles because it would show that he "desired the old way" of government. If the political nation failed to respond "cheerfully" to his needs, "the world might see he is forced, contrary to his own inclination, to use extraordinary means, rather than by the peevishness of some few factious spirits to suffer his State and Government to be lost" (quoted by Martin Butler, "Politics and the Masque," 65).

77. Lindley's translation.

and his struggling to and fro," Hermaphroditus cannot escape the clinging nymph (4.444). Sincere as it is, Salmacis' love is a form of violation. Even as she annihilates any claim that Hermaphroditus has to distinct agency or subjectivity, she "held and kissed him a hundred times and mo" (4.445). This is not just a transient urge, either, for Salmacis prays "that this same wilfull boy and I may never parted bee" (4.461). When Hermaphroditus realizes that "in the water sheene / To which he had entred in a man, his limmes were weakened so / That out fro thence but halfe a man he was compelde to go," he beseeches the gods that whoever enters this pool will be similarly effeminized (4.471–473). The Salmacian fountain represents the predatory, devouring side of eros, the wish to erase division or difference from which both love and hatred derive. If the pool on which the masque centers is a "fowle and filthy sinke" "which not the bodye only, but the mynd doo also chaunge" (15.34–349), then the apparent alternatives of conquest by love and conquest by violence end up being more similar than we like to think. Either, as the story of Hermaphroditus cautions, can dissolve not only resistance to another's will but also any identity distinct from it. As in the masques that I have discussed above, this loss of boundaries is expressed through the violation of gendered norms. Francis Beaumont's version of the story reminds us that Hermaphroditus' sexuality is ambiguous even before he encounters Salmacis. Not only does Hermaphroditus' name register the union of his father Mercury (Hermes) and his mother Venus (Aphrodite), but his extraordinary beauty enthralls both Diana and Apollo.[78] Like the male courtiers dancing for, and expressing their love for, male monarchs, Hermaphroditus is both masculine and feminine, an object of homo- and heteroerotic admiration. In political terms, such a loss of hierarchical and gendered boundaries may diminish subjects' ability to distinguish between the desires of the king and the good of the political nation.

The possibility that love may provoke obsession and violence, not redemption and harmony, was especially pertinent in the context in which *Salmacida Spolia* was produced, performed, and circulated. If *Coelum Britannicum* addresses Charles' lack of foreign triumphs, *Salmacida Spolia* considers the possibility that he might direct against his own people the military forces he had raised to suppress Scottish and Irish revolts. In the years between the performances of the two masques, a number of events increased subjects' mistrust not only of Charles' willingness to govern moderately but also of the ability of English law to protect subjects from royal will. In particular, 1637 had seen several ominous signs that the crown's power over both church and state was growing: Hampden's Case affirmed Charles' right to determine unilaterally what constituted a national emergency and to tax subjects accordingly; William Prynne, John Bastwick, and Henry Burton were publicly mutilated for their critiques of Laudian policy; and an Anglican Prayer Book was imposed on the Scottish Kirk. All of these events seemed to threaten traditional liberties of property and religion and therefore inspired organized resistance. Laud and many

---

78. Beaumont, *Salmacis and Hermaphroditus.*

of the sheriffs collecting ship money noticed links among puritanism, support of parliaments, and resistance to Charles' claims of royal emergency powers.[79] By refusing to withhold their criticism of Charles and Laud's policies, Prynne, Bastwick, and Burton had embraced the roles of martyrs who pushed the government to reveal that force, not love, upheld its power.[80] The Scottish Covenanters' pamphlets in particular sought to connect English and Scottish fears of royal tyranny, a connection that may well have existed. Scottish clergy and noblemen united to reject the Laudian Prayer Book in February 1638 and to expel bishops from the Kirk the following November, thereby establishing Presbyterianism. These actions directly assaulted the fiction that Charles ruled with the consent of his Scottish subjects and forced him into a position where he could reassert his authority only through military action. Charles' English subjects offered little support for his plan to subdue the Scottish rebels, and when his lack of supplies and forces compelled the king to accept the Pacification of Berwick in June 1639, few expected that this would be the end of hostilities.

Salmacida Spolia participates in debates surrounding the imminent gathering of the first parliament since 1629, which Charles had called to request supply for a second expedition against the Scots. Many had high hopes that this meeting would be, as Benjamin Rudyard put it, "the bedd of reconciliacion betwixt King and people," and at first glance, Davenant's masque seems to promise such harmony.[81] For it is not Charles alone, but the king "attended by his nobles" and with "his appearance prepared by a chorus, representing the beloved people" that quiets the fury of the antimasque (12–13, 14–15). Whereas earlier masques imagined Charles' personal rule as a product of his subjects' love and trust, *Salmacida Spolia* makes explicit two of the implicit anxieties of previous entertainments: first, that the king might use force against his people, and second, that such a violation of trust might foment rebellion. Even if Charles really is Philogenes, his love may be more aggressive and selfish than gentle and nurturing.

Salmacis, then, is not the opposite of the king, but the perversion of the erotic role Charles has played throughout the decade—and like this feminized double, Charles may refuse to allow any divergence from his own will. The first sign that

---

79. According to Burgess, it was a "crisis of the common law"—the anxiety that English law was inadequate to protect subjects' lives, liberties, and property from royal demands—that fomented conflict (*Politics*, 180, 190–195, 202–210). On the significance of Hamden's Case, see also Hirst, *Authority*, 178–180; Sharpe, *Personal Rule*, 721–728; and Russell, 137–144. For the connection between the Covenanters' opposition to the Prayer Book and the increased sense that to support parliamentary government was to resist royal prerogative, see Sharpe, *Personal Rule*, 731–737, 784–820; and Russell, 231–253. Cressy argues that the constitutional, political, religious, and social revolutions that occurred between 1640 and 1642 were the cause, not the effect, of the civil wars ("Revolutionary England").

80. Russell, 179–204; Sharpe, *Personal Rule*, 757–762; and McRae.

81. Quoted in Martin Butler, *Theatre and Crisis*, 74.

Charles may not be as open to counsel as the incoming parliament might wish is that the masque either demonizes or dismisses anyone who might criticize the king's policies. *Salmacida Spolia* presents Discord as a gruesome Fury, a characterization that identifies any dissatisfaction with Caroline rule as arising from the same "factious spirits" whose validity Charles dismissed after the 1629 parliament. In her song, Discord satirically embodies those who have challenged Charles' irenic foreign policies in her lament that "the world should everywhere / Be vexed into a storm save only here!" (113–114). In order to remedy this situation, she will generate domestic strife by arousing the suspicions of the great, the greed of the wealthy, and the ambitions of the poor, the last of whom will "make religion to become their vice, / Named to disguise ambitious avarice" (133–134). By implication, those who oppose the Prayer Book in Scotland or Laudian reform in England use religion as a cover for self-promotion. Even easier to dismiss are the twenty antimasques of what Sharpe has called "Politic Would-Bes" that take up the middle part of the masque.[82] The most prominent of these is Wolfgangus Vandergoose. As Karen Britland has shown, this character evokes Vangoose from Jonson's *Masque of Augers*, an Englishman whose native accent and identity has been obscured by his imitation of the Dutch.[83] Given the Tudor and Stuart suspicion of the Dutch Republic and its rebellion against the Spanish monarchy, Vandergoose may be a parody of the commitments to Protestantism and political liberty embraced not only by such men as Prynne, Milton, or John Pym but also by many members of the Privy Council, like Pembroke, Holland, and Northumberland. Vandergoose is accompanied by "the Invisible Lady Styled the Magical Sister of the Rosicross" (179–180), a pairing that associates him with a mystical, pan-European movement that threatened to divert allegiance from the monarch to an international religious alliance.[84] The quack cures he offers for England's ills—represented by ancient Irish- and Scotsmen, an "old-fashioned Englishman," "a country gentlemen," and various courtiers and cavaliers—discredit solutions other than those offered by Charles himself. Linking Vandergoose to such potential threats as the Irish or the Scots and to such foolish figures as "a jealous Dutchman, his wife, and her Italian lover" (243), the antimasque makes him a figure of hostility, impotence, and hypocrisy, one who uses the "magic" of religion for his own ends. Whereas Discord is deformed and frightening, Vandergoose is foolish and contemptible. This pairing collapses serious and trivial challenges to royal authority. It thereby justifies Charles' use of force against the Scots and their English compatriots even as it diminishes the threat they pose.

82. *Criticism*, 253.
83. Britland, "Marie de Médicis," 208.
84. See Pearl's discussion of Jonson's satire on the Rosicrucians in *The Fortunate Isles, and Their Union* ("Jonson's Masques," 71–73).

Between the antimasques of Discord and Vandergoose, Concord and the Genius of Great Britain briefly appear to bemoan the ingratitude of the English people. Casting Charles as a misunderstood martyr, the Genius complains that the people "lay too mean, too cheap a price / On every blessing they possess" (151–152). This complaint is also an implicit threat, however, as Concord offers to leave and promises that "I shall be valued when I'm gone" (157). Genius manages to persuade her to stay in order to please and comfort Philogenes, but Concord remains distressed that "'tis his fate to rule in adverse times, / When wisdom must awhile give place to crimes" (168–169). Like the traditional wounded lover, Philogenes' suffering makes him a martyr and, correspondingly, transforms aggression into self-defense. Here, the language of hagiography destabilizes identities of tyrant and victim, force and love. *Salmacida Spolia* reminds us of the polemical power of the stance of wronged innocence taken by men like Prynne, Bastwick, and Burton. Like his political opponents, Charles sought to demonstrate his virtue by advertising his suffering. Concord and the Genius model the proper response to such royal distress when they admire the magnanimity with which Philogenes bears his affliction:

> O who but he could thus endure
> To live and govern in a sullen age,
> When it is harder far to cure
> The people's folly than resist their rage? (173–176)

These lines transform Charles from an emblem of martial strength to a saint whose heroism is exhibited in his ability to endure. To resist the people's rage—to use force to create order—is far easier than to gain their love and obedience. Like that of a lover rejected by a haughty mistress, Charles' patience is no longer the behavior expected of a good ruler, but a mark of otherworldly virtue—a role that he would occupy with astounding success in *Eikon Basilike*. As *Salmacida Spolia* implies, the people's sullenness, folly, and rage would provoke a less patient man to use far harsher methods to achieve reunion. This song expresses the dilemma Charles faces: he can depend only on free expressions of compromise and good will, for if he compels submission he will exchange his role of suffering martyr for that of persecuting tyrant. This difficulty appears further in the scene that follows, which pictures "craggy rocks and inaccessible mountains . . . all of which represented the difficult way which heroes are to pass ere they come to the Throne of Honour" (256–257, 262–264). No longer capable of banishing lust and rage with his mere presence, Charles will have to acknowledge that his subjects' desires are distinct from his own. The real obstacle he must overcome is as much his own willfulness as the resistance of the political nation.

This willing subjection is modeled by the "chorus of beloved people" that welcomes Marie de Médici, who had been exiled from France in 1631 and living in England since 1638. As Britland has argued, *Salmacida Spolia* connects the

waters of Salmacis to Marie, the "spring" from which Henrietta Maria has originated, thereby registering the ambivalent relation between pacification and
emasculation.[85] The masque celebrates Marie's marriage to Henri IV, whom it
describes as "the chief and best / Of modern victors" (282–283). But, as we have
seen, Henri's reputation in England was hardly spotless. Despite his protection
of Huguenots, his conversion to Catholicism made him an emblem of political
expediency memorialized as Spenser's Bourbon, not the heroism of a Sidney or a
Gustavus. Moreover, even though Marie's own iconography depicted her as an
advocate for peace, she was widely regarded as a troublemaker whose presence was
unwelcome in England and whose pro-Spanish policies were associated in 1638
and 1640 with Laudian reform and ship money.[86] If Henrietta Maria, who was also
endorsing pro-Spanish policies by 1640, were to pattern herself after her mother,
then this "stream from whence our blessings flow" could prove a similar danger to
English religion and liberty, enervating those who would defend them. This impression was only amplified by Henrietta Maria's attempts to raise money for the
First Bishop's War—thus circumventing the need for parliamentary supply—by
requesting Catholic contributions (281).[87] The queen and her ladies' subsequent
appearance "in Amazonian habits" visualizes the sense that her influence had so
emasculated Charles that he was incapable of defending the political nation and
that she would do the same to Protestant subjects (353).[88] Indeed, it is precisely this
charge that the Long Parliament would stress in the 1645 publication of *The King's
Cabinet Opened*, a collection of the king and queen's private letters seized after the
Battle of Naseby.

In this context, it is more ominous than comforting that the final song in *Salmacida Spolia* (and, for that matter, the final masque song ever) insists that king and
people can still be reconciled if they can emulate the royal example of "turning
[their] thoughts to either's will" (424). Yet, as the second verse warns, this reciprocal obedience may be a product of delusion:

> All that are harsh, all that are rude,
> Are by your harmony subdued;
> Yet so into obedience wrought
> As if not forced to it, but taught. (425–428)

85. "Marie de Médicis," 213.
86. See Britland on the association of Marie with ship money (*Drama*, 205–216). White
describes a letter sent to Charles after the dissolution of the Short Parliament threatening to
"chase the Pope and the Devil from St. James's, where is lodged the Queene, [and] Mother
of the Queene" (40). Bailey describes Marie's arrival as part of the increasingly revived
Catholicism of Henrietta Maria's court (9–11, 175–207).
87. White, 35–36.
88. As Veevers observes, in *Salmacida Spolia* Charles and Henrietta Maria switch expected
gender roles, with king appearing as passive, forgiving Christ and queen as militant virgin
(203).

Rather than mutual compromise between king and political nation, the song envisions a unilateral capitulation on the part of the people. It is only "as if" they have been taught rather than forced. The trick may be to make subjects believe that they have chosen to be subdued, the illusion for which the decade's masques as a group strive, at least on the surface. If, as the song claims, Charles is "Loved even by those who should your justice fear," then the politics of conciliation and force, pedagogy and punishment, have merged into one another, like Hermaphroditus and Salmacis (436).

The fantasy of such erotic engulfment suggests the same pleasure in abjection that Spenser and Wroth analyze. *Salmacida Spolia* expresses not a fantasy of reconciliation, but a fear that discipline will be experienced as pleasure, subjection as choice. Such a blurring of boundaries will make prerogative and law one and the same—ending in a hermaphroditic absorption of native religion and liberty by royal will. As I argue in the following chapter, this was the last thing that even a devout royalist like Margaret Cavendish had in mind when she defended the monarchy. For Cavendish, as for many royalists, a strict adherence to impersonal law was the only way to contain the human passions depicted in the Caroline masque. Because monarch and subjects are equally vulnerable to these pulls of irrational desire, it is not revolution, but a return to the principles of the ancient constitution that will protect England from love's destructive potential.

CHAPTER 7

❧

"Honest Margaret Newcastle"

Law and Desire in Margaret Cavendish's Romances

S ince Margaret Cavendish is frequently described as one of absolutism's most staunch apologists, it may seem odd to claim that she soundly rejects just the vision of ceaseless devotion that is so often associated with the Stuart masque.[1] But Cavendish's opposition to absolutism should not be equated with a rejection of monarchy as such. Rather, she endorses a return to a Sidneian view that noble subjects have a duty to restrain both their own impulses and those of their sovereign. Cavendish is different from her predecessors, however, in that she wrote after a decade of civil war that had culminated in the abolition of monarchy itself, events that had made legible the extremes to which constitutionalist arguments for resistance could lead. Cavendish's historical situation complicated her view of the proper expression of the loyal opposition urged by the earlier writers I have examined. For Cavendish, suffering alone no longer provides the moral authority that justifies rebellion. Instead, subject and sovereign alike must strive to subordinate their private desires to the strictly impersonal, unsympathetic realm of public law, however difficult this may prove.

In two mid-century prose romances, *Assaulted and Pursued Chastity* and "The Contract," Cavendish repeatedly depicts heroines who regulate their passions and demand that their would-be lovers do the same. By stressing the necessity of legal

---

1. For readings that assume Cavendish's "absolutism," see, for instance, Mendelson, *Mental World of Stuart Women*; Gallagher, "Politics of the Female Subject"; Trubowitz, "Margaret Cavendish's Blazing World"; and Iyengar, "Rank, Gender, and Race."

and customary structures to contain individual will, Cavendish endorses the ancient constitutionalism that both Charles I and Cromwell had eschewed. After the Restoration, however, Cavendish's work manifests the pessimism voiced by Shakespeare and Wroth. For Cavendish, Charles II and his noble subjects exhibited just the license that her earlier fiction had condemned. She expresses her disillusionment with the prospect of limited monarchy by depicting in *The Blazing World* an Empress enthralled by the dream of mastery. Here, Cavendish herself occupies the role of chaste, controlled heroine: it is only the blunt counsel of one "honest Margaret Newcastle" that prevents the Empress from destroying her nation. Like Cavendish's mid-century romances, then, *The Blazing World* repudiates the passive obedience that had long been associated with moral and political virtue. Cavendish's work shows that by allowing the ruler to exceed the bounds of law, even the most virtuous of subjects may find themselves protecting a regime that endangers the public harmony they wish to promote.

Cavendish's own husband was subject to this charge of misplaced fidelity and self-sacrifice. In the dedicatory epistle to Charles II that precedes *The Life of the Thrice Noble, High and Puissant Prince William Cavendishe, Duke, Marquess, and Earl of Newcastle*, Cavendish promises a "short History (which is as full of Truths, as words) of the Actions and Sufferings of Your most Loyal Subject, my Lord and Husband," who, she assures the king, "loves Your Royal Person so dearly, that He would most willingly, upon all occasions, sacrifice his Life and Posterity for Your Majesty."[2] This narrative of Newcastle's unqualified devotion, as several readers have noted, functions largely as a "bill" to its royal dedicatee, for it lists in detail the unrewarded personal financial ruin that Newcastle had incurred serving the Stuart monarchy.[3] But Cavendish is interested in more than money. She aims to challenge the equation of love, virtue, and sacrifice that has so damaged her husband. In one oft-cited passage, for instance, Cavendish archly chides Newcastle for his continued dedication to an ungrateful king. "I have heard him say several times," she writes, "That his love to his gracious Master King *Charles* the Second, was above the love he bore to his Wife, Children, and all his Posterity, nay to his own life: And when, since His Return into *England*, I answer'd him, That I observed His Gracious Master did not love him so well as he lov'd Him; he replied, That he cared not whether His Majesty lov'd him again or not; for he was resolved to love him."[4] Newcastle, in Cavendish's account, has too credulously accepted a narrative in which voluntary suffering, even in the face of betrayal, proves true virtue. In Cavendish's hands, even Newcastle's

2. *Life of Newcastle*, n.p.

3. See, for instance, Mendelson, 41–50; Norbrook, "Identity, Ideology, and Politics," 194; and Fitzmaurice, "Margaret Cavendish's *Life of William*," 93–94.

4. *Life of Newcastle*, 179. Numerous critics have discussed the ambivalent dynamics of Cavendish's relation with her husband. See especially Hilda Smith, "Political Differences"; Raber, "Margaret Cavendish's *Playes* and the Drama of Authority"; and Masten, "Material Cavendish."

melodramatic announcement that he is "resolved to love" Charles no matter what becomes political protest, for it concedes that his "Gracious Master" hardly merits such loyalty.

In her fiction, Cavendish imagines a countermodel to Newcastle's resolute self-sacrifice. This countermodel appears most prominently in chaste heroines who reject ideals of ecstatic devotion in favor of the principle that private passion must be constrained by public law. Through these more restrained affective models, Cavendish pictures a political order in which common law and aristocratic counsel protect sovereign and subject alike from the kindred threats of tyranny and anarchy. In this regard, she draws on classical and Renaissance political models in which the tyrant embodies the worst tendencies in human nature more generally. The tyrant acts as irresponsibly as everyone secretly wants to, so the very self-indulgence that corrodes law and liberty may only accentuate his allure in that he becomes a narcissistic reflection of his subjects' own desires.[5] The blurring of boundaries between self and other that characterizes tyranny betrays the instability of sexual, as well as political, identities. Authority and submission, as we have seen, were respectively gendered male and female.[6] But hypermasculine sexual rapaciousness exposed the ruler's inability to defend himself against his own fantasies and passions. The abuse of masculine power, paradoxically, revealed a loss of masculine self-control. Because submission is gendered female, the ability to regulate—chastise—one's own fears and desires is imagined as feminine chastity that limits the virile pursuit of power.

In embracing such a dialectical vision of gender and power, Cavendish challenges the misogyny of both absolutist and republican polemic, each of which imagine an infectious femininity at the roots of their respective bogies, anarchy and tyranny.[7] Cavendish's depiction of resistant subjects as chaste women rejects visions

---

5. See Bushnell, *Tragedies*, 1–36.

6. In Thomas Hobbes' formulation, for instance, "though Man may be male and female, Authority is not" (quoted in Hilda Smith, "A General War," 154).

7. Misogyny was a favored polemical tool of both proponents of absolutism and defenders of regicide and republican rule. Robert Filmer, for instance, challenges arguments for mixed rule by satirically suggesting that women might participate in politics: "It cannot but be mischievous always at the least to all infants and others under age of discretion—not to speak of women, especially virgins, who by birth have as much natural freedom as any other and therefore ought not to lose their liberty without their own consent" (*The Anarchy of Limited or Mixed Monarchy* in *Patriarcha and Other Writings*, 142; all references to Filmer will be to this edition). Milton, similarly, marshals antifeminism in his attack on Salmasius: "naturally you want to force royal tyranny on others after being used to suffer so slavishly a woman's tyranny at home" (*First Defense*, CP, 4:382). For discussions of women in the civil war sects as emblems of anarchy, see Thomas, "Women in the Civil War Sects"; Nadelhaft, "Feminist Attitudes toward Men, Women and Marriage"; Hill, *World Turned Upside Down*, 306–321; Hawes, *Mania and Literary Style*, 1–21; and Davis, *Fear, Myth, and History*, 104–107. Suzuki shows that women petitioned parliament in the 1640s on behalf of both the royalist and the parliamentary cause (*Subordinate Subjects*, 165).

of an entirely masculine political sphere even as she scorns the vain, effeminate spectacle of the Caroline court. In place of these mid-seventeenth-century extremes, she insists on the principle of mixed rule that harks back to sixteenth-century models, in which female *concilium* restrains the destructive impulses of male *imperium*. In contemplating political questions through the lens of erotic relations, Cavendish resembles many Elizabethan and Jacobean authors who both served and criticized the crown. But because Cavendish had witnessed the brutality of the civil wars, she is far less optimistic about the possibility that resistance will lead to reform. Accordingly, her work admits that the rule of law she endorses may turn out to be just as much a fiction as the romance narratives of love and sacrifice it should replace.

Because Cavendish's reputation as an absolutist has been so entrenched, her criticism of tyranny and her endorsement of mixed rule were often overlooked by early criticism. But, as several recent studies have noted, the seeming incongruity between her royalism and her critique of excessive power disappears when we read her work as deliberation rather than polemic.[8] I would like to pursue this more cautious mode of reading, one encouraged by the unresolved series of political and moral debates staged in Cavendish's plays (1662, 1668), *Orations of Diverse Sorts* (1662), and *Sociable Letters* (1664). In particular, I suggest that by situating Cavendish's defense of monarchy within the conceptual frameworks of her own day, we can better appreciate the complexity not only of royalism but also of political thought in general during and after the English civil wars. Literary critics have frequently treated royalism and absolutism as though they are the same thing, supporting a system in which, in the words of the parliamentarian apologist Phillip Hunton, "the sovereignty is so fully in one, that it hath no limits or bounds under God but his own will."[9] In fact, in the seventeenth century support for monarchy frequently meant support for an ancient constitution in which royal power was limited by law and parliament. Until 1648, both sides in the civil war claimed to be conservatives defending England's ancient laws from the encroachments of the other side, and throughout the war both royalists and parliamentarians switched allegiances in the name of loyalty to an ideal of mixed

8. Scholors that have detected in Cavendish a more complex politics include Suzuki, *Subordinate Subjects*; Hilda Smith; "Political Differences"; and Jowitt, "Margaret Cavendish and the Cult of Elizabeth." While Norbrook acknowledges the difficulty of categorizing Cavendish, he nonetheless tends to align her with the self-serving egoism of absolutist discourse in contrast to the more public-spirited republicanism of Lucy Hutchinson and Anna Maria van Schurmann ("Women, the Republic of Letters, and the Public Sphere").

9. *A Treatise of Monarchy*, 6. Filmer is typically taken as the spokesperson for absolutism, but as Daly argues, Filmer's absolutism was unusual among royalists (*Sir Robert Filmer*).

rule.[10] Charles I, however disingenuously, challenged the Nineteen Propositions by insisting that their emphasis on parliamentary supremacy was "a total subversion of the fundamental laws, and that excellent constitution of this kingdome which hath made this nation so many years both famous and happy."[11] Meanwhile, the Commons resolved as late as 1648 not to "alter the fundamental government of the kingdom by King, Lords, and Commons," and Cromwell struggled to find a settlement by which Charles would abdicate in favor of one of his sons.[12]

Still, as numerous historians have shown, the broad consensus that the balance of the ancient constitution was the best form of government left a lot of room for controversy.[13] So once we relinquish the picture of the civil war as, in the words of Richard Cust and Ann Hughes, "a constitutional and political struggle between authoritarian, arbitrary monarchy and the rule of law, the property rights and liberties of individuals," we can see that the conflicts of the mid-seventeenth century took place not only between the royalist and parliamentary parties, but within the individuals who supported them.[14] William Prynne, for instance, notoriously had his ears cropped, his nose slit, and his cheeks branded for criticizing the crypto-Catholic theatrics of the Caroline court in the 1630s, and in 1643 he wrote the *Soveraigne Power of Parliaments and Kingdoms*, the definitive argument for parliamentary prerogative. But Prynne also opposed the trial and execution of Charles I in 1649, was imprisoned from 1650 to 1653 for his opposition to Cromwell's military rule, and was one of the most vocal proponents for the authority of the monarchy and House of Lords in the 1660s.[15] And while Newcastle himself was a long-standing servant of the crown who acted as governor to the future Charles II and who financed and led a

10. Hirst, for instance, notes that after John Pym blocked a peace initiative in 1643, the leaders of the parliamentary peace party defected to Oxford, while royalists like Edward Dering and Trevor Williams abandoned the royalist cause in response to Charles' Cessation with Ireland and the duplicity revealed in the letters seized at Naseby (*Authority*, 243–244, 257). Kenyon has shown that fully half of the upper classes, including half of the Long Parliament, took no part in the wars at all (*Stuart England*, 158).

11. Answer to the Nineteen Propositions, June 18, 1642 (Kenyon, ed., *Stuart Constitution*, 19). Burgess emphasizes that political writing of the 1640s was fundamentally rhetorical, as people on all sides sought to exploit the language of mixed monarchy, natural rights, common law, and counsel (*Absolute Monarchy*, 91).

12. Weston and Greenberg, *Subjects and Sovereigns*, 74.

13. Burgess, *Absolute Monarchy*, 127–164, 209–212. See also McIlwain, *Constitutionalism*; Pocock, *Ancient Constitution*; and Burgess, *Politics*.

14. Cust and Hughes, "After Revisionism," 2. For descriptions of the complexities of political discourse in the 1640s and 1650s, see Hirst, *Authority*, 234–241, 257–268, 344–348; Kenyon, *Stuart England*, 154–167, 190–197; Burgess, *Politics*, 179–211; and Weston and Greenberg, 35–123.

15. For details of Prynne's political life, see Lamont, *Marginal Prynne*. Veevers describes his opposition to the Catholicism of Henrietta Maria's court (*Images of Love and Religion*, 89–90, 108). For Prynne's political activities after the civil wars, see Ogg, *England in the Reign of Charles II*, 1:25–26; and Weston and Greenberg, 118–148.

significant part of the royalist army, he also recommended a mixed form of government in which the nobility restrains the potential excesses of both king and commons.[16] However much Cavendish's biography may stress her husband's loyalty in order to accentuate Charles II's betrayal, Newcastle was never an unambivalent champion of the Stuarts. He satirized the effeminate French fashions of Charles I and Henrietta Maria in his plays, blamed the outbreak of war on the errors of James I and Charles I, and attributed his military losses to Charles I's inept command. When the restored Charles II failed to reward decades of service, Newcastle withdrew to the country and was conspicuously absent from the king's coronation in 1661.[17]

Like Prynne or Newcastle, Cavendish endorses an ancient constitutionalism in which monarchal prerogative is balanced by parliamentary liberty. Since Cavendish's feminized subjects are capable of controlling their own passions, they provide external limits for their sovereigns, rather than vice versa. Cavendish's heroines embody the constitutional authority that many royalists considered the prerogative of the aristocracy. In this regard, Cavendish's political views are consistent with those of many of her contemporaries. For after Pride's Purge, the regicide, and the abolition of the Lords and the monarchy did away with traditional forms of government, only the royalists could claim to be defending the ancient constitution.[18] In imagining limited sovereignty, Cavendish's fiction challenges

16. In his *Letter of Advice* to Charles II, Newcastle assumes the nobility's deposing power over the kings they protect. "For the worste in the Nobility is," according to Newcastle, "but to pull downe one king, & sett up an other, so that they are always for monarkey, butt the Comons, pull downe Roote, & branch, & utterly destroyes monarky." And the "distraction," or violent dissolution, by the Long Parliament of "our Antiente kings" is, for Newcastle, of a piece with the destruction of "our setled Church & our old fundamentall, Lawes—& The Inslaveing the whole nation" (in *Ideology and Politics*, 47, 55). *OED*, 2d ed., s.v. "distraction."

17. Trease, *Portrait of a Cavalier*. In *The Varietie* the Elizabethan figure Manley responds to being mocked as the "ghost of Leister" by censuring the Frenchified manners of the courtier Galliard and defending his Elizabethan dress, which harks back to the days "when men of honour flourish'd. . . . It was never a good time since these cloathes went out of fashion; oh, those honorable dayes and persons!" See *The Country Captaine, And the Varietie, Two Comedies*. See also Martin Butler, *Theatre and Crisis*, 197–198; Jowitt, 388–389; Chalmers, *Royalist Women Writers*, 142; and Knowles, "Nostalgia, Politics, and Jonson's Use of the 1575 Kenilworth Entertainments," 247–267. Both Cavendish's *Life of Newcastle* and Newcastle's *Letter* depict on the whole a rather tense relation with successive Stuart rulers. Cavendish's biography recounts Newcastle's frustrations with what turned out to be disastrous royal interferences in his execution of the war (*Life of Newcastle*, 29, 41, 47, 119), Newcastle's departure from Charles II's court (*Life of Newcastle*, 88–89), and his awareness of his sacrifices (*Life of Newcastle*, 183–184, 188). In his unsolicited *Letter of Advice* to Charles II, Newcastle contrasts the mistakes of the Stuarts to the effective rule of Elizabeth I (9–10, 38, 44, 49–60). Lynn Hulse's DNB entry concludes by observing that, except for his three-year period as governor to the future Charles II, Newcastle remained on the fringes of court ("Cavendish, William," 15).

18. As Bushnell notes, tyranny was long associated with effeminacy and artifice, and by the mid-seventeenth century these charges were being applied to parliament as much as to the monarchy (7–20, 76–78). Herman describes in detail royalist claims of parliamentary tyranny ("Ancient Constitution," 994–1000).

the reasoning by which the Rump abolished monarchy in 1649: "usually and naturally any one person in such power makes it his interest to encroach upon the just freedom and liberty of the people, and to promote the setting up of their own will and power above the laws, that so they might enslave these kingdoms to their own lust."[19] This declaration assumes a populace whose symbiotic idolatry and self-interest makes it helpless to restrain its ruler's insatiable appetite. As Milton put it, those who wished for the return of monarchy could only be victims of "a besotted and degenerate baseness of spirit" or Machiavels eager "to set a face upon thir own malignant designes."[20] According to many mid-century republican tracts, this widespread servility to desire—whether the king's or one's own—meant that a truly popular system of government might endanger the common good. "If a people be depraved and corrupt, so as to conferre . . . power . . . upon wicked men," John Goodwin sternly warned, "they forfeit their power . . . unto those that are good, though but a few."[21] But as the series of failed government experiments of the 1650s demonstrates, those "few" could as easily be accused of tyranny as the "one person" they replaced. By the time that Cavendish published *Nature's Pictures* in 1656, many in the English nation had tired of Cromwell's military rule and grown anxious about its potential for abuse. On January 19, 1657, James Ashe anticipated the Humble Petition and Advice by moving that Cromwell "take upon him the government according to an ancient constitution."[22] For all but the most ideologically committed republicans, a return to monarchy seemed the best safeguard against arbitrary power.

Likewise, most royalists who hoped for the return of the Lords and the king did not endorse royal absolutism. They insisted on the wisdom of what Charles I had termed "regulated monarchy" in opposition to the military rule of the 1650s. At his trial, Charles I himself had warned that "if power without law may make laws, may alter the fundamental laws of the Kingdom, I do not know what subject he is in England, that can be sure of his life, or anything that he calls his own."[23] However insincere these claims were, they effectively replaced absolutist rhetoric with that of mixed rule, and before Charles II was declared king on May 8, 1660, the parliament announced that "according to the ancient and fundamental laws of the kingdom the government is and ought to be by king, lords, and commons."[24] Indeed, the language of mixed monarchy had become so habitual by 1660 that Charles II's Declaration at Breda took for granted the coordination of king and parliament, while the

---

19. "An Act for the abolishing the kingly office," in Kenyon, ed., *Stuart Constitution*, 306.

20. *Eikonoklastes, CP*, 3:344–345.

21. *Right and Might Well Met.*

22. Quoted in Kenyon, ed., *Stuart Constitution*, 304.

23. Wedgwood, *The Trial of Charles I*, 156.

24. Quoted by Greenberg, 243. See also Morrill and Baker, "Oliver Cromwell," 14–35; Gardiner, *History of the Great Civil War*, 4:116, 124; and Ogg, 1:32.

anonymous author of *The Dignity of Kingship* (1660) responded to Milton's *Readie and Easie Way* not with a defense of absolutism, but with an assurance that the English constitution limited the king's authority.[25]

Through narratives of ravishment and betrayal, *Assaulted and Pursued Chastity* and "The Contract" censure the arbitrary rule of the Interregnum regimes and urge limited, legal monarchy as its antidote. Cavendish introduces *Assaulted and Pursued Chastity* by situating it within a tradition of politicized rape narratives in which sexual violation both manifests tyranny and leads to its destruction. The classic example of such an equation is, of course, Livy's *History*, but Cavendish pointedly ignores the Livian tale of rape that Shakespeare had made so popular.[26] Livy's narrative insists that the best alternative to tyranny is republican government that replaces passive, effeminate suffering with decisive, masculine action. This opposition, as we have seen in Shakespeare's version of the story, forces subjects into either loathsome complicity or dangerous mutiny. In order to emphasize the vulnerabilities to which rebellion exposes its perpetrators, Cavendish takes as her example "Jacob's daughter Dinah, which Shechem forced. And others, whose enforcement mentioned in holy Scripture, and in histories of less authority (sans number) which shows, that Heaven doth not always protect the persons of virtuous souls from rude violences."[27]

Cavendish's choice of Dinah challenges the rape-revolution-republicanism trajectory offered by such "histories of less authority" as Livy's. After Shechem violates Dinah, his father Hamor approaches Jacob with an offer of marriage, but Jacob's sons demand that the entire Hivite tribe be circumcised first. They then treacherously attack the Hivites while the men are too "sore" to fight back, leveling their city and seizing their livestock, women, and children (Gen. 34:25–26). This invasion increases the hostility of the neighboring tribes, making Jacob's own tribe more vulnerable to attack. Dinah's story suggests that the violent overthrow of tyranny may as easily lead to constant war and chaos as to republican liberty. This narrative may equally work to dissociate the parliamentarians' self-identification with God's chosen people by engaging the royalist argument that puritan calls for religious reform hid more worldly ambitions: the Geneva Bible gloss states that Jacob's sons "made the holy ordinance of God a meane to compasses their wicked

---

25. See Weston and Greenberg, 150–152; and Keeble, *Restoration*, 65–70.
26. Cavendish was well aware of the history of interpretations of Livy's tale: *Sociable Letters* includes a debate over Lucretia's response to her violation (64–66).
27. *Assaulted and Pursued Chastity*, in *The Blazing World & Other Writings*, ed. Lilley, 47. All references to Cavendish's fiction will be to this edition unless otherwise noted. Leslie argues that Cavendish may draw on Dinah's story to imagine the restoration of English royalists ("Evading Rape").

purpose" (34:14) and that "their fault is the greater in that they make religion a cloke for their craft" (34:17).[28]

Assaulted and Pursued Chastity departs from its biblical, classical, and Shakespearean predecessors in its depiction of rape. Instead, Cavendish draws on Spenserian allegory to imagine a world in which female resistance can constrain male appetite and thereby prevent the tyranny that leads to revolution. As she sails to her native Kingdom of Riches after exile during its civil wars, the romance's protagonist, the thrice-baptized Miseria-Travellia-Affectionata, is shipwrecked in the Kingdom of Sensuality. There she is abandoned by her friends, robbed, and purchased by a bawd who in turn sells her to the Prince of Sensuality. Like Shakespeare's Lysimachus, the Prince is a "grand monopolizer of young virgins" whose private desires have so taken over his public office that he considers the bawd his "chief officer" (50). The Prince repeatedly attempts to violate Miseria, but she protects her virtue while avoiding the usual routes of rescue, death, or suicide. This narrative distinguishes self-defense from revolution, sanctioning the former even as it condemns the latter.

Miseria's very heroism, however, reveals the difficulty of sustaining any true balance between monarchal prerogative and aristocratic resistance. As Kathryn Schwarz has argued, since Miseria "abandons . . . the path of masochistic resignation," she emulates militant virgins who vanquish their rapists. She thereby reveals that chastity may destabilize the same gender hierarchies it is designed to protect.[29] Because Miseria defends her honor with a rigor that frequently shades into violence, she blurs the lines between proper resistance and improper revolt. This behavior confronts the question of how far subjects can go to resist unjust commands before anarchy ensues. And if Miseria's course of action is any guide, they can go surprisingly far.

The political dimension of Miseria's chastity becomes apparent when she resists the Prince's initial advances by describing her body as a piece of inviolable property of which she is sole owner. "It is an injustice to take the goods from the right owners without their consent," Miseria insists, "and an injustice is an act that all noble minds hate . . . and none but base or cruel tyrants will lay unreasonable commands, or require wicked demands to the powerless, or virtuous" (52). This argument gives a gendered dimension to the outrage of royalists whose estates were confiscated and decimated by the Republic and Protectorate, a situation with which Cavendish was personally familiar. In November 1651, shortly after Cromwell's victory at

---

28. In *A Declaration Made by the Earl of New-Castle . . . For his Resolution of Marching into Yorkshire*, Newcastle condemns the horrific bloodshed and destruction "exercised by a party who pretend nothing but the Religion of God, the Law of the Land, and the Liberty of the Subiect" (3).

29. Schwarz, "Cavendish's Romance," 278. Weitz argues that chastity's very position as the antithesis to lust also makes it "the inescapable partner of lust" ("Romance Fiction," 149–150). Jankowski examines the transgressive potential of militant virginity (*Pure Resistance*).

Worcester had extinguished all remaining hopes of a royalist resurgence, Cavendish had traveled to England with her brother-in-law, Charles Cavendish, to compound for her banished husband's property. When she appealed to the Parliamentary Committee for Compounding for the allowance that wives were to receive, she "found their hearts as hard as my fortunes, and their Natures as cruell as my miseries, for they sold all my Lords Estate, which was a very great one, and gave me not any part thereof, or any allowance thereout, which few or no other was so hardly dealt withall."[30] In Cavendish's experience, it is not parliamentary authority as such that is unjust, but the misuse of that power to appropriate private property.

Cavendish's individual attempt to retain her family's estates was emblematic of the larger constitutional anxieties that occupied the English throughout the 1650s. The events that followed her return to Antwerp in 1653 only increased the fears of royalists and republicans alike that English government was quickly abandoning even the pretence of representation and consent.[31] The Rump voted on April 19, 1653, to hold fresh elections without a mechanism for screening candidates, and the next day Cromwell led a company of soldiers into Westminster and forcibly expelled the parliament. His handpicked Nominated Assembly—the "Barebones Parliament"—fared little better when it convened in September 1654 only to be dissolved four months later. After royalists revolted in Penruddock's Rising in May 1655, conditions grew even grimmer. Cromwell responded to the revolt by dividing England and Wales into eleven regions, each to be governed by a Major General and militia funded by imposing fines of 10 percent on the estates of unyielding royalists. Cromwell's government justified this "decimation tax" by claiming the same "emergency powers" that Charles I had invoked to defend extraparliamentary taxation.[32] In the context of these Cromwellian policies, Miseria's description of her virtue as property gives political resonance to her charge that by threatening to deflower her the Prince becomes "a beast to appetite, a tyrant to innocence." Cavendish's description employs terms used to describe Cromwell by republicans like Lucy Hutchinson, who were similarly appalled by his abandonment of representative rule (52). Hutchinson repeatedly emphasizes Cromwell's "ambition" and "appetite" as she recounts how "Cromwell and his army grew wanton with their power, and invented a thousand tricks of government," calling "several sorts of mock parliaments, but not finding one of them absolutely for his turn, turned them off again." Once Lord Protector, he "at last exercised such an arbitrary power that the whole

---

30. *True Relation*, 51. Cavendish repeats this account in the *Life of Newcastle*, 71.
31. These fears had already been raised by the Levellers, particularly in the context of the Putney Debates. See Gentiles, "The *Agreements of the People*"; and Worden, "Levellers." During the interregnum, the political elite expressed similar anxieties about representation.
32. For a general overview of English politics from 1653 to 1657, see Hirst, *Authority*, 317–336; Kenyon, ed., *Stuart Constitution*, 179–185. For more detailed discussions of the rule of the major generals and the decimation tax, see Woolrych, "Military Dictatorship?" 61–89; and Anthony Fletcher, "Problem of Consent," 121–137.

land grew weary of him, while he set up a company of silly mean fellows, called major generals, as governors in every county, who ruled according to their wills, by no law but what seemed good in their own eyes."[33]

Though Cavendish, like Hutchinson, laments the injustices of the Cromwellian regime, she seems concerned to ground this objection not on questions of Cromwell's legitimacy, but on his misuse of power. Her sense that tyranny is behavioral rather than structural means that the Prince figures not only Cromwell but also misrule in general—and her designation of him by his royal title extends her argument for resistance to all figures of power. As Bushnell has suggested, "the tyrant figures a kind of improper authority that makes authority itself problematic."[34] In arguing that the tyranny of Cromwell or his army should be resisted, Cavendish implicitly sanctions opposition to any abuse of sovereign authority. So when Miseria, unable to repel the Prince with reason, resorts to force, her actions are all the harder to distinguish from those who had executed Charles I for the same "tyranny" and "treason" with which Miseria charges the Prince.[35] Seeing that he is "ready to seize on her," Miseria "drew forth the pistol, which she had concealed: bending her brows, with a resolute spirit [she] told him she would stand upon her guard: for[,] said she, it is no sin to defend myself against an obstinate and cruel enemy, and know said she, I am no ways to be found [ ] but in death; for whilst I live I will live in honour, or when I kill or be killed I will kill or die for security" (52). When the Prince attempts to disarm her, she shoots him, thus repudiating victimization in favor of active self-defense. By insisting that the Prince lost his royal sanctity when he unjustly assaulted her liberty and property, Miseria recalls the claims that MPs had been making against extraparliamentary taxation for decades. She thus affirms the limits of royal power even as she accepts monarchy as an institution.

Like the other authors I have examined, Cavendish knows that external force is only one mechanism of tyranny. A more insidious tool is seduction. In *Assaulted and Pursued Chastity*, Miseria is not immune to the Prince's charms, and her ability to withstand her own passions is far greater evidence of heroism than her rejection of the Prince. Once recovered from his gunshot wound, the Prince, "with an humble behavior and civil respect, craved pardon for his former faults, promising [Miseria], that if she would be pleased to allow him her conversation, he would never enforce that from her which she was not willing to grant" and begins "to insinuate himself into her favour by his person and services" (57). But when he urges Miseria to consummate their now-mutual attraction, "protesting his love, vowing his fidelity and secrecy, swearing his constancy to death," she rebuffs him, insisting that because he

33. *Memoirs*, 256–257. As Norbrook has observed, much of the polemical energy of Hutchinson's *Memoirs* is not against royalists but against enemies who had been on the parliamentary side during the civil wars ("Republican Civility").

34. Bushnell, 5.

35. For the official charges against Charles, see "The Sentence of the High Court of Justice upon the King," January 27, 1648/9, in Gardiner, ed., *Constitutional Documents*, 312.

is already married, "he might make all that good, but not the lawfulness." Despite his claim that their mutual desire is "lawful by nature," Miseria maintains that "it is as impossible to corrupt me, as to corrupt Heaven; but were you free, I should willingly embrace your love, in lawful marriage" (59). In insisting upon the Prince's lack of freedom, Miseria equates his marriage with the force of law. The move from the indicative description of her present steadfastness to the subjunctive mood of her possible consent accentuates Miseria's determination to subject her own feelings to the same rigor that she demands of the Prince. Divine decree, personal consent, and public law check the "natural" passions that threaten to confound beast and human. The Prince initially yields to her will, but soon afterward he assaults her a second time. This time, Miseria preserves her honor by poisoning herself. As we shall see, this shift from self-defense to self-destruction suggests that she may have come to share the Prince's treacherous desires. When she recovers, the Prince again seems to repent, "cursing himself, praying and imploring his pardon and her forgiveness, promising and protesting never the like again" (60). Unfortunately, however, his determination to imprison her in the Kingdom of Sensuality reveals the hollowness of these vows. Knowing that the Prince will make further attempts on her honor, Miseria cuts her hair, dons the clothes of a page, and flees aboard a ship whose master eventually adopts her as his "son" (61).

Cavendish has repeatedly described the Prince as a "beast to appetite, a tyrant to innocence" (52), and a "ravenous lion" (57), and she literalizes this conventional description of tyrant as beast when Travellia and her adopted father are shipwrecked on an island of cannibals.[36] Here, they quickly learn that "they had a custom in that country, to keep great store of slaves, both males and females, to breed on, as we do breed flocks of sheep, and other cattle[.] The children were eaten as we do lambs or veal, for young and tender meat; the elder for beef and mutton, as stronger meats" (69). While the slaves used as livestock initially appear to be distinct from—and possibly food for—the rest of the country's subjects, that distinction disappears by the end of the paragraph, when Cavendish tells us that "as for their government, it was tyrannical, for all the common people were slaves to the royal" (69). Cavendish uses the same word to describe "the great store of slaves" on which the rulers dine and the "common people" as such, which extends the condition of slavery to the population at large: monarchs may cannibalize any of their subjects.[37] Travellia makes a similarly explicit equation of tyranny with uncontrolled appetite in the letter that she leaves the Prince's aunt explaining that she must escape because "it is too dangerous for a lamb to live near a lion; for your nephew is of so hungry an appetite, that I dare not stay" (76). Like tyrant in Sidney's Ister Bank fable, and like

36. This characterization echoes Erasmus' depiction of the tyrant as both beast and cannibal (Bushnell, 51).
37. Iyengar reads Cavendish's description of the cannibals as a celebration of absolute authority (658).

the island rulers whose young slaves are "eaten as we do lambs or veal, for young and tender meat," the Prince is more beast than man. His excessive appetite has made Sensuality a state not unlike the one that Travellia and her adopted father confront on the island. Because the tyrant expects his subjects to mirror his own impulses, his brutish appetite equally dehumanizes his people. Nonetheless, by signing her letters to the Prince and his aunt with her "real" name, "Affectionata," our heroine makes clear that she flees her own passions as much as those of the Prince. Since she cannot reform Sensuality, she must escape its corrupting influence.

The ability of the law to subdue natural passion is further tested when Travellia and the Prince are kidnapped by the same group of pirates, then shipwrecked on an uninhabited island. Despite his exile from Sensuality, the Prince's character remains unchanged. As Travellia wryly observes, "he was not grown the chaster" after spending time with the pirates (who have, appropriately enough, made him their captain). On the island, the Prince soon recognizes that the boy he has abducted is actually the mistress he has pursued, and he makes a third attempt on Travellia's honor. Travellia threatens to kill herself, to which the Prince (apparently weary of this pattern) replies that "he would satisfy himself first, unless she would consent to live with him as his wife, in that island, wherein, said he, we may live free, and secure, without a disturbance" (83). The Prince envisions the virgin land where he will establish "his new and small monarchy" as a place where natural passion is unconstrained by human law. He muses "how that island might be made a paradise, and in what felicity they might live therein, if their peevish humours did not overthrow their pleasures" (85). For the Prince, law and virtue are "peevish humours" that arbitrarily impede a return to Eden. Travellia, however, insists that they follow the laws of her native kingdom rather than the impulses of nature, and she flees again rather than commit adultery.

In the romance's final episode, Travellia and the Prince end up leading the respective armies of the Kingdoms of Amity and Amour. This rather Spenserian battle between the moderation and compromise signified by "Amity" and the ambivalence and obsession represented by "Amour" is hardly a new event. But it does specify the political implications of the struggle both between the Prince and Travellia and within Travellia herself.[38] In Amour, the King has all of the marks of a tyrant. His inability to rule himself has infected his nobility, who are so "given to ease, and delighting in effeminate pleasures" that they "shunned the wars, sending out only the most vulgar people who were rather slaves than subjects" (89). Once his forces are defeated, he refuses to summon his councilors: he knows that "for their own securities" they will force him to surrender the Queen, whom he has taken prisoner (106). The King's willingness to place "his passion of love" above the safety of his people puts in political terms the Prince's own lack of regard for Travellia's consent. By contrast, the Queen of Amity repeatedly bows to her council's

38. Leslie, 193.

advice, leaving her beloved Travellia to rally her soldiers and waiting to marry until her council has agreed (91, 114).

Although Travellia leads the Kingdom of Amity to a victory of chaste love over willful desire, the details of the war and its resolution disrupt this allegory of restraint. If the Amitian nobility has the sort of conciliar sway recommended by ancient constitutionalists like Newcastle, this power is always on the verge of wresting sovereignty from the monarch. When the Queen leaves Travellia to govern in her stead, "the people knowing her commands, and pleasure by her proclamation, fell a-murmuring, not only in that she left a stranger, but a poor slave, who was taken prisoner and sold, and a person who was of no higher birth, than a shipmaster's son . . . whereupon they began to design his death" (92). Travellia, luckily, governs so "gently" that she "begot such love in every heart . . . and [the people] by their obedience showed their duty and zeal to all his commands, or rather to his persuasions" (92). Cavendish attempts to transform this popular election into noble assent when "all the chief of the kingdom" elect Travellia general. But the threat of rebellion locates authority in the obedience of subjects, not the command of the sovereign. Travellia can secure loyalty because she does not attempt to extend her power beyond its lawful bounds.

The potential for love to disrupt ideals of balanced rule appears even more ominous in the romance's resolution, which is made possible not by the Prince's moral reform but by the news that his aged wife has expired. When Travellia learns that her beloved is free to marry, the passion that she has long suppressed nearly explodes: "her heart did beat like to a feverish pulse, being moved with several passions, fearing it was not so, hoping it was so, joying if it were so, grieving that she ought not to wish it so" (113). Her unsettling, if ambivalent, joy at the news of another woman's death attempts to reconcile her former resistance with her present consent. If she has loved the Prince all along, Travellia's allegiance to the law has been the only thing keeping her from falling into the arms of a man who has repeatedly attempted to rape and kill her. It is precisely because that chastity has successfully withstood the assaults of heretofore invisible passion that its revelation is so jarring.

Cavendish never resolves these tensions in her narrative. Instead, she exacerbates them in the contradictory instructions the Queen of Amity offers for the viceregency of her kingdom after she has married the King of Amour. Initially, the Queen determines that "the Prince, and his Princess that was to be should be Viceroy, or rather she should rule; who was so beloved of the people, as if she had not only been a native born, but as if she had been born from the royal stock" (114). Her emphasis on the people's love would seem to mystify the conditions of rule by attributing power to affective choice. However, it also threatens to destabilize the balanced rule that Cavendish labors to envision. Though the Queen appears to determine her proxies, the source of this decision is rendered ambiguous when her royal decree is supplemented by popular demand: "when it was read that the Prince should be Viceroy in the Kingdom of Amity, all the soldiers, as if they had been one voice, cried out, Travellia shall be Viceregency; which was granted to pacify them. Whereupon there were great acclamations of joy" (116). Given these contradictory scenarios, it is difficult to tell first, whether the Prince or Travellia will rule, and second, whether the source of this authority is in Queen or people. Crucially, this army is not peopled by the Levellers and radicals that made up the New Model Army, but by virtuous soldiers reminiscent of Elizabethan forces. But even such an aristocratic troop can be pacified only by getting what they demand, and this vision of belligerent nobility poses the same problem for Cavendish's ideal of mixed monarchy as it did for her fifteenth- and sixteenth-century forbears. Moreover, as Schwarz notes, the text gives no clear sense of whether the viceroy is supported or supplanted by the viceregency here, an ambiguity reflected in the different understandings that Travellia and the Prince have of this settlement: "The Prince told his mistress, she should also govern him. / She answered, that he should govern her, and she would govern the kingdom" (116).[39] The Prince's offer of submission suggests joint rule in that it distinguishes himself from the kingdom. Travellia's reply, by contrast, assumes that she will have sole rule of Amity, a public superiority for which she coyly compensates by promising private submission to a man who has done nothing to deserve it. As we have seen, the events in *Assaulted and Pursued Chastity* suggest that only constant struggle can constrain tyranny. Tellingly, however, Cavendish cannot imagine the end of the struggle, only its abandonment in favor of the same romance ideals she has largely eschewed.

Like *Assaulted and Pursued Chastity*, "The Contract" explores the relation between rule and resistance through the trope of courtship, but it turns more explicitly to the law—again embodied in a previous wife—as the instrument for regulating sovereign authority. The story opens by describing a marriage contract to which neither party consents: a dying Duke and a wealthy gentleman betroth the Duke's rakish younger son to the gentleman's 6-year-old niece, Delitia. The young man is "very unwilling thereto, he being a man grown, and she a child," but he "seemed to consent, to please his father. Then they were as firmly contracted as the priest could make them, and two or three witnesses to avow it" (4). In time, the young man's elder brother also dies, so he inherits both title and property. Now Duke, he falls "extremely in love" with the wife of a rich grandee and, once her aged husband has expired, he marries her without giving a thought to his contract with Delitia. Years later, the Duke and Delitia meet and, unaware of one another's identities, fall instantly and passionately in love. Two obstacles, however, stand in the way of the happy ending that can be secured only through lawful marriage: the Duke, of course, already has

---

39. Schwarz, "Cavendish's Romance," 280. Rees argues that Travellia is aware that the army's support makes the Prince's authority over her purely nominal (*Margaret Cavendish*, 115).

a wife, and Delitia's uncle is determined to marry her to a wealthy Viceroy. The lovers take their dilemma to court, where Delitia pleads her "just interest" in the Duke based on the their original contract (30). The judges grant her suit and declare her legally married to the Duke, upon which the spurned Viceroy and the Duke's former wife agree to marry, the court adjourns, and the tale ends with "much rejoicings . . . of all sides" (43).

The conclusion of "The Contract" imagines a union in which law at once sanctions true love and renders it irrelevant. The very thing that makes affection a sign of freedom is its volatility, but this volatility also makes love alone an insufficient bond. So the narrative can only reconcile coercive authority (represented by arranged marriage) and individual volition (represented by spontaneous love) through a temporal displacement that effects the subordination of will to law. Delitia initiates her lawsuit only after she has fallen in love with the Duke. But she does not win because the judges sympathize with her feelings or her virtue, as might be the case in a more traditional romance that honors the spirit of the law above its letter. In fact, she and the Duke conceal their newfound affection during the trial, and the judge's decision to "award" the Duke to Delitia is based on the principle that law must control personal whims. This insistence on the sovereignty of public law may censure the arbitrary power of the Interregnum regimes, which, according to Charles II in a letter to General George Monck, were "assumed by passion and appetite and not supported by justice."[40] Yet by depicting law as a realm in which truth and justice are rhetorical and contingent, not transcendent or absolute, "The Contract" also allows that the law is itself vulnerable to the arbitrary desires it should restrain.

Although the argument that rulers must obey the law emerges from the experience of the Interregnum, its theoretical formulation has consequences for monarchy as well. Throughout "The Contract" Cavendish is at pains to distinguish true nobility from mere courtliness, and she does this most prominently by contrasting the vanities of the court, represented by the Duke, with Delitia's sober chastity. Cavendish's brief stint as a lady-in-waiting to Henrietta Maria has been treated as one source of her "absolutist" sympathies. But Delitia's disdain throughout "The Contract" for the "painted scenes" of masques (9) and the larger court culture of "splendrous vanities," "pomp and pride," and "factions, envies, and back-bitings" (41) may be more representative of Cavendish's actual experience.[41] Born Margaret Lucas into a minor gentry family in Colchester, Cavendish grew up in an atmosphere that embraced the values of honesty, sobriety, and modesty that were associated with the "country" in seventeenth-century polemic—values that writers like William Prynne so often opposed to the *préciosité* and ostentation that characterized

40. Quoted in Ogg, 1:32.
41. Chalmers, 141–142.

the court Cavendish would join at Oxford in 1643. As she tells us in *A True Relation of My Birth, Breeding, and Life,* Cavendish was miserable at court, where her concern for "loyal duty" and "honest reputation" earned only mockery.[42] According to her autobiography, Cavendish followed Henrietta Maria into exile in 1644 only because "my Mother said, it would be a disgrace for me to return out of the Court so soon after I was placed."[43] While in exile in Paris, Cavendish met Newcastle, and the couple married in spite of Henrietta Maria's opposition. The cruelty of such monarchal interference is the topic of Cavendish's narrative poem "The Description of Constancy" in which a haughty queen nearly executes a pair of faithful lovers in order to prevent their marriage.[44] In *A True Relation,* Cavendish presents her 1645 marriage as a reprieve from the court culture she found so oppressive: "so I continued almost two years, until such time as I was married from thence; for my Lord the Marquis of *Newcastle* did approve of those bashfull fears which many condemn'd."[45]

The effects of renouncing courtly ideals surface at the conclusion of "The Contract" when Delitia counters the Duke's wife's charge that she is "of too mean a breeding" for the Duke. Delitia asserts that she "can draw a line of pedigree five hundred years in length from the root of merit, from whence gentility doth spring." Moreover, she maintains, her honor "cannot be degraded by the displeasure of princes, it holds not the fee-simple from the crown ... and having such a father and mother as merit and time, gentry is a fit and equal match for any, were they rulers of the whole world" (41). Delitia's statement defends Cavendish's own marriage against those courtly detractors—including Henrietta Maria—who would have stopped it by denying innate superiority to noble, or even royal, birth. This principle was typical of both the "country" values of the Lucas family and of Cavendish and her husband in their exile and post-Reformation rustication. This "country" ideology encourages a social order based on virtue, not birth, a position coherent with the more general insistence on law in "The Contract."[46]

Cavendish's turn to judicial answers to Delitia's predicament registers the increasing association of law-making with sovereignty in the seventeenth century and the consequent debates over whether legislative power belonged to king or political community.[47] The early Stuarts had notoriously argued that because the king makes the law he is not subject to it. James I had pronounced that "the King is aboue the

---

42. In *Paper Bodies,* ed. Bowerbank and Mendelson, 46.

43. *True Relation,* 47. See also Grant, *Margaret the First;* and Kathleen Jones, *Glorious Fame.*

44. In *Natures Pictures,* 12–38. See also Grant, 82–85; and Battigelli, *Margaret Cavendish,* 23–37, 119.

45. *True Relation,* 47. For accounts of Cavendish and Newcastle's courtship, see Grant, 71–83; and Trease, 146–152.

46. For discussions of "country" ideology, see Zagorin's influential *The Court and the Country* and Sharpe's revisionist account (*Criticism,* 11–16).

47. Weston and Greenberg survey the different configurations that this question took. See also Cromartie, "Transformation of Political Culture."

law, as both the author and giuer of strength thereunto." And Charles I had main-
tained with his dying breath that subjects' "liberty and freedom consists in having
of government; those laws by which their life and other goods may be most their
own. It is not for having share in government, sir, that is nothing pertaining to
them."[48] In opposition to these claims of royal supremacy, MPs like Prynne had
cited medieval law and the ancient constitution to insist that "the whole kingdom
and parliament are the supreme sovereign authority, and paramount the king,
because they may lawfully, and do usually prescribe such conditions, terms, and
rules of governing the people to him, and bind them thus by oath, faithfully to perform the same, as long as he shall continue king." As representative of the political
nation, parliament "hath power ... so far as finally to oblige both king and subject."[49]

Given that such defenders of regicide as Milton and John Sadler invoked the
ancient constitutionalist claim that the coronation oath was a contract between
ruler and people—one that Charles I had broken—it may seem curious that a royalist like Cavendish would delineate an equally legalistic vision of marital and political bonds in "The Contract." But in asserting the inviolability of the law, "The
Contract" also argues against the Cromwellian regime, which in the cultural imagination had come to seem as autocratic a form of rule as the Caroline court it
replaced.[50] By 1655, increasing numbers of judges asserted that although for the
sake of good government they had accepted the Instrument of Government, which
they saw as an illegal constitution, they would not allow Cromwell as executive to
override that constitution.[51] For royalists and republicans alike, this tyranny was
manifested most prominently in Cromwell's contempt for England's laws, which
appeared to dispense with any standard but his own will and earned him the enmity
of most of the legal profession. In one widely reported case, for instance, the counsel of George Cony, a merchant and religious radical who refused to pay customs
duties, swayed the bench with arguments for ancient rights to property. In response,
Cromwell replaced the Chief Justice Henry Rolle and two other judges, furious at
their affirmation of what, as we have seen, he referred to as "Magna Farta."[52] Cromwell's impatience with English law and custom helps to explain why royalists like
Cavendish would identify monarchy with public law, the current regime with
private will. The role of the Lord Protector was constantly being redefined in

48. James I, *The Trew Law of Free Monarchies* in *Political Writings*, 75; and Charles I's final
    speech (which was published illegally on February 5, 1649), in Kenyon, ed., *Stuart Consti-
    tution*, 295.

49. *The Treachery and Disloyalty of Papists to Their Soveraignes*, 32, 43, 45.

50. Gaunt argues that Cromwell's reputation as tyrant was the result of the secrecy of his Coun-
    cilors, rather than their status as a sort of puppet regime ("Oliver Cromwell and His Protec-
    toral Councilors").

51. Kenyon, ed., *Stuart Constitution*, 304.

52. The incident is described by Hirst, *Authority*, 334.

documents like Lambert's 1653 Instrument and the third Protectorate Parliament's 1657 Humble Petition and Advice, and it was precisely the written nature of these constitutions that made them disposable: as the 1660 *A declaration of the freeborn people* put it, "if he [Cromwell] pleases to throw away (or burne by the hands of the hangman) his Limits in his paper of Government, who can trouble him?"[53] By contrast to the office of Protector, which was newly invented and therefore open to potentially limitless expansions of power, that of monarch was constrained by an ancient constitution that neither king nor people could alter.

As Victoria Kahn has observed, Cavendish's emphasis on law and consent aligns her with republican critics of absolutist theory. Whereas Kahn sees this as an accidental self-contradiction, however, I argue that it is in fact consistent with Cavendish's investment in mixed monarchy.[54] The view that monarchy was incompatible with republicanism was a comparatively recent position, one that even Cromwell himself never fully embraced and that parliamentary leaders like Thomas Fairfax abandoned by the end of the 1650s. Read in this light, the legalism of "The Contract" makes evident the need for a reciprocal relation between sovereignty and law, represented in this narrative through the relation of courtship. And, indeed, Cavendish was writing in a singular political moment in which the exiled Charles Stuart's accession was largely dependent on the consent and invitation of the collective body politic. This situation was not unlike courtship, in which the elective and uncertain nature of subjection is impossible to ignore. Courtship, at least in Cavendish's experience, is a moment in which a woman actively decides to subordinate herself, and it is this choice that is the basis of legitimate marriage.

But even legitimate obedience has its limits. Like Sidney and Wroth, Cavendish contemplates the limits of authority though the scenario of forced marriage. In "The Contract," Delitia's uncle—who has unquestionably legitimate authority— orders her to marry an aged Viceroy. The Duke's response to the news of her betrothal is the only assertion of absolutism in the romance, but its source and its logic tellingly undermine its persuasiveness. After he threatens to kill the Viceroy to prevent Delitia from marrying him, she responds that "it is an unheard of malice to me, or an impudent and vainglorious pride in you, neither to own me yourself, nor let another" (29). The Duke answers by appealing to a political analogy of inviolable kingship:

53. Quoted in Gaunt, 539. See also Hirst's discussion of the Humble Petition and Advice (*Authority*, 345–348), and Keeble's analysis of the importance of this line of argument in the restoration of monarchy (*Restoration*, 64–66).

54. Victoria Kahn, "Margaret Cavendish," 544–547. Kahn reads "The Contract" as an allegory for the Engagement Controversy, in which English subjects had to decide whether they could legitimately swear allegiance to the Commonwealth and break their earlier oath to Charles. As Hirst has argued, this Controversy not only tested loyalties but also encouraged people to think about the grounds of government in more theoretical ways (*Authority*, 297).

Said the Duke, you cannot want an owner whilst I live, for I had, nor have no more power to resign the interest I have in you, than Kings to resign their crown that comes by succession, for the right lies in the crown, not in the man, and though I have played the tyrant, and deserved to be uncrowned, yet none ought to take it off my head, but death, nor have I power to throw it from myself, death only must make way for a successor. (29)

Parliamentary apologists had described the king's office and person as divisible and consequently justified rebellion as itself a way of defending monarchy. By contrast, the Duke presents sovereignty as a mystical essence that even he himself is incapable of sacrificing at will. So when the Duke depicts his passion for Delitia as a divine right, he makes the unsettling suggestion that he will not allow the law to constrain him. But he also reveals the danger of such a view of sovereignty. Unlike Delitia, who is only bound by propriety—she "ought" not uncrown him—the Duke has no power over his own impulses. In arguing for an absolute power of affection, the Duke reveals the very royal willfulness that makes the rule of law essential.

Significantly, it is the Duke himself who recognizes that the same law that prevents his marriage to Delitia may ultimately sanction it. Delitia must "pardon" his fault and then plead her right to their original marriage contract in a court of law. The uncle agrees to join with his niece and the Duke in their lawsuit, and "advising all three together, they thought it fit, since the parties must plead their own cause, to conceal their agreements, and to cover it by the Duke's seeming dissent, lest he should be convicted as a breaker of the known laws, and so be liable to punishment, either by the hazard of his own life, or the price of a great fame" (37). In "acting" the parts of wrongly forsaken maiden and unregenerate cad, Delitia and the Duke do not invent new roles for themselves. They simply draw on recognizable tropes to make their legal positions more intelligible. They need not disguise the facts of the case, only the private desires that are immaterial to the law itself. As the judges finally rule, "humane justice sentences not the thoughts, but acts; wherefore those words that plead his thoughts, ought to be waived as useless, and from the bar of justice cast aside" (40). Far from arguing that desire is superior to law—as the Duke did in his speech on absolute sovereignty—the three conspirators recognize that love itself must be restrained in order to assure the impartial justice that gives public law its force. According to the logic of the case, it might be possible for Delitia to force the Duke into marriage even without his consent. Within the framework of "The Contract," this situation allows a romance narrative of true love to coexist with a legal power of coercion, as Victoria Kahn has argued.[55] But in light of Interregnum constitutional debates—and by the terms of the Duke's own analogy—Delitia's successful pleas suggest that the law must be capable of containing even royal passions.

55. "Margaret Cavendish," 529–530, 554–557.

The arguments offered in the trial are exactly what they would be if Delitia were claiming the Duke from his current wife based on purely legal, not affective, grounds. In insisting that their original betrothal means that the Duke's will is no longer his own, Delitia insists on the supremacy of law over will. This argument acquires the contours of contemporary debate when she contends that "should you caste aside your canon law, most pious Judges, and judge it by the common law, my suit must needs be granted, if Justice deals out right, and gives to truth her own" (38).[56] By appealing to common, rather than canon law, Delitia situates justice in the public realm of ancient tradition rather than the private one of ecclesiastical or prerogative courts.[57] She thus implicitly supports the claims of such lawyers as Coke that the common law could define and limit royal prerogative.[58] In opposition, the Duke pleads that the betrothal was invalid because he agreed to it "not with a free consent of mind; but being forced by duty to my father ... I ... yielded to those actions which my affections and free will renounced" (39). In light of the private intentions that drive the narrative of "The Contract," all of these pleas are disingenuous. But in light of the actual events they describe, they are entirely true. Even the Duke's wife unwittingly supports the lovers' case by protesting that "his consent was seeming, not real, as being forced thereunto, it could not be a firm contract" (40). The Judges' decision denies the relevance of such secret feelings and intentions: what matter are the objective actions that can be verified. The ruling that "the justice of your cause judges itself; for the severest judge, or strictest rules in law, would admit of no debate" (42) rejects both the Hobbesian dictum that the sovereign is not subject to the laws or the commonwealth and even the more moderate Baconian formulation that the king is beneath the law's directive power but above its corrective power.[59] This judgment insists that the transient passions that the Duke pleads are not above the law, but immaterial to it.

In both *Assaulted and Pursued Chastity* and "The Contract," the discrepancy between the heroines' purity and their lover's debauchery accentuates the superiority of the female heroines and the noble subjects that they represent, even as it situates their consent as the foundation of the order to which they submit. However, Cavendish's emphasis on the men's casual viciousness and infidelity also questions the wisdom of such voluntary submission. By insisting that subjects are as likely to consent to bad as to good rule, she pointedly refuses to idealize the hierarchy she

56. Seventeenth-century law was divided on the relative force of *de presenti* and *de futuro* marriage contracts (Victoria Kahn, "Margaret Cavendish," 534).
57. She also, perhaps, alludes to the 1654 parliamentary act that made marriage a civic rather than religious ceremony.
58. See Weston and Greenberg, 136–140; and Burgess, *Absolute Monarchy*, 151–159.
59. *Leviathan*, 224. Victoria Kahn argues that this ending reflects Cavendish's unwitting affiliation with Hobbes ("Margaret Cavendish," 558–562).

defends. Still, *Assaulted and Pursued Chastity* and "The Contract" offer at least the possibility that subjects, however drawn to royal charisma, are capable of subordinating passion to reason and law. Once the Restoration that she advocated actually occurred, however, Cavendish's fiction became markedly more satirical and pessimistic, a shift that suggests that England had yet to realize even the troubled balance imaged in her Interregnum romances.

Published a year before the *Life of Newcastle*, *The Blazing World* registers the widespread disillusionment and anxiety that set in after the initial euphoria of the Restoration. Charles II's return had ended the series of governmental experiments of the Interregnum, which by 1659 had come and gone in intervals of a few weeks, and it was widely hailed as, in John Evelyn's words, "the Lords doing . . . past all humane policy."[60] The hagiographic depiction of Charles I that had emerged during the Interregnum only underscored the sense that divine agency was at work. In Gilbert Burnet's account, it was Charles I's "serious and Christian deportment" on the scaffold that "made all his former errors be quite forgot, and raised a compassionate regard to him, that drew a lasting hatred on the actors, and was the true cause of the great turn of the nation in the year 1660." Abraham Cowley, even more dramatically, enthused that much as "The martyr's blood was said of old to be / The seed from whence the church did grow," so "The royal blood which dying Charles did sow / Becomes no less the seed of royalty."[61] In practice, however, Charles II's court neither practiced nor rewarded such self-sacrificing humility. And opponents of monarchy were not the only ones disappointed with the reality of the Restoration. For Cavendish, as for many royalists, the restoration of Charles Stuart was neither "the Lord's doing" nor the product of Charles I's "royal blood," but the result of the sacrifices of loyal Cavaliers like Newcastle. By erasing the role of such "humane policy," providential and hagiographic narratives of restoration implicitly justified Charles' failure to reward many of those who had suffered for their loyalty and his preference for former Cromwellians and unscrupulous libertines.[62] In such a context, the sober devotion of older courtiers like Newcastle was replaced by a dynamic

60. Evelyn's statement is quoted in Keeble, *Restoration*, 2. For the events following Cromwell's death, see Ogg and Keeble.

61. *Burnet's History of My Own Time*, 1.86–87; and Cowly, "Upon His Majesty's Restoration," 174–177. The popularity of *Eikon Basilike* can scarcely be overestimated: thirty-six editions were published in 1649 alone. For a discussion of its use in royalist propaganda of the period, see Potter, *Secret Rites*, chapter 5. Lacey describes the commemorative elegies that further solidified the myth of Charles the Martyr ("Elegies and Commemorative Verse"). After the Restoration, parliament reserved January 30 as a day of fasting and repentance (Kenyon, *Stuart England*, 209).

62. See Keeble, *Restoration*, 158–184; Ogg, 1:189, 204; and Grant, 178–180.

of self-interest and indulgence to which many attributed the domestic and foreign crises of the second half of the 1660s.[63]

In *The Blazing World*, Cavendish satirizes the royal ineptitude, noble cynicism, and popular delusion that pervade both the Blazing World and her own. Far from practicing the chaste, balanced rule that Cavendish had envisioned in her Interregnum romances, the Restoration court was, in Roger L'Estrange's words, "dangerously throng'd with *Parasites: Knaves* represented to the *King,* for *Honest* men, and *Honest* men for *Villeins*: a watch upon his Majesties Eare, to keep out better Enformation; *seditious Ministers* protected." Meanwhile, as Pepys put it, Charles minded "nothing but his ease."[64] *The Blazing World* contrasts such self-indulgence with the loyal counsel offered by a noble character none other than "honest Margaret Newcastle." According to the Elizabethan model that this autobiographical character follows, true servants to the crown do not slavishly adore the king in hopes of reward. Rather, they are willing to risk disfavor in order to keep the sovereign from destroying himself and his kingdom. As Cavendish's play on the dual meaning of "honesty" in her autobiographical epitaph stresses, seeing and speaking the truth require chastity, or the ability to resist the desires that power so often provokes. In repeatedly emphasizing that *The Blazing World* is itself a fiction, however, Cavendish also asserts that the efficacy of such chaste service is confined to the pages of romance—if it even exists there.

The Blazing World begins with a series of events that contrast the physical force of rape to the psychological coercion of ravishment. A foreign merchant abducts a beautiful Lady, but a tempest blows him into the North Pole, where he and his men quickly freeze to death. The Lady, preserved by her virtue, is rescued and brought before the Emperor of the Blazing World. At first glance, the Emperor

> conceived her to be some goddess, and offered to worship her; which she refused, telling him . . . that although she came out of another world, yet was she but a mortal; at which the Emperor rejoicing, made her his wife, and gave her an absolute power to rule and govern all that world as she pleased. But her subjects, who could hardly be persuaded to believe her mortal, tendered her all the veneration and worship due to a deity. (132)

Unlike the merchant, who uses physical force to acquire power, the Lady dominates the Emperor and his people by arousing their passions. The Emperor's ravishment

---

63. For discussions of the Restoration settlement, see Kenyon, ed., *Stuart England,* 195–197, 211–219; and Ogg, 1:31–33, 1:148–188. Ogg takes Newcastle as an example of the older generation of politicians whose Elizabethan ideals at once placed them out-of-step with the Restoration regime and enabled them "to set the social and political problems of the Restoration in sharper definition against the background of the older regime" (143–147; 143). Ng also discusses the clash between Cavendish's old Cavalier values and the sexual and state politics of the Restoration (*Literature and the Politics of the Family,* 169–194).

64. L'Estrange, *A Caveat to Cavaliers,* 19–20; Pepys quoted in Keeble, *Restoration,* 62.

is mirrored by that of his subjects, who are so blinded by the Lady's beauty that they can "hardly be persuaded to believe her mortal." Like the adulation for royalty expressed in the cultish devotion to Charles I's memory, the extravagance of the 1661 coronation ceremony, or the widespread belief in Charles II's ability to cure scrofula, the idolatry of the Blazing World supports the Empress's absolute power to "rule and govern all that world as she pleased."[65] The new Empress's erotic authority recalls the influence of Charles II's mistresses and his Merry Gang of favorites, who, many feared, could dominate the king by indulging his appetite for pleasure.[66] Perhaps this is why all of the priests and governors of the Blazing World are "made eunuchs for that purpose" (133). The voluntary affection that sanctioned rule in Cavendish's Interregnum romances has become a fascinated thralldom, and wisdom is possible only in the absence of such overwhelming desire. The eunuchs' emasculation protects them from the influence of the sexual drives.

The Blazing World is not without alternatives to a model of erotic devotion. The foremost countermodels of service are the Empress's scientists and, even more prominently, the Duchess of Newcastle. Significantly, the scientists seem unaware of the beauty that so beguiles the rest of the Blazing World's inhabitants. Unable to dazzle them into submission, the Empress is forced to debate and compromise. As Hirst has argued, science was in the Restoration an antidote to the religious and political zealotry of the previous two decades. Consequently, we can understand Cavendish's depiction of the markedly desexualized relation between the Empress and her philosophers as a model for the distance and moderation urged by her Interregnum romances.[67]

When the Duchess of Newcastle appears as a character halfway through *The Blazing World*, she offers the same measured rebuke and criticism. Her prominence indicates that the Empress is not an exact figure for Cavendish herself, for the Duchess proves far wiser than her royal mistress. This superiority is figured in terms of friendship that avoids the idolatry and domination that characterize the relationship of the Empress to both the Emperor and her subjects.[68] The Duchess is first introduced as the Empress's scribe, there to record the Empress's Cabbala. Far from merely taking dictation, however, the Duchess immediately warns the Empress

65. Ogg, 1:181.

66. On the influence of Charles' mistresses and his youthful Privy Council, see Keeble, *Restoration*, 171–177. Ogg sees two parties in embryo as early as 1662: a youthful party whose confidence in Charles' power led them to urge adoption of French-style absolutism and an older party who encouraged cautious and moderate rule (1:204).

67. Hirst, *Authority*, 360. Rogers (*Matter of Revolution*) and Keller ("Margaret Cavendish's Critique of Experimental Science") both examine the relation between Cavendish's science, feminism, and politics.

68. We might read the friendship of the Duchess and Empress in terms of Shannon's thesis that friendship in the Renaissance represented equitable political relations (Shannon, *Sovereign Amity*, 1–14).

that unless she is instructed by Moses or "one of the chief rabbis or sages of the tribe of Levi," she "will be apt to mistake, and a thousand to one, will commit gross errors." In other words, the Empress is neither god nor prophet. The Duchess then recommends that the Empress pursue the more modest goal of writing "a poetical or romancical Cabbala" that makes no claims to divine truth (182–183). The Empress, far from being insulted by this insistence on her human limitations, "thanked the Duchess, and embracing her soul, told her she would take her counsel: she made her also her favourite, and kept her sometime in that world, and by this means the Duchess came to know and give this relation of all that passed in that rich, populous, and happy world" (183). The Duchess's accession from humble scribe to favorite councilor reminds us that Cavendish is not just reporting the events of the Blazing World. She is also creating them and therefore exercises an authority that few beyond Charles' inner circle could claim in Restoration England.

The discrepancy between the Duchess's power in the Blazing World and Cavendish's—and Newcastle's—own lack of influence in Restoration England becomes pronounced when the Duchess takes the Empress on a tour of England. There, they see Charles II, whom the Duchess wryly calls "as powerful a monarch as the Grand Signior" (191). This description draws on long-standing analogies between Catholic and Ottoman lusts for power and implicitly charges the Merry Monarch with a similar ambition. At the English court the Empress, always willing to take appearance at face value, listens to Charles speak and concludes "that Mercury and Apollo had been his celestial instructors" (192). The Duchess, however, quickly explains the reality beyond this royal image. The conventional praise of royal divinity, she observes, is due neither to Charles himself, nor to some disembodied "celestial instructors." He owes his education to Newcastle, who was his governor from 1638 to 1641: "my dear lord and husband, added the Duchess, has been his earthly governor" (192). Here, the Duchess punctures the Empress's enthusiasm by insisting that if anyone resembles "Mercury and Apollo," it is Newcastle. Charles is merely a product of his wisdom—and an ungrateful one at that. Like Cavendish's more general rejection of providential narratives of the Restoration, this attention to the facts of history in which her husband has long served and influenced the Stuart court envisions a reciprocal bond between king and counselors. In *The Blazing World*, this bond is exemplified by the relation between the Empress and Duchess, where the Empress's higher rank is countered by the Duchess's greater wisdom.

Because by 1666 Newcastle had long been excluded from Charles II's circle, the "very magnificent show" at court quickly wears thin. Cavendish stresses her loyalty to her husband over her king when she observes that "after some short stay in the court, the Duchess's soul grew very melancholy; the Empress asking the cause of her sadness? she told her, that she had an extreme desire to converse with the soul of her noble lord and dear husband, and that she was impatient of a longer stay" (192). This opposition between the "show" of Charles and the "soul" of Newcastle reiterates Cavendish's 1662 comparison between "the Lord C.R." (Charles Rex) who "is an Effeminate Man, fitter to Dance with a Lady, than to Fight with an Enemy" and the "the Lord N.W." (William Newcastle) who "is an Heroick man, fitter to Conquer a Nation, than to Dance a Galliard or Courrant."[69] Charles' aggressive self-indulgence has not only made him helpless to contend with enemies but has caused him to dismiss the "Heroick" councilor whose advise and experience he needs. The journey from Charles' luxurious court to the Duke's impoverished country estates accentuate this contrast. Here, the Duchess describes the "great patience, by which [Newcastle] bears all his losses and misfortunes" in the present tense, suggesting that conditions are little better under Charles than under Cromwell. The present, far from a restoration of the Elizabethan ideals for which Newcastle fought, is a state to be endured.

The ending of the first part of the romance further reflects Cavendish's dissatisfaction with the Restoration order. Here, the Empress confesses that the changes she has made in the Blazing World have destroyed the peace that preceded her arrival. The Duchess advises her to "introduce the same form of government again, which had been before" (201). In response to the Empress's fear that "it would be an eternal disgrace to her to alter her own decrees, acts and laws," the Duchess assures her that "it was so far from a disgrace, as it would rather be for her Majesty's eternal honour, to return from a worse to a better, and would express and declare her to be more than ordinary wise and good; so wise, as to perceive her own errors, and so good, as not to persist in them, which few did" (202). In the Duchess's account, the recognition of limitations offers a way of getting beyond them, so that loyal criticism actually sustains authority. This advice has obvious application to Cavendish's England, where government had seen far more innovation than the restoration of the Elizabethan forms idealized by the generation to which Newcastle belonged. The Empress's pliability offers fictional compensation for Charles II's own disregard for Newcastle's advice even as it underscores its folly.

The Second Part of *The Blazing World* equally emphasizes the insecurity of absolutist government by asserting the monarch's dependence on both wise counsel and material support in matters of foreign policy. In this section, the Empress's native country ESFI is embroiled in a trade war clearly modeled on the Second Dutch War and is "like to be destroyed by numerous enemies that made war against it" (90).

---

69. *Sociable Letters*, 45–46. Cavendish makes the same point in *Orations of Diverse Sorts*: "put the case, *Noble Citizens*, that some noblemen did retire out of some discontent, as for example, imagine this kingdom or monarchy had been in a long civil war, and some noblemen had not only been so loyal as never to adhere to the rebels, but had served their prince to the last of their power, ventured their lives, lost their estates, and had endured great misery in a long banishment, and after an agreement of peace, and the proof of their honesty and loyalty, should be neglected or affronted instead of reward and favour; if these forsaken and ruined, although honest persons, should retire from court and city into the country, to bewail their misfortunes in solitary grans, or to pick up their scattered goods, broken inheritance, and tattered states, or to restore their half-dying posterity to some time of life, should they be railed and exclaimed against?" (165–166).

While the full scale of the English military disaster would not become apparent until 1667, by 1666 there was already a clear contrast between Cromwell's successes against the Netherlands a decade earlier and Charles' embarrassing inability to prevent his enemies from blockading the Thames.[70] Cavendish's portrayal of the war in *The Blazing World* implicitly contrasts Charles' naval failures with Elizabeth's military might when the Duchess advises the Empress to burn the enemies' ships and towns. Here, she evokes Newcastle's advice to Charles II that he protect his naval power by imitating Elizabeth I, who, seeing that Henri IV had "began to Increase his shiping, shee sent him word, to Disiste for shee would not loose her prorogative of the narrow seaes, & did Assure him if hee did not, Disist, shee would burne his shipps in their Havens, which hee knowing shee was able to Doe, for bore, & lefte that Designe."[71] Despite misgivings, the Empress follows the Duchess's plan to the letter, and as a result makes ESFI's previously helpless king master of the narrow seas.

Cavendish consistently describes the Empress's foreign conquests in language that lurches uneasily between love and fear. This juxtaposition underscores the distance between the cooperation required to triumph in warfare and the providential narratives that obscure such human effort. Cavendish spends several pages detailing the planning and operations of the Duchess, the Empress, and their followers, but once the conquest is complete the Empress arranges a spectacle that obscures such careful planning. When the Empress appears "like an angel," the vanquished Europeans all have "a desire to worship" the Empress not only because of the "splendid and transcendent beauty" she has theatrically augmented but also because they fear her "great . . . power . . . to destroy whatever she pleases" (215). And rather than grant that this power depends on the labor of her followers, the Empress describes herself as an agent of a "Heaven" "much displeased" with the assault on her king's rights to trade routes. This "Heaven," she claims, has responded by awarding the King "absolute power."

Cavendish's seeming celebration of absolute power is complicated in several ways by its context. First, the absolute domination over the seas that the King of ESFI now enjoys is a result not of his own strength, but of the help that the Empress has given him. And the Empress's assistance itself depended on the advice of the Duchess and the work of the scientists. Second, we as readers have

70. When war was declared on February 22, 1665, the English widely expected easy victory, an optimism that seemed justified by English success in the first battle in June. In October, however, the Dutch defeated the Earl of Sandwich and blockaded the Thames for three weeks, and Monck was beaten in the Four Days' Battle (June 1–4) in 1666. A year later, the Dutch burnt the English fleet at Chatham, towed away the Royal Charles, and again blockaded the Thames, forcing the English to surrender. See Keeble, *Restoration*, 102–103; and Ogg, 1:283–321.

71. *Letter*, 10. Jowitt has argued that these scenes bring together Cavendish's idealization of Elizabeth I as a specifically female ruler with contemporary anxieties about England's economic and mercantile future (393–393).

witnessed the careful planning and execution of the military and theatrical operations that have enabled both the imperial victory and the Empress's spectacular appearance before her foreign audience. Unlike these spectators, we are aware of the fictionality of her providential claims. The victory has been a group endeavor, not a sign of divine right.[72] Finally, the absolutism is itself limited to mercantile activities, not actual empire, and thus echoes Tudor theories of absolutism that saw the English monarch as "absolute" only insofar as he or she was free of papal domination.[73] Far from asserting unlimited dominance over England's laws and subjects, this claim of absolutism protected England from the tyranny of Rome and allowed the monarch to defend native religion and liberty—Charles' military failures signified his inability to defend his subjects. As David Armitage has shown, after the Restoration geopolitical competition between England and its Continental neighbors was cast in the idiom of universal monarchy. At the same time, attempts by Holland or France to achieve hegemony in Europe through maritime supremacy and commercial monopoly appeared to threaten English liberty and prosperity.[74] In imagining a scenario in which a ruler's receptiveness to noble counsel permits England to dominate the seas and thus foreign trade, Cavendish articulates the same policy that Newcastle had outlined in his *Letter* to Charles. She thereby links liberty, commerce, and empire.[75] In such a context, we can understand Cavendish's demystification of royal authority as an attempt to protect both monarch and kingdom. *The Blazing World* imagines a model of government that is more successful than the solitary rule that, as we saw in the Empress's case, cannot succeed.

In the Blazing World, no less than in Restoration England, Cavendish situates "honest Margaret Newcastle" as the lone voice opposing such absolutist fantasies. This isolation, she admits, confines her counsel to the realms of fiction, just as it has made ancient forms of rule the stuff of romance. The only solution for those who

72. Lilley argues that the ending of *The Blazing World* suggests that all power is self-perpetuating and imaginary (Introduction to Cavendish, *The Blazing World & Other Writings*, xxvii).

73. As Burgess has argued, most English writers claimed that absolute monarchy aimed more at the authority of the Pope than domestic subjects and that the Oath of Allegiance was itself a counter to papal power (*Politics*, 118, 129).

74. As Armitage shows, in the Sallustian and Machiavellian analysis of geopolitical history, *libertas* and *imperium* existed in an uneasy tension. History showed that the pursuit of empire inevitably destroyed republican liberty, but republics who eschewed expansionist policies would ultimately be conquered by foreign enemies (*Ideological Origins*, 100–145). See also Pincus, "English Debate over Universal Monarchy."

75. Newcastle emphasizes the centrality of foreign trade to a secure and peaceful kingdom and urges Charles to act aggressively against the Dutch, French, and Spanish navies (*Letter*, 35–42, 72–75).

"cannot endure to be subjects" in such a world is to "create worlds of their own, and govern them as they please" (225). Such a solution, however, makes even the fantasy of reform impossible. For, unlike the compromised relations of *Assaulted and Pursued Chastity* and "The Contract," the dream of world domination that concludes *The Blazing World* indulges the desire for absolute power. And it is such a desire, as Milton was painfully aware, that is the greatest threat to liberty and virtue.

CHAPTER 8

✥

"My self / Before Me"

The Erotics of Republicanism in Paradise Lost

Milton's *Paradise Lost* provides a fitting end to this study, for it offers perhaps the most explicit argument of all of the texts that I have discussed that private fantasies and desires invariably shape public decisions. Accordingly, for Milton, the best form of government will not attempt to ignore or abolish the passions. It will make them part of the formula for building a godly state. In the texts that I have discussed thus far, the perversity of erotic relations has registered a lack of faith in rationalist political narratives. In *Paradise Lost*, Milton's conception of godly rule rests on a nuanced view of the place of sexual desire and cross-gendered identification in legal and political structures. *Paradise Lost* attests to the dangers of treating human reason and perception as though they are separate from human desire and fantasy and therefore infallibly stable and objective.[1] A central concern for Milton is the ease with which the idealization of individual virtue can lead to the destruction of the republican order such virtue is supposed to support. While Milton had initially seen individual rectitude as a source of public justice, his experience of its failure during the Protectorate and Restoration encouraged a skepticism that colors his prose and poetry in the 1650s and 1660s. In these writings, Milton suggests that the perverse pride and ambition he had earlier identified as the hallmarks of tyranny are ineradicable aspects of the human condition as such.

Consequently, the political theory of Milton's later years—including *Paradise Lost*—bases its arguments for republican rule on the conviction of human

---

1. As Fish argues, Milton's work is deeply concerned with the difficulty of accurately evaluating the motives of oneself or others, since base and selfish actions may often appear noble and altruistic, even to one's own self (*How Milton Works*, 3–7, 85–87).

imperfection. Since behavior is often driven by perverse and ambivalent impulses that one is unable to recognize as such, even the wisest and best-meaning public servants are subject to delusions that threaten both self and state. Political subjects must therefore submit to a wider arena of conflict and debate that constrains their inevitably corrupt private wills. In *Paradise Lost*, scenes of erotic addiction and confusion indicate that republican rule must be based on the recognition of human frailty. And as in Milton's earlier work, the self-control and humility that republican government demand are represented as the feminine virtues of chastity and submission. Since republicanism has long been associated with the exclusion of women from the public sphere, the prominence of female humility as a model for political behavior in Milton's work encourages us to rethink our ideas of republican theory and the gender identities it is said to embrace.[2] By extension, reconsidering the erotics of republicanism compels us further to complicate our views of the place of eros in early modern politics more largely.

It is no surprise that *Paradise Lost* gives such a central role to the perverse intimacy of pleasures and pain, ascendancy and abjection, for Milton was almost certainly composing his epic during the same years that saw his republican ideals collapse in the face of Cromwell's increasingly autocratic rule, Charles Stuart's return to England, the brutal punishment of the regicides, and his own arrest and imprisonment.[3] In his contemporaneous prose tracts of the Protectorate and the Restoration, Milton modulates the optimistic rhetoric of the early Commonwealth years. In those earlier writings, he confidently divides the English majority, who "with a besotted and degenerate baseness of spirit" condemn Charles I's execution, from "some few, who yet retain in them the old English fortitude and love of freedom."[4] Milton's optimism had waned by the time he published the *Second Defense of the English*

---

2. Many scholars have noted that republican thought of the 1650s was often misogynistic, aligning femininity with the corrupt indulgence of private appetite and masculinity with noble service to the public good. See, for instance, Stallybrass, "Inversion, Gender, and the State"; Norbrook, "Women, the Republic of Letters, and the Public Sphere"; Hilda Smith, *All Men and Both Sexes*; Pateman, *Sexual Contract*, 1–38, 77–115; Magro, "Milton's Sexualized Women"; and Purkiss, *Literature, Gender, and Politics*, 52–97.

3. Norbrook cites Milton's nephew Edward Phillips and his friend Cyriack Skinner to argue that Milton began work in earnest on *Paradise Lost* sometime in the late 1650s and completed it sometime around 1663 (*Writing*, 433–434). Hill describes a similar dating, which he sees borne out by the poem's style (*Milton*, 402).

4. *Eikonoklastes*, *CP*, 3:344. On the evolution of Milton's political thought from support of the limited monarchy of the ancient constitution to the republican rejection of any government that included a single sovereign, see Mendle, *Dangerous Positions*, 38–122, 599–601; and Dzelzainis, "Milton's Classical Republicanism." Corns argues that Milton's writings do not express a consistent or univocal radicalism but a provisional and conflicted view of the diverse pressures and anxieties of the period, pressures which led many educated, propertied, English Protestants to "slip" into an oppositionalism that ended in war and regicide ("Milton before 'Lycidas,'" 35–36).

People in May 1654, a tract that scholars have almost unanimously seen as a subtle rebuke to Cromwell, who had been inaugurated as Lord Protector five months earlier.[5] Here, Milton acknowledges that even the exceptional few are vulnerable to the same internal corruption as the besotted many. The inevitable yearning for pleasure and power, he warns, means that the real battle for liberty is as much against the self as against the Stuarts:

> Many men has war made great whom peace makes small. . . . Unless you expel avarice, ambition, and luxury from your minds, yes, and extravagance from your families as well, you will find at home and within that tyrant who, you believed, was to be sought abroad and in the field—now even more stubborn. In fact, many tyrants, impossible to endure, will from day to day hatch out from your very vitals. Conquer them first.[6]

This passage suggests the inevitability of human corruption, casting as it does avarice, ambition, and luxury as internal tyrants constantly threatening to explode, like Sin's Cerberean brood, from the "very vitals" of even the most exemplary republicans.[7] Because they are part of us, these psychic enemies are more difficult to discern—and thus to defeat—than the tyrant "abroad and in the field." And because they will relentlessly appear "from day to day," the conquest that Milton advises is never single or complete, but rather an ongoing struggle with an ever-evolving enemy.[8]

5. See Hill, who sets this disillusionment earlier (*Milton*, 162–165, 193–194); Dzelzainis, "Milton and the Protectorate in 1658"; Armitage, "Poet Against Empire"; Worden, "John Milton and Oliver Cromwell"; and Keeble, "Milton's Later Vernacular Republican Tracts." Norbrook argues that for some republicans, Cromwell's 1653 coup signaled as crucial a political change as the regicide (*Writing*, 3). Loewenstein sees Milton's opposition to the increasing dominance of Cromwell and the army as a wider trend of disillusionment shared by radical groups like the Levellers and the Diggers (*Representing Revolution*, 33, 38–43, 47). Raymond locates Milton's praise of Cromwell in the genre of advice to princes ("The King is a Thing"). Robert Fallon, to the contrary, has seen the *Second Defense* as an expression of Milton's continued admiration of Cromwell ("Milton's Critique of Cromwell?").

6. *CP*, 4:180–181.

7. As Loewenstein shows, Milton's depiction of the internal origin of tyranny through gendered analogies aligns him with such thinkers as Gerard Winstanley, who likened one's own delusions to Circe's power, and Abeizer Croppe, who described charity as the conquest of the "harlot" within (64–78, 107–109). Sawday has demonstrated the prevalence of the language of psychic division during the civil wars, as exemplified by Richard Lovelace's Lucasta poems and Joseph Beaumont's *Psyche* ("Civil War, Madness, and the Divided Self").

8. The passage anticipates Satan's description of himself as the victim of his own desires, happy "Till Pride and worse Ambition threw me down" (4.40). It suggests his affinity with erstwhile republican leaders like Cromwell, who, as Norbrook has argued, embodied for contemporaries the general principle of that rule by a single person gives reign to corruption (*Writing*, 442).

As Milton would argue six years later in *The Readie and Easie Way to Establish a Free Commonwealth* (1660), it was the failure to recognize and therefore to resist the innate human desire for pleasure and power that assured the breakdown of government in the 1650s and thus the return of monarchy.[9] Here, Milton incredulously casts the imminent Restoration as a sadomasochistic scenario in which bondage and abjection have become sources of pleasure: "Is it such an unspeakable joy to serve, such felicitie to wear a yoke? to clink our shackles, lockt on by pretended law of subjection more intolerable and hopeless to be ever shaken off, then those which are knockt on by illegal injurie and violence?"[10] The prevalence of this "uspeakable joy" in the "pretended law of subjection" evinces the need for republican rule, which will prevent the indulgence permitted a single ruler and his sycophants. Such a vision of mutuality, compromise, and debate appears in domestic terms in the divorce tracts, and in public terms in *Areopagitica*. In the latter, Milton imagines a commonwealth in which all work together to gather the scattered and seemingly contradictory fragments of Truth, which is unavailable in its entirety to any single mortal. Such mutual cooperation and restraint characterizes the Grand Council that Milton envisions in the second edition of the *Readie and Easie Way*, where he insists that "The happiness of a nation must needs be firmest and certaintest in a full and free Councel of thir own electing, where no single person, but reason only swaies."[11] Milton's rejection of rule by a "single person," which may censure Cromwell as much as Charles, rests on the principle that even a good monarch, or "single person," will be "far easier corruptible by the excess of his singular power and exaltation, or at best, not comparably sufficient to beare the weight of government."[12] A single sovereign may not be uncommonly evil himself, but his singular power allows him unusual opportunity to indulge the avarice and abjection that tempt us all.[13] Good government, accordingly, is built on the assumption of innate human imperfection.

For Milton, so tantalizing is the fantasy of human mastery that the unrelenting need for mutual aid and compromise must be registered in the very name of

9. For discussions of the events between Cromwell's death in 1658 and the restoration of monarchy, see Woolrich, "A Military Dictatorship?" 86–88.

10. *CP*, 7:447. For the relation of Milton's language of slavery to Roman law and history, see Skinner, "John Milton and the Politics of Slavery," 19–21.

11. *CP*, 7:425.

12. *CP*, 7:448–449.

13. As Milton's prose attests, while he considered virtue difficult under a monarchical system, he did not deem it impossible. He praises Queen Christina of Sweden as "the most heavenly guardian of that course which prefers truth to the heat of partisans" and denies to her that "my attacks on tyrants in any way applied to you" in the *Second Defense* (*CP*, 4:603–604), and in 1674 he translated the celebratory announcement of Jan Sobieski's election as King of Poland ("Letters Patents of the Election of the Most Serene King of Poland," *CP*, 8:445–453). See also Worden's argument that Milton's unambiguous opposition to monarchy as such in 1659 represented only a brief interruption to his general equivocation on the subject ("Milton's Republicanism," 228).

England's governing institution. Although the Grand Council will ultimately act as a parliament "call'd, not as heretofore, by the summons of a king, but by the voice of libertie," the name of parliament itself should be abolished "as originally signifying but the *parlie* of our Lords and Commons with their *Norman* king when he pleasd to call them."[14] England's government must therefore take "the name of a Grand or Generall Councel" to register the absence of any single or permanent sovereign at its head. This name change will affirm that sovereignty is a structure rather than a person and that the Council is "chosen by the people to consult of public affairs from time to time for the common good. In this Grand Councel must the soverantie, not transferrd, but delegated only, and as it were deposited, reside."[15] The emphasis here on consultation and delegation underscores the provisional, cooperative nature of this form of government, one that insists on the inability of any single member of the body politic to ensure that "reason only swaies." All men are subject to the private ambition that characterizes the monarch, and recognition of this inevitable imperfection leads to the need for the selfless, communal rule of a Commonwealth, "wherein they who are greatest, are perpetual servants and drudges to the public at thir own cost and charges, neglect thir own affairs; yet are not elevated above thir brethren, live soberly in their families, walk the streets as other men, may be spoken to freely, familiarly, friendly, without adoration."[16] Those who rule are like everyone else in their creaturely limitations, and they must be constantly reminded of this by being treated like everyone else. They must live with restraint, inhabit the same public spaces as others, and converse with others "freely, familiarly, friendly"—accepting the candor due an equal, not the reverence due a superior.[17] Such humility requires precisely the painful recognition of individual imperfection that the tyrant, surrounded by self-serving flatterers, repudiates.

In *Paradise Lost*, Milton's analysis of the desires that undermine republican liberty finds its fullest articulation not in Satanic machinations, but in Edenic marriage.[18] Despite the narrator's idealizing claim to the contrary, our first parents' love

14. *CP*, 7:444. Herman has argued that this shift in name registered Milton's rejection of ancient constitutionalism, which by definition included a monarch, to a more radical republicanism (*Destabilizing Milton*, 61–81, esp. 78–80).

15. *CP*, 7:431.

16. *CP*, 7:425.

17. Both Schoenfeldt ("Gender and Conduct," 335–336) and Ng (*Literature and the Politics of the Family*, 144–160) see continuity between Milton's consistent replacement of birth order with merit, his rejection of hereditary rule, and his depiction of gender roles as contingent and fluid.

18. See Turner's detailed analysis of the assumptions about sex, gender, and marriage in which Milton intervened (*One Flesh*, 1–55). Luxon discusses Milton's efforts to articulate marriage in terms of classical doctrines of friendship, an effort that, Luxon argues, ultimately fails because of Milton's inability to imagine true equality between husband and wife (2). As Norbrook shows, the language of restoring "pristine beginnings," always central to English republican rhetoric, reached a height in 1658–1660, with writers like Thomas Scot comparing the Commons with Adam and the Lords with Eve (*Writing*, 474).

has much in common with the emotions expressed in the courtly "Serenate, which the starv'd Lover sings / To his proud fair, best quitted with disdain" (4.769–770).[19] As we have seen, since the Elizabethan era, Petrarchan courtship had offered an idiom for exploring the conflicting impulses of both private and political allegiance. In elaborately sketching the mutual ambivalence and aggression that characterize Adam and Eve's relationship, Milton acknowledges that this Petrarchan dynamic is latent in the vision of reciprocal love that his divorce tracts had taken as an analogy for political liberty. In *The Doctrine and Discipline of Divorce*, Milton argues that the original purpose of marriage was to "comfort and refresh [man] against the evil of solitary life," assuaging "God-forbidden loneliness" with "meet and happy conversation."[20] And, as Milton insists in *Tetrachordon*, such fulfillment is possible only in the heterosexual relation. "God," he argues, "could have created [for Adam] out of the same mould a thousand friends and brother *Adams* to have bin his consorts, yet for all this till *Eve* was given him, God reckn'd him to be alone" for "there is a peculiar comfort in the maried state besides the genial bed, which no other society affords."[21] This "peculiar comfort," as Milton understands it, is possible only with one who is entirely distinct from the imperfect self, an otherness that for him is most legible in sexual difference. Because man cannot experience "joy and harmles pastime . . . without company, so in no company so well as where the different sexe in most resembling unlikenes, and most unlike resemblance cannot but please best and be pleas'd in the aptitude of that variety."[22]

But this need for specifically female company signifies something lacking in both the individual man and in masculinity more generally. It thus places the desiring male subject at the mercy of a mate whose role as supplement conflicts with her role as subordinate.[23] Her singular ability to solace man's loneliness imbues woman with a potentially emasculating authority that Milton associates with tyranny in the *Defense*. Here, he denounces Salmacius' wife as "a barking bitch who rules your wretched wolf-mastership."[24] Female deference to male desire can disguise this treacherous erotic influence, but such submission is meaningful only insofar as it is voluntary. Accordingly, the "true consent of mind" that defines marriage necessarily implies the possibility of the female refusal that will reveal women

---

19. Kerrigan and Braden describe *Paradise Lost* as a "consummate expression" of the courtly love tradition ("Milton's Coy Eve").

20. *CP*, 2:247, 235, 246.

21. *CP*, 2:595, 596.

22. *CP*, 2:597. Halley argues that Milton's vision of marriage as the means of achieving wholeness depends on the ideology that woman freely chooses not only heterosexuality but the subordination that marriage demands of her ("Female Autonomy," 231–236, 243–244).

23. I am thinking here of Jacques Derrida's notion of the supplement as an external addition that enhances that which is whole and complete in itself, and a prosthetic that makes up for an intrinsic lack (see "White Mythology," in *Margins of Philosophy*). Shoaf offers a detailed analysis of this Derridean concept in Milton's work (*Milton, Poet of Duality*, 135–137).

24. *CP*, 4:380.

to be "neither fit helps, nor tolerable society."[25] And because such female autonomy threatens the dream of male perfection and mastery, heterosexual desire always seems to teeter between erotic enslavement and "*Hate*, not that Hate that sins, but that which onely is naturall dissatisfaction and the turning aside from a mistaken object."[26] A wife becomes a "mistaken object" when she refuses to enact the subjection that will conceal her husband's deficiency and so causes mutuality—"the golden dependence of headship and subjection"—to give way to rivalry, "counterplotting, and secret wishing one anothers dissolution."[27]

Critics have long noticed the conflicted relationship between desire and dependence in *Paradise Lost*, where Eve's very existence threatens Adam's identity as God's preeminent creation.[28] Such analyses of Edenic marriage have tended to focus exclusively on determining Milton's conception of women, but a feminist attention to the problem of gender relations can also make available a more complex view of Milton's political theory.[29] As a number of scholars have argued, Milton explores the psychology of religious faith and political allegiance through Adam and Eve's marriage, which many seventeenth-century thinkers saw as the origin of all society and governance.[30] What I would like to add to these discussions of political psychology is a more thorough analysis of the ways in which this union reveals that human action and allegiance are shaped as much by perverse fantasies and

25. *CP*, 2:445, 621.

26. *CP*, 2:253.

27. *CP*, 2:591, 607.

28. See, for instance, Stein, *Answerable Style*, 78; Grossman, "Milton and the Question of Woman"; and Stone, "Androgyny and the Divided Unity of Adam and Eve." Silver understands Adam and Eve's relation in terms of Lutheran theology in which Adam's understanding of himself as the image of God depends on an awareness of his difference from both God and Eve (*Imperfect Sense*, 283–345).

29. Milton's readers have long debated his views on women. Critics who have made seminal arguments for a consistently antifeminist, even misogynist, strain in Milton's work include Halley; Nyquist, "Gynesis, Genesis, Exegesis" and "Genesis of Gendered Subjectivity"; and Gilbert, "Reflections on Milton's Bogey". By contrast, Lewalski ("Milton on Women") and McColley (*Milton's Eve* and "Eve as Milton's Defense of Poesie") see in Milton a protofeminist defender of female virtue. There has also been considerable debate about Milton's reception among women of his own time. Wittrich has stressed Milton's early reputation as an advocate for women (*Feminist Milton*, 44–82). Norbrook notes that early feminists like Mary Astell found Milton was hostile to women (*Writing*, 482–483). Shannon Miller traces the mutual influence between Milton and women writers throughout the seventeenth century (*Engendering the Fall*).

30. Hill notes that in discussing Adam and Eve we must remember that contemporaries would have understood this relation as an analogy for that between ruler and subjects or Christ and his Church; accordingly, the moral defects of the original couple illuminate the failure of the English people (*Milton*, 375, 342–344). See also Quint, *Epic and Empire*, 268, 281–307; Nigel Smith, *Literature and Revolution*, 99, 218–235; Silver, *Imperfect Sense*, 311–316; Victoria Kahn, *Wayward Contracts*, 196–222; and Achinstein, "Contextualizing Milton's Divorce Tracts."

ambivalent desires as by sober calculations of self-interest or public duty.[31] As Milton's divorce tracts intimate, and as the interactions of Adam and Eve illustrate, the need for others may really express a narcissistic desire for mastery and coherence, so that any expression of difference or autonomy on the part of the beloved also inspires aggression and hate. This need for dominance threatens to dissolve not only marital bonds but also republican ideals of public service, debate, and compromise.

However, Milton's recognition of the universality of human imperfection does not lead to an argument against self-rule. Instead, it proves the necessity of a republican system in which all members accept that they need aid and opposition if they are to keep their inner tyrants at bay. In the *First Defense*, Milton had attacked Salmacius' claim that scripture sanctioned absolute monarchy by contending that such unlimited power was contrary to Christian values of humility and self-sacrifice. "Amongst Christians," Milton insists, "there will either be no king at all, or else one who is the servant of all; for clearly one cannot wish to dominate and remain a Christian."[32] This Christian ideal of humility reshaped the classical republican ideal of masculine *virtus* into the more androgynous *imitatio Christi*. The very same analogical argument that Milton had used in *Tetrachordon* to defend male domestic rule depended on male recognition of his own effeminacy before Christ, who was himself both masculine in relation to humanity and feminine in relation to God: "as God is the head of Christ, and Christ the head of man, so man is the head of woman."[33] In other words, man justifies his expectation of female obedience by asserting not only his own power but also his own submission as bride of Christ, who himself occupies a feminine position of subjection to God.[34]

According to Milton, the feminized submission common to Christ, man, and woman is a product of love, not reason. These analogous religious, political, and conjugal bonds were charged with the erotic ecstasy imagined in the Song of Songs, an overwhelming *jouissance*, which Milton evokes as the only true sign of love and consent in the *Doctrine*: "but this pure and more inbred desire of joyning to it self in conjugall fellowship a fit conversing soul (which desire is properly call'd love) *is stronger then death*, as the Spouse of Christ thought, *many waters cannot quench it, neither can the flouds drown it*."[35] Because these analogical relations of authority are

---

31. Corns cautions that the unified thought that many critics attribute to Milton is alien to most people at most times, since fantasy, pragmatism, and idealism all coexist and create conflicting polemical imperatives ("Plurality of Miltonic Ideology," 110–114).

32. *CP*, 4:379.

33. *CP*, 2:591. As Hill shows, early modern Protestants understood the simultaneously equal and unequal relation between the Father and the Son as a figure for that between the husband and wife (*Milton*, 285).

34. Shannon Miller persuasively argues that in *Paradise Lost* Milton's poetic voice takes the passive, instrumental position of seventeenth-century female prophecy in order to justify the epic's political and religious polemics (79–95).

35. *CP*, 2:251; Milton's emphasis. Milton quotes from the Geneva translation of the Song of Solomon 8:6–7.

understood in sexual terms, hierarchy itself becomes erotic, and thus brings with it all of the predatory and abject potential of eros, which is ultimately directed not at an external object, but at the narcissistic self. Such a wish for ecstatic union also signifies, in Julia Kristeva's analysis, the draw of the abjection that exists "at the fragile limits of the speaking being."[36] Such transgression is as attractive as it is terrifying—it is the possibility of *jouissance* that causes the abject to exist.[37] The promise of such rapture threatens the line between self and other, pleasure and pain, life and death, a collapse of meaning represented above all in the feminine. Woman, in this erotic context, is an object of both desire and repulsion, a sign of the ecstatic engulfment—the death—that will end the frustrations of individuality, difference, and limitation.[38] As Adam and Eve's relationship in *Paradise Lost* attests, the "joyning . . . in conjugall fellowship" that Milton celebrates thus threatens the compromise, counsel, and debate that upholds republican rule—for the tyrant's wish to dominate and devour is but the flip side of the yearning for ecstatic dissolution into an other. Indeed, much as Milton's defense of divorce emerged from his acknowledgment that he was himself subject to the same affective delusion and misplaced allegiance as the "common lump of men," so *Paradise Lost* acknowledges that even our unfallen parents, and therefore the most virtuous of postlapsarian political actors, are vulnerable to the pathologies that haunt eros.[39]

The republicanism that Milton championed has long been associated with the exclusion of women from the masculine, rational, public sphere, so it may seem strange to assert that Eve registers the dilemmas of male political subjects much as Adam does. But Milton himself had explicitly likened marriage to political allegiance in his divorce tracts. The most oft-cited equation occurs in the Preface to the *Doctrine*, where Milton equates his call for legalized divorce with the parliamentary rebellion, asserting that "He who marries, intends as little to conspire his own ruin as he that swears allegiance: and as a whole people is in proportion to an ill

---

36. Kristeva, *Powers of Horror*, 18.

37. Kristeva, 7.

38. Kristeva, 56–89, esp. 58–59, 82. Fish has called the death drive a perfect description of Milton's theology (2–4).

39. In the *Doctrine*, Milton argues that it is the awareness of one's own weakness and propensity to misjudgment that prevents the tyranny of forced marriage: "it is incredible, how cold, how dull, and farre from all fellow feeling we are, without the spurre of self-concernment" (*CP*, 2:226). He goes on to suggest that humans are destined to self-destruction, "for though it were granted us by divine indulgence to be exempt from all that can be harmfull to us from without, yet the perversness of our folly is so bent, that we should never lin hammering out of our own hearts, as it were out of a flint, the seeds and sparkes of new misery to our selves, till all were in a blaze again" (*CP*, 2:234). Such mistakes are not limited to the foolish, either: "for all the wariness that can be us'd, it may yet befall a discreet man to be mistak'n in his choice: and we have plenty of examples. The soberest and best govern'd men are lest practiz'd in these affairs" (*CP*, 2:249). For a discussion of Milton's anxious recognition of his own fallibility in the divorce tracts, see Barker, *Milton and the Puritan Dilemma*; Sirluck, "Milton's Idle Right Hand"; Stephen Fallon, "Milton in His Divorce Tracts"; and Patterson, *Milton's Words*, 34–39.

government, so is one man to an ill marriage."[40] Like the authors I have discussed in previous chapters, Milton and his republican compatriots consistently drew on the idioms of gender and romance to discuss relations of authority, agency, and consent.[41] These models were particularly useful given that the model of a government founded on the rational, open debate that Milton had idealized in *Areopagitica* had little to do with the reality of England, where the governments of the Interregnum were all, in Christopher Hill's words, "sitting on bayonets."[42] In order to validate this use of force, apologists for the governments of the 1650s contended that some— perhaps most—men are irrational, indulgent, and weak, and so must be ruled like women. But rather than imagine this hierarchy in terms of raw strength, republican polemics often described it in terms that transformed force into seduction. Milton's compatriot Henry Vane, for instance, argued that because the English populace was incapable of acting in its own best interest, "he would have some few refined spirits (and those of his own nomination) sit at the helm of state . . . til the people be made familiar with a Republique and in love with it."[43] In conflating physical coercion with passionate surrender, Vane acknowledges that the rational, public rule he defends demands the same affective engagement as the indulgent, private monarchalism it would replace. Milton repeats this sentiment in the *Readie and Easie Way*, where he hypothesizes that if a true Commonwealth had been formed immediately after Charles' execution, even those who initially opposed it "might have soon bin satisfi'd and delighted with the decent order, ease and benefit thereof."[44] The notion that a government established by force will eventually secure not only outward compliance but also reciprocal desire imagines the founding act of republican governance as something between seduction and rape. The use of such erotic analogies recognizes that the dream of a commonwealth in which private desire, aggression, and complexity have been magically dissolved into an unambivalent, altruistic

---

40. *CP*, 2:229. As Patterson argues, Milton's Commonplace Book shows that his thoughts on marriage and divorce were originally political in nature, and his views changed very little in his discussion of these topics in *De Doctrina Christiana* (*Milton's Words*, 32–33, 51). Hatten describes the shifts in uses of conjugal analogies to describe political allegiance during the civil wars ("Politics of Marital Reform," 95–113); Victoria Kahn analyzes Henry Parker's inversion of this analogy to place the king in the position of wifely subordination (*Wayward Contracts*, 95–104).

41. As early as *Comus* (1634) Milton had imagined the Caroline political subject as a Spenserian virgin assaulted by appetites and defended by reason, an analogy that he extended in the 1642 *Apology for Smectymnuus* (*CP*, 1:891).

42. *Century of Revolution*, 116. Resistance to the regimes of the 1650s was not limited to those who fought for Charles I; the tensions between what historians have designated the "peace party," the "war party," and the "middle group" of the parliamentary side became explicit in the Putney debates of 1647 and in the withdrawal of such men as Fairfax and Vane from Cromwell's government in the 1650s. See Hirst, *Authority*, 268, 273–278, 293; Kenyon, *Stuart England*, 167–180; Peacey, *Regicides*, 18, 29; and Jonathan Scott, *Algernon Sidney*, 92–142.

43. George Warner, ed., *Nicholas Papers*, 4:161.

44. *CP*, 7:430.

conviction of public duty is as false as the dream of royal beneficence depicted in the "Masking Scene[s]" Milton derided in *Eikonoklastes* (*CP*, 3:342).

Rather than cling to an impossible ideal of a passionless state, Milton acknowledges that these psychic pathologies cannot be conclusively cured. More specifically, by analyzing the tensions in Adam and Eve's love in *Paradise Lost*, he shows that the claim that governance can be founded on a purely rational calculation of public good is itself a dangerous fantasy.[45] Such rationalist theories fail to come to terms with the erotic vicissitudes that both drive and threaten political engagement. But this does not make *Paradise Lost* a poem of defeat.[46] To the contrary, we can see Milton's publication of his epic as a call for renewed struggle against the unacknowledged forces that had allowed the return of a corrupt monarchal government. Particularly in light of Charles II's blatant corruption and indulgence, the argument that human imperfection made communal rule necessary took on increased urgency. The first edition of *Paradise Lost* appeared in 1667, when the disillusionment of the early 1660s had evolved into widespread distrust for Charles II and his government after England's humiliation in the Second Dutch War and Clarendon's fall from power. This first edition was thus part of what N. H. Keeble has described as an atmosphere of renewed political protest.[47] The revised edition appeared in 1674 amidst debates over the monarchal ability to dispense with law. These debates had been sparked by Charles' attempt to impose a Declaration of Indulgence relaxing penalties against Catholics and nonconformists, a claim to absolutist prerogative that the parliament would crush in 1673.[48] Charles' withdrawal of the Declaration and acceptance of the Test Act implicitly acknowledged monarchal limitations. But the Test Act, which made public office contingent on professed allegiance to the Anglican Church, also revealed the threat to English Protestantism and liberty posed by Charles' brother, James, Duke of York. The future James II confirmed suspicions of his Catholicism by refusing to swear allegiance to the Anglican Church as the Test prescribed; made it clear that he saw the Test Act as a parliamentary assault

---

45. Schoenfeldt argues that Milton locates passion at the center of human experience both before and after the fall ("Passion in *Paradise Lost*"). In this chapter, I stress the political implications of this centrality.

46. Numerous critics have rejected Parker's claim that *Paradise Lost* represents a retreat from political engagement (cited in Corns, "Plurality of Miltonic Ideology," 111). They emphasize instead the public consequences and implications of the domestic and psychological dynamics of Milton's epic; see Hill, *Milton*, 213–221; Quint, 281–283; Corns, "Plurality of Miltonic Ideology," 111–113; and Norbrook, *Writing*, 434–437.

47. Keeble argues that the crises of Charles II's reign came to a head in 1667 and 1672, and that by the late 1670s the throne was almost as much at risk as it had been in the 1640s (*Restoration*, 85, 167–171).

48. See Ogg, *England in the Reign of Charles II*, 1:203–204; Mueller argues that the key issue was Charles' claim to the power to dispense with laws mandating Anglican conformity, which parliament saw as a claim to arbitrary power ("Samson as a Hero of London Nonconformity," 148). For the struggles over the dispensing power claimed by the Declaration of Indulgence, see Westin and Greenberg, *Subjects and Sovereigns*, 164–177.

on royal prerogative; seriously contemplated staging a military coup as a means of restoring sovereign authority; and married the Catholic Marie of Modena in 1673, ensuring that any male heir to the throne would be Catholic.[49]

We can understand the reappearance of *Paradise Lost* as a response to this renewed threat of tyranny.[50] In replacing his claims of exceptional individual virtue with an analysis of inevitable human pathology, Milton insists on the need for the painful confrontation with otherness. Debate, frustration, and compromise distinguish communal republican rule from the dynamic of ambition and abuse that characterizes tyranny—and Milton's recognition of inevitable human failure makes such self-examination all the more urgent. For Milton, the refusal to acknowledge the limits of human reason encourages the delusions of infallibility—whether of oneself or of others—on which ambition and tyranny thrive. An optimistic view of individual virtue thereby imperils commonwealth ideals. In making Eve's submission the model by which Adam regains his proper relation to God, Milton also suggests that such feminine humility offers a model for political subjects who wish to restore godly rule, which requires chaste leaders who act as servants and, accordingly, acknowledge their need for aid and counsel.

In *Paradise Lost*, Eve embodies not only the imperfection that characterizes men, as well as women, but the resentment and aggression so often aroused by the awareness of one's consequent dependence and need. Eve's birth narrative has been widely discussed by humanist, feminist, and psychoanalytic critics who see it as, alternately, a rape that wrenches her into a heterosexual universe that demands her subjugation, a divine rapture that extracts her from a superficial obsession with worldly pleasure, and a case study of Freudian narcissism.[51] But Eve's ambiguous submission to Adam, situated as it is between coercion and consent, also suggests the difficulty of accepting godly republican ideals of humility and service. Like the subjects imagined by Vane or Milton, Eve is unwilling to relinquish her fantasies of

49. James Stuart's first marriage to the Protestant Anne Hyde, the daughter of the Earl of Clarendon, produced only daughters (his Protestant eldest daughter Mary would rule after his forced abdication in 1688). For the international and political context, see Kenyon, ed., *Stuart Constitution*, 375–376, and *Stuart England*, 222–225; and Keeble, *Restoration*, 170–171.

50. Several critics have observed Milton's strategic choice of publication dates. Hill notes that *Paradise Lost* first appeared just when Clarendon's fall demonstrated the instability of the Restoration settlement (*Milton*, 402). Norbrook argues that Marvell's introductory poem engages the second edition in the controversies of the 1670s and links these controversies back to mid-century (*Writing*, 34, 491–493).

51. Feminist critics have been divided on this scene: Gilbert; Halley, and Froula argue that it depicts Eve's forcible induction into a heterosexual, patriarchal economy (see Gilbert; Halley, 247–249, and Froula, "Undoing the Canonical Economy"). By contrast, McColley understands it as Eve's escape from a paralyzing narcissism (*Milton's Eve*). Kerrigan reads Adam and Eve's marriage as a textbook case of Freud's argument that sexual overvaluation is derived from a primary narcissism transferred to a sexual object (*Sacred Complex*, 70–71).

perfection and coherence. These fantasies appear in *Paradise Lost* as a narcissistic attachment to her reflection's "answering looks / Of sympathy and love" 4.464–465). Eve's enthrallment with her own image emblematizes the reluctance to acknowledge a reality beyond the self that had long been associated with tyranny. It thereby pictures in gendered terms what the *Tenure of Kings and Magistrates* had described as the "boundless and exorbitant" will of the tyrant.[52] Such devotion to the self is "not freedom, but licence; which never hath more scope or indulgence then under Tyrants," who promote a culture in which servility and ambition are indistinguishable, "the falsifi'd names of *Loyalty*, and *Obedience*" deployed "to colour over . . . base compliances."[53] In *The Readie and Easie Way*, Milton sees this corruption exemplified by the "*French* court" in which Charles Stuart has spent his exile, "where enticements and preferments daily draw away and pervert the Protestant Nobilitie.[54] In this parasitic relation, favor is both lure and payment. The tyrant's generosity exposes his dependence on followers whose hopes of promotion lead them to collaborate in royal fictions of omnipotence.

If Eve is to avoid the self-destructive pursuit of pleasure and power to which she is instinctively drawn, she must conform to the godly republican values of sacrifice and compromise. Such a choice requires that she admit the insufficiency of her solitary self. Eve signifies her reluctant acceptance of the need for relation with an other in her marriage to Adam, with whom she shares her creaturely status. Adam's imperfection figures her own. Eve has to recognize as her true image one that is "less fair / Less winning soft, less amiably mild / than that smooth wat'ry image" with which she was initially smitten (4.478–480).[55] Before she actually sees Adam, Eve has been told that, in contrast to the image in the pool, Adam is "hee / Whose image thou art," an other whom Eve "shalt enjoy / Inseparably thine" (4.471–473). Eve's acceptance of Adam as her image is also her acceptance of the humility on which republican government depends and which royal absolutism denies. But her ambivalent feelings for Adam register the difficulty of sustaining this modesty, which always threatens to give into resentment, abjection, or egoistic delusion. Tellingly, Eve initially rejects Adam because his apparent inferiority threatens her own sense of perfection: if it is true that she is both image and part of Adam, then she is also "less" than the idealized vision in the water. Her initial flight from Adam, then, may be a flight from her own creaturely imperfection and mortality. If left to her own devices, Eve would choose the delusions of power and perfection that find political expression in the all-devouring

52. *CP*, 3:212.
53. *CP*, 3:190.
54. *CP*, 7:425.
55. Silver argues that in Eve, Milton evokes love for what is different, outside the self (*Imperfect Sense*, 317). I would add that Adam is both like and unlike Eve: they do not literally look alike, and they each have qualities that the other lacks, but each reflects the other's imperfection and consequent need for an other.

monarchal will, rather than the humble recognition of mutual need expressed in godly republicanism.

Cromwell was confident that "[g]overnment is for the people's good, not what pleases them," and Milton similarly defends force by appealing to the distinction between pleasure and interest.[56] Accordingly, like the feminized populace imagined by Milton, Vane, and Cromwell, Eve must be compelled to exchange love of self for duty to others. It is Adam's difference that persuades her of the disparity between herself and the outside world. As Eve acknowledges, she would have remained dangerously obsessed with her own reflection if God and Adam had not intervened. There, she would have "fixt / Mine eyes till now, and pin'd with vain desire" in an impossible pursuit of self-completion that anticipates Satan's complaint that he is "Still unfulfill'd with pain of longing pines" (4:465–466, 511). But this recognition that she needs Adam also instills in Eve a degree of resentment that is registered in her emphasis on the compulsory origins of their union. As she reminds Adam, she did not want to abandon the pool. But in the shadow of divine command, she asks, "what could I do, / But follow straight, invisibly thus led?" (4.475–476).[57] Even in retrospect, Eve stresses the reluctance with which she surrendered to her "other half" (4.488):

> thy gentle hand
> Seiz'd mine, I yielded, and from that time see
> How beauty is excell'd by manly grace
> And wisdome, which alone is truly fair. (4.488–491)

In Eve's memory, Adam's use of physical force—however "gentle"—succeeded in persuading her after his rhetorical pleas had failed. The breathless enjambment of "hand" and "Seiz'd" accentuates the latent violence of this moment, poetically mirroring Adam's physical breach of the boundary between them. Moreover, the line break between "grace" and "wisdome" makes even the "manly grace" of her husband inferior to "wisdome, which alone is truly fair." And while we can certainly read "manly" as modifying "wisdom," this does not make wisdom an essentially masculine attribute. Indeed, in Book 8 Raphael will admonish Adam to "be not diffident / Of Wisdom, *she* deserts thee not, if thou / Dismiss not *her*" (8.562–564; my emphasis). Evidently, wisdom can be at once feminine and "manly," like the androgynous angels. Wisdom's androgyny accentuates Adam's own distance from the "truly fair"—his very identity as a man limits his access to the full range of human virtues. Eve thereby reminds him that they are both mere images of deity:

56. Quoted by Morrill, "Introduction," 13.

57. Victoria Kahn has seen Eve's "drama of duress" as part of Milton's self-conscious explanation of the relation between coercion and consent in contractual obligation and of his recognition of the potential difficulty of distinguishing voluntary subjection from voluntary servitude (*Wayward Contracts*, 207–211).

even if Adam is structurally analogous to God with regard to Eve, he is not identical to him. By qualifying her submission to Adam, Eve suggests a latent hostility at the heart of their "conjugal attraction" (4.493). This hostility, as Milton well knew, could disrupt political as well as nuptial harmony.

Eve is not the only one who is ambivalent and resentful. Adam's conversation with Raphael in Book 8 makes even more explicit the distance between the idealized relationship of husband and wife as "one Flesh, one Heart, one Soul" and the threat that such union poses to his own sense of mastery and coherence (8.499). For Milton, erotic desire registers both an acknowledgment of imperfection and a longing to be perfected. Because the desire for another is also the desire for completion, it is, paradoxically, the desire not to need companionship—the wish either to be complete on one's own or to be absorbed into another. Consequently, mutual need and compromise threaten to give way to the dynamic of abjection and arrogance that characterizes tyranny. As Adam's feelings show, erotic desire reveals the strange affinity between divine aspiration and bestial desire. And for Milton, it is in claiming the powers of a god, in striving to erase all difference between his will and his world, that the tyrant becomes a beast, mired in the appetites and desires that drive him and his kingdom to destruction. In the *Tenure* Milton rehearses this classical definition of a tyrant as "he who regarding neither Law nor the common good, reigns only for himself and his faction. . . . And because his power is great, his will boundless and exorbitant, the fulfilling whereof is for the most part accompanied with innumerable wrongs and oppressions of the people, murders, massachers, rapes, adulteries, desolation, and subversion of Citties and whole Provinces."[58] The "boundless and exorbitant" will that the tyrant seeks to fulfill can best be sated with the destruction of alterity. The imposition of private desire on the public world turns others to pliant instruments of self-gratification and thereby obscures the ruler's own imperfection.

Such a will to emulate divine wholeness is not limited to the tyrant. Those who follow such rulers do so in order to indulge their own desires and ambitions, like the "chief . . . adherents" of Charles I, who, Milton claims in *Eikonoklastes*, may be "ready to fall flatt and give adoration to the Image and Memory of this Man," but in truth "never lov'd him, never honour'd either him or his cause, but as they took him to set a face upon thir own malignant designes; nor bemoan his loss at all, but the loss of thir own aspiring hopes: Like those captive women whom the Poet notes in his *Iliad*, to have bewaild the death of *Patroclus* in outward show, but indeed thir own condition."[59] The "love" that a tyrant and his effeminate followers feel for one another is based on the same aspiration to divine completion as the desire for companionship that figures godly republicanism. But under tyranny this aspiration

58. *CP*, 3:212.
59. *CP*, 3:344–345.

threatens to transform mutual need into mutual exploitation. And the more that the tyrant and his followers imagine themselves as limitless immortals, the more they resemble animals—a state that Milton himself had illustrated in Comus' dissolute rout, whose "human count'nance / Th' express resemblance of the gods, is chang'd / Into some brutish form" but who are "so perfect in their misery" that they "Not once perceive their foul disfigurement, / But boast themselves more comely than before" (68–70, 73–75). To forget one's imperfect, human status in an ecstatic pursuit of divine pleasure or power is to mire oneself in the creaturely being that desire seeks to transcend. Satan remarks this irony when he enters the serpent's body, noting that to contend "With Gods to sit the highest" is to find oneself "constrain'd / Into a Beast, and mixt with bestial slime" (9.164–165). The aspiration to equal deity denies creaturely limitations. As Milton repeatedly insists, to so forget one's mortal flaws is to sink to the unthinking level of a beast.

For Milton, the way to limit such brutalization is to understand that the approximation of divine immortality or wisdom is possible only through relation with others. And sexual difference plays a crucial role in imposing a recognition of human imperfection. So while scholars are right to detect in Milton's work a longing for a homosocial universe that excludes women and the threatening difference that they represent, *Paradise Lost* suggests that this longing it itself the problem, since it indicates a dangerous avoidance of alterity little different from Eve's initial enthrallment with her own reflection.[60] For Milton, confrontation with sexual otherness forces man to recognize his own needs and limitations, and this confrontation takes archetypal form in the heteroerotic relation. But, as Adam's feelings about Eve demonstrate, the humility that acknowledges individual need is never entirely stable. It may always veer into either a servile subjugation of oneself to an other or an arrogant treatment of others as mere instruments of one's own pleasure.

We see this danger in Adam's account of his request for a helpmeet. This request arises from his simultaneous recognition of his superiority to the beasts and his inferiority to God. Adam's dual impulses of humility and aspiration inspire his wish for a relationship and make that wish a painful sign that he is incomplete in himself. As Adam Phillips succinctly puts it, "no amount of redescription will alter the fact that if people can satisfy each other they can frustrate each other."[61] Desire all too easily becomes a source of resentment.

This tension will manifest itself in Adam's ambivalence toward Eve, for whom he feels both adoration and hostility. There is quite a distance between Adam's dream of mutual support between equals and the actual dynamic of subservience and hostility that he and Eve enact. And this distance registers the complexity of the private desire in which political commitment and allegiance begins. David Quint describes

60. For discussions of the homosocial program that haunts Milton's work, see Halley, 239–260; Victoria Kahn, *Wayward Contracts*, 206–207; and Herman, *Destabilizing Milton*, 142.
61. Bersani and Phillips, *Intimacies*, 109.

Book 8 as an exploration of how Adam's consciousness of being God's creature produces in him a sense of inferiority that Eve's initial indifference exacerbates. This insecurity, for Quint, leads to both the fall and the English Restoration, for it compels humanity to seek a secure, stable condition that is the opposite of the contingent and provisional condition that Milton associated with Christian faith and republican liberty.[62] What I would like to add to Quint's analysis is that the acceptance of contingency and imperfection that Quint sees Milton advocating is acknowledged by *Paradise Lost* itself to be infinitely difficult and unstable. As a result, an optimistic affirmation of the uncertainties of both Arminianism and republicanism must itself waver in order to produce the humility necessary to both salvation and liberty. As Martin Luther argued, weakness and failure are central to salvation. The Ten Commandments offer a salient example of the spiritual purpose of the gap between human ideals and abilities, for as Luther explains, they

> show us what we ought to do but do not give us the power to do it. They are intended to teach man to know himself, that through them he may recognize his inability to do good and may despair of his own ability. . . . For example, the commandment, "you shall not covet" [Exod. 20:17] is a command which proves us all to be sinners, for no one can avoid coveting no matter how much he may struggle against it. Therefore, in order not to covet and to fulfill the commandment, a man is compelled to despair of himself, to seek the help which he does not find in himself elsewhere and from someone else.[63]

In other words, failure is necessary to salvation. One must learn to despair of one's own virtue in order to turn to God. And republican government, no less than Christian faith, depends on the individual's choice "to seek the help which he does not find in himself elsewhere and from someone else."

Adam's request for a helpmeet acknowledges the unsatisfactory nature of his initial position of absolute mastery over the beasts that surround him. Such solitude is a sign of unqualified power, as God points out: "is not the Earth / With various living creatures, and the Air / Replenisht, and all these at thy command / To come and play before thee?" (8.369–372). But although all worldly creatures are ready to entertain Adam on command, his power over inferiors brings him no satisfaction. Despite God's advice, Adam cannot "Find pastime and bear rule" with the animals (8.375). Rather than enjoy his absolute dominion, Adam sadly wonders

> Among unequals what society
> Can sort, what harmony or true delight?
> Which must be mutual in proportion due
> Given and received. (8.383–386)

---

62. Quint, 288–302.
63. *The Freedom of a Christian*, in *Martin Luther: Selections from His Writings*, 57.

The "harmony or true delight" that Adam wants is expressly different from the "pastime" or "rule" possible with his animal inferiors. Unlike the pleasure or power that Adam would find with these nonhuman companions, "true delight" consists in mutuality. Relations with inferiors can only "prove / Tedious alike," breeding boredom, disgust, even pain (8.388–389).

It is, Adam quickly reveals, the wish to be more like God that grounds his desire for others. Adam's request is equally a confession of his own inferiority to God, and thus of the deficiencies he shares with the beasts. Desire, in Adam's formulation, is not only the yearning for an equal but also a sign of lack. As he explains to God,

> Thou in thyself art perfet, and in thee
> Is no deficience found; not so is Man
> But in degree, the cause of his desire
> By conversation with his like to help,
> Or solace his defects. (8.415–420)

As Adam recognizes, humanity is characterized by awareness of its own "deficience." This awareness of lack constitutes, perhaps, the "rational" orientation that distinguishes humanity both from the creatures who are blissfully ignorant of their deficiencies and from the tyrant who willfully ignores his own flaws. But because Adam is also like god "in degree"—that is, in the analogical chain that links him to both divinity and brutality—he aspires to be as "perfet" as his maker. His desire, then, at once acknowledges his creaturely status and seeks to escape it.

So even as his peculiarly human awareness of difference from God leads Adam to aspire to be more like God, it also means that love defeats its own ends. Yearning for divine plenitude inevitably produces pain and frustration. The presence of a helpmeet continuously forces Adam to recognize his failed aspirations to deity. This humiliation is necessary to both Christian faith and republican rule, but it may also inspire resentment that threatens them. The anxiety aroused by the erotic relation is exacerbated by the sexual, physical component of desire, the satisfaction of which simultaneously mimics divine ecstasy and mires humanity in bodily sensation. As Thomas Luxon has shown, the ambiguous status of Adam's desire emerges in the very word he uses to describe what he wants: "conversation." In the seventeenth century, this could mean engagement with society, discussion and debate, or sexual intercourse.[64] The latter, in particular, is for Adam a means of imitating God's infinity and immortality through procreation, the multiplication of the self promised to Eve as consolation for accepting her singular insufficiency. As Adam recognizes, God is "already infinite" and so has no need to reproduce. In contrast to this divine oneness,

---

64. Luxon, 58–61. Le Compt (*Milton and Sex*) and Patterson (*Milton's Words*, 47–48) both argue that Milton found sex distasteful, if not disgusting.

> Man by number is to manifest
> His single imperfection, and beget
> Like of his like, his Image multipli'd,
> In unity defective, which requires
> Collateral love, and dearest amity. (8.422–426)

Adam's wish to mimic divine infinitude and eternity through continuous self-duplication inevitably displays the impossibility of the end he seeks. Neither is the individual perfect in his single state, nor does relation with or creation of others—which can only be an imperfect union of persons "defective" in themselves—do anything but acknowledge this imperfection.

It is in this gap between love for others and love for the self that we see the limitations of the fantasy of union expressed in Adam's request for an equal and his initial view of Eve as "my Self / Before me" (8.495–496). In describing his feelings to Raphael, Adam oscillates between idealization and belittlement of Eve. His words evoke a Petrarchan discourse of ravishment, in which beauty arouses unruly passion in its male beholders and, by seducing them from their higher natures, becomes responsible for its own violation. For Adam, Eve is at once idol and inferior, helpmeet and rival, comforting reflection of self and alarming evidence of alterity. But, in Adam's own account, none of these roles have much relation to what Eve actually does. Rather, they are a product of Adam's own fantasies of mastery and coherence—and of their inevitable frustration.[65] In detailing the vicissitudes of Adam's love for Eve, Milton reveals that the society of "Collateral love and dearest amity" is never a simple, stable one, since it is easily disturbed by precisely the desire for wholeness that led to its creation. This speech demonstrates the power of the "enemy within" of which Milton warned in the *Second Defense*. This inner tyrant is the true enemy of the humility, compromise, and self-control on which godly republican government rests.

In his complaint to Raphael, Adam enacts the internal battle described in Milton's political works. Like the Presbyterians who, Milton charges in the *Tenure*, worship not Charles I himself but only "the useless bulk of his person," Adam's response to Eve's appearance—what Raphael will term her "outside" (8.568)—has little to do with objective reality.[66] For however much he might lament his susceptibility to "the charm of Beauty's powerful glance" (8.533), it is the narcissistic component of Adam's desire that makes it so intense.[67] Insofar as it is unquestionably other and inferior, the purely sensual delight offered by "Taste, Sight, Smell, Herbs, Fruits, and Flow'rs, / Walks, and the melody of Birds" is such that "us'd or not, works in the

---

65. As McColley argues, Adam learns that his other half is not merely an image but also a being that can enlarge and change him ("Eve as Milton's Defense of Poesie").

66. *CP*, 3:197.

67. Kerrigan, *Sacred Complex*, 69–71.

mind no change, / Nor vehement desire" (8.527–528, 525–526). Adam had already rejected these physical pleasures as inferior, so they cannot arouse "vehement desire." By contrast, Eve, in God's own account, is Adam's "likeness, thy fit help, thy other self, / Thy wish, exactly to thy heart's desire" (8.450–451). And because Adam himself recognizes Eve as "my Self / Before me" his desire for her is of a different order than that aroused by the five senses: Eve distinguishes Adam from the animals precisely because her existence is evidence of his desire for divine perfection. But such arousal also attests to an insufficiency of which the beasts remain happily ignorant.

As his complaint reveals, what Adam wants is not the fulfillment of desire but its absence. For he experiences the presence of desire as a humiliation that encourages both aggression (the desire to restore a sense of superiority or mastery) and servility (the desire to be incorporated into the fantasy of perfection he has projected onto Eve). Consequently, Adam understands the relationship between the two of them as a contest of wills, his attraction to Eve as an invasive ache that may reveal that God "left some part / Not proof enough such Object to sustain" (8.534–535). Eve becomes not a partner to be enjoyed but a test to be endured. Her existence opens a "wide . . . wound" that vitiates Adam's very self (8.467). Eve is a creation for which God "took perhaps / More than enough" of Adam (8.536–537).[68]

Adam responds to his sense that Eve is the cause of his defects by attempting to invert the hierarchy his obsession has created. In a description that contradicts his earlier desires for an equal with whom he can share "all rational delight," Adam assures Raphael that "well I understand in the prime end / Of Nature her th' inferior, in the mind / And inward Faculties, which most excel" (8.540–542). Moreover, in addition to deeming Eve inferior where it really matters, Adam insists that even the physical charms he earlier extolled signal her subordinate relation to deity. Eve is

> In outward also resembling less
> His Image who made both, and less expressing
> The character of that Dominion giv'n
> O'er other Creatures. (8.543–546)

Adam's critique of the appearance that arouses him echoes Eve's description of him in Book 4 as "less fair, / Less winning soft / less amiably mild." She is not only "in outward show / Elaborate, of inward less exact" but also reflects "less" of God's image, and thus has "less" of the analogical authority with which divine

---

68. For further discussions of Adam's reaction to Eve's beauty, see Silver (*Imperfect Sense*, 287) and Victoria Kahn, both of whom have noted what Kahn describes as Adam's "scarcity economy of desire" (*Wayward Contracts*, 212–213). Dolan similarly describes marriage as an "economy of scarcity in which there is only room for one full person" (*Marriage and Violence*, 3).

resemblance endows humanity.[69] Like Eve's response to Adam's appearance, however, this criticism is not without a narcissistic component. For if in seeing Eve,
Adam also sees "My self / Before me," then her distance from "His Image who made
both" must likewise remind Adam of his own difference from God. Both are only an
image. Adam's need to rank them suggests an uneasiness with this knowledge, a fear
that Eve may really be "wisest, virtuousest, discreetest, best" (8.550). Yet as Adam's
clumsy superlatives indicate, this anxiety that Eve may possess the very divine perfection he himself craves is not a product of calm reasoning. Rather, it stems from
the same unseemly desire for earthly perfection and assurance that, as Quint has
argued, Milton sees as the source of republicanism's failure in England.[70]

Raphael's response is inadequate to Adam's dilemma because it denies the force
of the human affect that Adam has just described. Raphael thus expresses the same
naïve idealization of the human reason that Milton rejects in *Paradise Lost*. Raphael
assumes a clear division between outside and inside, sensual and spiritual desire, in
his contemptuous question, "what admir'st thou, what transports thee so, / An outside?" He reiterates this assumption in his advice that "What higher in her society
thou find'st / Attractive, human, rational, love still; / In loving thou dost well, in
passion not" (8.567–568, 586–588). This condemnation of the bodily passions
ignores the duality of human nature that Adam's narrative has established. Raphael
therefore exhorts an angelic eros that is impossible in the creaturely sphere. Adam
hastens to retract his earlier confession to assure Raphael that what really delights
him in Eve is "Neither her out-side form'd so fair, nor aught / In procreation
common to all kinds," but rather the "Union of Mind" he experiences with her
(8.595–596, 604). But however much Adam may emphasize intellectual and spiritual oneness, he recognizes, as Raphael does not, the importance of sexual desire to
conjugal union. His notorious query about sex in heaven points to the limits of the
archangel's counsel:

> To Love thou blam'st me not, for Love thou say'st
> Leads up to Heav'n, is both the way and guide;
> Bear with me then, if lawful what I ask;
> Love not the heav'nly Spirits, and how their Love
> Express they, by looks only, or do they mix
> Irradiance, virtual or immediate touch? (8.612–617)

What we see here is less Adam's prurient curiosity than a genuine conceptual problem. If love is, as Raphael has claimed, "the scale / By which to heav'nly Love thou

---

69. As Silver has argued, to suppose that Milton makes likeness to God contingent on masculinity is to define that image as an exclusive appearance that corresponds to some attribute
in deity itself and thus misunderstand it as something finite and divisible (*Imperfect Sense*,
283).

70. Quint, 299–307.

may'st ascend," then angels must love (8.591–592). But the earthly expression of
love involves physical contact and desire that distinguish it from the "heav'nly
Love" it approximates. This mixed nature of love is central to the Platonic definition
of eros on which Raphael's description of love as a ladder draws.

So how do angels, lacking bodies and the physical passions they produce,
express love? Raphael's answer further underscores the disparity between ideals of
love and its reality, one caused by the same body that Adam imagines as the sole
vehicle of love's expression. The ideal of rational affection that Raphael describes is
possible only in absence of a body, which signifies human limits:

> Whatever pure thou in the body enjoy'st
> (And pure thou wert created) we enjoy
> In eminence, and obstacle find none
> Of membrane, joint, or limb, exclusive bars:
> Easier than Air with Air, if Spirits embrace,
> Total they mix, Union of Pure with Pure
> Desiring; nor restrained conveyance need
> As Flesh to mix with Flesh, or Soul with Soul. (8.622–629)

The body parts—"membrane, joint, or limb"—that make possible human intercourse
are obstacles to angelic pleasure, as Raphael's redundant term "exclusive bars" suggests. In contrast to angelic embraces, the "restrained conveyance" that is available to
human beings only reminds them of their division from one another. The difference
between the ideal and the actuality of sexual union is what makes it an expression of
subjection and brutality, rather than of the spiritual intercourse it should allegorize.
So when Raphael concludes their conversation by warning Adam to "take heed lest
Passion sway / Thy Judgment to do aught, which else free Will / Would not admit,"
he anticipates the consequences of the fall, in which doing whatever one wants—
license—is in fact the opposite of freedom and liberty (8.635–637).

Adam and Eve rarely talk to one another before the fall. Their entire relationship
appears to be, as William Kerrigan and Gordon Braden have observed, more of the
order of distant Petrarchan courtship than intimate companionate marriage. In this
light, the argument that Adam and Eve have at the opening of Book 9 is hardly a
rupture of perfect unity, but only one of many expressions of its failure, a continuation of the dynamic of reproach, critique, and resentment that we have already witnessed.[71] The rejection of mutual need becomes most explicit in the argument that

---

71. Kerrigan and Braden, 38–48. In addition to the conversations I have just discussed, we
   might compare Adam's response to Eve's inquiry as to why the stars shine even when living
   creatures are asleep (4.657–688) with his own repetition of this question (8.13–38). Both
   Herman and Luxon assume that Eve overhears Adam's conversation with Raphael
   (Herman, *Destabilizing Milton*, 140–141; and Luxon, 153–155).

opens Book 9. Here, our first parents reenact the rivalry we have already witnessed, with Eve striving to assert her self-sufficiency and Adam veering between adoring Eve and belittling her.[72] It is only after their fall forces them to recognize their mutual imperfection and need that Adam and Eve learn the compromise and humility necessary for real mutuality.

Adam's responses to Eve's desire to work apart express the same conflicted desires for mutuality and superiority as his request for and response to Eve's creation. Initially, he attempts to dissuade Eve from leaving by insisting that their united strength makes Satan "Hopeless to circumvent us join'd, where each / To other speedy aid might lend at need" (9.259–260). But, as in his earlier conversation with Raphael, Adam oscillates between an ideal of mutual support and a dream of his own superiority. We see this ambivalence when he begs Eve to stay with him on the grounds that his "faithful side / That gave thee being, still shades thee and protects" and he "guards her, or with her the worst endures" (9.265–266, 269).[73] Echoing Raphael's portrayal of humanity as creatures who are "Perfet within, no outward aid require," Adam argues that God has made man "Secure from outward force; within himself / The danger lies, yet lies within his power: / Against his will he can receive no harm" (9.348–350). But this internal danger, it seems, may not lie entirely within individual power. In Adam's account, Eve's wish to separate signifies a rejection of the "tender love" which "enjoins, / That I should mind thee oft, and mind thou me" (9.357–358). Accepting the care of another means accepting one's limited perspicacity and strength and therefore submitting to external judgment. Adam and Eve may be "Perfet within" and thus capable of resisting temptation, but they are more likely to remain virtuous if they recognize their human frailty and rely on one another.

After the fall, Eve's own desire to be "as Gods" appears in her new consciousness of competition with Adam (9.708). Eve considers whether she should "give [Adam] to partake / Full happiness with mee, or rather not, / But keep the odds of Knowledge in my power / Without Copartner?" (9.818–821). Here, she states more baldly the conflicted desires that we have seen in Adam all along: the wish for companionship and the wish for dominance. And, as in the Petrarchan structures that provide the subtext for Milton's meditation on human society, Eve understands love and desire as a means of subjugating others. If she does keep "the odds of Knowledge" to herself, it will be "so to add what wants / In Female Sex, the more to draw his Love" (9.821–822). Here, the love Eve has in mind is expressed not by mutual service, but by Adam's unilateral submission. The enhancement that the fruit offers will not only inspire love but also "render me more equal, and

---

72. Victoria Kahn argues that Adam's distrust and insecurity lead him to reject the testing that Milton endorses in *Areopagitica*, while Eve's desire to prove herself turns the search for truth into Hobbesian vainglory (*Wayward Contracts*, 214–215).

73. Nyquist has identified this move from mutuality to hierarchy as a larger principle of Milton's work ("Genesis of Gendered Subjectivity," 111–112).

perhaps, / A thing not undesirable, sometime / Superior: for inferior who is free?" (9.823–825). Desire and domination are hopelessly intertwined. The mark of Eve's superiority will be her ability to arouse desire while remaining immune to it herself.

Even when Eve recognizes her need for Adam, this need is expressed not as a generous desire for his good, but as a selfish wish to protect her own erotic power over him. Eve realizes that she is mortal and therefore fungible, and that upon her death Adam, "wedded to another *Eve*, / Shall live with her enjoying, I extinct" (9.828–829). It is this possibility that leads Eve to acknowledge her need for Adam. Rather than allow this, she resolves that "*Adam* shall share with me in bliss or woe: / So dear I love him, that with him all deaths / I could endure, without him live no life" (9.831–833). And Adam's decision to join in Eve's fall is as selfish as her decision to share the fruit: he does not want "To live again in these wild Woods forlorn" (9.910). We see in his claim that "to lose thee were to lose myself" (9.959). As Victoria Kahn has observed, Adam's absolute identification with Eve expresses a dangerous confusion between humble service to another and obsessive servitude to his own passions.[74]

After the fall, Adam's resentment of his creaturely imperfection—now conclusively established by his choice of Eve over God—takes explicitly misogynistic form. Adam's projection of his weakness onto Eve was already implicit in his conversation with Raphael. But like Eve's wish for superiority, it achieves conscious articulation only in the postlapsarian state. Once fallen, Eve learns the lesson of humility and compromise more readily than Adam. She therefore becomes an example for Adam to follow. Just as Eve's recognition of her imperfection compels her to submit to Adam, Adam must acknowledge his own human frailty so that he can learn to manage it. Eve's subordination becomes more official and extreme after the fall, with the Son's pronouncement that "to thy Husband's will / Thine shall submit, hee over thee shall rule" (10.195–196). But in order to deserve the rule that has been formally conferred on him, Adam will need to imitate Eve's newfound meekness, even as she imitates the humility of Christ. In the final books of *Paradise Lost*, the analogical chain linking God, Christ, man, and woman means that the feminine submission that the Son demands of Eve is not the opposite of masculine government. Rather, it exemplifies the humility required of the men who show their fitness to rule by acting as "perpetual servants and drudges to the public."

We see the first instance of Adam's emulation of humility in his reconciliation with Eve, which also provides the model for Adam's reconciliation to God. In contrast to Adam's furious despair at his own lack of mastery, Eve stresses her weakness in order to set things right with both Adam and God. Eve is "Not . . . repulst" by Adam's diatribe, but instead "at his feet / Fell humble, and imbracing them, besought / His peace" (10.910–913). In admitting her need for Adam's "gentle

74. *Wayward Contracts*, 219–220.

looks, thy aid, / Thy counsel," Eve also realizes that they can only overcome their misery by uniting. She demonstrates her willingness to sacrifice herself for Adam as a token of her sincerity, promising that she

> to the place of judgment will return
> There with my cries importune Heaven, that all
> The sentence from thy head remov'd may light
> On me, sole cause to thee of all this woe,
> Mee mee only just object of his ire. (10.932–936)

Eve's offer of self-sacrifice differs from Adam's death wish at the end of Book 9, for it is unselfishly directed at his good rather than her own. As critics have noted, Eve here echoes the Son's plea in Book 3 that the God "Behold mee then, mee for him, life for life, / I offer, on mee let thine anger fall" (3.236–237).[75] Eve differs from the Son, however, in her recognition that she is "sole cause" of humanity's woe and "only just object" of God's ire. Such awareness of guilt is important because, as in Luther's formulation, it leads her back to her proper relationship with God. Eve's confession and appeal echo Milton's rhetorical stress on his own imperfection in the divorce tracts. There, the argument for divorce—and for the ability to divorce as a figure for the right to depose an ineffective ruler—depends on "the spur of self-concernment," the recognition of human misprision and folly of which no one is free. It is Eve's acknowledgment of her weakness that leads Adam to recognize her again as "my Self / Before me" and so to imitate her humble posture. And his "com-miseration" with Eve's "lowly plight" allows Adam to make a similar appeal to God (9.940, 937).[76]

This recognition of shared suffering turns rivalry to cooperation. Rather than compete for dominance, Adam suggests, they should "strive / In offices of Love, how we may light'n / Each other's burden in our share of woe" (10.959–961). This new quest for humility is expressed in Adam's imitation of Eve's own promise that she "to the place of judgment will return" in order to "importune Heaven" as well as her own prostrate weeping. Drawing an analogy between his own position and that of God, Adam asks

---

75. Quilligan argues that Book 10 insists upon the centrality of Eve's submission to Milton's theological argument; because Eve is the first character to choose the prostration that Satan, and initially Adam, refuse, she is the embodiment of the "heroic martyrdom" that Milton takes as the subject of his epic in place of masculine heroism (*Milton's Spenser*, 237–242). See also Silver, *Imperfect Sense*, 342–344; and Schoenfeldt, "Passion in *Paradise Lost*," 65–67.

76. Schoenfeldt reads Eve's submission in the context of the courtly practice of *sprezzatura* and therefore sees it as an instance of the "simultaneously redemptive and manipulative powers of submission" ("Gender and Conduct," 318–333). I would argue that Eve is less artful than that here, however, for the very quality that gives force to her submission is its sincerity and lack of concern with reward.

> What better can we do, than to the place
> Repairing where he judg'd us, prostrate fall
> Before him reverent, and there confess
> Humbly our faults, and pardon beg, with tears
> Watering the ground, and with our sighs the Air
> Frequenting, sent from hearts contrite, in sign
> Of sorrow unfeign'd, and humiliation meek. (10.1086–1092)

Adam reconciles himself to God's will by replicating Eve's own posture of supplication. His imitation suggests that the female submission commanded by the Son is the model on which men must pattern their own behavior. The poem itself manifests this mimetic logic by replicating Adam's own words almost exactly in its description of their repentance. But here, the changed pronouns signify the move from private repentance to communal action:

> they forthwith to the place
> Repairing where he judg'd them prostrate fell
> Before him reverent, and both confess'd
> Humbly thir faults, and pardon begg'd, with tears
> Watering the ground, and with thir sighs the Air
> Frequenting, sent from hearts contrite, in sign
> Of sorrow unfeign'd, and humiliation meek. (10.1098–1104)

Emphasizing the exemplary role Eve takes in the final books of *Paradise Lost*, Quilligan has noted that the repetition of prostrate postures "insists upon the centrality of her submission to the whole series of relations that are clearer after the fall than before."[77] I would extend this argument to add that such an emphasis on feminine humility also challenges characterizations of republican thought as purely masculine or militaristic. Rather, Milton situates Eve's painful recognition of her own guilt and imperfection as the basis of godly government.

Such constant awareness of one's human fallibility checks the pride and ambition that led to the fall and that, in the political realm, enables tyranny. This stance of humility, however, can be surprisingly strenuous. That is the lesson of the last two books of *Paradise Lost*. As we see in Adam's responses to the vision of biblical history with which Michael attempts to educate him, the stance of humility that permits faith in God is under constant assault by the desire for pleasure and power. Accordingly, Michael's narrative is less concerned with external events than with the irrepressible inner tyrants that endanger true—spiritual—liberty. In Michael's representation of the future of the human race, the grisly sights of Cain's murder of

---

77. *Milton's Spenser*, 238.

Abel and the lazar-house are followed by the vision of "A Bevy of fair Women, richly gay / In Gems and wanton dress" (11.582–583). Rather than resist these tempt-resses, the initially righteous sons of Seth "though grave, ey'd them, and let thir eyes / Rove without rein, till in the amorous Net / Fast caught, they like'd, and each his liking chose" (11.585–587). This blurring of agency and objectification suggests how easily one's own desires can be experienced as external forces rather than inter-nal choices—the men vacillate from an active staring ("ey'd") to a passive loss of control ("let thir eyes / Rove without rein") to becoming objects of the women's seduction ("in the amorous Net / Fast caught") and back to active liking and choosing.

Given Adam's own predilection to value desire and beauty above all, it is unsur-prising that he mistakes this scene of debauchery for a good thing. Confusing the beautiful with the good, he fails to realize that moral laxity is just as bad as the phys-ical suffering of the lazar-house. In his misprision, Adam reveals his similarity to the "grave men" whose nuptials he has witnessed:

> Such happy interview and fair event
> Of love and youth not lost, songs, Garlands, Flow'rs,
> And charming Symphonies attach'd the heart
> Of *Adam*, soon inclin'd to admit delight
> The bent of Nature. (11.593–597)

Adam's reading of this "fair event / Of love and youth not lost" suggests the same choice of earthly pleasure over eternal salvation, body over soul, urged by a carpe diem lyric. It is because he already has an affinity with these men that Adam's heart becomes "attach'd" to this sight.

Adam's interpretation of this vision registers how difficult it is to remember that, as Raphael had warned him, "great / Or bright infers not excellence" (8.90–91). Addressing Michael as the "True opener of mine eyes," Adam naively enthuses that

> Much better seems this Vision, and more hope
> Of peaceful days portends, than those two past;
> Those were of hate and death, or pain much worse,
> Here Nature seems fulfill'd in all her ends. (11.599–603)

Adam's inability to distinguish between pleasure and pain, true and false harmony, indicates that he is still confused as to the true image of God. For, as Eve's supplica-tion evinced, true godliness is the acceptance of "hate and death, or pain much worse." The bevy of ladies and the pleasures they offer are a long way from "the better fortitude / Of patience and heroic martyrdom / Unsung" that Milton urges (9.31–33). Yet Adam fails to learn the correct lesson when Michael informs him that "The world erelong a world of tears must weep" as a result of the men's thrall-dom to these "fair Atheists" (11.627, 625). The point here is to guard oneself against the tendency to mistake pleasure and power for virtue and truth, to confuse one's own desires with those of God. But Adam does not blame the men themselves for their abandonment of the virtuous ways "to tread / Paths indirect, or in the midway faint!" Instead, he exclaims that "still I see the tenor of Man's woe / Holds on the same, from Woman to begin" (11.630–633). Michael, however, quickly rebukes Adam, assuring him that "From Man's effeminate slackness it begins" (11.634). Because this "effeminate slackness," as Milton's *Second Defense* and *The Readie and Easie Way* made clear, haunts all of humanity, consciousness of weakness becomes the foundation of strength.

The desire to deny imperfection and mutual need has political, as well as theological, consequences. Further on, Adam is appalled by Michael's description of Nimrod's tyrannous rule. In response to this tale of tyranny, he insists that while God may have given humanity dominion over the animals, "Man over men / He made not Lord; such title to himself / Reserving, human left from human free" (12.69–71). Adam's repetitive nouns (Man/men, human/human) and structure under-scores the "fair equality, fraternal state" that Nimrod's "proud ambitious heart"—like that of Satan—led him to reject and destroy in order to "arrogate Dominion undeserv'd / Over his brethren" (12.24,–27). *Paradise Lost* calls Nimrod a "mighty Hunter" (12.33), an epithet borrowed from Fortescue, whom Milton quotes in his *First Defense*. Fortescue explains that Nimrod earned his epitaph because "as a hunter compels beasts enjoying their liberty to obey him, so did he compel men."[78] But, as Fortescue had demonstrated in the previous paragraph, this compulsion itself could not be clearly separated from consent. For while greedy rulers "subjugated neigh-boring peoples to themselves, often by force," the people responded with the same choice of security over liberty that Hobbes would recommend. "As long as they were protected by their subjection against the injuries of others," Fortescue recounts, they "consented to the domination of their subduers, thinking it better to be under the government of one, whereby they were protected from others, than to be exposed to the oppressions of all those who wished to attack them." As a result, "certain king-doms, and the subduers of them ruling the subject people in this way, usurped to themselves the name of king, from the word 'ruling' [*rex a regendo*], and their domin-ion is described as only royal."[79] For Fortescue, as for many legal historians, Nimrod is an example of the absolute rule that runs contrary to the English ancient constitu-tion. Milton's inclusion of Nimrod in Michael's history lesson stresses that such usur-pation perpetuates itself not through mere external force, but through the internal weakness of its subjects. Nimrod is not acting alone. His destruction of "fair equality, fraternal state" is supported by "a crew, whom like Ambition joins, / With him or

---

78. Fortescue, "In Praise of the Laws of England," 19.
79. Fortescue, "In Praise of the Laws of England," 19. See Herman's analysis of Nimrod within the ancient constitutionalist that Milton eventually abandoned (*Destabilizing Milton*, 63–67).

under him to tyrannize" (12.38–39). The "like Ambition" of Nimrod's crew entails a mimetic loyalty in which they may be both victims and oppressors: they endure tyranny because it gives them the power to abuse their own inferiors. Michael describes this situation as a "Rebellion" against Heaven, an ambition epitomized in the tower of Babel. This refusal of humility, expressed in the worship of human prince rather than divine creator, is the theological corollary of the rejection of equality and compromise that permit republican liberty.[80]

As Michael informs Adam, Nimrod is only an external manifestation of the subjection of reason to passion that is both cause and effect of Adam's own fall. "Since thy original lapse," the archangel warns, "true Liberty / Is lost" (12.83–84). In this view,

> Reason in man obscur'd, or not obey'd,
> Immediately inordinate desires
> And upstart Passions catch the Government
> From Reason, and to servitude reduce
> Man till then free. Therefore since hee permits
> Within himself unworthy Powers to reign
> Over free Reason, God in Judgment just
> Subjects him from without to violent Lords;
> Who oft as undeservedly enthral
> His outward freedom: Tyranny must be,
> Though to the Tyrant thereby no excuse. (12.86–96)

Here, external servitude is understood as an allegory for loss of self-control, the tyrant an allegory for the "upstart Passions" that govern in place of reason. The distortion of this valuation is illustrated in the three words that stretch out into ten syllables: "Immediately inordinate desires." Michael's rebuke expresses in erotic terms the same ambivalent relation to bondage that Milton described in the *Second Defense*: "by the customary judgment and, so to speak, just retaliation of God, it happens that a nation which cannot rule and govern itself, but has delivered itself into slavery to its own lusts, is enslaved also to other masters whom it does not choose, and serves not only voluntarily but also against its will."[81] Self-indulgence is, paradoxically, the greatest sign of servitude, one that can be avoided by only recognizing the innate corruption of the will and instituting a government that limits its exercise. In the 1660s, such limitation appeared especially urgent, for the desire for pleasure and power that Milton condemned found expression in the bestial libertinism and tyrannous secrecy associated with Charles' government. The

---

80. As Keeble shows, writers from Foxe to Bunyan identified the Reformation world with Babel and Nebuchadnezzar's Babylon, aligning persecution of dissenters with Babylonian, Median, and Roman tyrants (*Restoration*, 137).

81. *CP*, 7:684.

Whitehall that Pepys called a "great bawdy-house" was also the seat of Charles' secret negotiations to secure a French alliance, a plot aimed at diminishing Charles' dependence on parliament and therefore his subjects' part in government.[82]

The crux of Adam's lesson is that he must submit to God's commands rather than to his own will and appetite. Adam has "attain'd the sum / Of wisdom" (12.575–576) only when he recognizes that

> to obey is best,
> And love with fear the only God, to walk
> As in his presence, ever to observe
> His providence, and on him sole depend. (12.561–564)

This obedience means a subordination of private will and desire, yet the ability "to walk / As in his presence" also means to acknowledge desire as the mark of human difference from God. And because this difference is a sign of inferiority and imperfection, obedience also entails constant mindfulness of one's imperfect knowledge and control of the world.[83] This is the "debt immense of endless gratitude / So burdonsome, still paying, still to owe" that Satan cannot stomach (4.52–53). As Stuart Curran observes, this perpetual burden of humble thanksgiving is the economy of God's universe after the fall.[84] The only way to serve God is to recognize that one is not God and therefore not self-sufficient or infallible. So Adam must learn to imitate not the omnipotent Father but the human Christ, who is

> Merciful over all his works, with good
> Still overcoming evil, and by small
> Accomplishing great things, by things deem'd weak
> Subverting worldly strong, and worldly wise
> By simply meek; that suffering for Truth's sake
> Is fortitude to highest victory. (12.565–570)

Such a valorization of feminine suffering, of the weak and the meek, is striking in light of the consistent misogyny of so many of Milton's characters in *Paradise Lost* and in republican rhetoric more widely. But the ability to imitate Christ's mercy requires the same "commiseration" that Eve's earlier confession of weakness elicited from Adam. In spiritual terms man must occupy this feminine position, which

82. Pepys, *Diary*, 7:377. For descriptions of Charles' political duplicity, particularly in his secret dealings with France, see Ogg, 1:322–354; Kenyon, *Stuart England*, 220–221; and Keeble, *Restoration*, 168–171. For a survey of the association of Charles' political corruption with the sexual license of his court, see Keeble, *Restoration*, 171–176.

83. As Norbrook argues, Adam has a tendency to premature optimism; Michael's aim is to teach him to face the world rather than seek to escape it (*Writing*, 466).

84. "God," 531.

means accepting his own inferior reason and need for the same "aid" and "counsel" for which Eve implores Adam after the fall. To fail to acknowledge such feminine need is, paradoxically, to express the "effeminate slackness" of the tyrant and his followers, who refuse to accept the pain of self-knowledge that makes self-control—what Milton elsewhere calls chastity—possible. In the context of the long tradition of monarchomach theory and Protestant martyrdom within which Milton writes, "suffering for Truth's sake" becomes the highest form of heroism.

While Adam may recite this lesson in its abstract form, it is Eve who actually performs it in *Paradise Lost*. Her wifely obedience offers a model of the proper human submission to God. Moreover, as Michael C. Schoenfeldt has observed, although Michael sends Adam to awaken Eve, Adam finds her already up, and it is she who utters the final words in the poem as Adam listens.[85] Initially, Eve had reacted with despair and resistance to the news that they must "wander down / Into a lower World, to this obscure / And wild" (11.282–284). But having been advised by God in her dreams, Eve expresses a new readiness to submit to divine will: "but now lead on; / In mee is no delay . . . Thou to mee / Art all things under Heav'n, all places thou" (12.614–615, 618–619). Her obedience emphasizes that the attitude of patience and humility that grounds true faith and good government is not easy or automatic, but a product of education and self-discipline. Here, the submission to divine decree is expressed in conjugal terms. In her assertion that Adam's presence makes the difference between heaven and hell, Eve rejects the solipsism of Satan's famous insistence that "The mind is its own place and in itself / Can make a Heav'n of Hell, a Hell of Heav'n" (1.254–255). Relation—the society and conversation that for thinkers at least from Sidney to Milton have their emblem and root in love—replaces egoism.[86] Virtue does not signify a banishment of desire, but its subordination to a greater good. We see this in Adam and Eve's obedience, which is painful rather than pleasant: "Some natural tears they dropp'd, but wip'd them soon" (12.645). Nor is this obedience complete, for as Michael's narrative has warned, it will fail time and again throughout human history.

In thus anatomizing the inevitable pulls of passion, Milton does not give up on the possibility of worldly reform. Rather, he redefines it. Like the serenity that so frequently eludes the human psyche, true restoration must be constantly pursued even if it cannot be conclusively obtained. Accordingly, a just and godly order will not require an ecstatic annihilation of desire that is as impossible as a return to Eden. It will demand a patient, if painful, struggle in which the darker forces of self and world remain forever before us—and in which godly rule is as conflicted and elusive as eros itself.

85. "Gender and Conduct," 334–335.
86. As Haskin has argued, the feminine and the domestic becomes even more prominent a paradigm for Christian virtue in *Paradise Regained*, where Milton takes Mary's humility as a model for all disciples ("Milton's Portrait of Mary," 176–181).

ᴄᴧᴐ

Conclusion

"Lives There Who Loves His Pain?"

Throughout this book, my analysis has been driven by a deceptively simple question. What happens to our understanding of early modern political thought if we take seriously two of the period's commonplaces: first, that true love hurts and second, that love—not fear or self-interest—is the source of sovereign authority? I began with the hypothesis that early modern writers' consciousness of love's sacrificial dimension significantly shaped their conceptions of power. Their emphasis on the masochistic, violent, and narcissistic structure of love suggests that desire is rarely rational or "normal." The very ideals of sacrifice and submission that were meant to regulate desire could also generate transgressive fantasies of eroticized torment and abjection. And if such desires—whose resistant, anti-normative potential I have been calling "queer"—motivates political investments, then politics has a queer side too. Because associations between love and pain, on the one hand, and love and loyalty, on the other, are so conventional, scholars have paid little attention to the political implications of early modern literature that stresses the queerness of the sexual instincts. As Richard Rambuss has noted, there is a critical tendency to assume that once a trope becomes recognizable, it ceases to convey complex meanings, "as if the status of being conventional would make a discursive construct or a sentiment any less thick with significance."[1] In the chapters above, I have sought to show just how "thick with significance" erotic conventions really were in the sixteenth and seventeenth centuries. I have argued that the intersection

---

1. *Closet Devotions*, 2.

of two of the period's most recognizable truisms—that real love is painful and self-less, and that love inspires political submission—shape the conception of sovereignty in ways that are anything but predictable.

The cliché that love hurts had power for political writers precisely because it allowed them to get at the latent contradictions of constitutionalist discourse. Epitomized in the Fortescuean political monarch, ancient constitutionalism taught that one could achieve true virtue and happiness only by sacrificing individual desire in favor of public duty. Ideally, this ethos of submission would assure a political bond of mutual service. Constitutionalist theory assumed that the political nation would cease to follow a ruler who failed to live up to his or her end of the bargain, so subjects' obedience could serve as a barometer of royal justice. In Elizabethan England, "love" increasingly named the popular volition and consent that distinguished the virtuous prince from the vicious tyrant. However, the Foxean and Petrarchan conventions that characterized Elizabethan discourse also uncovered a problem with the assumption that love was incompatible with injury. Hagiography and courtship defined true love as a feeling that was the opposite of self-interest, so that loving someone unconditionally was proof of sincerity and virtue. We might here recall Pamphilia's defense of her selfless devotion in the *Urania*: "To leave him for being false, would shew my love was not for his sake, but mine owne, that because he loved me, I therefore loved him, but when hee leaves I can doe so to. O no deere Cousen I loved him for himselfe, and would have loved him had hee not loved mee, and will love though he dispise me" (1.470). This insistence that pain is proof of love takes to its logical conclusion the Fortescuean maxim that submission is a sign of integrity and a source of power. By translating this maxim into erotic terms, the period's literature uncovers the masochistic dimension of a political imaginary based on an ideal of sacrifice. Subjects know that they are being abused, but they tolerate affliction because they enjoy the moral authority it gives them. This conceptual shift appears most strikingly in the period's literature, where scenes of eroticized pain and humiliation illustrate just how complex and disturbing political psychology can be.

A central premise of this book has been that if we treat early modern literature as part of the period's political history, political history itself will look very different. I have proceeded according to the assumption that we can appreciate the nuances of sixteenth- and seventeenth-century political thought if we begin with what the literature shows us, rather than allowing a preconceived historical context to determine our interpretive possibilities. History is lived in large part through fantasy, and memories acquire significance through narrative. As Christopher Lane has argued, strictly contextual interpretation may distort our understanding of not only what happened but also what it means.[2] In early modern

---

2. "The Poverty of Context."

England, the persistent literary recourse to scenarios of erotic violence suggests that even if events changed, the narrative structures through which those events were conceptualized remained remarkably constant. By tracing the recurrence of certain sexualized tropes across a wide range of historical moments, literary genres, and political loyalties, I have sought to reassess teleological accounts of English political thought that see it developing from royalist servility to republican rationality.

While the structure of this book might appear to tell a chronological story of political change, beginning with the reign of Elizabeth and ending with that of Charles II, my actual readings of this literature instead construct a narrative of nostalgia, repetition, and contingency. If we read this literature as though we already know what sides its authors were on—and what such "sides" would have meant to them—we miss much of the tension and complexity of early modern ideas of sovereignty. Most Elizabethan and Jacobean literature, for instance, is certainly "royalist" if we mean by that that it supports monarchy as a system. But many late sixteenth- and early seventeenth-century writers are invested in the same constitutionalist principles that we now tend to associate with civil war opposition. Accordingly, the work of Sidney, Spenser, Shakespeare, and Wroth compels us to rethink what it meant to "support" monarchy in the first place. Similarly, writers whom we have assumed to be servile royalists—Jonson, Carew, Townshend, Davenant, and Cavendish—appear much more critical of absolutist discourse if we take seriously their emphasis on sexual violence. Finally, we must temper our views of Milton's republicanism as purely rationalist and masculinist in light of Adam's misprision and Eve's exemplarity. Because Milton was such an important influence on later republican thought, he is often read in the context of a nascent Habermasian public sphere in which private desires have no place. Such a rationalist reading tends to overlook Milton's attention to the inherently perverse nature of political psychology. The picture of Milton as a misogynistic prude mistakenly excludes him from a tradition of political theory for which sexuality and sentiment is central—a tradition most powerfully enunciated in the romances, plays, and masques that Milton both imitated and transformed.

By way of conclusion, I want to look at Milton's Satan as an example of the consequences of treating human behavior as though it fits rationalist or redemptive ideas of psychic or political subjectivity. My analysis in chapter 8 focused on Adam and Eve, who achieve redemption only by learning to accept the inevitable failure of human reason to regulate human passion. For Milton, it is this sense of creaturely weakness that makes private faith and public compromise necessary. Eve is central to Milton's narrative of redemption, for she epitomizes the dutiful, feminized patience that is, counterintuitively, the true source of moral authority—and therefore political legitimacy. Eve registers the paradoxical interplay between strength and weakness, masculinity and femininity, that is central to both private and public virtue. It is this interplay that Satan rejects in his relentless attempts to assert absolute power and autonomy.

At the end of Book 4, Satan reveals just how insufficient individual human reason is to the task of forging a virtuous self and a just state. Here, having caught Satan
in Eden, Gabriel demands to know why Satan has defied God and "broke the
bounds prescrib'd / To thy transgressions" (4.878–879). In a "contemptuous"
reply, Satan explains his flight from hell in terms at once astute and ironic:

> *Gabriel*, thou had'st in Heav'n th' esteem of wise
> And such I held thee; but this question askt
> Puts me in doubt. Lives there who loves his pain?
> Who would not, finding way, break loose from Hell
> Though thither doom'd? Thou wouldst thyself, no doubt,
> And boldly venture to whatever place
> Farthest from pain where thou might'st hope to change
> Torment with ease, and soonest recompense
> Dole with delight, which in this place I sought. (4.885, 886–894)

Satan's initial question ("Lives there who loves his pain?") is one that troubled all of
the political thinkers that I have considered in *Erotic Subjects*. Recalling Spenser's
"Who can loue the worker of her smart?" Satan's words capture the strangeness
of human desire. The very quality that proves the integrity and truth of love—its
endurance in the face of pain and betrayal—also attests to its irrational, obsessive,
masochistic potential.

On the most literal level, it makes sense that Satan would mock Gabriel's question. Since the only "wise" response to pain is to avoid it, the reason for Satan's
flight should be self-evident. But this explanation ignores the larger lesson of *Paradise Lost*, which is that human beings cannot credit their own perceptions of right
and wrong, pleasure and pain. As Gabriel (and the reader of *Paradise Lost*) know,
Satan's "bold" challenge to divine will can only lead to more punishment. For in
the context of Milton's epic, breaking the "bounds prescrib'd" by God means that
Satan has placed his own will before that of his creator, momentary relief over eternal salvation. He has thereby taken the exact opposite course he should if he hopes
"to change / Torment with ease, and soonest recompense / Dole with delight."
There is a significant gap between what Satan thinks he is doing and what he actually does. In drawing our attention to this discrepancy, Milton insists that choices
that one experiences as obvious common sense, like seeking pleasure and avoiding
pain, may have hopelessly obscure motives and consequences. Indeed, what
counts as pleasure and pain may be determined by ideals and impulses that so distort both physical and psychic sensations that they cease to be stable, objective
phenomena.

Martyrdom, of course, is a case in point. As Marian exiles like Goodman, Ponet,
and Foxe taught generations of English subjects, earthly comfort and pleasure are
fleeting. Like these writers, Milton was well aware that the ability to love one's pain
might be the only real proof of submission to God's will—which is why he, like

Foxe, celebrates "the better fortitude / Of Patience and Heroic Martyrdom / Unsung" over more traditional military heroism (9.31–33). But because one can never be entirely sure of one's own motives, neither pleasure nor pain is a reliable indication of virtue. If both Protestants and Catholics, supporters and opponents of monarchy, are willing to die for their beliefs, even martyrdom loses its seemingly privileged relation to truth. As Spenser and Shakespeare's treatments of sexual coercion, or Townshend's equation of love and slavery, insist, it is harder than one would think to tell the difference between principled, virtuous endurance and shameful, self-serving abjection. Allowing oneself to be hurt or degraded may signify perversion rather than integrity, ambition rather than humility. As Milton repeatedly warns in his later poetry and prose, this human susceptibility to abject and narcissistic desires means that erotic and political subjects can never be entirely certain what the rational course of action would be, much less whether they are following it. One's worst enemies are within, and the fact that one rarely recognizes them as such makes them all the more fearsome.

In answering Satan's "Lives there who loves his pain?" with an unqualified "yes," *Erotic Subjects* has sought to understand victimization as a public fantasy that helped structure early modern political discourse, not a perversion limited to a disturbed or deluded few. I have attempted to estrange early modern literature from traditional definitions of both love and politics by reading the period's romances, plays, masques, and poetry as an extended study of the effects of hagiographic desire. Ultimately, I hope that this analysis will open up some new avenues for thinking about the relationships between private desire and public decision, the history of sexuality and the history of politics, and past and present views of political psychology.

By rethinking our definitions of early modern love and politics—by noticing just how resistant to normalization early modern ideas of love and politics were—we can complicate our understanding of the relation between sexuality and power. And by seeing this erotic literature as part of our historical records, we can refine our views of the relation between past and present. The erotic and political subjects of sixteenth- and seventeenth-century romances, plays, masques, or Christian epics might appear worlds away from our own political and sexual concerns. Early modern subjects exist in a conceptual space that is monarchal rather than democratic, religious rather than secular, one to which our modern ideas of sexuality, gender, and governance would be foreign. But, as numerous scholars have argued, we ought not to allow a sense of alterity to overwhelm the connections we might find with this past.[3] By practicing what Frances E. Dolan has called a "presentist historicism" in

---

3. Determining the proper relation between the present and the past, identification and alterity, has been a central concern for historians of pre-modern sexuality. Just a few instances include Dinshaw, *Getting Medieval*, 1–54; Traub, *Renaissance of Lesbianism*, 1–35; Halperin, *How to Do the History of Homosexuality*; Sedgwick, *Epistemology of the Closet*; Goldberg and Menon, "Queering History"; and Freccero, *Queer/Early/Modern*, 31-50.

our encounters with early modern erotic subjects, we can try "to denaturalize present arrangements by uncovering their roots in the past."[4] Erotic literature which examines the effects of hagiographic thinking is an important archive for scholars interested in the history of the relationships between affect, identity, and political investment. Recent studies of gendered, racial, and socioeconomic hierarchies have shown that sacrifice and injury continue to structure our definitions of ethics, legal rights, and the social contract.[5] This work has emphasized that the worlds of public law and private sentiment are mutually constitutive and that an ideal of what I have called secular martyrdom plays a vital role in both. As I have sought to show, early modern authors were especially sensitive to the potential of hagiographic desire to both reinforce and disrupt political hierarchies. Their work allows us to see how the relation between love and politics was conceived in a historical moment that was very different from our own, but whose stories continue to haunt modern experiences of power and desire.

4. *Marriage and Violence*, 17.
5. See Brown, "Suffering Rights as Paradoxes"; Paul Kahn, *Putting Liberalism in Its Place*, 143–290; Lupton, *Citizen-Saints*; and Berlant, *Female Complaint*.

BIBLIOGRAPHY

PRIMARY SOURCES

Aristotle. *Ethics*. Edited by Hugh Treddenick and Jonathan Barnes. Translated by J. A. K. Thomson. Harmondsworth: Penguin, 1976.

———. *Poetics*. Edited and translated by James Hutton. New York: Norton, 1982.

———. *Politics*. Edited by Stephen Everson. Translated by Jonathan Barnes. Cambridge: Cambridge University Press, 1996.

Aristotle's Master Piece. London, 1698.

Augustine. *St. Augustine, of the Citie of God: with the learned comments of Iohn Lodovico Vives*. Englished by J.H. London, 1610.

Aylmer, John. *An Harborowe for faithfull and trewe subiects, agaynst the late blowne Blaste, concerninge the Gouernment of Wemen*. London, 1559.

Beaumont, Francis. *Salmacis and Hermaphroditus*. London, 1602.

Bodin, Jean. *The Six Books of a Commonweale*. Translated by Richard Knolles. London, 1606.

Boétie, Étienne de la. *The Politics of Obedience: The Discourse of Voluntary Servitude*. Translated by Harry Kurz. New York: Free Life Editions, 1975.

———. *The Will to Bondage, Being the 1577 Text of the Discours de la Servitude volontaire in Parallel with the 1735 Translation as A Discourse of Voluntary Servitude*. Edited by William Flygare. Colorado Springs: Ralph Myles, 1974.

Buchanan, George. *A Dialogue of the Laws of Kingship among the Scots*. Translated and edited by Roger A. Mason and Martin S. Smith. Aldershot: Ashgate, 2004.

Burnet, Gilbert. *Burnet's History of My Own Time, Part I: The Reign of Charles the Second*, 2 vols. Edited by Osmund Airy. Oxford: Clarendon Press, 1897–1900.

Burton, Robert. *The Anatomy of Melancholy*, 2 vols. Translated by F. D. Kessinger and P. J. S. Kessinger. Kila, Mont.: Kessinger, 1991.

Camden, William. *Annales*. London, 1625.

Cavendish, Margaret. *The Blazing World & Other Writings*. Edited by Kate Lilley. Harmondsworth: Penguin, 1992.

———. *The Life of . . . William Cavendishe, Duke . . . of Newcastle*. London, 1667.

———. *Natures Pictures*. London, 1671.

———. *Orations of Diverse Sorts*. London, 1662.

———. *Paper Bodies: A Margaret Cavendish Reader*. Edited by Sylvia Bowerbank and Sara Mendelson. Ontario, Canada: Broadview, 2000.

———. *Sociable Letters*. Edited by James Fitzmaurice. New York: Garland, 1997.

Cavendish, William. *The Country Captaine, And the Varietie, Two Comedies*. London, 1649.

———. *A Declaration Made by the Earl of New-Castle . . . For his Resolution of Marching into Yorkshire*. London, 1642/3.

———. *Ideology and Politics on the Eve of Restoration: Newcastle's Advice to Charles II*. Edited by Thomas P. Slaughter. Philadelphia: American Philosophical Society, 1985.

Chambers, E. K. *The Elizabethan Stage*. 4 vols. Oxford: Clarendon Press, 1923.

Charles I. *Eikon Basilike*. Edited by Edward Almack. London: Chatto and Windus, 1907.

Cicero. *On Old Age, On Friendship, On Divination*. Translated by W. A. Falconer. Cambridge, Mass.: Harvard University Press, 1923.

Coke, Edward. *The Second Part of the Institutes of the Lawes of England*. London, 1642.

———. *The Third Part of the Institutes of the Lawes of England*. London, 1644.

Cowly, Abraham. *The Works of Mr. A. Cowley*. 2 vols. London: John Sharpe, 1809.

Crooke, Helkiah. *Mikrokosmographia: A description of the Body of Man*. London, 1615.

Dalton, Michael. *The Country Justice*. London, 1681.

Elizabeth I. *Elizabeth I: Collected Works*. Edited by Leah S. Marcus, Janel Mueller, and Mary Beth Rose. Chicago: University of Chicago Press, 2000.

Elyot, Thomas. *The Boke, Named the Governour*. London, 1580.

———. *The Castell of Health*. London, 1587.

Filmer, Robert. *Patriarcha and Other Writings*. Edited by Johann P. Sommerville. Cambridge: Cambridge University Press, 1996.

Fortescue, John. *On the Laws and Governance of England*. Edited by Shelley Lockwood. Cambridge: Cambridge University Press, 1997.

Foster, Elizabeth Read. *Proceedings in Parliament, 1610*. 2 vols. New Haven: Yale University Press, 1966.

Foxe, John. *The Acts and Monuments of John Foxe*. 8 vols. Edited by George Townsend. New York: AMS Press, 1965.

Franklin, Julian H., ed. *Constitutionalism and Resistance: Three Treatises by Hotman, Beza, Mornay*. New York: Pegasus, 1969.

Freud, Sigmund. *General Psychological Theory: Papers on Metapsychology*. Edited by Philip Rieff. New York: Touchstone, 1977.

———. *Totem and Taboo*. Translated and edited by James Strachey. New York: Norton, 1950.

Gardiner, Samuel Rawson. *History of the Great Civil War*. 4 vols. London: Longmans, Green, and Co., 1904.

———, ed. *The Constitutional Documents of the Puritan Revolution, 1625–1660*. 3d ed. Oxford: Clarendon Press, 1906.

The Geneva Bible: A Facsimile of the 1560 Edition. Edited by Lloyd Eason Berry and William Whittingham. Madison: University of Wisconsin Press, 1969.

Goodman, Christopher. *How Superior Powers ogt to be Obeyd*. Geneva, 1558.

Goodwin, John. *Right and might well met*. London, 1649.

Gower, John. *Confessio Amantis*. Edited by Russell A. Peck. Translated by Andrew Galloway. Kalamazoo, Mich.: Medieval Institute Publications, 2000.

Greville, Fulke. *Fulke Greville's Life of Sir Philip Sidney*. Edited by Nowell Smith. Oxford: Oxford University Press, 1907.

———. *The Prose Works of Fulke Greville, Lord Brooke*. Edited by John Gouws. Oxford: Oxford University Press, 1986.

Herbert, Thomas. *Vox secunda populi*. London, 1641.

History of the Thrice Illustrious Princess Henrietta Maria de Bourbon, Queen of England, The. London: E.C. for Philip Chetwind, 1660.

Hobbes, Thomas. *Leviathan*. Edited by Richard Tuck. Cambridge: Cambridge University Press, 1996.

Hunton, Philip. *A Treatise of Monarchy*. London, 1643.

Hutchinson, Lucy. *Memoirs of the Life of Colonial Hutchinson*. Edited by N. H. Keeble. London: Everyman, 1995.

Jacob, Giles. *New Law-Dictionary, A*. London, 1772.

James VI and I. *Political Writings*. Edited by Johann P. Sommerville. Cambridge: Cambridge University Press, 1994.

Jonson, Ben. *Ben Jonson: The Complete Masques*. Edited by Stephen Orgel. New Haven: Yale University Press, 1969.

———. *Ben Jonson: The Complete Poems*. Edited by George Parfitt. Harmondsworth: Penguin, 1996.

Journals of the House of Commons. Vols 1-9. London: H. M. Stationary Office, 1808.

Knox, John. *The First Blast of the Trumphet against the Monstrous regiment of women*. Geneva, 1558.

Languet, Hubert, and Philippe Duplessis-Mornay. *Vindiciae, Contra Tyrannos*. Edited and translated by George Garnett. Cambridge: Cambridge University Press, 1994.

Lawes Resolution of Women's Rights, The. London, 1632.

L'Estrange, Roger. *A Caveat to the Cavaliers*. London, 1661.

Lindley, David, ed. *Court Masques: Jacobean and Caroline Entertainments, 1605–1640*. Oxford: Oxford University Press, 1995.

Livy. *History of Rome*. Translated by B. O. Foster. Cambridge, Mass.: Harvard University Press, 1919.

Luther, Martin. *Martin Luther: Selections from His Writings*. Edited by John Dillinger. New York: Anchor, 1962.

Marx, Karl. *The Ethnological Notebooks of Karl Marx*. Edited by Lawrence Krader. Assen: Van Gorcum, 1972.

Milton, John. *Complete Prose Works of John Milton*. 8 vols. Edited by Don M. Wolfe. New Haven and London: Yale University Press, 1962.

———. *John Milton: Complete Poems and Major Prose*. Edited by Merritt Y. Hughes. New York: Macmillan, 1957.

Nichols, John. *The Progresses and Public Processions of Queen Elizabeth*. 3 vols. New York: AMS, 1969.

Ovid. *Ars amoratia*. Translated by Thomas Heywood. London, 1640.

———. *Fasti*. Translated by James G. Frazer. Cambridge, Mass.: Harvard University Press, 1989.

———. *Metamorphoses: The Arthur Golding Translation of 1567*. Edited by John Frederick Nims. Philadelphia: Paul Dry Books, 2000.

Painter, William. *The Palace of Pleasure*. London, 1575.

Parker, Henry. *Observations upon some of His Majesties Late Answers*. 2d ed. London, 1642.

Pepys, Samuel. *The Diary of Samuel Pepys*. 9 vols. Edited by Henry B. Wheatley. New York: Crosscup and Sterling, 1900.

Ponet, John. *A Shorte Treatise of politic power*. Geneva, 1556.

Prynne, William. *Independency Examined*. London, 1644.

———. *The Treachery and Disloyalty of Papists to Their Soveraignes*. London, 1643.

Quarles, Francis. *Argalus and Parthenia*. London, 1629.

Rushworth, J. *Historical Collections of Private Passages of State*. 8 vols. London, 1659–1701.

Seneca the Elder. *Declamations*. 2 vols. Volume Two: *Controversiae, Books 7-10, Suasoriae, Fragments*. Translated by Michael Winterbottom. Cambridge, Mass.: Harvard University Press, 1974.

Shakespeare, William. *Pericles*. Edited by Susanne Gossett. London: Arden, 2004.

———. *The Riverside Shakespeare*. 2d ed. Edited by G. Blakemore Evans. Boston: Houghton Mifflin, 1997.

Sidney, Algernon. *Discourses Concerning Government*. Edited by Thomas G. West. Indianapolis: Liberty Fund, 1996.

———. *The Essence of Algernon Sidney's Work on Government*. 2d ed. Edited by William Scott. London, 1797.

Sidney, Philip. *The Countess of Pembroke's Arcadia.* Edited by Maurice Evans. New York: Penguin, 1977.

———. *The Countess of Pembroke's Arcadia.* 10th ed. Edited by William Dugard. London, 1655.

———. *The Poems of Sir Philip Sidney.* Edited by William A. Ringler, Jr. Oxford: Clarendon Press, 1962.

———. *The Prose Works of Sir Philip.* 4 vols. Edited by Albert Feuillerat. Cambridge: Cambridge University Press, 1969.

———. *Sir Philip Sidney: The Major Works.* Edited by Katherine Duncan-Jones. Oxford: Oxford University Press, 2002.

Smyth, Thomas. *De Republica Anglorum.* London, 1583.

Spenser, Edmund. *The Faerie Queene.* Edited by A. C. Hamilton, Hiroshi Yamashita, and Toshiyuki Suzuki. Harlow: Longman, 2001.

———. *The Shorter Poems.* Edited by Richard A. McCabe. Harmondsworth: Penguin, 1999.

Starkey, Thomas. *Dialogue Between Reginald Pole and Thomas Lupset.* Edited by Kathleen M. Burton. London: Chatto & Windus, 1948.

St. German, Christopher. *The secu[n]d dyaloge in Englisshe wyth new addycyons.* London, 1531.

Tacitus. *The Ende of Nero and the Beginning of Galba. Fower Bookes of the Histories of Cornelius Tacitus. The Life of Agricola.* Translated by Henry Savile. London, 1591.

Tilney, Edmund. *A Brief and Pleasant Discourse of Duties in Mariage, called the Flower of Friendshippe.* Edited by Valerie Wayne. Ithaca, N.Y.: Cornell University Press, 1992.

Twine, Lawrence. *The Patterne of Painefull Adventures.* London, 1594.

Vicary, Thomas. *The English-Man's Treasure.* London, 1586.

Warner, George F., ed. *Nicholas Papers.* 4 vols. London: Camden Society, 1886–1920.

Wilkins, George. *The Painfull Adventures of Pericles Prince of Tyre.* Edited by Kenneth Muir. Liverpool: University Press of Liverpool, 1953.

Wilson, Jean. *Entertainments for Elizabeth I.* Woodbridge: D. S. Brewer, 1980.

Wroth, Mary. *The First Part of the Countess of Montgomery's Urania.* Edited by Josephine A. Roberts. Binghampton, N.Y.: Center for Medieval and Early Renaissance Studies, 1995.

———. *The Second Part of the Countess of Montgomery's Urania.* Edited by Josephine A. Roberts, completed by Suzanne Gossett and Janel Mueller. Tempe: Arizona Center for Medieval and Renaissance Studies, 1999.

———. *The Poems of Lady Mary Wroth.* Edited by Josephine A. Roberts. Baton Rouge: Louisiana State University Press, 1983.

SECONDARY SOURCES

Achinstein, Sharon. "'A Law in this Matter to Himself': Contextualizing Milton's Divorce Tracts." In *The Oxford Handbook to Milton,* edited by Nicholas McDowell and Nigel Smith, 174–185. Oxford: Oxford University Press, 2009.

Adamson, J. S. A. "Chivalry and Political Culture." In *Culture and Politics in Early Stuart England,* edited by Kevin Sharpe and Peter Lake, 161-197. Stanford, Calif.: Stanford University Press, 1993.

Akrigg, G. P. V. *Shakespeare and the Earl of Southampton.* London: Hamish Hamilton, 1968.

Adelman, Janet. *Suffocating Mothers: Fantasies of Maternal Origin in Shakespeare's Plays, "Hamlet" to "The Tempest."* London: Routledge, 1992.

Alexander, Gavin. *Writing after Sidney: The Literary Response to Sir Philip Sidney.* New York: Oxford University Press, 2006.

Allen, M. J. B., Dominic Baker-Smith, and Arthur F. Kinney, with Margaret M. Sullivan, eds. *Sir Philip Sidney's Achievements.* New York: AMS, 1990.

Amussen, Susan Dwyer. *An Ordered Society: Gender and Class in Early Modern England.* New York: Columbia University Press, 1993.

Anderson, Judith. "'Nor Man it Is': The Knight of Justice in Book V of Spenser's *Faerie Queene*." *PMLA* 85 (1970): 65–77.

———. *Reading the Allegorical Intertext: Chaucer, Spenser, Shakespeare, Milton*. New York: Fordham University Press, 2008.

Andrea, Bernadette. "Pamphilia's Cabinet: Gendered Authorship and Empire in Lady Mary Wroth's *Urania*." *ELH* 68 (2001): 335–358.

Archer, Jayne Elizabeth, Elizabeth Goldring, and Sarah Knight, eds. *The Progresses, Pageants, and Entertainments of Queen Elizabeth I*. Oxford: Oxford University Press, 2007.

Armitage, David. *The Ideological Origins of the British Empire*. Cambridge: Cambridge University Press, 2000.

———. "John Milton: Poet Against Empire." In *Milton and Republicanism*, edited by David Armitage, Armand Himy, and Quentin Skinner, 206–225. Cambridge: Cambridge University Press, 1995.

Armitage, David, Armand Himy, and Quentin Skinner, eds. *Milton and Republicanism*. Cambridge: Cambridge University Press, 1995.

Arnold, Oliver. *The Third Citizen: Shakespeare's Theater and the Early Modern House of Commons*. Baltimore: Johns Hopkins University Press, 2007.

Arrizabalaga, Jon, John Henderson, and Roger French. *The Great Pox: The French Disease in Renaissance Europe*. New Haven: Yale University Press, 1997.

Ashton, Robert. *James I by His Contemporaries*. London: Hutchinson, 1969.

Atherton, Ian, and Julie Sanders. "Introducing the 1630s." In *The 1630s: Interdisciplinary Essays on Culture and Politics in the Caroline Era*, edited by Ian Atherton and Julie Sanders, 1–27. Manchester: Manchester University Press, 2006.

Bach, Rebecca Ann. *Shakespeare and Renaissance Literature before Heterosexuality*. New York: Palgrave MacMillan, 2007.

Bailey, Rebecca A. *Staging the Old Faith: Queen Henrietta Maria and the Theatre of Caroline England, 1625–1642*. Manchester: Manchester University Press, 2009.

Baines, Barbara J. *Representing Rape in the English Early Modern Period*. Lewiston, N.Y.: Edwin Mellen Press, 2003.

Baker, David. "Historical Contexts: Britain and Europe." In *The Cambridge Companion to Spenser*, edited by Andrew Hadfield, 37–59. Cambridge: Cambridge University Press, 2001.

Bamford, Karen. *Sexual Violence on the Jacobean Stage*. New York: St. Martin's Press, 2000.

Barber, C. L., and Richard Wheeler. *The Whole Journey: Shakespeare's Power of Development*. Berkeley: University of California Press, 1986.

Barker, Arthur. *Milton and the Puritan Dilemma*. Toronto: University of Toronto Press, 1942.

Bashar, Nazife. "Rape in England between 1550 and 1700." In *The Sexual Dynamics of History*, edited by London Feminist History Group, 28–42. London: Pluto Press, 1983.

Bates, Catherine. *Masculinity, Gender, and Identity in the English Renaissance Lyric*. Cambridge: Cambridge University Press, 2008.

Battigelli, Anna. *Margaret Cavendish and the Exiles of the Mind*. Lexington: University of Kentucky Press, 1998.

Beilin, Elaine V. "'The Onely Perfect Vertue': Constancy in Mary Wroth's *Pamphilia to Amphilanthus*." *Spenser Studies* 2 (1981): 229–245.

———. *Redeeming Eve: Women Writers of the English Renaissance*. Princeton: Princeton University Press, 1987.

———. "Winning 'the Harts of the People': The Role of the Political Subject in the *Urania*." In *Pilgrimage for Love: Essays in Early Modern Literature in Honor of Josephine A. Roberts*, edited by Sigrid King, 1–17. Tempe: Arizona Center for Medieval and Renaissance Studies, 1999.

Belsey, Catherine. "Tarquin Dispossessed: Expropriation and Consent in *The Rape of Lucrece*." *Shakespeare Quarterly* 52 (2001): 315–335.

Benjamin, Jessica. *The Bonds of Love: Psychoanalysis, Feminism, and the Problem of Domination.* New York: Pantheon, 1988.

Benson, Pamela J. "Florimell at Sea: The Action of Grace in *The Faerie Queene*, Book III." *Spenser Studies* 6 (1986): 83–94.

Berger, Harry, Jr. *The Allegorical Temper: Vision and Reality in Book II of Spenser's "Faerie Queene."* New Haven: Yale University Press, 1957.

———. *Revisionary Play: Studies in Spenserian Dynamics.* Berkeley: University of California Press, 1988.

———. "Writing Out the Old: Squeezing the Text, 1951–2001." *Spenser Studies* 18 (2003): 81–121.

Bergeron, David M. *Shakespeare's Romances and the Royal Family.* Lawrence: University Press of Kansas, 1985.

Berlant, Lauren. *The Female Complaint: The Unfinished Business of Sentimentality in American Culture.* Durham, N.C.: Duke University Press, 2008.

———. "Love, A Queer Feeling." In *Homosexuality and Psychoanalysis*, edited by Tim Dean and Christopher Lane, 432–451. Chicago: University of Chicago Press, 2001.

Berlant, Lauren, and Michael Warner. "Sex in Public." *Critical Inquiry* 24 (1998): 547–566.

Berry, Philippa. *Of Chastity and Power: Elizabethan Literature and the Unmarried Queen.* London: Routledge, 1989.

Bersani, Leo. "Is the Rectum a Grave?" *October* 43 (1987): 197–222.

Bersani, Leo, and Adam Phillips. *Intimacies.* Chicago: University of Chicago Press, 2008.

Bevington, David, and Peter Holbrook, "Introduction." In *The Politics of the Stuart Court Masque*, edited by David Bevington and Peter Holbrook, 1–19. Cambridge: Cambridge University Press, 1998.

———, eds. *The Politics of the Stuart Court Masque.* Cambridge: Cambridge University Press, 1998.

Bone, Quinton. *Henrietta Maria: Queen of the Cavaliers.* Chicago: University of Illinois Press, 1972.

Borris, Kenneth. *Spenser's Poetics of Prophecy in "The Faerie Queene" V.* Victoria: University of Victoria English Literary Studies, 1991.

Bowers, Toni. *Force or Fraud: British Seduction Stories and the Problem of Resistance, 1660–1760.* Oxford: Oxford University Press, 2011.

Bowman, Mary R. "Distressing Irena: Gender, Conquest, and Justice in Book V of *The Faerie Queene*." *Spenser Studies* 17 (2003): 151–182.

Breitenberg, Mark. *Anxious Masculinity in Early Modern England.* Cambridge: Cambridge University Press, 1996.

Brennan, Michael G. "Creating Female Authorship in the Early Seventeenth Century: Ben Jonson and Lady Mary Wroth." In *Women's Writing and the Circulation of Ideas*, edited by George L. Justice and Nathan Tinker, 73–93. Cambridge: Cambridge University Press, 2002.

———. *Literary Patronage in the English Renaissance: The Pembroke Family.* London: Routledge, 1988.

———. *The Sidneys of Penshurst and the Monarchy, 1500–1700.* Aldershot: Ashgate, 2006.

Britland, Karen. *Drama at the Courts of Henrietta Maria.* Cambridge: Cambridge University Press, 2006.

———. "Marie de Médicis and the Last Caroline Court Masque." In *Women and Culture at the Courts of the Stuart Queens*, edited by Clare McManus, 204–223. New York: Palgrave Macmillan, 2003.

Bromley, Laura G. "Lucrece's Re-Creation." *Shakespeare Quarterly* 34 (1983): 200–211.

Brown, Wendy. "Suffering Rights as Paradoxes." *Constellations* 7 (2000): 230–241.

Burgess, Glen. *Absolute Monarchy and the Stuart Constitution.* New Haven: Yale University Press, 1996.

———. *The Politics of the Ancient Constitution: An Introduction to English Political Thought, 1603–1642.* University Park: Pennsylvania State University Press, 1993.

Burks, Deborah G. "'I'll Want My Will Else': *The Changeling* and Women's Complicity with Their Rapists." *ELH* 62 (1995): 759–779.

Bushnell, Rebecca. *Tragedies of Tyrants: Political Thought and Theater in the English Renaissance.* Ithaca, N.Y.: Cornell University Press, 1990.

Butler, Judith. "Against Proper Objects. Introduction." *differences* 6.2–3 (1994): 1–26.

———. *Bodies that Matter: On the Discursive Limits of "Sex."* New York: Routledge, 1993.

———. *Gender Trouble: Feminism and the Subversion of Identity.* New York: Routledge, 1999.

———. *The Psychic Life of Power: Theories in Subjection.* Stanford, Calif.: Stanford University Press, 1997.

Butler, Martin. "Ben Jonson and the Limits of Courtly Panegyric." In *Culture and Politics in Early Stuart England*, edited by Kevin Sharpe and Peter Lake, 91–115. Stanford, Calif.: Stanford University Press, 1993.

———. "Courtly Negotiations." In *The Politics of the Stuart Court Masque*, edited by David Bevington and Peter Holbrook, 20–40. Cambridge: Cambridge University Press, 1998.

———. "Late Jonson." In *The Politics of Tragicomedy: Shakespeare and After*, edited by Gordon McMullan and Jonathan Hope, 166–188. London: Routledge, 1992.

———. "Politics and the Masque: *Salmacida Spolia.*" In *Literature and the English Civil War*, edited by Thomas Healy and Jonathan Sawday, 59–74. Cambridge: Cambridge University Press, 1990.

———. *The Stuart Court Masque and Political Culture.* Cambridge: Cambridge University Press, 2008.

———. *Theatre and Crisis: 1632–1642.* Cambridge: Cambridge University Press, 1987.

Carey, Vincent P., and Clare L. Carroll. "Factions and Fictions: Spenser's Reflections on Elizabethan Politics." In *Spenser's Life and the Subject of Biography*, edited by Judith Anderson, Donald Cheney, and David A. Richardson, 31–44. Amherst: University of Massachusetts Press, 1996.

Carroll, Clare. "The Construction of Gender and the Cultural and Political Other in *The Faerie Queene* and *A View of the Present State of Ireland*: The Critics, the Context and the Case of Radigund." *Criticism* 32 (1990): 163–192.

Cassirer, Ernst, Paul Oskar Kristeller, Jr., and John Herman Randall, eds. *The Renaissance Philosophy of Man.* Chicago: University of Chicago Press, 1956.

Catty, Jocelyn. *Writing Rape, Writing Women in Early Modern England: Unbridled Speech.* New York: St. Martin's Press, 1999.

Cavanagh, Sheila T. *Cherished Torment: The Emotional Geography of Lady Mary Wroth's "Urania."* Pittsburgh: Dusquesne University Press, 2001.

———. *Wanton Eyes and Chaste Desires: Female Sexuality in "The Faerie Queene."* Bloomington: Indiana University Press, 1994.

Chalmers, Hero. *Royalist Women Writers, 1650–1689.* Oxford: Clarendon Press, 2004.

Chaytor, Miranda. "Husband(ry): Narratives of Rape in the Seventeenth Century." *Gender and History* 7 (1995): 378–407.

Cheney, Patrick. "'O, Let My Books Be . . . Dumb Presagers': Poetry and Theater in Shakespeare's Sonnets." *Shakespeare Quarterly* 52 (2001): 222–254.

Chibnall, Jennifer. "'To that Secure Fix'd State': The Function of the Caroline Masque." In *The Court Masque,* edited by David Lindley, 78–93. Manchester: Manchester University Press, 1984.

Clark, Peter, Alan G. R. Smith, and Nicholas Tyacke, eds. *The English Commonwealth, 1547–1640.* Leicester: Leicester University Press, 1979.

Clarke, Danielle. *The Politics of Early Modern Women's Writing.* Harlow, England: Pearson Education Ltd, 2001.

Cohen, Walter. Introduction to *Pericles.* In *The Norton Shakespeare,* edited by Stephen Greenblatt, et al. New York: Norton, 1997.

———. "Prerevolutionary Drama." In *The Politics of Tragicomedy: Shakespeare and After,* edited by Gordon McMullan and Jonathan Hope, 122–150. London: Routledge, 1992.

Colclough, David. *Freedom of Speech in Early Stuart England.* Cambridge: Cambridge University Press, 2005.

Coles, Kimberly Anne. "'Perfect Hole': Elizabeth I, Spenser, and Chaste Productions." *ELR* 32 (2002): 31–61.

———. *Religion, Reform, and Women's Writing in Early Modern England.* Cambridge: Cambridge University Press, 2008.

Collinson, Patrick. "Ecclesiastical Vitriol: Religious Satire in the 1590s and the Invention of Puritanism." In *The Reign of Elizabeth I: Court and Culture in the Last Decade,* edited by John Guy, 150–170. Cambridge: Cambridge University Press, 1995.

———. "Pulling the Strings: Religion and Politics in the Progress of 1578." In *The Progresses, Pageants, and Entertainments of Queen Elizabeth I,* edited by Jayne Elizabeth Archer, Elizabeth Goldring, and Sarah Knight, 122–141. Oxford: Oxford University Press, 2007.

———. "Puritans, Men of Business, and Elizabethan Parliaments." *Parliamentary History* 7, pt. 2 (1988): 187-211.

Cooper, Helen. *The English Romance in Time.* Oxford: Oxford University Press, 2008.

Corns, Thomas. "Milton before 'Lycidas.'" In *Milton and the Terms of Liberty,* edited by Graham Parry and Joad Raymond, 23–36. Cambridge: D. S. Brewer, 2002.

———. "'Some Rousing Motions': The Plurality of Miltonic Ideology." In *Literature and the English Civil War,* edited by Thomas Healy and Jonathan Sawday, 110–126. Cambridge: Cambridge University Press, 1990.

Cottegnies, Line, and Nancy Weitz, eds. *Authorial Conquests: Essays on Genre in the Writings of Margaret Cavendish.* Cranbury, N.J.: Associated University Presses, 2003.

Coughlin, Patricia, ed. *Spenser and Ireland: An Interdisciplinary Perspective.* Cork: Cork University Press, 1989.

Craig, Hugh. "Jonson, the Antimasque, and the 'Rules of Flattery.'" In *The Politics of the Stuart Court Masque,* edited by David Bevington and Peter Holbrook, 176–196. Cambridge: Cambridge University Press, 1998.

Cressy, David. "Revolutionary England, 1640–1642." *Past and Present* 181 (2003): 35–72.

Cromartie, Alan. "The Constitutionalist Revolution: The Transformation of Political Culture in Early Stuart England." *Past and Present* 1663 (1999): 76–120.

Curran, Stuart. "God." In *The Oxford Handbook to Milton,* edited by Nicholas McDowell and Nigel Smith, 525–533. Oxford: Oxford University Press, 2009.

Cust, Richard. *Charles I: A Political Life.* Harlow: Pearson, 2007. "God

Cust, Richard, and Anne Hughes. "After Revisionism." In *Conflict in Early Stuart England: Studies in Religion and Politics, 1603–1642,* edited by Richard Cust and Anne Hughes, 1–46. London: Longman, 1989.

Daly, James. *Sir Robert Filmer and English Political Thought.* Toronto: University of Toronto Press, 1979.

Dasenbrock, Reed Way. "Wyatt's Transformation of Petrarch." *Comparative Literature* 40 (1988): 122–133.

Davis, J. C. *Fear, Myth, and History: The Ranters and the Historians.* Cambridge: Cambridge University Press, 1986.

Dawson, Lesel. *Lovesickness and Gender in Early Modern English Literature.* Oxford: Oxford University Press, 2008.

Deleuze, Gilles. *Masochism: Coldness and Cruelty and Venus in Furs.* Translated by Jean McNeil. New York: Zone, 1989.

Derrida, Jacques. *Margins of Philosophy.* Translated by Alan Bass. Chicago: University of Chicago Press, 1982.

Dillon, Anne. *The Construction of Martyrdom in the English Catholic Community.* Aldershot: Ashgate, 2002.

Dinshaw, Carolyn. *Getting Medieval: Sexualities and Communities, Pre- and Postmodern.* Durham, N.C.: Duke University Press, 1999.

Dolan, Frances E. *Marriage and Violence: The Early Modern Legacy.* Philadelphia: University of Pennsylvania Press, 2008.

———. *Whores of Babylon: Catholicism, Gender, and Seventeenth-Century Print Culture.* Ithaca, N.Y.: Cornell University Press, 1999.

Dollimore, Jonathan. *Sexual Dissidence: Augustine to Wilde, Freud to Foucault.* Oxford: Oxford University Press, 1991.

Donagan, Barbara. "Casuistry and Allegiance in the English Civil War." In *Writing and Political Engagement in Seventeenth-Century England,* edited by Derek Hirst and Richard Strier, 89–111. Cambridge: Cambridge University Press, 1999.

Donaldson, Ian. *The Rapes of Lucretia.* Oxford: Clarendon Press, 1982.

Douglas, Mary. *Purity and Danger: An Analysis of Concepts of Pollution and Taboo.* New York: Routledge, 2002.

Dubrow, Heather. *Captive Victors: Shakespeare's Narrative Poems and Sonnets.* Ithaca, N.Y.: Cornell University Press, 1987.

———. *Echoes of Desire: English Petrarchism and Its Counterdiscourses.* Ithaca, N.Y.: Cornell University Press, 1995.

Duncan-Jones, Katherine. *Sir Philip Sidney: Courtier-Poet.* New Haven: Yale University Press, 1991.

———. *Ungentle Shakespeare: Scenes from His Life.* London: Arden Shakespeare, 2001.

Dzelzainis, Martin. "Milton and the Protectorate in 1658." In *Milton and Republicanism,* edited by David Armitage, Armand Himy, and Quentin Skinner, 181–205. Cambridge: Cambridge University Press, 1995.

———. "Milton's Classical Republicanism." In *Milton and Republicanism,* edited by David Armitage, Armand Himy, and Quentin Skinner, 3–24. Cambridge: Cambridge University Press, 1995.

Edelman, Lee. *No Future: Queer Theory and the Death Drive.* Durham, N.C.: Duke University Press, 2004.

Eggert, Katherine. "'Changing All that Form of Common Weale': Genre and the Repeal of Queenship in *The Faerie Queene,* Book 5." *English Literary Renaissance* 26 (1996): 261–285.

———. "Spenser's Ravishment: Rape and Rapture in *The Faerie Queene.*" *Representations* 70 (2000): 1–26.

Ellis, Stephen. *Tudor Frontiers and Noble Power: The Making of the British State.* Oxford: Clarendon Press, 1995.

Elton, G. R. *The Tudor Constitution: Documents and Commentary.* Cambridge: Cambridge University Press, 1982.

Escobedo, Andrew. "Daemon Lovers: Will, Personification, and Character." *Spenser Studies* 22 (2007): 203–225.

Fallon, Robert. "*A Second Defence*: Milton's Critique of Cromwell?" *Milton Studies* 39 (2000): 167–183.

Fallon, Stephen M. "The Spur of Self-Concernment: Milton in His Divorce Tracts." *Milton Studies* 38 (2000): 220–242.

Ferguson, Margaret, Maureen Quilligan, and Nancy Vickers, eds. *Rewriting the Renaissance: The Discourses of Sexual Difference in Early Modern Europe*. Chicago: University of Chicago Press, 1986.

Fienberg, Nona. "Mary Wroth's Poetics of the Self." *SEL* 42 (2002): 121–136.

Fineman, Joel. "Shakespeare's Will: The Temporality of Rape." *Representations* 20 (1987): 25–76.

Fish, Stanley. *How Milton Works*. Cambridge, Mass.: Harvard University Press, 2001.

Fitzmaurice, James. "Margaret Cavendish's *Life of William*, Plutarch, and Mixed Genre." In *Authorial Conquests: Essays on Genre in the Writings of Margaret Cavendish*, edited by Line Cottegnies and Nancy Weitz, 80–102. Cranbury, N.J.: Associated University Presses, 2003.

Fletcher, Angus. *Allegory: The Theory of a Symbolic Mode*. Ithaca, N.Y.: Cornell University Press, 1964.

Fletcher, Anthony. "Oliver Cromwell and the Localities: The Problem of Consent." In *Cromwell and the Interregnum: The Essential Readings*, edited by David L. Smith, 121–138. Malden, Mass.: Blackwell, 2003.

Fogarty, Anne. "The Colonization of Language: Narrative Strategy in *A View of the Present State of Ireland* and *The Faerie Queene*, Book VI." In *Spenser and Ireland: An Interdisciplinary Perspective*, edited by Patricia Coughlin, 75–108. Cork: Cork University Press, 1989.

Foucault, Michel. *The History of Sexuality*. Vol. 1. Translated by Robert Hurley. New York: Vintage, 1990.

Fowler, Elizabeth. "The Failure of Moral Philosophy in the Work of Edmund Spenser." *Representations* 51 (1995): 47–76.

Freccero, Carla. *Queer/Early/Modern*. Durham, N.C.: Duke University Press, 2006.

Froula, Christine. "When Eve Reads Milton: Undoing the Canonical Economy." *Critical Inquiry* 10 (1983): 321–347.

Frye, Northrop. *Anatomy of Criticism*. Princeton: Princeton University Press, 1957.

———. *The Secular Scripture: A Study of the Structure of Romance*. Cambridge, Mass.: Harvard University Press, 1976.

Frye, Susan. *Elizabeth I: The Competition for Representation*. New York: Oxford University Press, 1993.

Fuchs, Barbara. *Romance*. New York: Routledge, 2004.

Gallagher, Catherine. "Embracing the Absolute: The Politics of the Female Subject in Seventeenth-Century England." *Genders* 1 (1988): 24–39.

Gaunt, Peter. "'The Single Person's Confidants and Dependants'? Oliver Cromwell and His Protectoral Councilors." *Historical Journal* 32 (1989): 537–560.

Gearhart, Suzanne. "The Taming of Michel Foucault: New Historicism, Psychoanalysis, and the Subversion of Power." *New Literary History* 28 (1997): 457–480.

Gentiles, Ian. "The *Agreements of the People* and Their Political Contexts, 1647–1649." In *The Putney Debates of 1647*, edited by Michael Mendle, 148–174. Cambridge: Cambridge University Press, 2001.

Gilbert, Sandra. "Patriarchal Poetry and Women Readers: Reflections on Milton's Bogey." *PMLA* 93 (1978): 368–382.

Godshalk, William Leigh. "Sidney's Revision of the *Arcadia*, Books III–V." In *Essential Articles for the Study of Sir Philip Sidney*, edited by Arthur F. Kinney, 311–326. Hamden, Conn.: Archon Books, 1987.

Goldberg, Jonathan. *James I and the Politics of Literature: Jonson, Shakespeare, Donne, and Their Contemporaries*. Baltimore: Johns Hopkins University Press, 1983.

Goldberg, Jonathan, and Madhavi Menon. "Queering History." *PMLA* 120.5 (2005): 1608–1617.

Goldie, Mark. "The Unacknowledged Republic: Officeholding in Early Modern England." In *The Politics of the Excluded, c. 1500–1850*, edited by Tim Harris, 153–194. New York: Palgrave, 2001.

Gordon, D. J. "Poet and Architect: The Intellectual Setting of the Quarrel between Ben Jonson and Inigo Jones." *Journal of the Warburg and Courtauld Institutes* 12 (1949): 152–178.

Gossett, Suzanne. "Introduction." In *Pericles*, edited by Susanne Gossett, 1–163. London: Arden, 2004.

———. "'Man-maid, Begone!' Women in Masques." In *Women in the Renaissance*, edited by Kirby Farrell, Elizabeth H. Hageman, and Arthur F. Kinney, 118–135. Amherst: University of Massachusetts Press, 1990.

Gowing, Laura. *Common Bodies: Women, Touch, and Power in Seventeenth-Century England*. New Haven: Yale University Press, 2003.

Grant, Douglas. *Margaret the First*. London: Rupert Hart-Davis, 1957.

Gray, Catharine. *Women Writers and Public Debate in Seventeenth-Century Britain*. New York: Palgrave Macmillan, 2007.

Greenberg, Janelle. *The Radical Face of the Ancient Constitution*. Cambridge: Cambridge University Press, 2001.

Greenblatt, Stephen J. *Learning to Curse: Essays in Early Modern Culture*. New York: Routledge, 1990.

Greenhalgh, Darlene. "Love, Chastity, and Woman's Erotic Power: Greek Romance in Elizabethan and Jacobean Contexts." In *Prose Fiction and Early Modern Sexualities in England, 1570–1640*, edited by Constance Relihan and Goran Stanivukovic, 15–42. New York: Palgrave Macmillan, 2003.

Greenlaw, Edwin A. "Sidney's *Arcadia* as an Example of Elizabethan Allegory." In *Essential Articles for the Study of Sir Philip Sidney*, edited by Arthur F. Kinney, 271–285. Hamden, Conn.: Archon Books, 1987.

Gregory, Brad S. *Salvation at Stake: Christian Martyrdom in Early Modern Europe*. Cambridge, Mass.: Harvard University Press, 1999.

Gregory, Tobias. "Shadowing Intervention: On the Politics of *The Faerie Queene* Book 5 Cantos 10–12." *ELH* 67 (2000): 365–397.

Grossman, Marshall. "Servile/Sterile/Style: Milton and the Question of Woman." In *Milton and the Idea of Woman*, edited by Julia M. Walker, 148–168. Urbana and Chicago: University of Illinois Press, 1988.

Guy, John. "The 1590s: The Second Reign of Elizabeth I?" In *The Reign of Elizabeth I: Court and Culture in the Last Decade*, edited by John Guy, 1–16. Cambridge: Cambridge University Press, 1995.

———. "The Henrician Age." In *The Varieties of British Political Thought, 1500–1800*, edited by J. G. A. Pocock, 13–46. Cambridge: Cambridge University Press, 1993.

———. "Monarchy and Counsel: Models of the State." In *The Sixteenth Century, 1485–1603*, edited by Patrick Collinson, 113–131. Oxford: Oxford University Press, 2002.

———, ed. *The Reign of Elizabeth I: Court and Culture in the Last Decade*. Cambridge: Cambridge University Press, 1995.

Habermas, Jürgen. *The Structural Transformation of the Public Sphere: An Inquiry into a Category of Bourgeios Society*. Translated by Thomas Burger. Cambridge, Mass.: MIT Press, 1989.

Hackett, Helen. "The Torture of Limena: Sex and Violence in Lady Mary Wroth's *Urania*." In *Voicing Women: Gender and Sexuality in Early Modern Writing*, edited by Kate Chedgzoy, Melanie Hansen, and Suzanne Trill, 93–110. Keele, Staffordshire: Keele University Press, 1996.

———. *Women and Romance Fiction in the English Renaissance*. Cambridge: Cambridge University Press, 2000.

Hadfield, Andrew. "Duessa's Trial and Elizabeth's Error: Judging Elizabeth in Spenser's *Faerie Queene*." In *The Myth of Elizabeth*, edited by Susan Doran and Thomas S. Freeman, 56–76. New York: Palgrave Macmillan, 2003.

———. *Shakespeare and Renaissance Politics*. London: Arden Shakespeare, 2004.

———. "Tarquin's Everlasting Banishment: Republicanism and Constitutionalism in *The Rape of Lucrece* and *Titus Andronicus*." *Parergon: Journal of the Australian and New Zealand Association of Medieval and Early Modern Studies* 19 (2002): 77–104.

———. "Was Spenser Really a Republican After All? A Reply to David Scott Wilson-Okamura." *Spenser Studies* 17 (2003): 275–290.

Hageman, Elizabeth, and Katherine Conway, eds. *Resurrecting Elizabeth in Seventeenth-Century England*. Madison, N. J.: Fairleigh Dickenson University Press, 2007.

Hager, Alan. "The Exemplary Mirage: Fabrication of Sir Philip Sidney's Biographical Image and the Sidney Reader." In *Essential Articles for the Study of Sir Philip Sidney*, edited by Arthur F. Kinney, 1–16. Hamden, Conn.: Archon Books, 1987.

Haigh, Christopher. *Catholics Writing the Nation in Early Modern Britain and Ireland*. Oxford: Oxford University Press, 2008.

Halley, Janet E. "Female Autonomy in Milton's Sexual Poetics." In *Milton and the Idea of Woman*, edited by Julia M. Walker, 230–253. Urbana and Chicago: University of Illinois Press, 1988.

Halperin, David M. *How to Do the History of Homosexuality*. Chicago: University of Chicago Press, 2002.

Hammer, Paul E. J. "Patronage at Court, Faction and the Earl of Essex." In *The Reign of Elizabeth I: Court and Culture in the Last Decade*, edited by John Guy, 65–86. Cambridge: Cambridge University Press, 1995.

———. *The Polarisation of Elizabethan Politics: The Political Career of Robert Devereux, 2nd Earl of Essex, 1585–1597*. Cambridge: Cambridge University Press, 1999.

Hannay, Margaret P. *Mary Sidney, Lady Wroth*. Burlington, V.T.: Ashgate, 2010.

———. "'My Daughter Wroth': Lady Mary Wroth in the Correspondence of Robert Sidney, first Earl of Leicester." *Sidney Journal* 22 (2004): 47–72.

———. *Philip's Phoenix: Mary Sidney, Countess of Pembroke*. Oxford: Oxford University Press, 1990.

———. "'Your Vertuous and Learned Aunt': The Countess of Pembroke as Mentor to Mary Wroth." In *Reading Mary Wroth: Representing Alternatives in Early Modern England*, edited by Naomi J. Miller and Gary Waller, 15–34. Knoxville: University of Tennessee Press, 1991.

Hanson, Elizabeth. *Discovering the Subject in English Renaissance Literature*. Cambridge: Cambridge University Press, 1998.

Hardison, O. B., Jr. "The Two Voices of Sidney's 'Apology for Poetry.'" In *Essential Articles for the Study of Sir Philip Sidney*, edited by Arthur F. Kinney, 83–99. Hamden, Conn.: Archon Books, 1987.

Harris, Jonathan Gil. *Sick Economies: Drama, Mercantilism, and Disease in Shakespeare's England*. Philadelphia: University of Pennsylvania Press, 2004.

Harvey, Elizabeth D. "Sensational Bodies, Consenting Organs: Helkiah Crooke's Incorporation of Spenser." *Spenser Studies* 18 (2003): 295–314.

Haskin, Dayton. "Milton's Portrait of Mary as Bearer of the Word." In *Milton and the Idea of Woman,* edited by Julia M. Walker, 169–184. Urbana and Chicago: University of Illinois Press, 1988,

Hatten, Charles. "The Politics of Marital Reform and the Rationalization of Romance in *The Doctrine and Discipline of Divorce.*" *Milton Studies* 27 (1991): 95–113.

Hawes, Clement. *Mania and Literary Style: The Rhetoric of Enthusiasm from the Ranters to Christopher Smart.* Cambridge: Cambridge University Press, 1996.

Hay, Millicent. *The Life of Robert Sidney, Earl of Leicester (1563–26).* Washington, D.C.: Folger Shakespeare Library, 1984.

Hayden, Deborah. *Pox, Madness, and the Mysteries of Syphilis.* New York: Basic Books, 2003.

Haynes, Henrietta. *Henrietta Maria.* London: Metheun, 1912.

Heale, Elizabeth. "Contesting Terms: Loyal Catholicism and Lord Montague's Entertainment at Cowdray." In *The Progresses, Pageants, and Entertainments of Queen Elizabeth I,* edited by Jayne Elizabeth Archer, Elizabeth Goldring, and Sarah Knight, 189–206. Oxford: Oxford University Press, 2007.

Healy, Margaret. "Pericles and the Pox." In *Shakespeare's Late Plays: New Readings,* edited by Jennifer Richards and James Knowles, 92–107. Edinburgh: Edinburgh University Press, 1999.

Healy, Thomas, and Jonathan Sawday, eds. *Literature and the English Civil War.* Cambridge: Cambridge University Press, 1990.

Heaton, Gabriel. "Elizabethan Entertainments in Manuscript: The Harefield Festivities (1602) and the Dynamics of Exchange." In *The Progresses, Pageants, and Entertainments of Queen Elizabeth I,* edited by Jayne Elizabeth Archer, Elizabeth Goldring, and Sarah Knight, 227–244. Oxford: Oxford University Press, 2007.

Heffner, Ray. "Essex and Book Five of the *Faerie Queene.*" *ELH* 3 (1936): 67–82.

Heinemann, Margot. "Political Drama." In *The Cambridge Companion to English Renaissance Drama.* 2d ed. Edited by A. R. Braunmuller and Michael Hattaway, 164–196. Cambridge: Cambridge University Press, 2003.

Held, Julius S. "Flora, Goddess and Courtesan." In *Essays in Honor of Erwin Panofsky,* 2 vols. Edited by Millard Meiss, 1: 201–216 and 2: 72–74. New York: New York University Press, 1961.

Helgerson, Richard. *Forms of Nationhood: The Elizabethan Writing of England.* Chicago: University of Chicago Press, 1992.

Helms, Lorraine. "The Saint in the Brothel: Or, Eloquence Rewarded." *Shakespeare Quarterly* 41 (1990): 319–332.

Hendricks, Margo, and Patricia Parker, eds. *Women, "Race," and Writing in the Early Modern Period.* New York: Routledge, 1993.

Herman, Peter C. "'Bastard Children of Tyranny': The Ancient Constitution and Fulke Greville's *A Dedication to Sir Philip Sidney.*" *Renaissance Quarterly* 55 (2002): 969–1004.

———. *Destabilizing Milton: "Paradise Lost" and the Poetics of Incertitude.* New York: Palgrave Macmillan, 2005.

Herrup, Cynthia B. *A House in Gross Disorder: Sex, Law, and the 2nd Earl of Castlehaven.* New York: Oxford University Press, 1999.

Hickerson, Megan. *Making Women Martyrs in Tudor England.* New York: Palgrave Macmillan, 2005.

Hill, Christopher. *Century of Revolution: 1603–1714.* 2d ed. New York: Norton, 1982.

———. *Milton and the English Revolution.* New York: Viking, 1977.

———. *The World Turned Upside Down: Radical Ideas during the English Revolution.* Harmondsworth: Penguin, 1972.

Hillman, Richard. "Shakespeare's Gower and Gower's Shakespeare: The Larger Debt of *Pericles*." *Shakespeare Quarterly* 36 (1985): 427–437.

Hirst, Derek. *Authority and Conflict: England, 1603–1658*. Cambridge, Mass.: Harvard University Press, 1986.

Hirst, Derek, and Richard Strier, eds. *Writing and Political Engagement in Seventeenth-Century England*. Cambridge: Cambridge University Press, 1999.

Holbrook, Peter. "Jacobean Masques and the Jacobean Peace." In *The Politics of the Stuart Court Masque*, edited by David Bevington and Peter Holbrook, 67–87. Cambridge: Cambridge University Press, 1998.

Hulse, Lynn. "Cavendish, William, First Duke of Newcastle." In *Oxford Dictionary of National Biography*, edited by H. C. G. Matthew and Brian Harrison. Oxford: Oxford University Press, 2004.

Israel, J. I. *The Dutch Republic: Its Rise, Greatness, and Fall, 1477–1806*. Oxford: Oxford University Press, 1998.

Iyengar, Sujata. "Royalist, Romancist, Racialist: Rank, Gender, and Race in the Science and Fiction of Margaret Cavendish." *ELH* 69 (2002): 649–672.

James, Mervyn Evans. *Society, Politics, and Culture: Studies in Early Modern England*. Cambridge: Cambridge University Press, 1988.

Jameson, Fredric. *The Political Unconscious: Narrative as a Socially Symbolic Act*. Ithaca, N.Y.: Cornell University Press, 1981.

Jankowski, Theodora A. *Pure Resistance: Queer Virginity in Early Modern English Drama*. Philadelphia: University of Pennsylvania Press, 2000.

Jardine, Lisa. *Still Harping on Daughters: Women and Drama in the Age of Shakespeare*. Sussex: Harvester Press, 1983.

Jayne, Sears. *Plato in Renaissance England*. Dordrecht: Kluwer, 1995.

Jed, Stephanie. *Chaste Thinking: "The Rape of Lucretia" and the Birth of Humanism*. Bloomington: Indiana University Press, 1989.

Jones, Ann Rosalind, and Peter Stallybrass. "Courtship and Courtiership: The Politics of *Astrophil and Stella*." *Studies in English Literature* 24 (1984): 53–68.

———. "Dismantling Irena: The Sexualization of Ireland in Early Modern England." In *Nationalisms and Sexualities*, edited by Andrew Parker, Mary Russo, Doris Sommer, and Patricia Yaeger, 157–171. London: Routledge, 1992.

Jones, Kathleen. *A Glorious Fame: The Life of Margaret Cavendish, Duchess of Newcastle, 1623–73*. London: Bloomsbury, 1990.

Jordan, Constance. *Renaissance Feminism: Literary Texts and Political Models*. Ithaca, N.Y.: Cornell University Press, 1990.

———. *Shakespeare's Monarchies: Ruler and Subject in the Romances*. Ithaca, N.Y.: Cornell University Press, 1997.

Jowitt, Claire. "Imperial Dreams? Margaret Cavendish and the Cult of Elizabeth." *Women's Writing* 4 (1997): 383–399.

Kahn, Coppélia. *Man's Estate: Masculine Identity in Shakespeare*. Berkeley: University of California Press, 1981.

———. "The Rape in Shakespeare's *Lucrece*." *Shakespeare Studies* 9 (1976): 45–72.

———. *Roman Shakespeare: Warriors, Wounds, and Women*. London: Routledge, 1997.

Kahn, Paul. *Putting Liberalism in Its Place*. Princeton: Princeton University Press, 2004.

Kahn, Victoria A. "Margaret Cavendish and the Romance of Contract." *Renaissance Quarterly* 50 (1997): 526–566.

———. *Wayward Contracts: The Crisis of Political Obligation in England, 1640–1674*. Princeton: Princeton University Press, 2004.

Kalstone, David. "Sir Philip Sidney and 'Poore *Petrarchs* Long Deceased Woes.'" In *Essential Articles for the Study of Sir Philip Sidney*, edited by Arthur F. Kinney, 241–254. Hamden, Conn.: Archon Books, 1987.

Kantorowicz, Ernst. *The King's Two Bodies: A Study in Medieval Political Theology*. Princeton: Princeton University Press, 1997.

Kay, Dennis. "'She Was a Queen, and Therefore Beautiful': Sidney, His Mother, and Queen Elizabeth." *Review of English Studies*, n.s. 43 (1992): 18–39.

Keeble, N. H. "'Nothing Nobler Then a Free Commonwealth': Milton's Later Vernacular Republican Tracts." In *The Oxford Handbook to Milton*, edited by Nicholas McDowell and Nigel Smith, 305–324. Oxford: Oxford University Press, 2009.

———. *The Restoration: England in the 1660s*. Malden, Mass.: Blackwell, 2002.

Keir, David Lindsay. *The Constitutional History of Modern Britain, 1485–1937*. London: Adam and Charles Black, 1938.

Keller, Eve. "Producing Petty Gods: Margaret Cavendish's Critique of Experimental Science." *ELH* 64 (1997): 447–471.

Kelley, Donald R. "Elizabethan Political Thought." In *The Varieties of British Political Thought, 1500–1800*, edited by J. G. A. Pocock, 47–79. Cambridge: Cambridge University Press, 1993.

Kelly, Kathleen Coyne. *Performing Virginity and Testing Chastity in the Middle Ages*. New York: Routledge, 2000.

Kennedy, Gwynne. *Just Anger: Representing Women's Anger in Early Modern England*. Carbondale: Southern Illinois University Press, 1999.

Kennedy, William J. *The Site of Petrarchism: Early Modern National Sentiment in Italy, France, and England*. Baltimore: Johns Hopkins University Press, 2003.

Kenyon, J. P. "Queen Elizabeth and the Historians." In *Queen Elizabeth I: Most Politik Princess*, edited by Simon Adams, 52–55. London: History Today, 1984.

———. *Stuart England*. Harmondsworth: Penguin, 1985.

———, ed. *The Stuart Constitution: Documents and Commentary*. 2d ed. Cambridge: Cambridge University Press, 1993.

Kerrigan, William. *The Sacred Complex: On the Psychogenesis of Paradise Lost*. Cambridge, Mass.: Harvard University Press, 1983.

Kerrigan, William, and Gordon Braden. "Milton's Coy Eve: *Paradise Lost* and Renaissance Love Poetry." *ELH* 53 (1986): 27–51.

King, John N. "Elizabeth I: Representation of the Virgin Queen." *Renaissance Quarterly* 43 (1990): 30–74.

Kinney, Arthur F., "Puritans Versus Royalists: Sir Philip Sidney's Rhetoric at the Court of Elizabeth I." In *Sir Philip Sidney's Achievements*, edited by M. J. B. Allen et al., 42–56. New York: AMS, 1990.

———. ed. *Essential Articles for the Study of Sir Philip Sidney*. Hamden, Conn.: Archon Books, 1987.

Kinney, Clare R. "'Beleeve This Butt a Fiction': Female Authorship, Narrative Undoing, and the Limits of Romance in *The Second Part of the Countess of Montgomery's Urania*." *Spenser Studies* 17 (2003): 239–250.

———. "Chivalry Unmasked: Courtly Spectacle and the Abuses of Romance in Sidney's *New Arcadia*." *SEL* 35 (1995): 35–52.

Kishlansky, Mark. "Charles I: A Case of Mistaken Identity." *Past and Present* 189 (2005): 41–80.

Knott, John R. *Discourses of Martyrdom in English Literature*. Cambridge: Cambridge University Press, 1993.

Knowles, James. "'In the Purest Times of Peerless Queen Elizabeth': Nostalgia, Politics, and Jonson's Use of the 1575 Kenilworth Entertainments." In *The Progresses, Pageants, and*

       Entertainments of Queen Elizabeth I, edited by Jayne Elizabeth Archer, Elizabeth Gold-
       ring, and Sarah Knight, 247–267. Oxford: Oxford University Press, 2007.

Kogan, Stephen. *The Hieroglyphic King: Wisdom and Idolatry in the Seventeenth-Century Masque.*
       London and Toronto: Associated University Press, 1986.

Kristeva, Julia. *Powers of Horror: An Essay on Abjection.* Translated by Leon S. Roudiez. New
       York: Columbia University Press, 1982.

Kroll, Richard W. F. *Restoration Drama and "The Circle of Commerce": Tragicomedy, Politics, and
       Trade in the Seventeenth Century.* Cambridge: Cambridge University Press, 2007.

Krontiras, Tina. *Oppositional Voices: Women as Writers and Translators of Literature in the English
       Renaissance.* London: Routledge, 1992.

Lacey, Andrew. *The Cult of King Charles the Martyr.* Rochester, N.Y.: Boydell Press, 2003.

———. "Elegies and Commemorative Verse in Honour of Charles the Martyr, 1649–60." In
       The Regicides and the Execution of Charles I, edited by Jason Peacey, 225–246. New York:
       Palgrave, 2001.

Lake, Peter. "Constitutional Consensus and Puritan Opposition in the 1620s: Thomas Scott
       and the Spanish Match." *Historical Journal* 25 (1982): 805–825.

Lake, Peter, and Michael Questier. "Agency, Appropriation, and Rhetoric under the Gallows:
       Puritans, Romanists, and the State in Early Modern England." *Past and Present* 153
       (1996): 64–107.

———. "Margaret Clitherow, Catholic Nonconformity, Martyrology, and the Politics of
       Religious Change in Elizabethan England." *Past and Present* 185 (2004): 43–87.

Lamb, Mary Ellen. "Exhibiting Class and Displaying the Body in Sidney's *Countess of Pem-
       broke's Arcadia.*" *SEL* 37 (1997): 55–72.

———. *Gender and Authorship in the Sidney Circle.* Madison: University of Wisconsin Press,
       1990.

Lamont, William M. *Marginal Prynne, 1600–1669.* London: Routledge, 1963.

Lane, Christopher. "The Poverty of Context: Historicism and Nonmimetic Fiction." *PMLA* 118
       (2003): 450–469.

Lanham, Richard. "*Astrophil and Stella*: Pure and Impure Persuasion." In *Essential Articles for the
       Study of Sir Philip Sidney*, edited by Arthur F. Kinney, 223–240. Hamden, Conn.: Archon
       Books, 1987.

Largier, Niklaus. *In Praise of the Whip: A Cultural History of Arousal.* Translated by Graham
       Harman. New York: Zone Books, 2007.

Le Compt, Edward. *Milton and Sex.* New York: Columbia University Press, 1978.

Lees-Jeffries, Hester. "Location as Metaphor in Queen Elizabeth's Coronation Entry (1559):
       Veritas Temporis Filia." In *The Progresses, Pageants, and Entertainments of Queen Elizabeth
       I*, edited by Jayne Elizabeth Archer, Elizabeth Goldring, and Sarah Knight, 65–85.
       Oxford: Oxford University Press, 2007.

Lei, Bi-Qi Beatrice. "Relational Antifeminism in Sidney's *Arcadia.*" *SEL* 41 (2001): 25–48.

Leslie, Marina. "Evading Rape and Embracing Empire in Margaret Cavendish's *Assaulted and
       Pursued Chastity.*" In *Menacing Virgins: Representing Virginity in the Middle Ages and
       Renaissance*, edited by Kathleen Coyne Kelly and Marina Leslie, 179–197. London:
       Associated University Press, 1999.

Lesser, Zachary. *Renaissance Drama and the Politics of Publication.* Cambridge: Cambridge
       University Press, 2004.

Levin, Richard. "What? How? Female–Female Desire in Sidney's *New Arcadia.*" *Criticism* 39
       (1997): 463–479.

Levy, J. F. "Philip Sidney Reconsidered." In *Essential Articles for the Study of Sir Philip Sidney*,
       edited by Arthur F. Kinney, 1–18. Hamden, Conn.: Archon Books, 1987.

Lewalski, Barbara. "Milton on Women—Yet Once More." *Milton Studies* 16 (1982): 3–20.

Lewis, C. S. *The Allegory of Love: A Study in the Medieval Tradition.* Oxford: Oxford University Press, 1959.

Lilley, Kate. "Contracting Readers: 'Margaret Newcastle' and the Rhetoric of Conjugality." In *A Princely Brave Woman: Essays on Margaret Cavendish, Duchess of Newcastle,* edited by Stephen Clucas, 19–39. Aldershot: Ashgate, 2003.

Lindley, David, "The Politics of Music in the Masque." In *The Politics of the Stuart Court Masque,* edited by David Bevington and Peter Holbrook, 273–295. Cambridge: Cambridge University Press, 1998.

———. ed. *The Court Masque.* Manchester: Manchester University Press, 1984.

Lochrie, Karma. *Heterosyncrasies: Female Sexuality When Normal Wasn't.* Minneapolis: University of Minnesota Press, 2005.

Loewenstein, David. *Representing Revolution in Milton and His Contemporaries.* Cambridge: Cambridge University Press, 2001.

Loughlin, Marie H. *Hymeneutics: Interpreting Virginity on the Early Modern Stage.* Lewisburg: Bucknell University Press, 1997.

Lucas, Caroline. *Writing for Women: The Example of Woman as Reader in Elizabethan Romance.* Philadelphia: Open University Press, 1989.

Lupton, Julia Reinhard. *Citizen-Saints: Shakespeare and Political Theology.* Chicago: University of Chicago Press, 2005.

Luxon, Thomas H. *Single Imperfection: Milton, Marriage and Friendship.* Pittsburgh: Duquesne University Press, 2005.

MacCaffrey, Wallace T. "The Anjou Match and the Making of Elizabethan Foreign Policy." In *The English Commonwealth, 1547–1640,* edited by Peter Clark, Alan G. R. Smith, and Nicholas Tyacke, 59–75. Leicester: Leicester University Press, 1979.

MacKinnon, Catharine A. "Feminism, Marxism, Method, and the State: An Agenda for Theory." *Signs* 7 (1982): 515–544.

Maclean, Hugh, ed. *Ben Jonson and the Cavalier Poets.* New York: Norton, 1974.

Magro, Maria. "Milton's Sexualized Women and the Creation of a Gendered Public Sphere." *Milton Quarterly* 35 (2001): 98–112.

Marcus, Leah S. *The Politics of Mirth: Jonson, Herrick, Marvell, Milton, and the Defense of Old Holiday Pastimes.* Chicago: University of Chicago Press, 1986.

Marcus, Sharon. "Queer Theory for Everyone: A Review Essay." *Signs* 31 (2005): 192–218.

Marenco, Franco. "Double Plot in Sidney's Old 'Arcadia." In *Essential Articles for the Study of Sir Philip Sidney,* edited by Arthur F. Kinney, 248–263. Hamden, Conn.: Archon Books, 1987.

Marotti, Arthur F. "'Love is not Love': Elizabethan Sonnet Sequences and the Social Order." *ELH* 49 (1982): 396–428.

———. *Religious Ideology and Cultural Fantasy: Catholic and Anti-Catholic Discourses in Early Modern England.* Notre Dame, Ind.: University of Notre Dame Press, 2005.

Marshall, John. *Locke, Toleration and Early Enlightenment Culture.* Cambridge: Cambridge University Press, 2006.

Masten, Jeffrey. "Material Cavendish: Paper, Performance, 'Sociable Virginity.'" *Modern Language Quarterly* 65 (2004): 49–68.

———. "'Shall I Turn Blabb': Circulation, Gender, and Subjectivity in Mary Wroth's Sonnets." In *Reading Mary Wroth: Representing Alternatives in Early Modern England,* edited by Naomi J. Miller and Gary Waller, 67–87. Knoxville: University of Tennessee Press, 1991.

Maus, Katherine Eisman. "Taking Tropes Seriously: Language and Violence in Shakespeare's *The Rape of Lucrece.*" *Shakespeare Quarterly* 37 (1986): 66–82.

McCabe, Richard. "The Fate of Irena: Spenser and Political Violence." In *Spenser and Ireland: An Interdisciplinary Perspective,* edited by Patricia Coughlin, 109–125. Cork: Cork University Press, 1989.

McColley, Diane. *Milton's Eve*. Urbana: University of Illinois Press, 1983.

———. "Subsequent or Precedent? Eve as Milton's Defense of Poesie." *Milton Quarterly* 20 (1986): 132–136.

McCoy, Richard. *The Rites of Knighthood*. Berkeley: University of California Press, 1989.

———. *Sir Philip Sidney: Rebellion in Arcadia*. New Brunswick, N.J.: Rutgers University Press, 1979.

McDowell, Nicholas, and Nigel Smith, eds. *The Oxford Handbook to Milton*. Oxford: Oxford University Press, 2009.

McIlwain, Charles H. *Constitutionalism Ancient and Modern*. Ithaca, N.Y.: Cornell University Press, 1940.

McKeon, Michael. *The Origins of the English Novel, 1600–1740*. Baltimore: Johns Hopkins University Press, 1987.

McLaren, A. N. *Political Culture in the Reign of Elizabeth I*. Cambridge: Cambridge University Press, 1999.

McManus, Clare. *Women on the Renaissance Stage: Anna of Denmark and Female Masquing in the Stuart Court*. Manchester: Manchester University Press, 2002.

———, ed. *Women and Culture at the Courts of the Stuart Queens*. New York: Palgrave Macmillan, 2003.

McMullan, Gordon, and Jonathan Hope, eds. *The Politics of Tragicomedy: Shakespeare and After*. London: Routledge, 1992.

McRae, Andrew. "Stigmatizing Prynne: Seditious Libel, Political Satire, and the Construction of Opposition." In *The 1630s: Interdisciplinary Essays on Culture and Politics in the Caroline Era*, edited by Ian Atherton and Julie Sanders, 171–188. Manchester: Manchester University Press, 2006.

Mendelson, Sarah Heller. *The Mental World of Stuart Women*. Amherst: University of Massachusetts Press, 1987.

Mendle, Michael. *Dangerous Positions: Mixed Government, the Estates of the Realm, and the Making of the "Answer to the XIX Propositions."* Tuscaloosa: University of Alabama Press, 1985.

———, ed. *The Putney Debates of 1647*. Cambridge: Cambridge University Press, 2001.

Miller, Naomi J. *Changing the Subject: Mary Wroth and Figurations of Gender in Early Modern England*. Lexington: University of Kentucky Press, 1996.

Miller, Naomi J., and Gary Waller, eds. *Reading Mary Wroth: Representing Alternatives in Early Modern England*. Knoxville: University of Tennessee Press, 1991.

Miller, Shannon. *Engendering the Fall: John Milton and Seventeenth-Century Women Writers*. Philadelphia: University of Pennsylvania Press, 2008.

———. "Textual Crimes and Punishment in Mary Wroth's *Urania*." *Journal of Medieval and Early Modern Studies* 35 (2005): 385–427.

Minogue, Sally. "A Woman's Touch: Astrophil, Stella, and 'Queen Virtue's Court.'" *ELH* 63 (1996): 555–570.

Monta, Susanna Brietz. *Martyrdom and Literature in Early Modern England*. Cambridge: Cambridge University Press, 2005.

Montrose, Louis Adrian. "'Shaping Fantasies': Figurations of Gender and Power in Elizabethan Culture." *Representations* 2 (1983): 61–94.

———. "Spenser and the Elizabethan Political Imaginary." *ELH* 69 (2002): 907–911.

———. *The Subject of Elizabeth: Authority, Gender, and Representation*. Chicago: Chicago University Press, 2006.

Morrill, John. "Introduction." In *Revolution and Restorations: England in the 1650s*, edited by John Morrill. New York: Collins and Brown, 1992.

Morrill, John, and Philip Baker. "Oliver Cromwell, the Regicide and the Sons of Zeruiah." In *The Regicides and the Execution of Charles I*, edited by Jason Peacey, 14–35. New York: Palgrave, 2001.

Mueller, Janel. "The Figure and the Ground: Samson as a Hero of London Nonconformity, 1662–1667." In *Milton and the Terms of Liberty*, edited by Graham Parry and Joad Raymond, 137–162. Cambridge: D. S. Brewer, 2002.

Mullaney, Steven. *The Place of the Stage: License, Play, and Power in Renaissance England.* Chicago: University of Chicago Press, 1988.

Munden, R. C. "James I and 'the Growth of Mutual Distrust': King, Commons, and Reform, 1603–1604." In *Faction and Parliament: Essays on Early Stuart History*, edited by Kevin Sharpe, 43–72. Oxford: Clarendon Press, 1978.

Nadelhaft, Jerome. "The Englishwoman's Sexual Civil War: Feminist Attitudes toward Men, Women and Marriage, 1650–1740." *Journal of the History of Ideas* 43 (1982): 555–579.

Neely, Carol Thomas. *Distracted Subjects: Madness and Gender in Shakespeare and Early Modern Culture.* Ithaca, N.Y.: Cornell University Press, 2004.

Newcomb, Lori Humphrey. "The Sources of Romance, the Generation of Story, and the Patterns of Pericles Tales." In *Staging Early Modern Romance*, edited by Mary Ellen Lamb and Valerie Wayne, 21–46. New York: Routledge, 2008.

Newman, J. "Inigo Jones and the Politics of Architecture." In *Culture and Politics in Early Stuart England*, edited by Kevin Sharpe and Peter Lake, 229–255. Stanford, Calif.: Stanford University Press, 1993.

Newman, Jane O. "'And Let Mild Women to Him Lose Their Mildness': Philomela, Female Violence, and Shakespeare's *Rape of Lucrece*." *Shakespeare Quarterly* 45 (1994): 304–326.

Ng, Su Fang. *Literature and the Politics of the Family in Seventeenth-Century England.* Cambridge: Cambridge University Press, 2007.

Norbrook, David. "Margaret Cavendish and Lucy Hutchinson: Identity, Ideology, and Politics." *In-Between* 9 (2000): 179–204.

———. *Poetry and Politics in the English Renaissance.* London: Routledge, 1984.

———. "The Reformation of the Masque." In *The Court Masque*, edited by David Lindley, 94–110. Manchester: Manchester University Press, 1984.

———. "Women, the Republic of Letters, and the Public Sphere in the Mid-Seventeenth Century." *Criticism* 46 (2004): 223–240.

———. "'Words More than Civil': Republican Civility in Lucy Hutchinson's 'The Life of John Hutchinson.'" In *Early Modern Civil Discourses*, edited by Jennifer Richards, 68–84. Basingstoke: Palgrave Macmillan, 2003.

———. *Writing the English Republic: Poetry, Rhetoric, and Politics, 1627–1660.* Cambridge: Cambridge University Press, 1999.

Notestein, Wallace. *The House of Commons, 1604–1610.* New Haven: Yale University Press, 1971.

———. *The Winning of the Initiative by the House of Commons.* Oxford: Oxford University Press, 1924.

Nyquist, Mary. "The Genesis of Gendered Subjectivity in the Divorce Tracts and *Paradise Lost*." In *Re-membering Milton: Essays on the Texts and Traditions*, edited by Mary Nyquist and Margaret W. Ferguson, 99–127. New York: Routledge, 1988.

———. "Gynesis, Genesis, Exegesis, and the Formation of Milton's Eve." In *Cannibals, Witches, and Divorce: Estranging the Renaissance*, edited by Marjorie Garber, 147–208. Baltimore: Johns Hopkins University Press, 1987.

O'Callaghan, Michelle. *The "Shepheards Nation": Jacobean Spenserians and Early Stuart Political Culture, 1612–1625.* Oxford: Oxford University Press, 2000.

O'Farrell, Brian. "Politician, Patron, Poet: William Herbert, Third Earl of Pembroke, 1580–1630." Ph. D. diss, University of California, Los Angeles, 1966.

Ogg, David. *England in the Reign of Charles II.* 2d ed. 2 vols. Oxford: Clarendon Press, 1955.

Oman, Carola Lenanton. *Henrietta Maria.* London: Hodder and Stoughton, 1936.

Oram, William Allan. *Edmund Spenser.* New York: Twain, 1997.

————. "Elizabethan Fact and Spenserian Fiction." *Spenser Studies* 4 (1984): 33–47.

Orgel, Stephen. *The Illusion of Power: Political Theatre in the English Renaissance.* Berkeley and Los Angeles: University of California Press, 1975.

————. *Impersonations: The Performance of Gender in Shakespeare's England.* Cambridge: Cambridge University Press, 1996.

Orgel, Stephen, and Roy Strong. *Inigo Jones and the Theatre of the Stuart Court.* 2 vols. Berkeley and Los Angeles: University of California Press, 1973.

Osborne, J. M. *Young Philip Sidney.* New Haven: Yale University Press, 1972.

Palfrey, Simon. *Late Shakespeare: A New World of Words.* Oxford: Clarendon Press, 1997.

Parry, Graham. *The Golden Age Restor'd: The Culture of the Stuart Court, 1603–42.* New York: St. Martin's Press, 1981.

————. *The Trophies of Time: English Antiquaries of the Seventeenth Century.* Oxford: Oxford University Press, 1995.

Parry, Graham, and Joad Raymond, eds. *Milton and the Terms of Liberty.* Cambridge: D. S. Brewer, 2002.

Pateman, Carole. *The Sexual Contract.* Stanford, Calif.: Stanford University Press, 1989.

Patterson, Annabel. *Censorship and Interpretation: The Conditions of Reading and Writing in Early Modern England.* Madison: University of Wisconsin Press, 1984.

————. *Milton's Words.* Oxford: Oxford University Press, 2009.

Peacey, Jason, ed. *The Regicides and the Execution of Charles I.* New York: Palgrave, 2001.

Peacock, John. "The Image of Charles I as a Roman Emperor." In *The 1630s: Interdisciplinary Essays on Culture and Politics in the Caroline Era,* edited by Ian Atherton and Julie Sanders, 50–73. Manchester: Manchester University Press, 2006.

Pearl, Sara. "Sounding to Present Occasions: Jonson's Masques of 1620–5." In *The Court Masque,* edited by David Lindley, 60–77. Manchester: Manchester University Press, 1984.

Peck, Linda Levy. "Kingship, Counsel and Law in Early Stuart Britain." In *The Varieties of British Political Thought, 1500–1800,* edited by J. G. A. Pocock, 80–115. Cambridge: Cambridge University Press, 1993.

Peltonen, Markku. *Classical Humanism and Republicanism in English Political Thought, 1570–1640.* Cambridge: Cambridge University Press, 1995.

Pincus, Steven. "The English Debate over Universal Monarchy." In *A Union for Empire,* edited by John Robertson, 37–62. Cambridge: Cambridge University Press, 1995.

Pocock, J. G. A. *The Ancient Constitution and the Feudal Law: A Study of English Historical Thought in the Seventeenth Century.* Cambridge: Cambridge University Press, 1987.

————, ed. *The Varieties of British Political Thought, 1500–1800.* Cambridge: Cambridge University Press, 1993.

Pollen, John H. *The English Catholics in the Reign of Queen Elizabeth.* London: Longmans, Green, and Co., 1920.

Pooley, Roger. "Writing, Love, and Action: Algernon Sidney and Sir Philip Sidney." *Sidney Newsletter and Journal* 14 (1996): 56–64.

Porter, Roy. "Rape—Does It Have a Historical Meaning?" In *Rape,* edited by Sylvana Tomaselli and Roy Porter, 216–236. Oxford: Basil Blackwell, 1986.

Potter, Lois. *Secret Rites and Secret Writing: Royalist Literature, 1641–1660.* Cambridge: Cambridge University Press, 1989.

Poynting, Sarah. "'In the Name of all the Sisters': Henrietta Maria's Notorious Whores." In *Women and Culture at the Courts of the Stuart Queens,* edited by Clare McManus, 163–185. New York: Palgrave Macmillan, 2003.

Prescott, Anne Lake. "Foreign Policy in Fairyland: Henri IV and Spenser's Burbon." *Spenser Studies* 14 (2000): 189–214.

———. "The Stuart Masque and Pantagruel's Dream." *ELH* 51 (1984): 407–430.

Preston, Claire. "Sidney's Arcadian Poetics: A Medicine of Cherries and the Philosophy of Cavaliers." In *English Renaissance Prose: History, Language, Politics*, edited by Neil Rhodes, 91–108. Tempe: Arizona Medieval and Renaissance Texts and Studies, 1997.

Purkiss, Diane. *Literature, Gender, and Politics during the English Civil War*. Cambridge: Cambridge University Press, 2005.

Quay, Sara E. "'Lucrece the Chaste': The Construction of Rape in Shakespeare's *The Rape of Lucrece*." *Modern Language Studies* 25 (1995): 3–17.

Quilligan, Maureen. *Incest and Agency in Elizabeth's England*. Philadelphia: University of Pennsylvania Press, 2006.

———. "Lady Mary Wroth: Female Authority and the Family Romance." In *Unfolded Tales: Essays on Renaissance Romance*, edited by George M. Logan and Gordon Teskey, 257–280. Ithaca, N.Y.: Cornell University Press, 1989.

———. *The Language of Allegory: Defining the Genre*. Ithaca, N.Y.: Cornell, University Press, 1979.

———. *Milton's Spenser: The Politics of Reading*. Ithaca, N.Y.: Cornell University Press, 1983.

Quint, David. *Epic and Empire: Politics and Generic Form from Virgil to Milton*. Princeton: Princeton University Press, 1993.

Raber, Karen L. "'Our Wits Join'd as in Matrimony': Margaret Cavendish's *Playes* and the Drama of Authority." *ELR* 28 (1998): 464–493.

Rambuss, Richard. *Closet Devotions*. Durham, N.C.: Duke University Press, 1998.

Ravelhofer, Barbara. "'Virgin Wax' and 'Hairy Men-Monsters': Unstable Movement Codes in the Stuart Masque." In *The Politics of the Stuart Court Masque*, edited by David Bevington and Peter Holbrook, 244–272. Cambridge: Cambridge University Press, 1998.

Raymond, Joad. "The King is a Thing." In *Milton and the Terms of Liberty*, edited by Graham Parry and Joad Raymond, 88–92. Cambridge: D. S. Brewer, 2002.

Read, Conyers. *Mr. Secretary Cecil and Queen Elizabeth*. London: Cape, 1955.

Rees, Emma L. E. *Margaret Cavendish: Gender, Genre, Exile*. Manchester: Manchester University Press, 2003.

Relihan, Constance, and Goran Stanivukovic. "Introduction." *Prose Fiction and Early Modern Sexualities in England, 1570–1640*, edited by Constance Relihan and Goran Stanivukovic, 1–13. New York: Palgrave Macmillan, 2003.

———, eds. *Prose Fiction and Early Modern Sexualities in England, 1570–1640*. New York: Palgrave Macmillan, 2003.

Rhodes, Neil. "Wrapped in the Strong Arms of the Union: Shakespeare and King James." In *Shakespeare and Scotland*, edited by Willy Maley and Andrew Murphey, 37–52. Manchester: Manchester University Press, 2004.

Roberts, Josephine A. "Introduction." In *The First Part of The Countess of Montgomery's Urania*, edited by Josephine A. Roberts. Binghampton, N.Y.: Center for Medieval and Early Renaissance Studies, 1995.

———. "'The Knott Never to Bee Untide': The Controversy Regarding Marriage in Mary Wroth's *Urania*." In *Reading Mary Wroth: Representing Alternatives in Early Modern England*, edited by Naomi J. Miller and Gary Waller, 109–132. Knoxville: University of Tennessee Press, 1991.

Roberts, Katherine J. *Fair Ladies: Sir Philip Sidney's Female Characters*. New York: Peter Lang, 1993.

Roche, Thomas P. *The Kindly Flame: A Study of the Third and Fourth Books of Spenser's "Faerie Queene."* Princeton: Princeton University Press, 1964.

———. *Petrarch and the English Sonnet Sequences*. New York: AMS Press, 1989.

Rogers, John. *The Matter of Revolution: Science, Poetry, and Politics in the Age of Milton*. Ithaca, N.Y.: Cornell University Press, 1996.

Rose, Mark. *Heroic Love: Studies in Sidney and Spenser*. Cambridge, Mass.: Harvard University Press, 1968.

Rose, Mary Beth. *Gender and Heroism in Early Modern English Literature*. Chicago: University of Chicago Press, 2002.

Rudolph, Julia. "Rape and Resistance: Women and Consent in Seventeenth-Century English Legal and Political Thought." *Journal of British Studies* 39 (2000): 157–184.

Russell, Conrad. *Unrevolutionary England, 1603–1642*. London: Hambledon Press, 1990.

Salmon, J. H. M. "Seneca and Tacitus in Jacobean England." In *The Mental World of the Jacobean Court*, edited by Linda Levy Peck, 169–188. Cambridge: Cambridge University Press, 1991.

Salzman, Paul. *Literary Culture in Jacobean England: Reading 1621*. New York: Palgrave, 2002.

Sanchez, Melissa E. "Romance and Libertinism in Rochester's Poetry." *Eighteenth-Century Studies* 38 (2005): 441–460.

Sandy, Amelia Zurcher. *Seventeenth-Century English Romance: Allegory, Ethics, and Politics*. New York: Palgrave Macmillan, 2007.

———. "Untimely Monuments: Stoicism, History, and the Problem of Utility in *The Winter's Tale* and *Pericles*." *ELH* 70 (2003): 903–927.

Sawday, Jonathan. *The Body Emblazoned: Dissection and the Human Body in Renaissance Culture*. London: Routledge, 1995.

———. "'Mysteriously Divided': Civil War, Madness, and the Divided Self." In *Literature and the English Civil War*, edited by Thomas Healy and Jonathan Sawday, 127–143. Cambridge: Cambridge University Press, 1990.

Scarry, Elaine. *The Body in Pain: The Making and Unmaking of the World*. New York: Oxford University Press, 1985.

Schlichter, Annette. "Queer At Last? Straight Intellectuals and the Desire for Transgression." *GLQ* 10 (2004): 543–564.

Schoenfeldt, Michael C. "'Commotion Strange': Passion in *Paradise Lost*." In *Reading the Early Modern Passions: Essays in the Cultural History of Emotion*, edited by Gail Kern Paster, Katherine Rowe, and Mary Floyd-Wilson, 43–67. Philadelphia: University of Pennsylvania Press, 2004.

———. "Gender and Conduct in *Paradise Lost*." In *Sexuality and Gender in Early Modern Europe: Institutions, Texts, Images*, edited by James Grantham Turner, 310–338. Cambridge: Cambridge University Press, 1993.

Schultz, James A. *Courtly Love, the Love of Courtliness, and the History of Sexuality*. Chicago: University of Chicago Press, 2006.

Schwarz, Kathryn. "Chastity, Militant and Married: Cavendish's Romance, Milton's Masque." *PMLA* 118 (2003): 270–285.

———. *Tough Love: Amazon Encounters in the English Renaissance*. Durham, N.C.: Duke University Press, 2000.

Scott, Joan W. "Gender: A Useful Category of Historical Analysis." *American Historical Review* 91 (1986): 1053–1075.

Scott, Jonathan. *Algernon Sidney and the English Republic, 1623–1677*. Cambridge: Cambridge University Press, 1988.

Sedgwick, Eve Kosofsky. *Epistemology of the Closet*. Berkeley and Los Angeles: University of California Press, 1990.

Shannon, Laurie. *Sovereign Amity: Figures of Friendship in Shakespearean Contexts*. Chicago: Chicago University Press, 2001.

Shapiro, James S. *A Year in the Life of Shakespeare, 1599*. New York: Harper Collins, 2005.

Sharpe, Kevin. *Criticism and Compliment: The Politics of Literature in the England of Charles I*. Cambridge: Cambridge University Press, 1987.

————. "Introduction: Parliamentary History, 1603–1629: In or Out of Perspective?" In *Faction and Parliament: Essays on Early Stuart History*, edited by Kevin Sharpe, 1–42. Oxford: Clarendon Press, 1978.

————. *The Personal Rule of Charles I*. New Haven: Yale University Press, 1992.

————. *Sir Robert Cotton, 1586–1631: History and Politics in Early Modern England*. Oxford: Oxford University Press, 1979.

————, ed. *Faction and Parliament: Essays on Early Stuart History*. Oxford: Clarendon Press, 1978.

Sharpe, Kevin, and Peter Lake, eds. *Culture and Politics in Early Stuart England*. Stanford, Calif.: Stanford University Press, 1993.

Shaver, Anne. "A New Woman of Romance." *Modern Language Studies* 21 (1991): 63–77.

————. "Woman's Place in the *New Arcadia*." *Sidney Newsletter* 10, no. 2 (1990): 3–15.

Shepherd, Robert. "The Political Commonplace Books of Sir Robert Sidney." *Sidney Journal* 21 (2003): 1–30.

Shoaf, R. A. *Milton, Poet of Duality*. New Haven: Yale University Press, 1985.

Shohet, Lauren. "The Masque in/as Print." In *The Book of the Play: Playwrights, Stationers, and Readers in Early Modern England*, edited by Marta Straznicky, 176–202. Amherst: University of Massachusetts Press, 2006.

————. "Reading/Genres: On 1630s Masques." In *Spectacle and Public Performance in the Late Middle Ages and the Renaissance*, edited by Robert E. Stillman, 231–248. Leiden: Brill, 2006.

————. "Reading Triumphs: Localizing Caroline Masques." In *Localizing Caroline Drama: Politics and Economics of the Early Modern English Stage, 1625–1642*, edited by Adam Zucker and Alan B. Farmer, 69–96. New York: Palgrave Macmillan, 2006.

Shuger, Debora K. "Castigating Livy: *The Rape of Lucretia* and *The Old Arcadia*." *Renaissance Quarterly* 51 (1998): 526–548.

Silberman, Lauren. "*The Faerie Queene*, Book V, and the Politics of the Text." *Spenser Studies* 19 (2004): 1–16.

————. *Transforming Desire: Erotic Knowledge in Books III and IV of "The Faerie Queene."* Los Angeles: University of California Press, 1995.

Silver, Victoria A. *Imperfect Sense: The Predicament of Milton's Irony*. Princeton: Princeton University Press, 2001.

————. "Sidney's *Discourses* on Political Images and Royalist Iconography." In *Writing and Political Engagement in Seventeenth-Century England*, edited by Derek Hirst and Richard Strier, 165–187. Cambridge: Cambridge University Press, 1999,

————. "Totem and Taboo in the Tribe of Ben: The Duplicity of Gender in Jonson's Satires." *ELH* 62 (1995): 729–757.

Sinfield, Alan. *Faultlines: Cultural Materialism and the Politics of Dissident Reading*. Berkeley: University of California Press, 1992.

Sirluck, Ernest. "Milton's Idle Right Hand." *JEGP* 60 (1961): 749–785.

Skeele, David. *Pericles: Critical Essays*. New York: Routledge, 2000.

Skinner, Quentin. *The Foundations of Modern Political Thought*. 2 vols. Cambridge: Cambridge University Press, 1978.

————. "John Milton and the Politics of Slavery." In *Milton and the Terms of Liberty*, edited by Graham Parry and Joad Raymond, 1–22. Cambridge: D. S. Brewer, 2002.

Skretkowitz, Victor. "Algernon Sidney and Philip Sidney: A Continuity of Rebellion." *Sidney Journal* 17, no. 2 (1999): 3–18.

Smith, Alan G. R. "Crown, Parliament and the Great Contract of 1610." In *The English Commonwealth, 1547–1640*, edited by Peter Clark, Alan G. R. Smith, and Nicholas Tyacke, 111–127. Leicester: Leicester University Press, 1979.

Smith, David L., ed. *Cromwell and the Interregnum: The Essential Readings*. Malden, Mass.: Blackwell, 2003.

Smith, G. C. Moore. "Aurelian Townshend." *Modern Language Review* 12 (1917): 422–427.

Smith, Hilda L. *All Men and Both Sexes: Gender, Politics, and the False Universal in England, 1640–1832*. University Park: Pennsylvania State University Press, 2002.

———. "'A General War amongst the Men but None amongst the Women': Political Differences between Margaret and William Cavendish." In *Politics and the Political Imagination in Later Stuart Britain*, edited by Howard Nenner, 143–160. Rochester: University of Rochester Press, 1997.

Smith, Nigel. *Literature and Revolution in England, 1640–1660*. New Haven: Yale University Press, 1994.

Smith, Rosalind. *Sonnets and the English Woman Writer, 1560–1621: The Politics of Absence*. Basingstoke: Palgrave Macmillan, 2005.

Smuts, Malcolm. "Court-Centered Politics and the Uses of Roman Historians, c. 1590–1630." In *Culture and Politics in Early Stuart England*, edited by Kevin Sharpe and Peter Lake, 21–43. Stanford, Calif.: Stanford University Press, 1993.

———. "Force, Love, and Authority in Caroline Political Culture." In *The 1630s: Interdisciplinary Essays on Culture and Politics in the Caroline Era*, edited by Ian Atherton and Julie Sanders, 28–48. Manchester: Manchester University Press, 2006.

———. "The Political Failure of Stuart Cultural Patronage." In *Patronage in the Renaissance*, edited by G. F. Lytle and Stephen Orgel, 165–187. Princeton: Princeton University Press, 1981.

———. "The Puritan Followers of Henrietta Maria in the 1630s." *English Historical Review* 93 (1978): 26–45.

Spelman, Elizabeth. "Anger and Insubordination," in *Women, Knowledge, and Reality: Explorations in Feminist Philosophy*, edited by Ann Garry and Marilyn Pearsall, 263–274. New York: Routledge, 1992.

Stallybrass, Peter. "Patriarchal Territories: The Body Enclosed." In *Rewriting the Renaissance: The Discourses of Sexual Difference in Early Modern Europe*, edited by Margaret Ferguson, Maureen Quilligan, and Nancy Vickers, 123–142. Chicago: University of Chicago Press, 1986.

———. "The World Turned Upside Down: Inversion, Gender, and the State." In *The Matter of Difference*, edited by Valerie Wayne, 201–220. Ithaca, N.Y.: Cornell University Press, 1991.

Stanton, Shirley. "Reading Spenser's *Faerie Queene*—In a Different Voice." In *Ambiguous Realities: Women in the Middle Ages and Renaissance*, edited by Carole Levin and Jeanine Watson, 145–162. Detroit: Wayne State University Press, 1987.

Stein, Arnold. *Answerable Style: Essays on Paradise Lost*. Minneapolis: University of Minnesota Press, 1953.

Stephens, Dorothy. "Into Other Arms: Amoret's Evasion." *ELH* 58 (1991): 523–544.

Stewart-Steinberg, Suzanne. "Girls Will Be Boys: Gender, Envy, and the Freudian Social Contract." *differences* 18 (2007): 24–71.

Stillman, Robert E. *Philip Sidney and the Poetics of Renaissance Cosmopolitanism*. Aldershot: Ashgate, 2008.

———. "The Politics of Sidney's Pastoral: Mystification and Mythology in *The Old Arcadia*." *ELH* 52 (1985): 795–814.

Stone, James W. "'Man's Effeminate S(lack)ness': Androgyny and the Divided Unity of Adam and Eve." *Milton Quarterly* 31 (1997): 33–42.

Strier, Richard. *Resistant Structures: Particularity, Radicalism, and Renaissance Texts*. Berkeley: University of California Press, 1995.

Strong, Roy C. *The Cult of Elizabeth*. London: Thames and Hudson, 1987.

———. *Henry, Prince of Wales and England's Lost Renaissance*. London: Thames and Hudson, 1986.

Stroud, Angus. *Stuart England*. London: Routledge, 1999.

Stump, Donald. "Fashioning Gender: Cross-Dressing in Spenser's Legend of Britomart and Artegall." *Spenser Studies* 15 (2001): 95–119.

———. "The Two Deaths of Mary Stuart: Historical Allegory in Spenser's Book of Justice." *Spenser Studies* 17 (2003): 81–105.

Sullivan, Margaret Mary. "Getting Pamela Out of the House: Gendering Genealogy in the *New Arcadia*." *Sidney Newsletter* 9 no. 2 (1989): 3–18.

Suzuki, Mihoko. "Scapegoating Radigund." In *Critical Essays on Edmund Spenser* edited by Mihoko Suzuki, 183–198. New York: G. K. Hall, 1996.

———. *Subordinate Subjects: Gender, the Political Nation, and Literary Form in England, 1588–1688*. Aldershot: Ashgate, 2003.

Swift, Caroline Ruth. "Feminine Identity in Lady Mary Wroth's Romance *Urania*." *ELR* 14 (1984): 328–346.

Tennenhouse, Leonard. "Arcadian Rhetoric: Sidney and the Politics of Courtship." In *Sir Philip Sidney's Achievements*, edited by M. J. B. Allen et al., 201–213. New York: AMS, 1990.

Teskey, Gordon. *Allegory and Violence*. Ithaca, N.Y.: Cornell University Press, 1996.

Thomas, Keith. "Women in the Civil War Sects." *Past and Present* 13 (1958): 42–62.

Thompson, Christopher. *The Debate on the Freedom of Speech in the House of Commons in February 1621*. Essex: Orchard Press, 1985.

Thrush, Andrew. "The Personal Rule of James I, 1611–1620." In *Politics, Religion, and Popularity*, edited by Thomas Cogswell, Richard Cust, and Peter Lake, 84–102. Cambridge: Cambridge University Press, 2002.

Tilmouth, Christopher. *Passion's Triumph Over Reason: A History of the Moral Imagination from Spenser to Rochester*. Oxford: Oxford University Press, 2007.

Tomlinson, Sophie. "She that Plays the King: Henrietta Maria and the Threat of the Actress in Caroline Culture." In *The Politics of Tragicomedy: Shakespeare and After*, edited by Gordon McMullan and Jonathan Hope, 189–207. London: Routledge, 1992,

———. "Theatrical Vibrancy on the Caroline Court Stage: *Tempe Restored* and The Shepherds' Paradise." In *Women and Culture at the Courts of the Stuart Queens*, edited by Clare McManus, 186–203. New York: Palgrave Macmillan, 2003.

Tompkins, J. M. S. "Why Pericles?" *Review of English Studies* 3 (1952): 315–324.

Traub, Valerie. *The Renaissance of Lesbianism in Early Modern England*. Cambridge: Cambridge University Press, 2002.

Trease, Geoffrey. *Portrait of a Cavalier: William Cavendish, First Duke of Newcastle*. New York: Taplinger, 1979.

Trevor, Douglas. *The Poetics of Melancholy in Early Modern England*. Cambridge: Cambridge University Press, 2004.

Trevor, Douglas, and Carla Mazzio, "Introduction." In *Historicism, Psychoanalysis, and Early Modern Culture*, edited by Douglas Trevor and Carla Mazzio, 1–18. New York: Routledge, 2000.

Trubowitz, Rachel. "The Reenchantment of Utopia and the Female Monarchical Self: Margaret Cavendish's *Blazing World*." *TSWL* 11 (1992): 229–245.

Truman, James C. "John Foxe and the Desires of Reformation Martyrology." *ELH* 70 (2003): 35–66.

Turner, James Grantham. *One Flesh: Paradisal Marriage and Sexual Relations in the Age of Milton*. Oxford: Clarendon, 1987.

Tyacke, Nicholas. "Wroth, Cecil, and the Parliamentary Session of 1604." *Bulletin of the Institute of Historical Research* 50 (1977): 120–125.

Underdown, David. "Yellow Ruffs and Poisoned Possets: Placing Women in Early Stuart Political Debate." In *Attending to Early Modern Women*, edited by Susan D. Amussen and Adele Seef, 230–242. Cranbury, N.J.: Associated University Press.

Van Nierop, H. "Alva's Throne—Making Sense of the Revolt of the Netherlands." In *The Origins and Development of the Dutch Revolt*, edited by G. Darby, 29–47. London: Routledge, 2001.

Veevers, Erica. *Images of Love and Religion: Queen Henrietta Maria and Court Entertainments.* Cambridge: Cambridge University Press, 1993.

Vickers, Nancy. "'The Blazon of Sweet Beauty's Best': Shakespeare's *Lucrece*." In *Shakespeare and the Question of Theory*, edited by Patricia Parker and Geoffrey Hartman, 95–115. New York: Methuen, 1985.

———. "Diana Described: Scattered Women and Scattered Rhyme." *Critical Inquiry* 8 (1981): 265–279.

Walker, Garthine. "Rereading Rape and Sexual Violence in Early Modern England." *Gender and History* 10.1 (1998): 1–25.

Walker, Julia M., ed. *Dissing Elizabeth: Negative Representations of Gloriana.* Durham, N.C.: Duke University Press, 1998.

———, ed. *Milton and the Idea of Woman.* Urbana and Chicago: University of Illinois Press, 1988.

Waller, Gary. "Mary Wroth and the Sidney Family Romance: Gender Construction in Early Modern England." In *Reading Mary Wroth: Representing Alternatives in Early Modern England*, edited by Naomi J. Miller and Gary Waller, 35–63. Knoxville: University of Tennessee Press, 1991.

Warner, Michael. "Introduction." In *Fear of a Queer Planet: Queer Politics and Social Theory*, edited by Michael Warner, vii–xxxi. Minneapolis: Minnesota University Press, 1993.

Watkins, John. *Representing Elizabeth in Stuart England: Literature, History, Sovereignty.* Cambridge: Cambridge University Press, 2002.

Watt, Diane. *Amoral Gower: Language, Sex, and Politics.* Minneapolis: University of Minnesota Press, 2003.

Wedgwood, C. V. *The King's Peace: 1637–1641.* London: C. Nicholls, 1966.

———. *Oliver Cromwell and the Elizabethan Inheritance.* London: Jonathan Cape, 1970.

———. *The Trial of Charles I.* London: Collins, 1964.

Weidemann, Heather L. "Theatricality and Identity in Mary Wroth's *Urania*." In *Reading Mary Wroth: Representing Alternatives in Early Modern England*, edited by Naomi J. Miller and Gary Waller, 191–209. Knoxville: University of Tennessee Press, 1991.

Weitz, Nancy. "Romantic Fiction, Moral Anxiety, and Social Capital in Cavendish's 'Assaulted and Pursued Chastity.'" In *Authorial Conquests: Essays on Genre in the Writings of Margaret Cavendish*, edited by Line Cottegnies and Nancy Weitz, 145–160. Cranbury, N.J.: Associated University Presses, 2003.

Weston, Corrine, and Janelle Greenberg. *Subjects and Sovereigns: The Grand Controversy over Legal Sovereignty in Stuart England.* Cambridge: Cambridge University Press, 1981.

Westrup, C. W. *Introduction to Early Roman Law.* Copenhagen: Levin and Munksgaard, 1944.

White, Michelle Anne. *Henrietta Maria and the English Civil Wars.* Aldershot: Ashgate, 2006.

Wikander, Matthew H. *Princes to Act: Royal Audience and Royal Performance, 1578–1792.* Baltimore: Johns Hopkins University Press, 1993.

Wilcox, Helen, ed. *Women and Literature in Britain, 1500–1700.* Cambridge: Cambridge University Press, 1996.

Williams, Kathleen. *Spenser's World of Glass: A Reading of the "Faerie Queene."* Berkeley: University of California Press, 1966.

Wilson-Okamura, David Scott. "Republicanism, Nostalgia, and the Crowd." *Spenser Studies* 17 (2003): 253–273.

Wind, Edgar. *Pagan Mysteries in the Renaissance.* London: Faber and Faber, 1968.

Wiseman, Susan. *Conspiracy and Virtue: Women, Writing, and Politics in Seventeenth-Century England.* Oxford: Oxford University Press, 2006.

Wittrich, Joseph. *Feminist Milton.* Ithaca, N.Y.: Cornell University Press, 1987.

Woods, Suzanne. "Freedom and Tyranny in Sidney's *Arcadia.*" In *Sir Philip Sidney's Achievements,* edited by M. J. B. Allen et al., 165–175. New York: AMS, 1990.

Woolrych, Austin. "The Cromwellian Protectorate: A Military Dictatorship?" In *Cromwell and the Interregnum: The Essential Readings,* edited by David L. Smith, 61–89. Malden, Mass.: Blackwell, 2003.

Worden, Blair. "Ben Jonson among the Historians." In *Culture and Politics in Early Stuart England,* edited by Kevin Sharpe and Peter Lake, 67–89. Stanford, Calif.: Stanford University Press, 1993.

———. "John Milton and Oliver Cromwell." In *Soldiers, Writers, and Statesmen of the English Revolution,* edited by Ian Gentiles, John Morrill, and Blair Worden, 243–264. Cambridge: Cambridge University Pres, 1998.

———. "The Levellers in History and Memory, c. 1660–1960." In *The Putney Debates of 1647,* edited by Michael Mendle, 256–282. Cambridge: Cambridge University Press, 2001.

———. "Milton's Republicanism and the Tyranny of Heaven." In *Machiavelli and Republicanism,* edited by Gisela Bock, Quentin Skinner, and Maurizio Viroli, 225–245. Cambridge: Cambridge University Press, 1990.

———. *The Sound of Virtue: Philip Sidney's "Arcadia" and Elizabethan Politics.* New Haven: Yale University Press, 1996.

Wright, Nancy E. "'Rival Traditions': Civic and Courtly Ceremonies in Jacobean London." In *The Politics of the Stuart Court Masque,* edited by David Bevington and Peter Holbrook, 197–217. Cambridge: Cambridge University Press, 1998.

Yates, Frances A. *Astraea: The Imperial Theme in the Sixteenth Century.* London: Routledge, 1975.

Zagorin, Perez. *The Court and the Country.* New York: Atheneum Press, 1970.

Zouch, Thomas. *Memoirs of the Life and Writings of Sir Philip Sidney.* 2d ed. York, 1809.

INDEX

CPSIA information can be obtained at www.ICGtesting.com
Printed in the USA
LVOW08s2043071013

355882LV00001B/1/P